MONTREAL
CITY OF SECRETS

Barry Sheehy
Images Arranged by Cindy Wallace

MONTREAL
CITY OF SECRETS

CONFEDERATE OPERATIONS IN MONTREAL
DURING THE AMERICAN CIVIL WAR

Baraka
Books

Montréal

© Baraka Books 2017
ISBN 978-1-77186-123-6

Book Design and Cover by Folio infographie
Editing and proofreading by Bronwyn Averett and Robin Philpot

Legal Deposit, 4th quarter 2017
Bibliothèque et Archives nationales du Québec
Library and Archives Canada

Published by Baraka Books of Montreal
6977, rue Lacroix
Montréal, Québec H4E 2V4
Telephone: 514 808-8504
info@barakabooks.com
www.barakabooks.com

Printed and bound in Quebec

We acknowledge the support from the Société de développement des entreprises culturelles (SODEC) and the Government of Quebec tax credit for book publishing administered by SODEC.

Funded by the Government of Canada
Financé par le gouvernement du Canada   Canadä

Trade Distribution & Returns
Canada and the United States
Independent Publishers Group
1-800-888-4741 (IPG1);
orders@ipgbook.com

Prologue

Silence: The Confederacy and Montreal

T<small>HE</small> S<small>TATUE OF</small> "S<small>ILENCE</small>" at Laurel Grove's Gettysburg cemetery in Savannah, Georgia marks the beginning of the journey that led to the writing of this book, *City of Secrets*. In researching our Civil War Savannah books *Immortal City* and *Brokers, Bankers and Bay Lane,* we took a keen interest in the Confederate Monument in Forsyth Park, the largest in the South. Savannah is full of beautiful statues and works of art, and the Confederate monument, which dominates the old "common" that served as a transit military encampment during the Civil War, is among the most impressive. But my absolute favorite has always been the haunting statue of "Silence," an angel holding her finger to her lips calling for quiet and respect as she watches over her Confederate dead at Laurel Grove. I have always thought the Angel's whisper signaled not just Silence but suggested something yet to be discovered.

When we investigated the origins of the Confederate Monument and the "Silence" statue we were stunned to learn they had been sculpted in Canada at the Montreal Marble Works by artist Robert Reid. Sourcing a major work of art from far away Montreal during the lean years of Reconstruction was akin to sourcing it from the far side of the moon. We learned the statues had been shipped to Savannah via Halifax without ever putting into a Northern port. The shipping and import duties exceeded the costs of the original art.

I asked myself, why Montreal? We investigated and discovered deep, fascinating, and unexpected links between Montreal and the Confederacy, including the beautiful city of Savannah. This was a historic journey like no other, out of which emerged a story of sedition, intrigue, violence and greed, but also one of fidelity and courage unto death. Stepping back, it all took one's breath away. For someone raised on the existing calcified and simplistic American Civil War narrative of a battle between good and evil, as defined by slavery, this turned the world upside down. The information was more than disconcerting. It was disorienting. This was particularly so for a Canadian who had lived in and loved the Deep South but had dared write about the institution of slavery as it operated as a business in Savannah. The book, while an award winner, was not universally welcomed locally. As for the author, here was someone born and raised in Montreal but who joined the great Anglophone diaspora, moving abroad while also somehow drawn back to his beloved Montreal. Although now and forever an exile, this is still a city I love.

As for the story, the more facts that poured in, the more the tale of Montreal and the Confederacy became deeper, richer, darker, more complex and riddled with contradictions. ∾

Barry M. Sheehy

Table of Contents

Montreal in 1866 from Notre Dame Basilica, looking east. McCord Museum, Notman Collection, Montreal, QC, 1866. I-21048.1

Introduction

DURING THE CIVIL WAR (1861-1865), the largest Confederate Secret Service base outside of Richmond was located in Montreal. This organization was funded by the Confederate Congress to the tune of a million dollars in gold or hard currencies in 1864. The Secret Service reported to Secretary of State Judah Benjamin. This was one of the reasons why Jefferson Davis and his family immediately fled to Montreal after the war. Varina Davis first took the family north and Jefferson Davis followed as soon as he was freed on bond from Fortress Monroe. The Confederacy had friends and the remnants of an organization in Montreal. We were able to identify and map the large Confederate Secret Service apparatus operating in Montreal and discovered that many key Confederates stayed at the same hotel, Montreal's prestigious St. Lawrence Hall, and had their photos taken at the same studio: Notman's Studio on Bleury Street. Notman's collection was later donated to the McCord

◄ St. Lawrence Hall, St. James Street, Montreal. McCord Museum, Notman Collection, Montreal, QC, about 1890. VIEW-1876

Museum in Montreal and represents perhaps the largest single repository of surviving Confederate Secret Service photographs.

As we delved into the surviving Guest Books from Montreal's leading hotel, St. Lawrence Hall, and the recently recovered registers of the Barnett's Niagara Falls Museum, the story took on a darker hue.[1] Not only were the Confederates present in strength in Montreal, but many of Lincoln's enemies from the North were as well, including Copperhead Democrats and Radical Republicans. We discovered much of Wall Street and America's nascent military industrial complex in Montreal, apparently doing business with the Confederacy. The level of corruption in the Northern war effort suggested by these American power brokers in Montreal is at once breathtaking and disquieting. Also present in the Montreal and Niagara areas were key members of the War Department, the Judge Advocate General's Office, the Federal National Detective Police, and the Treasury Department. Much of Secretary of the Treasury Salmon Chase's presidential committee appears to be on hand.

William Notman, Montreal's most prominent photographer, was a favorite of the Confederate community in the city. Confederate agents, commissioners, and operatives went to his studio at 17 Bleury Street to have their photographs taken. Notman donated his entire collection to Montreal's McCord Museum. It provides a priceless reservoir of Civil War and post-Civil War images. Notman Studio, 17 Bleury Street, McCord Museum, Notman Collection, Montreal, QC, 1859-60. N-0000.157

What business called these senior American officials to Montreal, and to a hotel known to be closely associated with the Confederate Secret Service? Civil War super banker Jay Cooke and Edwin Stanton's chief telegraph operator and confidant Thomas T. Eckert were in Canada along with Radical Republicans like James Ashley, James Harlan, James Wilson, John Bingham, John Sherman, and Alexander R. Shepard, to name but a few. Lincoln haters like New York Mayor Fernando Wood and his brother, Congressman and newspaper editor Benjamin Wood, were regulars at St. Lawrence Hall. Benjamin Wood was on the Confederate payroll. It is evident that, by 1864, opposition to Lincoln was deeper, more strident and more bipartisan, than is generally acknowledged. The full list of those present in Montreal will stagger anyone familiar with the era and certainly challenge the existing mainstream American narrative regarding the Civil War and Lincoln. (*See Appendices A and B the names of those in Canada 1864-1865.*)

It's not just America's mainstream Civil War narrative that will be buffeted by these new facts. Canadian history will be likewise bruised. Most Canadians naively assume Canada was supportive of Lincoln's war because of their collective opposition to slavery. This is simply not true. Although Canada was the last stop on the underground railway, the number of slaves who made it safely to Canada from 1840-1865 was relatively small, somewhere between 30,000 and 100,000, with the lower number being more likely.[2] Most settled in Ontario. There was certainly a committed abolitionist movement in Canada, espe-cially in Southern Ontario, but the general view of slavery was agnostic. Britain had abolished slavery decades earlier and this was now viewed as an American rather than a Canadian problem. Even in the states that elected Lincoln there was no great appetite for emancipation. This is clearly reflected in Lincoln's first inaugural address.

As for Lincoln's war effort, Canada's Tory government, along with British authorities, viewed a permanently divided United States as being in the best interests of British North America. A unified, militarized United States represented an existential threat to Canadian and British interests. Great Britain had declared official neutrality in the war, recognizing both North and South as legitimate and equal belligerents with whom they could do business; the same rules applied to Canada. Not surprisingly, Canadian businessmen and bankers readily did business with the Confederacy. Montreal played host to blockade running and contraband for cotton trading on an enormous scale. Arguably, the single largest cotton deal of all time, worth half a billion dollars or more in Greenbacks, was orchestrated out of Montreal in 1864. This enormous contraband for cotton trade had the support of both Richmond and Washington and, in particular, Lincoln's White House.

Meanwhile, the Confederate Secret Service was allowed to deepen and expand operations in Canada while authorities looked the other way. It was only after the St. Albans Raid thoroughly embarrassed the colonial government in Canada that steps were finally taken to rein in Confederate operatives in Canada.

Canadian banks had no difficulty holding rich Confederate deposits in their vaults. Cashier's checks for thousands of dollars issued by Canadian banks were found in possession of Confederate agents and raiders arrested in the U.S. The Ontario Bank on Place d'Armes in Montreal and the Niagara and District Bank in St. Catharines were effectively controlled by the Confederates. The Ontario Bank regularly laundered money for the Confederate Secret Service, making cashier's checks out to employees who endorsed them to the intended recipients, which included senior American politicians. A cashier's check signed by Ontario Bank President Henry Starnes, soon to be Mayor of Montreal, was found on the body of John Wilkes Booth after he was shot to death at the Garrett farm in Virginia. It was entered into the record during the trial of the Lincoln Conspirators in 1865.

Starnes, like Canada's first Prime Minister, John A. Macdonald, hailed from Kingston, Ontario. He was also a close school friend of George-Étienne Cartier. Macdonald and Cartier are considered to be the fathers of Canadian Confederation.

These are just some of the many secrets Montreal has kept hidden for 150 years. The picture presented is hardly comforting. This is not *Gone with The Wind*. *City of Secrets* is a raw, sordid story, riddled with greed and treachery but not without redemption. There are certainly villains here but also genuine heroes and, more notably, heroines. This is a tale of war, intrigue and betrayal but also one of courage and love. In its human dimensions, it is almost Shakespearean. This was not what we expected when we set out to discover the links between Savannah's haunting statues and Montreal but this is the story we discovered and it is ours to tell. ❧

This is an early photograph of the beautiful neoclassical Bank of Montreal building taken from the tower of Notre Dame Basilica. The building was designed by architect John Wells. This incredible photo predates 1859 as the Dome was removed that year and the new headquarters of the Bank were constructed adjacent to the branch in the space on the left in this photo. (A new dome was added early in the twentieth century.) The Bank of Montreal and the nearby Ontario Bank would play important roles in the story of Confederate Montreal. This beautiful structure still graces the Place d'Armes today. McCord Museum, Notman Collection, Montreal, QC, 1858-1859. MP-0000-2901

CHAPTER 1

Montreal and the Confederacy

**HUB OF CONFEDERATE
SECRET SERVICE ACTIVITY**

During the American Civil War, the Confederate government had a substantial presence in Canada, centered in St. Catharines, Toronto, and especially Montreal. Inside the vaults of the Bank of Montreal, the Ontario Bank, and other Canadian financial institutions as far away as the Niagara and District Bank in St. Catharines, the Confederates kept on deposit a million dollars or more in hard currencies and gold to fund clandestine activities.[1] This was an enormous sum for the time. Room and board at Montreal's best hotels ranged from $1.75-$2.50 per day and a major in the Confederate army was paid $1200 a year. The Ontario Bank, located on Place d'Armes in Montreal, was so closely associated with the Confederate Secret Service that Southern bankers were sometimes perceived as employees or direct associates of the bank. The Confederate Secret Service effectively controlled the institution.

The Confederate Secret Service rented entire suites of rooms in grand hotels such as the St. Lawrence Hall on St. James Street (now Saint-Jacques) and the Donegana Hotel on Notre Dame Street. Dooley's bar in St. Lawrence Hall offered Mint Juleps year round, and the *Montreal Gazette* and the *Montreal Telegraph* were always available at the hotel's newsstand. Both papers were generally sympathetic to the Confederacy's call for independence. St. Lawrence Hall had its own telegraph office to provide current war news from America. On the main floor of the hotel was an elegant lobby, which included both ladies' and men's smoking rooms, a purser's office, a mail room, and a first-class barber shop. Downstairs was Dooley's Bar and a large billiards room.

On any given day, Confederate couriers, raiders, blockade runners, businessmen, and refugees could be found in the parlors and bars of the Donegana, St. Lawrence Hall, the nearby Ottawa Hotel, and other hostelries throughout the city.

The grand Ottawa Hotel still graces Old Montreal today, the last of the City's Civil War spy hotels. McCord Museum, Notman Collection. Montreal, QC, 1874. II-10908

Montreal, like Halifax, was generally sympathetic to the Confederacy. This did not necessarily reflect support for slavery but rather a cold calculation by Canada's ruling elite that a permanently divided United States was less of a threat to British North America than a united, militarized neighbor. It didn't help that American politicians and some members of the press openly called for the annexation of Canada.[2] As a result, agents representing U.S. Secretary of State William Seward and Secretary of War Edwin Stanton sometimes found it tough going when seeking local cooperation or even lodging in Montreal. U.S. Federal agents usually stayed at the still-standing Ottawa Hotel on St. James Street, just a few blocks from St. Lawrence Hall. It was one of the few hotels where they were welcome.

The Ottawa Hotel was a safe haven not only for Federal agents, but also for the Confederate Secret Service who sometimes used the hotel, which offered affordable, comfortable accommodations. Some senior Confederates like George Sanders and Edwin Lee took up lodgings there from time to time. The mix of Federal and Confederate operatives in this neutral setting must have made for curious conversation over breakfast.

Today, locals and visitors pass by the former Ottawa Hotel, a grand old structure on St. James/Saint-Jacques, without knowing its story as the last of Montreal's great Civil War spy hotels.

CONFEDERATE OPERATIONS MOUNTED OUT OF CANADA

The Confederate Secret Service mounted numerous operations out of Canada. This included raids on Union prisoner-of-war camps, attempts to burn major hotels in New York City, blowing up ships along the Mississippi, and finally, the infamous raid on St. Albans, Vermont in October 1864, the most northerly action of the Civil War. They also launched a successful assault on the new American currency, the "Greenback," which nearly created a run on the dollar. This was orchestrated out of Montreal and executed right under the noses of federal authorities in New York City. The massive scheme to "short" the dollar and drive up the price of gold involved Canadian banks and American financiers like J.P. Morgan. The Lincoln kidnapping plot, which mutated into an assassination, also involved Montreal. The presence of John Wilkes Booth in Montreal in the fall of 1864 is well established historically but has never been adequately examined. Booth's presence at Montreal's St. Lawrence Hall becomes more intriguing when we consider who else frequented the hotel in 1864. The Confederate Secret Service is foremost on this list but the story does not end there. St. Lawrence Hall also played host to powerful American politicians, both Democrats and Republicans, including anti-Lincoln Radicals. America's most powerful bankers, businessmen, and financiers stayed at the St. Lawrence Hall. Representatives of the War Department and the Treasury Department along with much of Salmon P. Chase's presidential committee were also there. Cotton speculators and much of America's nascent military industrial complex were in the city most likely to do business with the Confederate Secret Service because the British Army equipped itself and the brand new Canadian military was small. The South was where the supplies were needed and they had the means to pay for it with cotton.

What happened in Montreal in the summer and fall of 1864 was unprecedented. It was arguably the largest gathering of American political and economic power outside of Washington in the nineteenth century.[3] Nothing like it had happened before and it would never happen again.

They left a trail of registrations at St. Lawrence Hall and Barnett's Museum in Niagara. Many of those present, particularly the Confederates, went to Notman's Studio on Bleury Street to have their photographs taken. All three original historical sources have survived: St. Lawrence Hall's Guest Books in Canada's National Archives, Notman's Photographic Collection at the McCord Museum in Montreal, and Barnett's Museum Guest Books recently acquired by the Niagara Falls Museums. The information gleaned from these sources and others represents part of Montreal's secret Civil War history.

Hints of Montreal's role began to emerge as early as the trial of the Lincoln Conspirators in June 1865, but Judge Advocate Joseph Holt's case against the Confederates in Canada collapsed when his star witness, Montreal-based Sanford Conover (Charles Dunham), was exposed as a perjurer. Worse still, there was strong evidence this perjury had been suborned by Holt and the Judge Advocate General's Office with the support of the War Department.

Those Americans who had been in Montreal doing business with the Confederates went to ground following Lincoln's assassination. Lincoln's support of cotton-for-contraband trading, if exposed, would have tainted his national deification. This transformation of Lincoln from a gifted politician into a secular saint was a self-serving, cynical political strategy driven largely by Radical Republicans who despised

John Wilkes Booth signed the St. Lawrence Hall Hotel Guest Book on 18 October 1864.[4]

him in life. Their scheming to force Lincoln off the Republican Ticket, some of it taking place in Montreal, was not something they wanted discussed. Copperhead Democrats, who had been in Montreal dealing with the Confederates, were especially vulnerable to public outrage. Congressman Fernando Wood, who had plotted against Lincoln at every turn, left for an extended stay in Europe. The British Government and their colonial counterparts in Canada, faced with a victorious, militarized, and angry United States, wanted no discussion of the tolerance that had been extended to Confederate operations in Canada. After the collapse of Judge Advocate Joseph Holt's case against the Confederates in Canada, no one on either side of the border wanted to explain what John Wilkes Booth had been up to in Montreal. And so a veil of silence descended on the subject. It has not been lifted for the past 150 years.

The concentration of American power and influence in Montreal, especially in 1864, reflected potent economic and political forces.[5] At the time, an enormous cotton-for-contraband deal was being negotiated by Confederate Commissioner Beverley Tucker, with the tacit support of both Richmond and the White House. The value of the deal was half a billion dollars or more in 1864 currency. Lincoln was particularly supportive of this inter-belligerent trade as it slowed the drain of gold flowing out of the United States and buttressed the Greenback. The Military and many in Congress opposed this inter-belligerent trade because the contraband reaching the South, especially military supplies and food, clearly length-

ened the war. This was why Montreal, located in foreign territory but linked by rail to New York and Washington, was chosen as the venue for these shady negotiations. This mega cotton deal attracted American and British bankers, businessmen, and cotton speculators in droves to Montreal. It also explains the presence of such a large contingent of Treasury Department officials in the city as the Treasury Department was supposed to regulate this inter-belligerent trade. American arms dealers and military suppliers were also present, presumably selling their wares to the Confederacy in exchange for cotton. Democrats were there collecting money from the Confederate Secret Service to defeat Lincoln in the November 1864 election. Republicans, on the other hand, are harder to explain. Some were possibly speculating in cotton, but others, especially the Radicals, were there, planning to replace Lincoln as the Republican nominee. Meanwhile, the presence in the city of important members of the War Department, especially Lafayette Baker and the National Detective Police and members of the Judge Advocate General Office, remains unexplained.

Dozens of buildings in Montreal have historical ties to the Civil War. Each site has its own history, its own story to tell. The McCord Museum's William Notman Collection contains a number of original photographs of Confederates who lived in or passed through Montreal during the war years. Each photograph represents a compelling story. In the intervening 150 years, most of these historically significant photographs have gone unrecognized. Prominent shots of Confederate

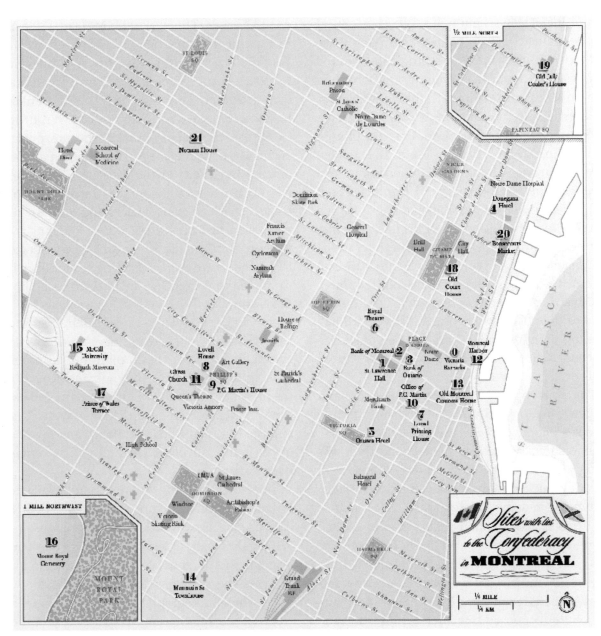

Montreal was the hub of Confederate secret service activity outside the United States. For the key to these twenty-one buildings with links to the Civil Wars see the key in Appendix F.

President Jefferson Davis and his family have occasionally made their way into publications but the rest have remained largely unrecognized and the history behind them untold.[6] The combination of photographs, hotel registrations, and other supporting historical data provides a unique window on Montreal at a time when the city played a fascinating and thus far unexplored role in America's Civil War and its immediate aftermath.

From 1861 until the end of the war in 1865, clandestine activities in Montreal closely resembled what occurred in places such as spy-riddled Casablanca, Lisbon or Geneva during the Second World War. The city was alive with refugees, soldiers-of-fortune, blockade-runners, U.S. army recruiters ("crimps"), and spies; all of them afloat on a sea of illicit money flowing from Confederate bank accounts, cotton trading, blockade running, and the sale of arms, food, and equipment to Richmond.

Canada could not avoid being buffeted by the bloody events of the American Civil War, the deadliest conflict North America had ever witnessed. American casualties dwarfed that of later conflicts, including the Second World War. 640,000 soldiers died, along with very likely as many civilians who perished from illness and deprivation, especially in the South. One third or more of all the youth in the Confederacy were killed, wounded, or debilitated, and an enormous part of the U.S. economy was destroyed, perhaps as much as a third.[7] In the South, some counties lost half the serving age population to war or disease.

The Civil War saw the birth of the United States as a nation with a highly centralized gov-

Ontario Bank next to the Pilot-Office on Place d'Armes. This shot is taken from the steps of beautiful Notre Dame Basilica. Bank President Henry Starnes had living quarters on the top floor but appeared to take rooms from time to time at St. Lawrence Hall. The Confederate Secret Service had $700,000 or more on deposit. Given capital-to-loan ratios at the time this would have given the Confederates effective control of the institution. Money laundering was a regular practice. Jacob Thompson would make out a large cashier's check in the name of a trusted bank employee, who would immediately countersign it over to the true beneficiary. The Pilot-Office, west side of Place d'Armes, McCord Museum, Notman Collection, Montreal, QC, 1868, copied before 1932. MP-0000.39.7

ernment and an immense military establishment. The counterbalance to expanding Federal power had been swept away on the battlefield. The U.S. fiat currency, the Greenback, as well as modern-day Wall Street trace their roots to the Civil War.

The harbor today is much expanded but the scene on the landward side, including many of the buildings in this 1865 photograph, remains largely unchanged. Note the sailors in the rigging. Montreal Harbour near Custom House, QC. McCord Museum, Notman Collection, Montreal, QC, 1865. 75MP-000.1452.51

With the defeat of the Southern Confederacy in 1865, British authorities in London and in Canada recognized that a victorious American super state represented an existential threat to the survival of British North America. Something had to be done. In many ways, the American Civil War helped create the Dominion of Canada. It was during these years of crisis that a political consensus favoring Canadian Confederation took root. Canada's obsession with east-west railroads is also a direct legacy of this era. As historian Oscar Skelton wrote soon after the turn of the century, "If the Civil War did not bring forth a new nation in the South, it helped make one in the far North."

New and, at times disturbing, information regarding the concentration of American power in Montreal in 1864 and early 1865 has come to the fore. The presence of so many powerful constituencies in Montreal raises a host of historical questions, not all of which can be answered in a single book. Some require further research. Some broad conclusions, however, can be drawn. We know, for example, that the Confederate Secret Service apparatus in Canada was large and well funded, and that its activities were largely winked at by British and Canadian authorities. This only changed with the St. Albans Raid in October 1864, which finally embarrassed the Canadian government into taking action to make it illegal to plan or undertake acts of war from or on Canadian soil. We also know powerful American banking, business, and political interests turned up in Montreal and their presence has never been fully explored or explained. Many were there to "trade with the enemy," but astonishingly, some of this illicit trade had the support of the White House. The implied level of corruption in the Union war effort exemplified by American powerbrokers in Montreal is extraordinary and disturbing. It calls into question many of the assumptions on which the existing American Civil War narrative rests. The presence of so many Democratic and Republican politicians, including many anti-Lincoln Radicals, in Canada, all rubbing elbows with the Confederate Secret Service, suggests that opposition to Lincoln in 1864 and 1865 was deeper, stronger, and more strident than is acknowledged in the mainstream Lincoln narrative. Other questions surrounding the presence of War Department officials in Montreal remain disturbing and unanswered. But because questions are unanswered or unsettling does not mean they should not be asked. These are precisely the questions we should pursue most vigorously. ❧

CHAPTER 2

Confederate Montreal
1861-1865

IN THE YEARS 1861-1865, and indeed for some time following the Civil War, hundreds of Confederate exiles, soldiers, blockade runners, and agents flocked to Montreal. They formed a distinct community in exile, welcomed into the upper crust of Montreal society. Montreal was then Canada's largest city and its undisputed banking and business center. It was also Canada's busiest inland port, hosting as many as eighty ocean-going ships in the harbor at the height of the St. Lawrence River's open season, which lasted on average 238 days.

The population was 100,000 and growing. It was a city on the move, made largely of stone, with very steep slate roofs to withstand Montreal's legendary winter snowfall.

Founded in 1642, Montreal was an old city by North American standards. Confederate visitors could not help but note the many buildings in the old quarter that were already a century or more old. The city had two hospitals, four col-leges, one university, a working sewer and water system, and an effective omnibus transit system. Montreal real estate in the early 1860's was valued at nearly thirty-five million dollars and the city was experiencing a boom in construction. Everywhere in the core city, streets were being paved with stone. Montreal had an excellent system of cabs (wheels and sleighs), a well-organized police and fire department, and boasted the continent's first YMCA and Fireman's Cemetery. The Crystal Palace was North America's first enclosed skating rink. For Confederates in the city, Richmond would have seemed smaller and a touch provincial in comparison.

The Lachine Canal, allowing vessels to access the Great Lakes while bypassing the fearsome Lachine Rapids, had been in operation since 1835 and was considered an engineering marvel.

The same was true for the newly completed Victoria Bridge, which spanned the mighty St. Lawrence, emptying the Great Lakes into

Crystal Palace on St. Catherine Street was the first enclosed skating rink in North America. Crystal Palace, St. Catherine Street, Montreal, QC. McCord Museum, Notman Collection, Montreal, QC, 1866. I-20722.2

the Atlantic. Second only to the Amazon River, the St. Lawrence River carries the largest flow of fresh water in the world. The Victoria Bridge was more than three kilometers long and was supported by twenty-four ice-breaking piers. It was the longest suspension bridge in the world at the time and carried both train and road traffic. It was an engineering wonder and even today remains Montreal's most reliable, trouble-free bridge.

The influx of thousands of British troops in 1861 following the Trent Crisis placed the military at the center of Montreal's social life. Officers' Messes hosted events in the winter social season at which Confederate exiles and officers were always welcome. Public opinion in the city was largely supportive of the Confederacy, especially following the Trent Crisis when Britain and the United States came to the brink of war. The *Montreal Evening Telegraph* and *The Gazette* both supported the Conservative government and George E. Cartier's *Parti Bleu* and both papers tended to be pro-Southern editorially. *The Gazette* and the *Telegraph* were always available in the lobby of the St. Lawrence Hall Hotel on Greater St. James Street—a Confederate favorite.

In Canada East and Canada West (effectively Quebec and Ontario) there was a tug of war going on for increased representation in the legislature, while to the east, the Maritime colonies were considering a union of their own, including perhaps economic affiliation with the New England States. Economically, this was the logical path. The endless political bickering between the regions made British North America a sometimes difficult and tiresome place to govern for the London-appointed Governor General and his staff. Canadian leaders like John A. Macdonald, George-Étienne Cartier, George Brown, and Thomas D'Arcy McGee were beginning to lay the groundwork for Canadian Confederation but momentum was slow and uneven.

The bloodiness of the American Civil War and the quick resort to violence as a solution gave pause to those who viewed affiliation with the United States as the logical long-term course for Canada. Other factors militated against joining the United States. The natural antipathy of the United Empire Loyalists toward the U.S.

Entrance to Lachine Canal, an early photo 1826-1830 http://www.mccord-museum.qc.ca/en/collection/artifacts/MP-1976.288.2

was inbred and the Catholic Church feared the corrupting secular influence of Republicanism. The Trent Crisis in 1862 further soured relations between British North America and the U.S.

In the end, it was the threat of U.S. invasion and the prospect of losing access to U.S. markets that drove Canada toward Confederation. The Civil War had a profound impact on Canadian policy and politics. It is fair to say that the Canadian Confederation in 1867, including use of the word "Confederation," was a direct by-product of the war.

The evolution of Canadian public opinion and policy during the Civil War is a fascinating subject. Few Canadians realize the extent to which the American Civil War transformed British North America into the Dominion of Canada. Fewer still realize that much of the Canadian political elite quietly hoped for a Southern victory in the war.

British North America did not participate directly in the American Civil War but more than forty thousand Canadians signed up to fight, mostly for the North, which offered rich signing bounties and bonuses. Four U.S. Generals were born in Canada and twenty-nine Canadians would win the U.S. Medal of Honor.[1] During the war, Canada was overrun with illegal Federal recruiters called "crimps," looking for able-bodied men and willing to pay a premium for trained soldiers. These bounties ranged from $200 to as high as $800.[2] Crimping, or recruitment by foreign agents of Canadians, was illegal in Canada but it was so pervasive that Canadian authorities found it nearly impossible to stop the unscrupulous but well-funded recruiters. The Catholic

View of Montreal from Mount Royal, 1865. Note the waterworks in the foreground and Notre Dame Basilica and the Victoria Bridge in the background. McCord Museum, Notman Collection, Montreal, QC, I-16524.1

Church and the government railed against the crimps and many were arrested, but the money driving the need for "substitutes" was too powerful to suppress.

It's clear that in the beginning, both English and French Canadian public opinion, being instinctively conservative, favored preservation of the Union. It was a typical "devil you know" mentality. Canada was the last stop on the Underground Railroad and opposition to slavery was generally the prevailing view, especially in Upper Canada. But when the Lincoln administration made clear that emancipation was not a war aim, Canadian opinion became uneasy.[3] Lincoln could not have been clearer in his first inaugural address. He had no inclination and indeed, according to his own words, no legal right to interfere with slavery where it existed. It was the spread of slavery to new territories that Lincoln objected to. Broad-based emancipation was not an aim of his administration. If the war was not about emancipation, then what was driving this terrible bloodshed? The answer was again provided by Lincoln in his first inaugural address. He made it clear that the issue of war or peace centered not on emancipation but on preservation of the Union at whatever cost.[4]

But to fight and win this war, the United States would have to transform itself into a centralized and militarized nation state. Such a transformation was perceived as a threat to the security of British North America.[5]

Meanwhile Canadian and British leaders looked on with alarm as the Lincoln administration set about closing opposition newspapers and imprisoning opponents without recourse to due process, even going so far as to abrogate the writ of *Habeas Corpus*. To many in British North America, the U.S. looked increasingly like a nascent military dictatorship. Britain had experienced one such dictatorship under Oliver Cromwell and the aftertaste was still bitter 200 years later. This made Britain wary of Lincoln's plans to expand the power of the central government and dramatically increase the size of the military. Secretary of State William Seward boasted to British Ambassador Richard Lyons that by ringing a small bell on his desk, he could have anyone in the United States arrested and held without trial. The assertion was frightening because it was essentially true.[6]

If there is an exemplary and compelling example of the turning of Canadian public opinion against the Northern war effort, it is surely Thomas D'Arcy McGee, Member of Parliament for Montreal

Hon. Thomas D'Arcy McGee, politician, author, newspaper editor, and a fierce advocate of Canadian Confederation. McCord Museum, Notman Collection, Montreal, QC, 1863. I-7383.1

West, author, historian, publisher, and Irish Nationalist. He was one of the Fathers of Canadian Confederation even though he was under threat of arrest had he returned to Ireland. While he hated the Crown for its harsh rule of Ireland, he was conflicted regarding British influence in Canada. He found his loyalties and logic locked in conflict. He had fought against the Crown in Ireland but could see that its influence in Canada had been generally benign and even nurturing. The two experiences were contradictory.

McGee was above all a realist. If British North America was to avoid being swallowed up by the United States, it needed British support and protection. Over time he became convinced that British North America would be more secure if it remained tied to Britain.

McGee regularly warned his colleagues in Parliament and his constituents at home that Canada's increasingly militarized neighbor was a threat. McGee had originally emigrated in 1848 to the United Sates where he became a prominent newspaper editor in Boston. But he soon grew disillusioned with American republicanism and the surrounding political corruption driven by money. Discouraged by his American experience he moved north to Montreal.

McGee came to the conclusion, no doubt after some difficult soul searching, that Canada's best hope for security lay in her ties with Great Britain. He strongly opposed the secretive Fenian movement, centered in the U.S. northeast, which he viewed as a threat to Canadian sovereignty and stability. His opposition to this radical movement would ultimately lead to his assassination in 1868.

When anti-Lincoln Democratic Congressman Clement Laird Vallandigham visited Canada, McGee introduced him on the floor of the House of Commons, then sitting in Quebec City. In a speech McGee made in support of Canadian Confederation, he proclaimed of the United States: *"She coveted Florida and seized it, they coveted Louisiana and purchased it; they coveted Texas and stole it, and then they picked a quarrel with Mexico which ended by their getting California."*[7] McGee believed Canada was next.

His willingness to reconcile with the Crown in the interests of his new, fledgling nation would cost him his life. His assassination has always been shrouded in controversy but it is clear that Fenian forces were directly or indirectly responsible. He is buried at Notre-Dame-des-Neiges (Our Lady of Snows) Cemetery on Mount Royal overlooking his beloved Montreal.[8]

Meanwhile, the Federal blockade of Southern ports dramatically reduced the flow of cotton to English mills, setting off an economic depression in parts of Great Britain. The Confederacy, on the other hand, proposed freer trade and lower tariffs, exactly the policy advocated by Great Britain, then at the height of its competitiveness.

Great Britain and British North America also looked over the border nervously at the buildup of U.S. military power. It wasn't a big leap from there to the sober realization that a centralized, militarized United States, capable of conquering the hard-fighting South, was more than capable of conquering much of the land mass of Canada. The Maritime colonies might be saved by the power

This extraordinary photograph shows the rear of the Victoria Barracks, Le Royer Street, Montreal, Quebec, shortly after the Civil War. This was the nerve center of the British operations in Central Canada during the Civil War. This impressive structure still stands between Le Royer and St. Paul Streets in the shadow of the beautiful Notre Dame Basilica. McCord Museum, Notman Collection, Montreal, QC, 1866 I-20772.1

of the Royal Navy but the rest of the country was at hazard.

Thus a permanently divided United States looked more and more like the safest outcome for Great Britain and British North America. The leadership class in Canada was slowly coming to see the obvious—a unified United States represented a very real threat to the survival of British North America. And soon begrudging admiration for the beleaguered, outnumbered Confederates, who chalked up one military success after another, began making itself felt in cities like Montreal and Halifax as well as the editorial pages of Canadian newspapers.

Many in British North America did not see why America's Southern states should not be allowed to *voluntarily* leave a union they had *voluntarily* entered. It was individual states who together had created the United States and not the other way around. Yet the absurd concept that Washington created the Union or the Union created itself, was precisely Lincoln's legal argument for raising an army to invade the South. It was a facile legal case but it justified the use of force to coerce the South into remaining in the Union. Canada's United Empire Loyalists, descendants of Americans loyal to Great Britain who had been driven from the United States during the American Revolution (1775-1783), could not see how Southern secession was all that different from the thirteen colonies throwing off their allegiance to Britain. It was viewed by many as the inevitable by-product of this original sin. They saw the United States as a nation inherently rooted in a tradition of rebellion and the chickens had come home to roost. Many recalled that the original American Revolution had also been a Civil War, one that the Loyalists had lost.

Meanwhile cities like Halifax and Montreal benefitted from trade with both Northern and Southern parties during the war. McGill University received rich endowments from William C. Macdonald whose tobacco empire drew upon raw material from slave states like Kentucky. His business boomed during the war, indicating that he had little difficulty obtaining tobacco—notwithstanding shortages caused by the Federal blockade of the South.[9]

Americans, both Northerners and Southerners, were quick to recognize the advantage offered by cities like Montreal, located on neutral territory, for conducting business which often involved trading with the enemy.

TURNING POINT — THE TRENT CRISIS

From the start of the war, Washington's primary foreign policy aim was to keep Europe's great powers out of the conflict. It wasn't lost on either side in the war that French intervention had tipped the scales in favor of the American revolutionaries at Yorktown in 1781. Like the war that erupted in 1861, the American Revolution had been very much a *civil war* with colonists ranged on both sides. In the end, French intervention and British fatigue proved decisive. These memories were still fresh at the start of the Civil War. Washington wanted European powers to stay out but Richmond was desperate to drag them in. The Confederacy was constantly seeking opportunities to solicit assistance and recognition from Great Britain, France, Mexico, and other nations.

Many political leaders in Washington—including some in Lincoln's cabinet—were convinced that Great Britain wanted to jump headlong into the great American bloodbath. Nothing was further from the truth. The spectacle of America's revolutionary legacy coming back to bite them provided some smug satisfaction at dinner parties in select London neighborhoods but this did not contaminate British foreign policy, which remained decidedly unsentimental and self-interested. For Britain, the American Civil War came as an unwanted development on the international scene. With the world's most productive economy and the largest merchant fleet, trade and market access were the centerpieces of British foreign policy.[10] When Lord Palmerston suggested the transfer of additional troops to Canada early in the war to garrison the Great Lakes, he was dissuaded by his cabinet colleagues precisely because it might be viewed in Washington as belligerent. There was considerable sympathy for the South in many circles in Great Britain but this did not translate into a desire to join the war. This reluctance to enter the fray did not mean that Great Britain would fail to defend its interests in British North America or on the high seas if they were challenged.

For its part, the Lincoln administration was far less focused on foreign policy than domestic politics, and when politics dictated, Washington did not hesitate to adopt policies hostile to British interests. For example, in response to pressure from Northern manufacturers, Lincoln signed into law the punitive Morrill Tariff, which effectively doubled the tax on British goods entering the United States. This tariff provided a protected market for Northern manufacturers and was a blow to the British economy. High tariffs were hated in the South as much as they were resented in Great Britain. The South accounted for two thirds of American exports and thus was disproportionally harmed by tariffs and the higher costs of imported manufactured goods. Yet another blow came with the Federal blockade, which severely restricted the flow of cotton to the great mills so vital to British prosperity. The blockade drove up the price of cotton and resulted in tens of thousands of British mill workers losing their jobs.

Despite these irritants, Prime Minister Lord Palmerston and Foreign Secretary Lord Russell tacked a decidedly middle course regarding the American Civil War. If they sympathized with pro-free trade South it did not demonstrably alter British foreign policy. Britain was determined to remain aloof from the bloody American struggle. In May 1861 Britain deferred Confederate requests for formal recognition and declared a policy of neutrality, recognizing both the Federal Government and the Confederacy as equal belligerents. This meant that vessels from both sides could enter British ports for repairs, refueling, or to pick up cargoes. Washington was not happy with this policy but it was consistent with Britain's aim of supporting trade and commerce, while staying aloof from the war.

DRAMA ON THE HIGH SEAS

Then in the autumn of 1861, British-American relations took a decided turn for the worse. The man responsible for the crisis was Captain Charles Wilkes of the *USS San Jacinto*. Wilkes had a well-earned reputation as a hothead and was known in government circles as a man with "a super abundance of self-esteem and deficiency of judgment."[11] In the fall of 1861, Wilkes confirmed this sorry assessment when, as Captain of the *USS San Jacinto,* he intercepted the *RMS Trent* in the Old Bahamas Channel. The *Trent* was sailing under the Union Jack in international waters, carrying passengers, mail, and cargo from the neutral port of Havana to Great Britain. Wilkes' aim in intercepting the British vessel was to seize two Confederate diplomats, James Mason and John Slidell, who were on their way to London to seek formal recognition of the new Confederacy.

Wilkes announced to his officers that he not only intended to intercept the *Trent* and arrest Mason and Slidell but also take the British vessel as a prize of war. This news was received with alarm by many of his officers who understood that such an act on the high seas was illegal under maritime law. More importantly, it was nearly certain to lead to war with Great Britain. Plunging America into a war with Great Britain was surely beyond the purview of a frigate captain. True to form the cranky Wilkes promptly arrested those voicing objections and proceeded full speed ahead with his plan. As the *San Jacinto* approached the *Trent*, loudhailers were used to order the British vessel to heave to. The captain of the unarmed *Trent* refused and shots were fired

across the bow of the Royal Mail Ship.[12] When the *Trent* finally complied, a boarding party was dispatched under the *San Jacinto*'s second in command, Lieutenant D.M. Fairfax. Fairfax, a man of more prudence than his Captain, understood his actions could well lead to war. He was especially concerned about taking the *Trent* as a prize and sailing her to an American port, even though that was the protocol after intercepting a ship carrying so-called "contraband." Fairfax may also have doubted that passengers, even Confederate ones, sailing from a neutral port to Great Britain on the high seas could be considered contraband.

Once they were aboard the *Trent*, the scene grew ugly. Captain James Moir was outraged and refused to hand over his passenger manifest or indeed any of his passengers. He warned Fairfax that he was committing an act of war. The Royal Mail agent on board, Richard Williams, a veteran of the Royal Navy, could not be restrained and confronted Fairfax on the open deck assuring him that the Royal Navy would smash the U.S. fleet and lift the Federal blockade of Southern ports in twenty days. Other angry passengers joined in the verbal barrage. Before confronting Fairfax, Williams went below to hide the Confederate diplomats' confidential correspondence and other documents. Eventually Mason and Slidell were taken by force—something they insisted on—to the *San Jacinto*. With his prisoners in hand Fairfax decided enough harm had been done to American foreign policy interests for one day and ignored his orders to seize the *Trent* as a prize, thus allowing the vessel to carry on to Great Britain. It was rank insubordination but probably saved the United States from a war with Great Britain ... but only just.

Given the implications for U.S. foreign policy, Captain Wilkes should have been court-martialed upon returning to the United States. Instead he was treated to a hero's welcome. Wilkes was lionized in the press amid a spasm of jingoism. In the face of setbacks on the battlefield, there was a general feeling of satisfaction at poking a stick in the eye of the British lion. Even Lincoln, anxious for some good news and always sensitive to public opinion, went along with the celebrations. Secretary of State Seward, whose job it was to advise the President on issues of foreign policy and international law, failed to remind him that freedom of passage on the high seas was the reason the U.S. entered the War of 1812 and had been a cornerstone of U.S. foreign policy ever since. Seward of all people should have known better.

When news reached Great Britain, Frederick Engels wrote to Karl Marx, "To take political prisoners by force, on a foreign ship, is the clearest *casus belli* there can be. The fellows must be sheer fools to land themselves in a war with England."[13] Meanwhile, the Confederacy was jubilant. Jefferson Davis proclaimed to Congress, "These gentlemen were as much under the jurisdiction of the British Government upon that ship and beneath its flag as if they had been on its soil." According to Davis, Wilkes' high-handed actions were akin to kidnapping Slidell and Mason in Piccadilly Circus.[14]

No great power, especially not the world's leading naval power, was prepared to have its ships intercepted and boarded in international waters.[15]

Captain Charles Wilkes, captain of the *USS San Jacinto*, intercepted the British *RMS Trent* in the Old Bahamas Channel in international waters and almost provoked war between the United States and Great Britain. (Library of Congress)

The British were furious. Even France, America's indispensable ally in the revolution, sided with Britain on this issue. With France neutralized, Britain prepared for war. Prime Minister Lord Palmerston formed a six-member war committee and ordered troops and ships immediately dispatched to British North America. By early in the New Year, Halifax harbor was crowded with the Royal Navy's iron warships, while transports unloaded eleven thousand British Regulars with their gear and artillery, the first contingent of what was planned to be an army of seventy thousand men. Prime Minister Lord Palmerston assured Queen Victoria that Britain was about to "read a lesson to the United States that will not soon be forgotten."[16] The first British transport sailing for Canada passed the Confederate raider *CSS Nashville* in Southampton Water. A British regimental band struck up the song "Off to Charleston" to cheers from the crew of both vessels.[17]

The swift and angry British reaction came as a shock to Washington, which was still celebrating Captain Wilkes' triumph. The crisis had apparently been good politics but was fast proving a foreign policy debacle. The British Government had its own public opinion to contend with and this was decidedly aroused.

Like most crises, this one soon took on a life of its own. With the arrival of British troops and warships it gained momentum, like a giant snowball rolling downhill. At some point, it would be impossible to avoid an impact. Ships and men trained to fight and keen to strike would soon be in dangerously close proximity. A clash seemed inevitable.

Britain's war plans were aggressive and called for the navy to strike quickly at sea. The Royal Navy's steam-driven ironclads would attack and sink the all-wooden American navy and break the blockade of the South, allowing the Confederacy to resume shipping cotton and thus pay for armaments. The Confederacy would be recognized as an ally and joint military operations were to be undertaken. Boston and New York were to be bombarded and a blockade imposed on all ports north of the Mason-Dixon Line thus cutting the United States off from foreign trade. In the interior of Canada, British troops would take the offensive and seize American forts on the traditional invasion routes into Canada along Lake Champlain and the Great Lakes. The region's fierce weather and inhospitable geography were expected to slow any American military response until the following summer, by which time the war would have been decided at sea. Meanwhile a resurgent and rearmed Confederacy was expected to attack Washington. In retrospect, this may have been the closest the Confederacy ever came to winning independence.

Attorney General Edward Bates was the first to sense the danger. He saw that the United States, in the midst of a terrible Civil War that had strained the nation to the limit, was about to throw itself into an unnecessary conflict with the world's greatest naval power. If Britain entered the war, the balance of power would shift decisively against the North. Bates recognized that Great Britain viewed the interception and boarding of the *Trent* as a legitimate *casus belli* and so did the rest of the world. Bates wrote in his diary, "I ... urged that to go to war with Great Britain is to abandon all hope of suppressing the rebellion ... the maritime superiority of Britain would sweep us from Southern waters. Our trade would be utterly ruined and our treasury bankrupt ... there is great reluctance on the part of some members of the cabinet to acknowledge these obvious truths."[18] This was not Lincoln's finest moment.

He responded to the crisis like a politician rather than a statesman. Lincoln's primary concern was managing American public opinion, which was in favor of war rather than surrendering the Confederate diplomats.[19] Lincoln had painted himself into a corner.

The British wasted no time presenting Washington with an ultimatum: apologize and release the Confederate diplomats or face immediate war. This was no bluff—ships and troops were already pouring into Canada. Britain halted the sale of all military equipment and vessels to the North. If American public opinion was aroused, it was nothing compared to that of Great Britain. The son of the newly arrived American Ambassador, Charles Francis Adams, complained bitterly that all his father's work in building relationships in London had been undone almost overnight; he lamented "We have friends here still, but very few."[20] In the United States, American public opinion, Congress, and most of Lincoln's cabinet, were ready to fight rather than back down. Financial markets panicked. On the New York Exchange investors dumped stocks and bonds and raced to buy commodities. A run on the banks forced many to close their doors. This in turn held up a major loan the Treasury Department had been expecting to float in order to fund the war. Worse still, banks and investors became leery of the Greenback and began to put money into gold. As gold prices soared, the value of the dollar plummeted.[21] It was all bad news for the Lincoln administration.

The President slowly came to the realization that Bates' painful assessment was correct.

Captain Wilkes' ill-advised adventure was about to lose them the Civil War. In this view, he finally had the support of Secretary of State Seward, who in the past had advocated war with Britain as a way of reuniting the country.[22] Recognizing the inevitable, Lincoln is said to have pronounced to his cabinet "one war at a time Gentlemen, one war at a time." He asked Seward to write a reply to the British ultimatum and arrange for the release of the Confederate envoys. He then called in friendly newspaper editors for advice on how to prepare the American public for the release of Slidell and Mason.[23]

Britain never did receive the apology demanded—in its place came a long-winded, self-serving explanation of events—but Mason and Slidell were soon on their way to Britain and everyone on both sides of the Atlantic heaved a sigh of relief. In the Confederacy, the disappointment was palpable. The lifting of the blockade on Southern ports alone would have been decisive, opening the floodgates for millions of bales of cotton to reach Europe. The resulting profits would have supplied the Confederacy with more than enough arms, munitions, and ships to win Southern independence. It had all come that close.

Diplomacy moved slowly in this era. It took two weeks for the *Trent* to reach England and a further two weeks for the British ultimatum and accompanying angry British editorials to reach Washington, knocking the Lincoln administration out of its political reverie. Time was then needed for the American government to grasp the gravity of the situation and formulate a response. And then it was another two weeks before the reply was received in London. Had the Atlantic telegraph been in place at the time of the incident, shortening the decision cycle, Britain and the United Sates would likely have been at war by January 1862.

Railway over suspension bridge, Niagara, ON, 1869, with a walkway located on the second level. This bridge was used regularly by Confederate agents moving in and out of Canada. Many registered at Barnett's Museum overlooking Niagara Falls before proceeding to St. Catharines and Montreal. Confederate operative John Yates Beall was arrested near the bridge after an abortive operation to free captured Confederate officers. He was executed at Fort Lafayette in New York Harbor shortly before the end of the war. (See *Evolution of the Confederate Secret Service in Canada*.) McCord Museum, Notman Collection, Montreal, QC,1869 I-37304

The residual effects of the crisis saw the stationing of tens of thousands of British Troops in Canada and the presence of an expanded Royal Navy fleet in Halifax for the duration of the war. The United States spent close to a million dollars, money badly needed elsewhere, to refurbish fortifications along the Canadian border that would never be used. Distrust on both sides remained high. The Trent Crisis marked a turning point in Canadian and British public opinion regarding the war. Slavery remained a contentious issue but more and more people came to see a unified and militarized United States as a threat to British North America.

The Trent affair remains one of the great "what if's" of the Civil War. In the end, the crisis was defused and the course of the Civil War continued unabated—becoming the bloodiest conflict in American history. The one place on which the Trent Affair had a lasting effect was Canada, for it started Canada along the road to developing an east-west railroad system. The only railroad from the Atlantic to Montreal, The Grand Trunk, traveled via Maine. For a time, the British considered capturing Portland to get their hands on this vital railhead but this plan was abandoned. Instead, thousands of British regulars were transported overland to Quebec in the dead of winter. The lesson was clear: Canada could not be defended without an east-west railroad system. No one realized this more than the minister responsible for defense, John A. Macdonald, who would later become Canada's first Prime Minister and a driving force behind the building of a transcontinental railroad.

The prospect of war with the United States forced the bickering colonies in Canada to begin thinking seriously about the need for a confederation of their own. Faced with the conflagration to the south, Canada reluctantly established an expanded militia, supported by a small permanent force. The numbers proposed in the "Militia Bill" were too small, given the threat, but it was all that the squabbling Canadians seemed prepared to fund, and even this brought down the government. British authorities were appalled at the feckless manner in which Canadian politicians looked to their own defense—essentially relying on the mother country to do the heavy lifting. The lesson was not lost on the British. Once the danger had passed, it was clearly time for Great Britain to nudge her diffident, parsimonious North American subjects out of the nest. The countdown to Canadian Confederation had begun.

THE EVOLUTION OF THE CONFEDERATE SECRET SERVICE IN CANADA

During the American Civil War, Montreal was much like Lisbon or Geneva during the Second World War—a center of intrigue and espionage, a city awash in shady money, desperate refugees, soldiers of fortune, spies, and even a few assassins. Few of the Confederate operatives in the city were professional spies; most were amateurs learning their tradecraft on the go under the direction of Senior Confederate Commissioners such as Jacob Thompson, C.C. Clay, and Edwin Lee. Most Confederate agents in the "Secret Service" were businessmen, mariners, soldiers, diplomats, lawyers, doctors, clergymen, and politicians. Few were in it for the money as no formal compensation was offered unless they were already serving soldiers eligible for Confederate military pay, which was notoriously unreliable. Couriers sometimes received a small bonus upon completing a particularly dangerous mission. Many of the Confederacy's most successful spies and couriers were women. In addition to being primarily amateurs, Confederate spies and couriers were almost all volunteers and they understood the risks. Several Confederate agents working out of Montreal were captured during the war. Some died in captivity, such as Reid Sanders, son of Confederate Commissioner George Sanders. Others like Robert Kennedy and John Yates Beall were executed.[24] Sam Davis was captured and sentenced to die, but his sentence was commuted by Lincoln. Theirs was a dangerous business.

Despite the threat of exposure, many Confederate operatives and spies took the time to go to Notman's Studio on Bleury Street in Montreal to have their photographs taken. Clearly, concepts of operational security were different in the 1860's. These photographs have miraculously survived in Montreal's McCord Museum, providing historians with an incredibly rich new source of primary material about the Confederate Secret Service and its supporters in Canada.

The Civil War photographs in the McCord Museum's Notman Collection have gone largely unrecognized and unheralded for a century and a half. The stories behind the faces have been too long forgotten. Surprisingly, when the Museum recently held its excellent exhibition of William Notman's photos and equipment covering his entire life, the only sign of Notman's work with the Confederates in Montreal was a small photo of Jefferson Davis and his family in Montreal.

The Beginning

The evolution of the Confederate Secret Service in Canada, and especially in Montreal, can be traced to the struggle between pro-Southern activists and Federal authorities in slave-holding border states whose allegiance was uncertain in 1861. Delaware, Kentucky, Maryland, Missouri, and Tennessee were among these swing states. Lincoln recognized immediately how important these border states would be in the coming struggle and acted decisively and ruthlessly to keep them from seceding. He sent in troops, arrested whole legislatures, and closed down newspapers, not just in border states but across the Union. He suspended the writ of *Habeas Corpus,* allowing critics to be arrested and held without trial or forced into exile. Lincoln used the military and the police, including the newly formed National Detective Police, to round up known pro-Confederacy leaders, activists, and anyone whose loyalty was suspect. Even those who simply advocated neutrality in the war were subject to arbitrary arrest. To avoid harassment and outright incarceration, many leaders and businessmen from turbulent border states fled. Many went south but others went north to Canada and settled in Halifax, Toronto, and especially Montreal, which was then Canada's largest city and banking center. By 1862, we find people like Captain Patrick C. Martin and George Kane of Baltimore, both strident Confederate sympathizers, living in exile in Montreal.

Like many other refugees, Martin brought his wife and children with him to the city. A skilled, courageous mariner and ardent rebel, Martin was wanted by Federal authorities for smuggling and blockade running. Martin earned his living in Baltimore as a liquor merchant who also sold Catholic bibles and other religious items. Once in Montreal he set up a liquor importing business with another important exile, General William Carroll of Tennessee. Their office and storehouse was on St. Jean Street in the shadow of beautiful Notre Dame Basilica and only a few blocks from the Custom House, which they often frequented. (See Appendix F: Map of Confederate Montreal.) George Kane served as Provost Marshal of Baltimore before the war, and in 1861 tried to raise a private army to keep Federal troops out of the city. When word of his impending arrest reached Kane, he fled north to join Martin and his family in Montreal. Martin, Kane, Carroll, and others stayed in touch with Richmond, and especially Secretary of State Judah Benjamin. They soon became semi-official emissaries for the Confederacy in Canada. British officers looking for passes to visit Lee's Army of Northern Virginia went to Martin and Kane for letters of introduction. Canadian businessmen, bankers, and even politicians looking to participate in lucrative blockade running also needed introductions and contacts in the South.

As more and more escaped POW's made their way to Canada, the fledgling Confederate Secret

Service found itself with newfound "muscle" at their disposal. This was especially true when a large number of John Hunt Morgan's men, fresh from their raid into Ohio, crossed the border into Canada. These Kentucky cavalrymen, as exemplified by Thomas Hines and Bennett Young, evolved into a sort of armed wing of the Confederate Secret Service, capable of carrying out raids including the St. Albans Raid in 1864, which resulted in the most northerly engagement of the war.[25]

By 1862, many Confederate officers and officials were sending their families to Canada to shield them from arrest or harassment. During the war the community of Confederate exiles swelled and became a recognized element of Montreal society. Halifax and Montreal were "secesh" friendly with pronounced Southern sympathies. The size of the Confederate exile community in Montreal was estimated by the city's Police Chief at between 300 and 500 people.[26] This included General William Preston of Kentucky. He was on a diplomatic assignment for Judah Benjamin in Europe but sent his wife, Margaret, and their family to Canada, where they were warmly received by the upper crust of Montreal society. A friend commented that, "Mag Preston is flourishing in Montreal with lordlings (sic) and generals in her train."[27] Like the Davis family who would follow, the Preston girls went to a nearby Catholic convent school while the General's son, "Wick," attended Bishop's College in Lennoxville just southeast of the city. General Preston himself arrived in Montreal in the fall of 1864 at a time when Confederate Secret Service activ-

Bishop's College in Lennoxville in the Eastern Townships, where some children of the Confederate exile community were schooled, including Jefferson Davis' children. McCord Museum MP-0000. 1566, ca. 1855 http://collections.musee-mccord.qc.ca/en/collection/artifacts/MP-0000.1566

ities were at a fever pitch. Preston, like so many Secret Service operatives in the city, lodged at St. Lawrence Hall on St. James Street.

Businessmen and Southern bankers soon followed Martin and Kane to Montreal. Broker Davis (B.A. Davis, H. Davis, or S. Davis) set up shop on St. James Street across from St. Lawrence Hall, unofficial Confederate headquarters in Montreal. Confederate bankers such as John Porterfield, and George and Hezekiah Payne, came north and became associated with the Montreal Branch of the Ontario Bank. Other important Confederate exiles in Montreal included Dr. M.A. Pallen of St. Louis, Dr. Luke Blackburn of Kentucky, General Daniel M. Frost of Missouri, Senator James Westcott of Florida, and General William Carroll of Tennessee.

Mrs. General Preston, called "Mag" by her friends, fit easily into the upper crust of Montreal Society. Mrs. Gen. Preston, Montreal, QC. McCord Museum, Notman Collection, Montreal, QC, 1865. I-14753.1

Captain P.C. Martin and George Kane were recognized as representing the interests of the Confederacy in Montreal early in the war. Martin became close friends with many British officers in the city and provided letters of introduction for those wanting to visit Lee's Army of Northern Virginia. These letters enabled them to travel via the Confederate courier lines through southern Maryland. These were the same routes used by Montreal-based couriers John Surratt, Sarah Slater, and Josephine Brown, and later by John Wilkes Booth. Booth and Martin spent considerable time together when the actor was in Montreal in October 1864. Martin operated two blockade-running schooners out of Montreal. McCord Museum, Notman Collection, Montreal, QC, copied 1862. I4041.0.1

Mrs. R.W. (Josephine) Brown was one of the most successful Confederate couriers of the war. This picture was taken in 1866 when the Browns remained in exile after the war. The reason for Josephine's and her husband Robert's extended stay in Montreal may have had to do with Robert's brief posting at Andersonville Prison and the subsequent execution of commander Henry Wirz who was held responsible for the camp's high POW mortality rates. An equally plausible explanation, however, is that Josephine, by virtue of her role, was privy to Booth's and George Sanders' plotting in Canada. (See "Confederate Couriers" and "The Hidden Hand—John Wilkes Booth in Montreal.") Mrs. R.W. Brown, Montreal, QC. McCord Museum, Notman Collection, Montreal, QC, 1866. I-20023.1

Confederate banker John Porterfield, taken at Notman's Studio, Montreal in 1862. Porterfield was an important player in the Confederate Secret Service. He and others set up an operation in New York designed to "short" the new American paper currency. They bought gold on margin and shipped it to England. This sapped already weak U.S. gold supplies, drove up gold, and put downward pressure on the dollar. Their plan was to create a run on the dollar, and it very nearly worked. Canadian banks and American financiers like J.P. Morgan also played the gold market and shorted the dollar. Porterfield later played a role in spiriting John Surratt out of St. Lawrence Hall and hiding him at his townhouse at Prince of Wales Terrace located on the western end of McGill University's campus. One of his neighbors was tobacco magnate William C. Macdonald, McGill's greatest benefactor. After the war, Porterfield settled in Niagara-on-the-Lake, where a small colony of Confederate exiles took up residence. John Porterfield. McCord Museum, Notman Collection, Montreal, QC, 1862. I-3606.1

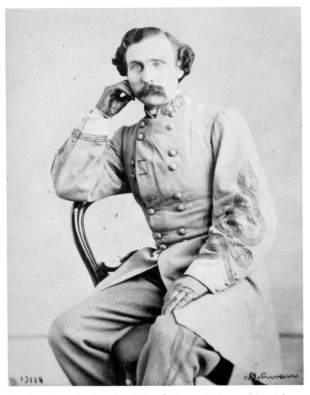

Dr. M.A. Pallen of Missouri was originally sent north to check on the health of Confederate prisoners held in Federal POW Camps. This included Johnson's Island, Ohio. Pallen wrote to Secretary of War Edwin Stanton complaining of the harsh conditions under which Southern soldiers were held, particularly given the bitter, cold climate. Pallen's medical visits also allowed him to scout these camps, which were targets for attack by the Confederate Secret Service looking to free badly-needed veterans who would then be returned to the Confederacy via Canada. He was a regular at St. Lawrence Hall. Doctor M.A. Pallen. McCord Museum, Notman Collection, Montreal, QC, 1864. I-12201.1

Coming from the border state of Missouri, General Daniel M. Frost is typical of the Confederate refugees and soldiers who made Montreal their home during the Civil War. Here we see him posing in Notman's Studio in his resplendent Confederate Officer's uniform, including leather gloves. Gen. D.M. Frost, CSA. McCord Museum, Notman Collection, Montreal, QC, 1864. I13179.1

It was these early exiles and escaping POW's who laid the groundwork for Confederate Secret Service activities in Canada. Men like Kane, Carroll, and especially P.C. Martin, were soon looked upon as the Confederacy's consuls in Montreal. Newly arrived exiles went to them for help, advice, or money. British officers looking to visit the Army of Northern Virginia as military observers went to them for letters of introduction enabling them to reach Virginia via secret courier lines through southern Maryland. Anyone wanting to do business with the Confederacy also called on them, and this trickle of commercial interest in trading with the Confederacy grew as the profits from blockade running became apparent. The Confederacy may have had little manufacturing infrastructure but it was hardly poor. The South had a stranglehold on the most valuable commodity in the world: cotton. They also had tobacco, turpentine, and rice. Before the war, the South accounted for two thirds of American exports and provided most of the tariff and excise revenue funding the Federal government.

The value of a bale of cotton increased nearly one thousand percent on the European market by the middle of the war. Meanwhile, the Confederacy was willing to pay huge premiums for imported food, munitions, uniforms, arms, and medicines. A barrel of salt worth $7.50 in Nassau sold for $1,700 in Charleston.[28] One single successful round trip through the blockade would pay for the ship and produce a profit for its owner and investors. With cotton commanding $500-$600 a bale or more, a cargo of 800 bales would be worth at least $400,000. The inbound cargo of food, uniforms, medicines, or munitions would be worth half that much again, producing round trip revenue of nearly $600,000. With most ships costing $40-50,000 and maritime insurance available against loss—at least for British (and Canadian) registered vessels—the potential profits were breathtaking. British and Canadian entrepreneurs were soon joined by investors from places like New York, creating a fleet of blockade runners that numbered more than 1,500 vessels.[29] Half to two thirds of these ships would eventually be caught or destroyed but only after making multiple runs through the blockade. Savannah entrepreneur and banker Gazaway Lamar and his slave-trading son, Charles Lamar, were typical of those involved in the trade. At the start of the war, Lamar sold his Northern assets and transferred the money to places like Montreal beyond the reach of the U.S. government.[30] The Lamars helped Confederate agent Captain P.C. Martin obtain his first blockade-running schooners based out of Montreal through the Confederate-controlled Ontario Bank.[31] Charles Lamar appears to have been in Montreal at St. Lawrence Hall in August 1864 when the hotel was full of American cotton traders, bankers, and anti-Lincoln politicians of all stripes.[32]

The Lamars maintained agents and business contacts in New York throughout the war. Gazaway Lamar even proposed going into the blockade-running business with New York Mayor Fernando Wood, who was another regular at St. Lawrence Hall. With so much money on the table, bankers, financiers, railroad tycoons, political powerbrokers, shipping magnates,

John Yates Beall was a larger-than-life Confederate agent who operated out of Canada and was often in Montreal. Beall was a swashbuckler willing to take on just about any assignment no matter how dangerous. He seized the *SS Philo Parsons* on the Great Lakes in an effort to capture the POW camp on Johnson's Island, Lake Erie. The Federal garrison had advance warning of the attack and so the plan was aborted. Beall and Lt. Robert Kennedy, another agent with close ties to St. Lawrence Hall, participated in raids in the United States, including attempting to burn New York's largest hotels and hijacking trains carrying confederate POW's. Both Beall and Kennedy were ultimately captured and executed in early 1865: Kennedy at Fort Lafayette in New York Harbor and Beall at Fort Columbus on Governor's Island, New York Harbor.[33] J. Y. Beall. McCord Museum, Notman Collection, 1865. I-16771.0.1

One of at least two Payne brothers from Kentucky who went into exile in Montreal. The Paynes were bankers specializing in currency and gold transactions. George and his brother, Hezekiah, participated in John Porterfield's assault on the Greenback. All three had such close association with the Ontario Bank on Place d'Armes that they were thought to be employees. G.B. Payne. McCord Museum, Notman Collection, Montreal, QC, 1864. I-12644.1

and anyone with cash sought to have a hand in the game. Eventually, Lamar's agent in New York, Connecticut-born slave trader Nelson Trowbridge, was arrested and charged with treason. He was pardoned near the end of the war and immediately fled to Montreal where he registered at St. Lawrence Hall.[34] Trowbridge told U.S. Consul John Potter in April 1865 that he was in Montreal to meet Lafayette Baker, head of the War Department's National Detective Police.[35] What business Trowbridge had with the War Department's chief spy is unclear, but it may have had to do with cotton.

Gazaway Lamar and his son set up their own blockade-running company, "The Importing and Exporting Company of Georgia." They purchased six fast ships and were actively running the blockade, including regular runs between Nassau and New York.[36] They maintained close ties with the Confederates in Canada throughout the war.[37]

By 1863, the Confederate Secret Service was well entrenched in Canada. Funding came from Richmond via couriers and was supplemented by profits from blockade running. There was sufficient money available to undertake raids into the United States to free Confederate POW's.[38] P.C. Martin was in the middle of these clandestine activities, with his wife carrying messages to Confederate officers imprisoned in these camps.[39] Two full-fledged expeditions were made to free Confederate POW's on Johnson's Island in Ohio—both ended in failure but nevertheless represented serious, well-organized, well-funded operations. Some of the Confederates captured in Ohio were carrying on them $5,000 cashier's checks issued by the Bank of Montreal.[40] The first raid on the island was staged in 1863, led by blockade-running legend Captain John Wilkinson. The second raid in 1864 was led by Secret Service agent John Y. Beall.[41] In 1864, Confederate Secret Service agents Robert Martin, John Headley, Robert Kennedy, John Price, and others orchestrated the fire-bombing of hotels in New York City.[42] The Confederate Secret Service also took credit for the destruction of Federal shipping on the Mississippi.[43]

In 1864, Montreal-based Confederate bankers John Porterfield and George Payne set up an operation in New York to undermine the U.S. Greenback. With a budget of $100,000, they began buying gold and selling Greenbacks. The gold was then shipped to Great Britain. The Lamars also participated in this assault on the Greenback, as did a number of Canadian banks and New York financiers such J.P. Morgan.[44] It appears Morgan alone shipped as much as a billion dollars in gold to London driving up the price of the commodity against the Greenback from $1.30 to $1.71 and eventually as high as $2.85. The resulting profits were staggering.[45] Morgan was getting rich betting against his own country.

1864: The Confederacy Shifts Strategy

By 1864 the leadership of the Confederacy recognized that military victory was beyond their reach. From 1861 through early 1863, the outnumbered Confederate Army of Northern Virginia under Robert E. Lee inflicted a series of crushing defeats on the Army of the Potomac but these victories, such as the Seven Days' Battles outside Richmond, Manassas, Fredericksburg and Chancellorsville, as well as the bloody stand-off at Sharpsburg/Antietam, had surprisingly little impact on policy in Washington. Lincoln simply buried the dead, raised new regiments, and renewed the fight. Conscription was introduced, allowing the North to tap a manpower reservoir many times larger than that of the South. By 1864, the Confederacy no longer had the resources to take the offensive, which was always General Lee's preferred course of action. He once commented that Richmond was "never so safe as when its defenders were absent" fighting elsewhere. But by 1864, the South's days of seizing the initiative were almost over. From behind their miles of entrenchments outside Richmond, the Confederates hoped to inflict such high casualties on the Army of the Potomac that Northern public opinion would insist on an armistice.

The first part of the plan more or less worked. Lee inflicted more casualties on Grant's forces from the Wilderness through Cold Harbor and the early stages of the Petersburg campaign, than Lee had men in his whole army. But Grant, with seemingly unlimited manpower, just kept flanking south and attacking. Jefferson Davis and his Secretary of State Judah Benjamin recognized that Lincoln was *never* going to allow Southern independence, no matter what the cost in blood. Lincoln was willing to compromise on just about anything except fracturing the Union. Meanwhile the South was fast running out of everything needed to sustain the war effort, including munitions, arms, manpower, and food.

By 1864, the Northern public was certainly growing weary of the war but no credible peace movement had taken form. Jefferson Davis, Judah Benjamin, and even Lee, recognized the need to influence the upcoming election. The issue could not be won on the battlefield. A political solution was required.

Millions of dollars were appropriated for the Confederate Secret Service to launch operations into Northern states and promote an antiwar movement. Influencing the Democratic convention planned for Chicago in August 1864 was essential. The South wanted a negotiated peace or at least an armistice that allowed room for Southern independence. Lincoln was the chief obstacle to achieving this aim. It was during this period of desperation that plans for kidnapping the President or killing him outright were set in motion. There were several such schemes being considered and funded in 1864-1865 but only one, the plot involving John Wilkes Booth, struck home. In addition to kidnapping, there were plans afoot to blow up the White House during a Cabinet meeting.[46] One of John Hunt Morgan's men in Canada, Lt. W. Alston, who was shipped home via Halifax, wrote to Confederacy President Davis offering to go north and "rid my country of some of her deadliest enemies by striking at the very hearts blood."[47] The letter has survived but not Davis' reply. Interestingly, there is an Alston registered at St. Lawrence Hall on 6 August 1864.[48]

Violence against Lincoln was being planned and funded but many thought the best way to get rid of Lincoln remained the ballot box. The ever-rising casualty rates made the war increasingly unpopular, as did conscription. Lincoln himself admitted that without a victory on the battlefield he was likely to be defeated in the fall 1864 election.[49] The Confederates were not the only ones aware of Lincoln's vulnerability and declining popularity in the summer of 1864. Radical Republicans and die-hard war Democrats were concerned that a strong "peace candidate" might emerge and bring the war to an early end. Those engaged in war profiteering certainly did not want to see an end to the fighting. The Radicals, in contrast, wanted the South utterly defeated, crushed and totally reconstructed. Lincoln's position was different. He sought restoration of the "old Union" but preferably without slavery. In addressing slavery, Lincoln constantly had to take into account the slave-holding states that stayed loyal to the Union.

The Radical Republicans meanwhile viewed Lincoln as incompetent and hopelessly weak when it came to harsh business of reconstruction. Lincoln was a conservative regarding the Constitution. He wanted the country reunited as it had been but without slavery, and even on this issue he proceeded cautiously. In rejecting the Wade Davis Bill, Lincoln set off a firestorm within Radical circles. The Radicals did not want the country united in its old form. They sought a revolution. The Radicals wanted a social revolution that would transform the South. In pocket vetoing the Wade Davis Bill, Lincoln was rejecting their plans for harsh reconstruction. He also rejected their plans to treat the South as a conquered territory to be governed by the military.

Ontario Bank President Henry Starnes was Mayor of Montreal both before and after the Civil War. Starnes was the favorite Canadian banker of the Confederate Secret Service in Canada. Confederate deposits in the bank were so large that they effectively controlled the institution. Starnes allowed large bank drafts from the Confederate account to be issued in the name of bank employees and then endorsed to the real recipients to hide the paper trail, an early form of money laundering. Starnes and American banker J. Cooke would later become involved in the "Pacific Scandal" which brought down the Conservative government of John A. Macdonald. A bank draft for 61 Pound Sterling (about $450-$550 dollars given exchange rates in the first quarter of 1865) signed by H. Starnes, Ontario Bank, was found on the body of John Wilkes Booth after he was killed at the Garrett farm in Virginia. In the Lincoln trial transcript H. Starnes was misinterpreted as H. Stanus and the error remains uncorrected. Mayor Starnes. McCord Museum, Notman Collection, Montreal, QC, 1866. I20691.1

Anyone who had served the Confederacy was to lose the right to vote and have their large estates confiscated. Newly freed Blacks would be enfranchised and organized to support the Radical Republican agenda. It was a recipe for poisoned race relations but would have guaranteed Radical control of Congress for a generation.

Under the Radical plan, Confederate states were not to be readmitted to Congress without the approval of the Republican majority. Keeping Democratic Southern states out of Congress would have given the Radical Republicans a stranglehold on power. Particularly dangerous to Radical plans was Lincoln's intention to readmit Southern states as quickly and painlessly as possible. The balance of power in Congress would have swung decidedly against the Radicals, who were always a minority, even within their own party. Democrats and conservative Republicans would have had the votes to defeat Radical Reconstruction. With Lincoln in the White House the whole Radical agenda was at risk. Everything the Radicals had fought for would slip from their grasp on the very cusp of victory. After the fall of Richmond, when Lincoln proposed recalling the Virginia Assembly, the Radicals almost lost their minds. One of their leaders, Senator Ben Wade, commented on rumors about plans to assassinate Lincoln, which abounded in Washington, and added, "the sooner he was assassinated the better."[50]

Against this volatile backdrop, Judah Benjamin sent a new group of senior Commissioners to Canada under the leadership of Jacob Thompson to hurry along Lincoln's demise politically or otherwise. An accomplished statesman and former member of President Buchanan's administration, Jacob Thompson carried with him bills of exchange in gold and hard currencies worth a million dollars. These funds would be supplemented with blockade running, bank robberies ($200,000 was seized during the St. Albans Raid), and additional advances from Richmond. All of this money was used to fund Confederate activities in Canada and Northern states.[51] This money was held on deposit in various banks, including the Bank of Montreal and the Ontario Bank. Thompson's deposits in the Ontario Bank alone amounted to nearly three quarters of a million dollars. A further $100,000 was deposited in the Niagara and District Bank in St. Catharines and an account was set up in the Bank of Montreal.[52] Given capital ratios for banks at the time, the money deposited in the Ontario Bank (Montreal) and Niagara and District Bank (St. Catharines) gave the Confederates enormous influence, if not effective control, over these institutions. Ontario Bank President Henry Starnes allowed Jacob Thompson to issue bank drafts in the names of bank employees, who then endorsed them to the real intended recipients of the money. This was an early example of money laundering and shows how *New York Daily News* editor, Congressman, and Lincoln opponent Benjamin Wood received a $25,000 payment.[53] When John Wilkes Booth's dead body was searched at the Garrett Farm in Virginia, they found in his possession a negotiable cashier's check from the Ontario Bank signed by *H. Stanus.*" This was clearly a misreading of the signature of Henry Starnes, the manager and

Bank of Montreal's main branch and its headquarters next door facing Place d'Armes 1860. The Bank held deposits of Confederate Secret Service money and was active in the New York gold market.[54] Varina Davis stored Jefferson Davis' personal papers, smuggled out of Richmond, in the bank's vault. She hoped he might write his memoirs as a means of combatting melancholia. Davis demurred, telling his wife he "could not look on his dead so soon." It would be twenty years before he would write his memoirs. Old and new Bank of Montreal buildings, City Bank. McCord Museum, Notman Collection, Montreal, QC, about 1860, copied 1928. MP-0000.364

Ontario Bank blank check on the Ottawa Branch. McCord Museum, Notman Collection, Montreal, QC, M930.50.5.169

The purser's and mail office at St. Lawrence Hall where business was transacted. A special line from the Telegraph Office directly across St. James Street was set up here so Southern guests could stay abreast of war news. Note the spittoons. Chewing tobacco was an American predilection and these spittoons reflected the predominately American clientele at St. Lawrence Hall. St. Lawrence Hall Office, Montreal, QC. McCord Museum, Notman Collection, Montreal, QC, about 1890. VIEW-1883 president of the Montreal branch of the Ontario Bank, who had been Mayor of Montreal before the Civil War and who would hold that position again.[55]

While Jacob Thompson was the leader of the Confederate Secret Service in Canada, there were other members of the *Confederate Cabinet* in Canada, including Clement Clay, George Sanders, Beverley Tucker, J.C. Holcombe, and William Cleary. The latter was Thompson's secretary and had taken up exile in Canada earlier in the war and knew the country. All of these "Commissioners" had considerable latitude to conduct their own operations. Tucker focused on recruiting Northern entrepreneurs and bankers for blockade running and massive cotton-for-food schemes. While in Montreal during 1864-1865, Tucker orchestrated what was perhaps the largest cotton deal in history up to that time. This exchange of cotton for contraband involved at least half a billion dollars in 1864 Greenbacks and would have provided the North with badly-needed cotton and the South with desperately needed food and munitions. This inter-belligerent trade, which certainly extended the war, was supported by both the Treasury Department and the White House.

James Holcombe was responsible for arranging a system to return escaped Confederate POW's arriving in Canada to the Confederacy. Clement Clay, stationed at St. Catharines, focused on attacking Federal POW camps and raiding areas along the Great Lakes and New England. George Sanders led abortive peace initiatives in Niagara Falls designed to embarrass Lincoln in the run up to the American elections. While at Niagara's Clifton House during these negotiations, Sanders was overheard loudly calling for the assassination of President Lincoln. Sanders was obsessed with the idea of assassinating tyrants and he considered Lincoln the greatest tyrant of all. He would spend considerable time with John Wilkes Booth during the actor's stay in Montreal in October 1864.

The proposed kidnapping of Lincoln was the boldest and surely the most complex operation undertaken by the Confederate Secret Service. There were coordinating meetings with Booth in Boston and later in Montreal in the fall of 1864 and very likely in early 1865.[56]

Daniel Lucas and General Edwin Lee became close friends of Montreal publisher and Confederate sympathizer John Lovell. Lovell published Lucas' biography of John Yates Beall who was executed at Fort Lafayette in New York Harbor in February 1865.[57] (Jefferson Davis and his family were later supported by Lovell during their exile in Montreal following the war.) The *Montreal Gazette* published Lucas' poem *"In the Land Where We Were Dreaming"* about the South's lost dream of independence.[58] It became part of the South's "lost cause" mythology.

W.W. Finney was a larger-than-life character and a key member of the Confederate Secret Service in Canada. He operated between Halifax and Montreal in the years leading up to and during the Civil War. Finney and his lifelong friend, Major Benjamin F. Ficklin, were among the founders of the famous "Pony Express," which incidentally was based on the feats of another man hailing

William Cleary came to Canada as the private secretary of Senior Commissioner Jacob Thompson. He was assigned this role, in part, because he had been exiled to Canada earlier in the war and knew the country and its people. William W. Cleary. McCord Museum, Notman Collection, Montreal, QC, 1865. I-15278.1

James P. Holcombe was a distinguished legal scholar from Virginia sent to Canada originally to organize legal efforts to prevent the captured *USS Chesapeake* being turned over to the U.S. Federal authorities. The *Chesapeake* had been captured at sea by Confederate privateers (most of them British subjects) and sailed into Canadian waters. The vessel was tracked down by the U.S. Navy and recaptured; but since this second seizure took place in Canadian territorial waters, the vessel was taken to Halifax where its fate was adjudicated by an admiralty court. The Confederate government desperately wanted to keep the *Chesapeake* but Holcombe soon realized their case was hopeless and he so advised Richmond. Holcombe was then sent to Canada West via Montreal to organize a system for returning escaped Confederate POW's to the South through Halifax. Here he had the support of important Haligonians like Dr. William Almon and Benjamin Wier, and the Catholic Archbishop of Halifax, Thomas Connolly. Holcombe also played a central role in the abortive peace negotiations at Niagara Falls in the fall of 1864. James P. Holcombe. McCord Museum, Notman Collection, Montreal, QC, 1864. I-11708.1

George N. Sanders was a Confederate Commissioner in Canada whose primary job was recruiting and nurturing anti-Lincoln politicians in the Republican and Democratic Parties. Many of those on Sanders' "client list" turn up at St. Lawrence Hall in the summer and fall of 1864. Sanders was determined to elect a peace candidate such as New York Governor Horatio Seymour to lead the Democratic Party into the 1864 election. Part of his plan called for the Democrats to expand their base by bringing in delegates from the western territories. Sanders' plan had considerable merit and Lincoln himself confessed in the summer of 1864 that, in the absence of a change in fortune on the battlefield, he was likely to lose the 1864 election. Sherman's capture of Atlanta shifted the tide in the nick of time. Sanders was a life-long advocate of assassinating tyrants, of whom he considered Lincoln the greatest. Sanders' son, Reid Sanders, was a Confederate Courier captured in 1864 who subsequently died in a Federal POW camp. Sanders spent considerable time with John Wilkes Booth when the latter was in Montreal in October 1864. George N. Sanders. McCord Museum, Notman Collection, Montreal, QC, 1864. I-13580.1

Beverley Tucker was sent North to Canada by the Confederate government to organize a cotton-for-contraband scheme valued at between five hundred million and a billion dollars in 1864 currency. The "who's who" of the banking and cotton trading world was soon in Montreal's St. Lawrence Hall, meeting with Tucker. Astonishingly, this massive exercise in inter-belligerent trade had the support of the White House. (See Chapter: *Trading with the Enemy*.) Mr. Beverley Tucker. McCord Museum, Notman Collection, Montreal, QC, 1865. I-14268.1

Brigadier General Edwin G. Lee was a cavalry veteran of the Army of Northern Virginia who had been wounded in battle and suffered from lung ailments. He had early dealings with John Yates Beall and had proposed setting up a "destructionist corps" to attack the North as a fifth volume. He was also aware of Rev. J.K. Stewart's early proposals to kidnap Lincoln. Jefferson Davis sent Lee to Canada in late 1864/early 1865 to take over as senior Confederate Commissioner from Jacob Thompson. Gen. Edwin Gray Lee. McCord Museum, Notman Collection, Montreal, QC, 1865. I-17038.1

Daniel B. Lucas was a cousin to General Edwin Gray Lee, who was posted to Canada in 1864 to assume command of the Confederate Secret Service from Jacob Thompson. Lucas had earlier begun his service in paramilitary operations and privateering in the Chesapeake Bay area. There, he worked closely with John Yates Beall, another agent who would play an important role in Confederate Secret Service operations in Canada.

Before coming to Canada, Lucas interrogated Federal prisoners of war captured during the "Dahlgren Raid" to obtain intelligence. This establishes him as a Secret Service operative even before he arrived in Montreal. One authoritative glimpse at the activity of Confederate intelligence personnel at a moment when retaliation for the infamous Dahlgren raid must have been on everyone's mind survives in a pass to Libby prison for 30 March 1864.[59] It authorized B.G. Burley, John Maxwell, and *Daniel Lucas* to visit Libby prison to interrogate prisoners from the Parnell Legion captured on the eastern shore of Virginia.[60] Both Burley and Lucas would be assigned to Canada as part of Confederate Secret Service operations. D.B. Lucas. McCord Museum, Notman Collection, Montreal, QC, 1865. I-17573.1

9190

W.W. Finney was a man of action and a key member of the Confederate Secret Service in Canada. This 1863 photograph was likely taken when the first raid on Johnson's Island POW camp was being staged. Finney and his partner Benjamin Ficklin helped create the original Pony Express. Ficklin was apparently in Montreal in 1865. He was also in Washington the day Lincoln was assassinated. He was arrested but ultimately released through the intervention of Washington powerbroker Orville H. Browning. W. W. Finney. McCord Museum, Notman Collection, Montreal, QC, 1863. I-9190.1

from the Montreal area, François-Xavier Aubry. During the war, Finney served as a Lieutenant Colonel commanding the 51st Virginia Volunteer Infantry. He was captured and imprisoned in the POW camp on Johnson's Island, but was later exchanged and returned south where he and Ficklin focused their energies on blockade running. They purchased the fast blockade runner, *Robert E. Lee,* for the Confederacy. Under the command of famed blockade runner John Wilkinson, the *Robert E. Lee* became one of the Confederacy's most successful raiders.[61] In 1863, Wilkinson was assigned the task of leading twenty-six experienced sailors to Canada to capture the POW camp on Johnson's Island in the fall of 1863. Because of his familiarity with the camp, W.W. Finney joined the expedition. From Halifax, they made their way to Montreal where their plans were coordinated by Confederate Secret Service agents P.C. Martin and George Kane. Martin's wife acted as a courier to Confederate officers inside the camp, alerting them to the planned breakout. The plan was ultimately betrayed to Canadian authorities by a Canadian Confederate sympathizer. With the plan discovered, the raid on Johnson's Island had to be abandoned.[62] Finney had this photograph taken at Notman's studio during his stay in Montreal in the run up to the raid. He is also found registered at Barnett's Museum in Niagara on 3 August 1864. He and his partner Ficklin remained active in blockade-running activities and had offices in Wilmington and also possibly Nassau.[63] Ficklin was active in cotton trading and involved in Beverley Tucker's mega cotton-for-contraband trade centered in Montreal in 1864-1865. He was

This is a particularly interesting and important photograph. Left to right: the small man standing with his hand in his coat is either Rev. J.K. Stewart or S.F. Cameron, both of whom had been trained by the British in spycraft.[64] Trained spies were a rarity in the Confederate Secret Service. The man seated to Stewart's left is senior Confederate Commissioner Jacob Thompson and across from him is his secretary William Cleary. The man standing in the middle is Confederate officer and agent Robert Brown, husband of successful courier Josephine Brown. The man standing on the far right bears a remarkable resemblance to confederate sea raider John Wilkinson, who was then in Canada. The picture appears celebratory and may have to do with the successful defense of the St. Albans Raiders. Mr. Cameron's group. McCord Museum, Notman Collection, Montreal, QC, 1865. I-8504.l in Washington the day of the assassination and was arrested and questioned. He was ultimately released upon the intervention of powerbroker Orville Browning.[65]

The leadership of the Secret Service in Canada followed a series of fragmented agendas. Jacob Thompson, for example, focused on a range of priorities, including a proposed uprising of Copperheads in the Northwest, manipulating the Democratic Convention to elect a peace candidate, and buying influence with various newspaper editors. The goal was to rob Lincoln of the nomination or at least to defeat him at the polls with a Democratic "peace" candidate. This was the last, best hope for the beleaguered Confederacy and necessitated spending considerable amounts of money from Thompson's rich Montreal Bank accounts. Jacob Thompson's contacts with U.S. politicians during this period remain largely in the shadows but are historically significant. It has long been assumed his contacts were primarily with Democrats, particularly anti-Lincoln Copperheads, but a review of the St. Lawrence Hall Guest Book indicates Thompson, or others in the Secret Service, were having back-channel discussions with disaffected Republicans, including some anti-Lincoln Radicals. More astonishingly, it appears Thompson and others were also in discussion with persons representing members of Lincoln's own cabinet, such as Secretary of State Seward and Secretary of War Stanton.

No less a Radical Republican than the mighty and cantankerous Thaddeus Stevens turned up at St. Lawrence Hall in August 1864 and he was not alone. Stevens was accompanied by a host of other disaffected Republicans. In the summer of 1864, with Grant stalled outside Richmond and Sherman bloodily rebuffed at Kennesaw Mountain, Lincoln's prospects for re-election were at their nadir. It was precisely at this time that St. Lawrence Hall was flooded with Democratic and Republican politicians, all rubbing elbows with the Confederate Secret Service. Everyone was scrambling for safe ground.

Even hardline Secretary of War Edwin Stanton, whom Lincoln nicknamed "Mars" after the god of war, panicked at the prospect of losing the November election. He sent a friend, Judge Jeremiah Black, to explore the possibility of a negotiated peace prior to the election or at least prior to the inauguration. Interestingly, there is a Dr. Cha(z) Black at St. Lawrence Hall on 16 August, exactly when Judge Black was known to be in Canada. Black was a senior Democrat and respected judge from Thaddeus Stevens' home state of Pennsylvania. Stanton, like most of Lincoln's cabinet, believed their administration was headed for imminent defeat.[66] Stanton was thoroughly unnerved by the prospect of being out of power and unprotected. Considering that he and Secretary of State Seward had imprisoned as many as 20,000 American citizens without trial, some backlash was expected once they were out of office.[67] Stanton would later try to distance himself from Black's mission but Judge Black had a sterling reputation for integrity. Even the Confederates trusted him. Black, who was a Democrat, participated in the 1864 August Conspiracy to dump Lincoln that was centered in New York.

With the fall of Atlanta, the military victory Lincoln so desperately needed, the political momentum shifted in the President's favor. When Stanton tried to scapegoat Black for going to Canada, Black calmly reaffirmed that he had indeed been in Canada at Stanton's request to hold talks with the Confederates.[68] For the Secretary of War, who was a close ally of the Radicals, it was all very embarrassing. Even Lincoln's closest ally in the Cabinet, Secretary of State Seward, appears to have opened up a back channel to the Confederates in Canada in the form of Detroit District Attorney Halmar H. Emmons. The U.S. Consul in Montreal wrote to Seward saying Emmons had identified himself as an agent for Secretary of State Seward.[69] Emmons' peace negotiations with the Confederate Secret Service were supposed to have taken place in 1865 but we find him at St. Lawrence Hall as early as 4 November 1864.[70]

One last set of abortive peace negotiations was undertaken by the Honorable R.J. Walker in early 1865. Walker was a distinguished member of Congress and a former Secretary of the Treasury. During the Civil War, he was called to Washington to provide advice on stabilizing the new U.S. fiat currency. The Greenback was under considerable pressure abroad, with the faith and credit of the war-torn United States being questioned by European investors. Confederate bonds backed by cotton were being oversubscribed while the U.S. could not raise a dime in foreign credit markets. (This currency weakness was exploited by the Confederate Secret Service who used New York as a base for undermining the

Colonel George Steele of Kentucky, was responsible for organizing Copperhead resistance to the Lincoln administration. In Windsor, Steele organized meetings with leaders of American groups like the Sons of Liberty and Sons of the Golden Circle. Jacob Thompson attended some of these meetings and the Secret Service funneled considerable sums of money to these groups. Lafayette Baker's National Detective Police had infiltrated these organizations with spies and informers. The anticipated uprising in the North West never materialized. Steele operated primarily out of Hamilton where he was in frequent contact with anti-Lincoln dissidents from the North West states who proposed a rebellion against the President's war policies. George Steele. McCord Museum, Notman Collection, Montreal, QC, 1864. I-11743.1

currency by buying gold and selling Greenbacks.) Walker wrote a series of treatises on the soundness of the U.S. currency and the bright prospects for post-war America aimed primarily at European audiences. He made little headway in Great Britain and France but was successful in convincing German investors to buy U.S. bonds.

Walker was a Lincoln supporter but one who maintained his independence from the White House. He was very much his own man. He saw the war as a national tragedy and looked for ways to end it. He represented a growing constituency within the country that wanted to end the slaughter on terms short of entirely crushing the South. Whether Walker acted with Lincoln's approval is unclear. Always a consummate politician, Lincoln had a way of winking at peace feelers without ever committing himself to their outcome.

Walker communicated with Confederate Commissioners in Canada about the possibility of a compromise settlement. He spent a month in Montreal in February 1865, negotiating terms with Confederate Commissioner George N. Sanders. The negotiations took place at St. Lawrence Hall. In his letter to the *New York Times* about the negotiations, George Sanders asks readers who may want to comment to send their letters to St. Lawrence Hall care of proprietor, Henry Hogan. Like so many other American visitors to Montreal, Walker took the time to have his photograph taken at Notman's Studio. In one of these photos, he posed with the wife of Confederate General William Preston. Preston was a Confederate diplomat and agent, reporting to Confederate Secretary of State Judah

Benjamin. This indicates, if nothing else, the social circle in which Walker was traveling while in Montreal.

The proposed compromise emerging from these meetings makes for interesting historical reading. It called for the reduction of tariffs and duties—a longstanding Southern demand. It also called for a diminution of executive power which was largely unrestrained by this stage of the war. Even the rulings of the Supreme Court were regularly ignored by the White House. The proposed peace document further stated that no section of the country should be allowed to dominate another section—a longstanding Southern fear. Slavery was ended. The amendment to the Constitution abolishing slavery was recognized as law but individual states rather than the Federal government would be charged with implementation. As to universal suffrage, the Federal government would undertake to leave this question to the jurisdiction of the states. In return, the Confederate States would willingly re-enter the Union and fighting would cease. In 1863, or even 1864, these terms might have ended the bloodshed but by 1865 it was too late. The Confederacy was losing the war and had little leverage. Radical Republicans, who were then in political ascendency, were intent on crushing the South and imposing a harsh reconstruction regime. They already despised and distrusted Lincoln for his inclination to be lenient toward the defeated South. That Walker's proposals were printed in the *New York Times* and made public would have driven some Radical Republicans to distraction.

Sanders wrote an open letter to the editor of the *New York Times* explaining the proposed compromise and inviting anyone interested to send their comments to him, care of Mr. Henry Hogan, proprietor of St. Lawrence Hall in Montreal. It was clear early on that the Lincoln Administration had little interest in Walker's terms at this point in the war. The White House could sense that the South was nearly exhausted and the war winding down.[71] Lincoln was open to some compromise but only after achieving complete victory; this is what worried the Radicals. Lincoln's willingness to entertain compromise with the Confederates was anathema to Radical Republicans.

Complementary and Conflicting Agendas

The 1864 arrival in Canada of Clement Clay, Beverley Tucker, James Holcombe, and especially the forceful and mercurial George Sanders, did not sit well with Jacob Thompson, who always liked to be in control. In that regard, George Sanders was particularly troublesome. He was persuasive, full of ideas, and not inclined to take orders. All this unnerved the cautious Thompson. But since all these new "helpers" had official sanction from Judah Benjamin and Jefferson Davis, Thompson did his best to make the situation work, however awkward. He supported Clay, Holcombe, and Tucker when they set up shop at St. Catharines (Ontario) near Niagara in a house provided by Robert Cox, a protégé of Republican powerbroker Orville Browning. Thompson transferred nearly $100,000 to Clement Clay's bank account in St. Catharines in the Niagara and District Bank, in the center

Here we see Hon J.R. Walker posing for a photo with Mag Preston, wife of Confederate General William Preston, who was involved in Confederate Secret Service and diplomatic activities. General Preston was in Montreal in October 1864 and both he and John Wilkes Booth had rooms at St. Lawrence Hall. Hon. R. J. Walker and Mrs. Preston. McCord Museum, Notman Collection, Montreal, QC, 1865. I-14750.

of town directly across from their safe house on St. Paul Street.

The role of St. Catharines as an adjunct headquarters and forward operating base of the Confederate Secret Service has never been fully explored because the documentation is sketchy. The Clay Papers at Duke University have some documents relating to Clement Clay's time in St. Catharines, including details regarding the funding of the St. Albans Raid and dealings with Confederate spy and courier Josephine Brown. Interestingly, St. Catharines was also a destination point on the Underground Railway. Harriet Tubman stayed here for a time and there was a small colony of escaped slaves who lived in the North Street area and worshipped at Salem Chapel British Methodist Episcopal Church, which still stands today. This enclave of escaped slaves was located not far from the Confederate headquarters. St. Catharines was ideally located, with rail connections to Toronto, Montreal, Windsor, and Niagara. Once across the suspension bridge at Niagara Falls, rail lines ran west, south, and east across the United States. Local hotels like the Welland House provided ready accommodations for Confederates heading into or out of Canada. The list of people arriving at St. Lawrence Hall from St. Catharines from August 1864 through April 1865 includes the usual suspects: Beverley Tucker, Clement C. Clay, Josephine (Mrs. Robert) Brown, and Governor Horatio Seymour, who was in Canada frequently in the run up to the U.S. elections. Other names are more mysterious.[72] We know that Republican "fixer" Orville Browning crossed into Canada at Windsor on 28 September and returned the next day via the Niagara suspension bridge. Browning was orchestrating a cotton play involving himself, Senator Edwin Morgan, Judge James Hughes, James Singleton, and Robert Cox, in which the President may have had an interest.[73]

The so-called Confederate "Canadian Cabinet" was a mixed bag of individualists who were all used to getting their own way. This group was anything but cohesive. Holcombe remained what he had always been, a cerebral law professor from Virginia, capable but fussy. He arrived in Montreal from Halifax accompanied by the widow of Major Smith Stansbury, one of the Confederacy's senior logistics officers in Nassau who had died in Halifax from a liver ailment.[74] During his stay in Montreal, the U.S. Consul described Holcombe as being constantly in the company of a "vixen named Stansbury."[75] Holcombe was accompanied to Canada by Beverley Tucker, who sought to stay out of clandestine operations in order to focus on the historic cotton-for-contraband deal he was charged with executing. Clement Clay, the least likely man to be a spy, set in motion the St. Albans Raid. He was soon horrified at the explosive diplomatic repercussions of the cross-border raid and sought to distance himself from the affair. The St. Albans Raiders never forgave Clay for what they saw as his betrayal. To his credit, Clay kept Jacob Thompson out of the planning cycle for the raid, thus providing plausible deniability when the diplomatic storm broke.

In late 1864, General Edwin Lee was sent north to take over from Jacob Thompson and provide military leadership for future operations primarily aimed at rescuing Confederate POW's. E.G. Lee had fought in Stonewall Jackson's Brigade through the Battle of Fredericksburg. He briefly commanded the famed Brigade before developing a severe lung infection from which he never fully recovered. Jefferson Davis posted him to Canada to take over from Jacob Thompson following the St. Albans Raid in October 1864. Edwin Lee was already familiar with Confederate Secret Service operations in Canada.[76]

Upon arrival in Canada, Lee inherited an informal, sometimes factious but still impressive clandestine apparatus. It consisted of spies, couriers, safe houses, hotels, friendly bankers, armed raiders, a host of Canadian supporters, and a small army of hangers on willing to do just about anything for the "cause." From faraway Montreal, the Confederate Secret Service managed to bribe and influence a significant part of the Democratic Party into considering "peace" candidate Horatio Seymour. For McClellan and the so called "war Democrats," the Confederate Secret Service was a menace on par with Lincoln. By now the Secret Service had operational bases in Halifax, Quebec City, Montreal, Toronto, Hamilton, and St. Catharines. In addition to the million dollars Thompson brought to Canada, Beverley Tucker's cotton deal gave the Confederates enormous leverage with both American politicians and the press. In this period, newspaper editorial pages could be readily bought and very often were. Lincoln's tacit support of the cotton deal may have provided him with a ready source of patronage but it also did the same for Beverley Tucker

and the Confederates in Canada and they used it to full advantage.

P.C. Martin (who died at sea while blockade running) and Jacob Thompson may not have always met Judah Benjamin's high expectations in running the Confederate Secret Service in Canada; very few people lived up to Benjamin's expectations, but Martin and Thompson had nevertheless built an organization with considerable reach and capabilities.

Confederate Secret Service Fades Away

Just before Lincoln's assassination in April 1865, Jacob Thompson emptied the Confederate account at the Ontario Bank and headed for Europe. What happened to funds held by other banks is unclear. Without funds, the Confederate Secret Service operations in Canada began to wither. The human apparatus began disintegrating the minute key operatives returned to the shattered South or fled to Europe or Mexico. Without a war, a cause, or money, the Secret Service machinery atrophied. The agents and operatives who once crowded St. Lawrence Hall and the common rooms of the Donegana and Ottawa hotels were suddenly gone, as if they had never been there. Montreal's role in the American Civil War was soon encapsulated in a conspiracy of silence. The Canadian government, facing a hostile and victorious neighbor to the south, was anxious to downplay support of the Confederacy during the war. The U.S. sued the British government for damages and the matter was eventually settled in 1871 for $15,000,000 with the British admitting no guilt.[77] Those American bankers, arms manufacturers, and politicians who had been in Montreal in 1864-1865 wanted the subject dropped. Trading with the enemy, war profiteering, secret negotiations with the Confederacy, plans to dump Lincoln, interactions with the Confederate Secret Service, all of this and more had happened in Montreal but no one wanted to talk about it. As for the presence of John Wilkes Booth in Montreal, no one wanted to discuss it, never mind have to explain it. The Confederates who stayed behind in Canada were fugitives and were naturally reluctant to discuss what had gone on in Montreal during the war. A wall of silence grew around the facts that has endured for 150 years.

With most of the money gone, there were barely sufficient resources to support those who chose not to return or could not return home. Some, like Jefferson Davis and his family, John Porterfield, Jubal Early, James Mason, George Pickett, John Breckenridge, Beverley Tucker, Bennett Young, Robert Brown and his brave wife, courier Josephine Brown, and others, remained in Canada for a period after the war. It was not an easy time for Confederate exiles. The center of gravity for the remaining Confederates shifted away from Montreal and St. Catharines, toward beautiful Niagara-on-the-Lake, which allowed them to view the United States flag across the Niagara River. When Jefferson Davis visited Niagara-on-the-Lake, he looked at the U.S. flag flying across the river and said to James Mason, "There is the gridiron on which we have been fricasseed."[78] Today, many of the Confederate exiles' homes remain standing in beautiful Niagara-on-the–Lake, a haunting legacy of Canada's role in America's bloodiest war.[79] ༄

Confederate Secret Service
in Canada 1864

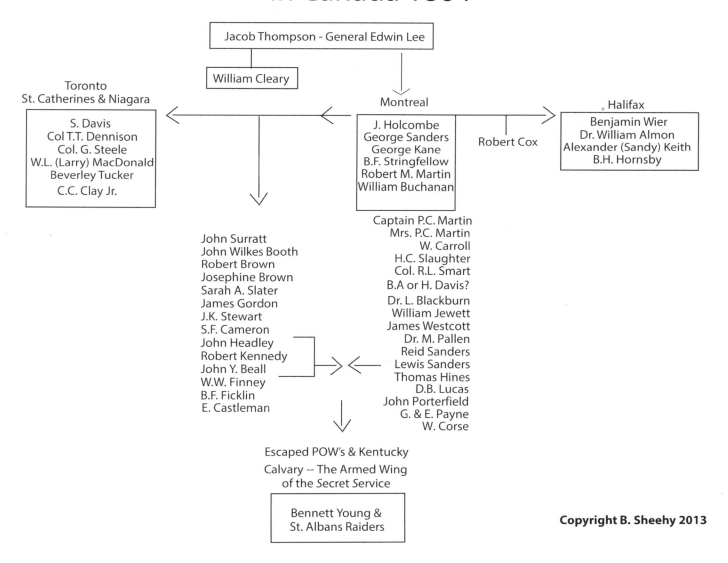

Jacob Thompson - General Edwin Lee

William Cleary

Toronto
St. Catherines & Niagara

S. Davis
Col T.T. Dennison
Col. G. Steele
W.L. (Larry) MacDonald
Beverley Tucker
C.C. Clay Jr.

Montreal

J. Holcombe
George Sanders
George Kane
B.F. Stringfellow
Robert M. Martin
William Buchanan

Robert Cox

Halifax
Benjamin Wier
Dr. William Almon
Alexander (Sandy) Keith
B.H. Hornsby

John Surratt
John Wilkes Booth
Robert Brown
Josephine Brown
Sarah A. Slater
James Gordon
J.K. Stewart
S.F. Cameron
John Headley
Robert Kennedy
John Y. Beall
W.W. Finney
B.F. Ficklin
E. Castleman

Captain P.C. Martin
Mrs. P.C. Martin
W. Carroll
H.C. Slaughter
Col. R.L. Smart
B.A or H. Davis?
Dr. L. Blackburn
William Jewett
James Westcott
Dr. M. Pallen
Reid Sanders
Lewis Sanders
Thomas Hines
D.B. Lucas
John Porterfield
G. & E. Payne
W. Corse

Escaped POW's & Kentucky
Calvary -- The Armed Wing
of the *Secret Service*

Bennett Young &
St. Albans Raiders

Copyright B. Sheehy 2013

CHAPTER 3

Confederate Couriers

*The Story of Montreal-Based Confederate Couriers
and Agents Josephine Brown, Mrs. P.C. Martin,
Sarah Slater, and John Surratt*

McGILL UNIVERSITY's McCord Museum, as mentioned, contains within its Notman Collection hundreds of photographs of Confederate agents and sympathizers who operated in Canada, and particularly in Montreal, during and immediately after the Civil War. These photographs were taken at Notman's Studio on Bleury Street on the eastern end of historic Old Montreal, or as it is called today, Vieux Port de Montréal. One such set is that of Confederate courier Josephine Brown and her husband, Lieutenant Robert W. Brown (CSA), taken in Montreal shortly after the Civil War. Both Browns were deeply involved in the Confederate Secret Service in Canada.

As a result of her work as a courier, Josephine Brown was familiar with those who operated the North-South courier routes through Maryland, some of whom were later implicated in the Lincoln assassination. This list includes: John Surratt;

his mother, Mrs. Mary Surratt; George Andreas Atzerodt; John Wilkes Booth; Augustus (Gus) Spencer Howell; Thomas Conrad, almost certainly Thomas A. Jones; Lewis Powell (who was known as Lewis Paine or Payne); David Edgar Herold; Michael O'Laughlen; Samuel Arnold; and Olivia Floyd.[1] Also part of this spy network were Preston Parr, Maggie Branson, and Thomas Green.[2] Brown carried correspondence to Richmond and back for Confederate Commissioners in Canada such as Jacob Thompson, George Sanders, Beverley Tucker, Clement C. Clay, and General Edwin Lee. The recipient in Richmond was usually Secretary of State Judah Benjamin, who was responsible for the Confederate Secret Service.

The photographs of Josephine—known to her friends as Josie—were taken when she was thirty years old and already the mother of two. The photos show a woman of striking beauty and bearing. Her husband, Confederate Officer

Robert Brown, also posed for a set of photographs at Notman's Studio, where most Confederate exiles and operatives went to have their photographs taken.

Along with Sarah Slater and John Surratt, Josephine Brown was among the most interesting and successful Confederate couriers operating out of Canada. Slater and Surratt have attracted some historical attention. Surratt was the last Booth conspirator to be captured, and his unfortunate mother was executed for her role in the assassination. The courier Sarah Antoinette Slater has also attracted the attention of historians, in part because of the way she walked off the pages of history following the Lincoln assassination, never to be heard from again. She took with her inside knowledge of Booth's plot against Lincoln. Born in Connecticut in 1843, she had three brothers and a sister. Both her mother and grandmother were French speaking.[3] In 1861 she married Rowan Slater of North Carolina, an accomplished musician and dance instructor. In 1863, Rowan enlisted in the Confederate Army and took leave of his wife. It was the last time they would see each other for the duration of the war. Not content with married life, Sarah, called Nettie by her friends, set out for Richmond on her own. She was pretty, full of life, and unafraid. These qualities, along with her bilingualism, attracted the attention of Secretary of War Seddon. At some point, early in 1864, he offered Slater a job carrying dispatches from Richmond to New York and Montreal. Slater was a natural for this kind of clandestine work. She was disciplined in maintaining her cover and seemed to revel in the excitement. It wasn't long before she became a regular on the courier routes between Richmond and Montreal. This brought her into contact with many of those involved in John Wilkes Booth's plan to kidnap President Lincoln. Among the many insiders she came to know were John Surratt and his mother, Mary Surratt. She certainly had inside knowledge of the plot against Lincoln hatched in Montreal. A handsome woman, Slater became Surratt's lover and also caught the attention of Booth, with whom she spent considerable time.[4]

Josephine Brown was another successful Confederate Courier but one who has attracted less historical attention. When researching the historical records for Josephine Brown, one cannot help but be startled by how closely her story intertwines with that of Sarah Slater.[5] Their paths crossed again and again during the war and their physical features were similar—so much so that they were often mistaken for one another. To add to the confusion, they also sometimes used the same aliases. There are times when they are almost indistinguishable, creating a nightmare for modern historians. Scholars seeking to understand these two extraordinary women must pursue them through a hall of mirrors.

Brown's and Slater's travels as couriers took them from Montreal and New York to Washington and from there, through southern Maryland to Richmond, Virginia, and back. Both were described as pretty, in their twenties, and having fair complexions with black hair and eyes.[6] Both women claimed to have family in New York and both spoke French fluently. In the event of

Mrs. R.W. Brown. Robert Brown wrote of his wife, *"Josie is smart, pretty and afraid of nothing."* McCord Museum, Notman Collection, Montreal, QC, 1866. I-20086.1

R.W. Brown served in the Confederate Army and was for a short time assigned to Andersonville Prison. He was affiliated with the Confederate Secret Service and his name appears along with that of his wife, Josephine, in the St. Lawrence Hall Guest Book. R.W. Brown. McCord Museum, Notman Collection, Montreal, QC, 1866. I-20066.1

arrest, *both* Slater and Brown planned to appeal to the French Embassy for assistance by feigning French citizenship.[7] Both Slater and Brown are found registered at Montreal's St. Lawrence Hall, which acted as the unofficial headquarters of the Confederate Secret Service in Canada. They almost certainly knew each other or at least about each other.

Josephine Brown was born Josephine Lovett in New York in 1836. Her father died when she was

young and Thomas Ridder and his wife Charlotte adopted her. Thomas Ridder was a wealthy tobacco merchant in the city and Josephine had every advantage growing up.[8] She spoke fluent French, having learned it either from the Lovett family—Lovett is a common French name—or at finishing school. In her youth she was one of the most beautiful debutantes in New York City.

In 1857 she married handsome Robert W. Brown, son of Confederate sympathizer John

Potts Brown of New York. The Browns were originally from North Carolina, but patriarch John Potts Brown moved his prosperous ship chandlery business to New York in 1846.[9] Despite the move north, Potts Brown remained a committed Southerner and during the Civil War took up blockade running and smuggling military material and medicines to the Confederacy.[10] Brown set up the original smuggling and courier line from New York through southern Maryland and into Virginia. This "hidden way to Dixie" was said to begin at Brown's office on Beaver Street in downtown New York City not far from famed Delmonico's Restaurant, another favorite Confederate haunt.[11] Confederate couriers and agents passing through New York could always count on the help and support of John Potts Brown.[12] Like many prominent New Yorkers, it appears Brown was involved in illicit cotton trading during the war and continued in the trade afterwards. We know that in 1866 he went into the cotton business with R.R. Cuyler of Savannah, one of the founders of the Central Georgia Railroad.[13]

With the start of the Civil War, Robert went south to join the Confederate Army and left Josephine and their two children behind in New York. He fought in the Seven Days' Battles outside Richmond and was later briefly stationed at infamous Andersonville Prison Camp. Here, he served under Captain Wirz, who was destined to hang for the terrible conditions and high mortality rate at the camp.[14]

Like so many American families, the Ridders and Browns found themselves divided by the war. The Ridders wanted to preserve the Union, whereas members of the Brown family were strident Confederates. Charlotte Ridder always blamed young Robert Brown for introducing Josephine to the Confederate Secret Service, but the facts point to Josephine as the driving force behind her espionage career.[15] She was very much her own woman. One observer wrote that she "was willing to do anything" for the Confederacy.[16]

Left behind in New York, Josephine soon tired of domesticity and set out with her children in tow for Fort Monroe, Virginia, seeking to obtain a pass through the lines. She spent several months cooling her heels at Fort Monroe before she was allowed to go on to Richmond and join her husband.[17] The delay was triggered by a letter General John Dix received from a New Yorker named "Williams" who accused Josephine of being a Confederate sympathizer. He wrote that, "This woman is in full sympathy with the rebellion."[18] Eventually, Brown's persistence paid off and she was allowed to pass south through military lines. Once she arrived in Richmond, it wasn't long before someone recognized that the "pretty Mrs. Brown" would make a fine courier.[19] After all, her father-in-law, John Potts Brown, had established the first courier and smuggling routes from New York to Virginia and she no doubt knew them well.[20] And so by mid-1863, Josephine, accompanied sometimes by her daughter as part of her cover story, was carrying dispatches to New York and transporting contraband medicines and official correspondence back south.[21]

The Brown family apparently had close pre-war ties to Alabama statesman Clement C. Clay and the couple named their first-born son Clement Clay Brown, after the former senator.[22] In correspondence, Josephine referred to Clement and Virginia Clay as "uncle and auntie."[23] Virginia Clay, herself an acknowledged beauty only ten years older than Brown, wrote admiringly of Josephine's filling her boots with medicinal quinine on each return trip to Richmond.[24] When Clement Clay was dispatched to Canada in 1864 as a senior Confederate Commissioner, Robert Brown was assigned to his staff. Robert's attractive wife soon joined him in Canada and both became deeply involved in Confederate Secret Service activities, with Josephine continuing her courier work carrying messages between Montreal, New York, Washington, and Richmond.[25] She apparently relied on her good looks and feminine charm to avoid being stopped and searched. Josephine carried dispatches sewn into her clothing or hidden in her bonnet. After one of her missions, Robert Brown wrote of his wife, "Josie is smart, pretty and afraid of nothing."[26] In December 1863, he wrote to Virginia Clay, "Josie has returned, came to me the morning before Christmas, having accomplished all she hoped for. My wife is a great woman."[27]

Josephine Brown's surviving family includes members living in and around Greenwood, South Carolina and Dalton, Georgia. They possess a number of documents related to their great-grandmother, Josephine Brown, who is referred to in family circles as the "spy." They remember in some detail the oral history passed on to them about Josephine. For example, they recall that she could speak French fluently, had gone to finishing school, and sometimes took her children with her on missions as part of her cover story.[28] She apparently once carried dispatches for someone she described as a "Yankee."[29] We know for certain that Josephine once carried documents and letters from former President Franklin Pierce to Confederate Commissioner C.C. Clay.[30]

Brown was one of those women who cast a spell over men. This special attraction is hard to quantify or qualify but whatever the ingredients, Josephine possessed them in abundance and so apparently did her fellow courier, Sarah Slater. The latter attracted the attention of John Surratt, George Atzerodt, Louis Weichmann, and even John Wilkes Booth. We know Brown attracted the attention of British Member of Parliament Thomas Conolly during his visit to Richmond in 1864.[31] While in the Confederate capital, she was his near-constant companion.[32] He referred to her as the "pretty" Mrs. Brown.[33] We know from her own letters that senior Confederate Commissioner in Canada Beverley Tucker, a married man, "fell in love" with Brown.[34] It all ended badly as such affairs generally do but the story illustrates the aura Brown seemed to exude in her dealings with men.

Mrs. P.C. Martin, the wife of the senior Confederate agent in Montreal Captain P.C. Martin, was herself an active courier and spy.[35] When John Wilkes Booth visited Montreal in October 1864, he apparently spent considerable time with Martin and his family who lived on Union Street near Phillips Square in Montreal.

Martin helped Booth open bank accounts at the Ontario Bank and provided letters of

Mrs. P.C. Martin, Confederate Courier. McCord Museum, Notman Collection, Montreal, QC, 1863. I-6548.1.

introduction to the "Doctors' Courier Line" in southern Maryland to facilitate Booth's escape from Washington after having kidnapped or murdered President Lincoln. The "Doctors' Line" included Dr. William Queen and Dr. Samuel Mudd. Martin also provided similar letters of introduction to British officers wanting to visit the Army of Northern Virginia. (See Chapter 9, British Players in Montreal.)

As a result of her husband's activities on behalf of the Confederacy, Mrs. Martin was soon acting as an agent and courier. She almost certainly knew Sarah Slater and Josephine Brown but there is no evidence of her having worked with them. Being a courier was a very solitary business. The first mention of Mrs. Martin as a courier comes from famed Confederate raider and blockade runner, Captain John Wilkinson, who was sent to Montreal in 1863 with an experienced team of sailors to capture the *USS Michigan*. They planned to use the captured vessel to help liberate thousands of Confederate prisoners-of-war on Johnson's Island, Ohio.

Upon arriving in Montreal with his team, Wilkinson went immediately to Captain P.C. Martin for assistance. Also living with Martin at the time was former Baltimore Provost Marshal George P. Kane. Like Martin, Kane was a Confederate sympathizer who had taken refuge in Canada. Kane and Martin immediately went to work assisting Wilkinson and his team. Mrs. Martin and her daughter were soon running dispatches into the United States and making contact with senior Confederates inside the prisoner-of-war camp.[36] As Wilkinson recorded in his memoirs, "the brave and devoted Mrs. M and her daughter" carried these vital dispatches.[37] Wilkinson's plan might have worked had it not been betrayed by a Canadian Confederate supporter, James S. McCraig, who panicked and informed Canadian authorities. The Governor General, Lord Monck, then informed the American government and the jig was up.[38]

Mrs. P.C. Martin is almost certainly the mysterious female agent 'Mrs. Wilson' arrested at Rouses Point, NY carrying more than eighty letters and dispatches from Montreal to Richmond. Mrs. Wilson's cover story was that she was selling religious tracts and prior to the war, Martin and his wife were indeed active in selling religious items. The description of Mrs. Wilson as dark haired, dark eyed and about forty-five years old is also a near perfect fit.[39] Furthermore, we know that by 1863 or perhaps earlier, she had been an active Confederate courier. When offered amnesty if she would divulge the names of her cohorts, Mrs. Wilson made it clear she would rather die in prison than give up her Confederate colleagues.[40] How long Mrs. Wilson was held is not clear but it was the norm to exile female spies after a short imprisonment so she was probably back in Montreal soon after her arrest.

Lincoln apparently reviewed the captured letters, setting aside those that were clearly personal. He was interested to see that one of the letters was addressed to a former president of the United States "then residing in New Hampshire."[41] This was clearly President Franklin Pierce who was from New Hampshire and retired there after leaving office. This incident rings true as we know

Confederate courier Josephine Brown once carried letters from President Pierce to Confederate Commissioner Clement C. Clay.

Captain P.C. Martin was an experienced mariner heavily involved in blockade running using his own vessels, including the *Marie Victoria*. Martin and two of his vessels were lost somewhere between Quebec City and Halifax in the winter of 1865. The *Victoria* was carrying John Wilkes Booth's wardrobe as part of the cargo. The circumstances surrounding the sinking of Martin's vessels were highly suspicious. It was suspected that Martin's disreputable partner in Halifax, Alexander 'Sandy' Keith, was behind the tragedy. Keith made off with the insurance money leaving Mrs. Martin and her children to fend for themselves in Montreal.[42] She remained for a time in the city, presumably through the generosity of friends. What happened to Mrs. Martin and her family is unclear, but they probably returned to their native Baltimore where a family friend, George Kane, was elected mayor after the war.

Meanwhile, Sarah Slater, using Kate Thompson and Mrs. Brown as aliases, had apparently charmed Lincoln conspirators Louis Weichmann, and George Atzerodt, as well as John Surratt. Even the worldly, womanizing John Wilkes Booth appears to have been taken with Slater and was often seen in her company.[43]

Sarah Slater's name first became prominent during the trial of the Lincoln conspirators in 1865. She was mentioned in the testimony of George Atzerodt and Louis Weichmann.[44] Atzerodt identified Slater as a skilled agent who had inside knowledge of Booth's plans. In the trial

Dr. L.J. McMillan befriended John Surratt during his escape to Europe on the *SS Peruvian* from Montreal and learned a great deal about Surratt's relationship with Courier Sarah Slater. McCord Museum, Notman Collection, Montreal, QC, 1866. I-17397.1

of John Surratt two years later, the same stories about Sarah Slater were repeated. New testimony in the second trial came from a stable boy, David Barry, and Dr. Louis J. McMillan, the surgeon on the *SS Peruvian*, who befriended John Surratt during his escape from Canada to Europe.[45]

During Surratt's 1867 trial for his involvement in the Lincoln assassination, McMillan was able to repeat a harrowing tale told to him by Surratt about killing four Yankee soldiers, probably escaped POW's, who surprised Surratt, Slater, and their party on the road somewhere near Fredericksburg, Virginia. Fredericksburg was a regular crossing point for couriers and was

used by both Slater and Brown. Slater urged her companions to "shoot the Yankees," which they apparently did, leaving their bodies by the side of the road.[46] While the story is both bloody and bizarre, there is no reason to believe Dr. McMillan lied under oath about something as serious as murder. The bigger question is why Surratt would admit to a capital crime in the presence of a stranger in the middle of the Atlantic Ocean?[47] If the story is true it shows the level of brutality and hatred four years of war had inflicted on the nation. And also, if true, the story provides an insight into Sarah Slater's capacity for cold-bloodedness.[48]

In his last confession, George Atzerodt discussed a mysterious Confederate courier who visited the Surratts, and whom he identified not as Sarah Slater but as Kate Thompson, also known to him as Kate Brown.[49] In his memoirs, written after the trial, Louis Weichmann remembered meeting Slater when she was using the alias Kate Thompson at Mary Surratt's boarding house in Washington City. "Kate Thompson stopped at Mrs. Surratt's and also at the National and Kimmel Hotels."[50] The National was one of Booth's favorite hotels and the Kimmel House was part of John Potts Brown's original courier line to Dixie.[51] So here again we see Slater's and Brown's narratives overlapping.

The woman Weichmann described meeting was in her twenties, "spruce, and neat of medium size, black eyes and fair complexion. She had a sister in New York...Surratt then met her in New York...and went with her south."[52] On Saturday, 25 March 1865, as Weichmann went down to breakfast, he remembered seeing "in front of the house John Surratt, Mrs. Surratt and the mysterious Mrs. Slater, who had been at the house in February."[53] In his confession Atzerodt reported, "Kate Thompson or Kate Brown, as she was known by both names, put up at National and was well known at Penn [Pennsylvania] House. She knew all about the affair [the Lincoln plot]. Surratt went with her to Richmond last March and Gust [Confederate agent Augustus Spencer Howell] made a trip with her to the same place."[54] On another occasion a Confederate agent introduced Kate Thompson as "Mrs. Brown."[55] George Atzerodt recorded that she had been instrumental in smuggling critical documents into Canada, which resulted in the release of the St. Albans Raiders.[56] Her cover story in Montreal was that she was a widow from Kentucky—at other times she claimed to be from North Carolina. The story about being a widow serving the Confederacy remained constant no matter which alias she was employing.[57]

Slater/Thompson/Brown consistently wore a veiled hat, or mask, as it was then called, and those who met her variously guessed her age at between twenty and twenty-nine years.[58] John Headley added that she was a true Southern patriot, refusing all offers of remuneration for her dangerous work. George Atzerodt's testimony provides a clear linkage between Kate Thompson and Kate Brown. Another link comes from the testimony of David Barry at John Surratt's trial. He identified Mrs. Slater as using the alias Mrs. Brown when she accompanied Surratt on his trip to Richmond in March 1865. For his part,

Surratt remarked to Barry that he had a "woman on the brain."[59] We can assume the woman in question was Mrs. Brown, whom Barry described as "slim and delicate."[60] Barry also described Mrs. Brown as being "under thirty" years of age.[61]

A HALL OF MIRRORS

Anyone studying this subject cannot help but be struck by how often Slater and Brown are mentioned in tandem, running dispatches from Montreal through New York and Washington to Richmond and then returning.[62] They appear to have been doing exactly the *same* job, at about the *same* time, in concert with many of the *same* individuals and visiting the *same* places. Slater and Brown also shared a common connection with the venerable St. Lawrence Hall in Montreal. Here we find both couriers' names in the hotel Guest Book on various dates from the summer of 1864 through April 1865. During this same period, John Wilkes Booth's and John Surratt's names also appear in the hotel Guest Book.[63]

We know that both Slater and Brown were remarkably disciplined about cover stories. Even when visiting the adoring St. Albans Raiders, who viewed her as a heroine, the Confederate courier maintained her "Confederate widow" story.[64]

The one supposed photo we have of Slater appeared in John Headley's 1906 book about Confederate operations in Canada and New York.[65] Published forty years after events, he could not remember the woman's name but he vividly remembered her story as a Kentucky widow and brave courier. The photo in Headley's book is a poor one caused perhaps by inadvertent

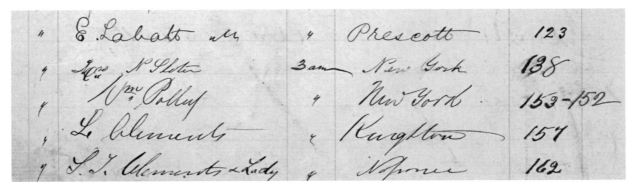

Signature for Mrs. S. Slater in room 138, St. Lawrence Hall Guest Book 15 February 1865. Note that National Detective Police agent W. Pollack, brother-in-law of National Detective Police Chief Lafayette Baker, apparently signed right after Slater. If so, they both traveled to Montreal on the train from New York City. Was Pollack following Slater or is the side-by-side registration just a coincidence? (Like his boss Lafayette Baker and so many others, Walter Pollack sometimes used aliases or altered his initials in registration, so we find W. Pollack, A. H. M Pollack, W^m. Pollack or simply Pollack.) (National Archives of Canada, Ottawa).

Supposed photograph of Sarah Slater from a *carte de visite* left with the St. Albans raiders and reproduced in John Headley's 1906 book *Confederate Operations in Canada and New York*.[66]

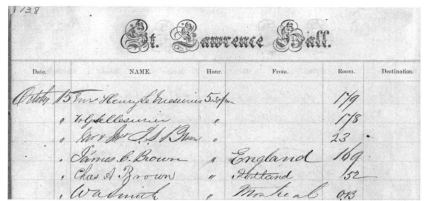

Signature for Mr. and Mrs. J. L. Brown in room 23, St. Lawrence Hall Guest Book 15 October 1864. This was just days before John Wilkes Booth and John Surratt registered at the hotel. (National Archives of Canada, Ottawa)

Here is a photograph of Josephine Brown taken some years after the war and still in the possession of her family. One can see how Brown and Slater could have been easily confused with one another. They were similar in age and size. Both were pretty, had dark hair, and were fluent in French. They used the same or similar aliases and traveled the same courier routes from Montreal to Richmond.

Signature for Mrs. Robert Brown in room 182 arriving from St. Catharines, St. Lawrence Hall Guest Book 12 December 1864. St. Catharines, on the rail line to Niagara and the United States, was a forward operating center for the Confederate Secret Service. Senior Confederate Commissioner C.C. Clay used this as his headquarters. (National Archives of Canada, Ottawa) movement during the photo session; given the photographic technology of the day, subjects were required to stay perfectly still for an excruciatingly long time for the photograph to be accurate. One twitch and the photo would be distorted.[67]

SEPARATING SLATER FROM BROWN

Any historian studying Brown and Slater will at some point confront the possibility that they might be the same person. Historian James O. Hall, who spent a lifetime studying Sarah Slater, admitted that at one point he entertained the idea.[68] We too wrestled with this question. In the end, we concluded, as did Hall, that Slater and Brown were indeed two fascinating but different people. It was also clear that they were sometimes confused with one another when traveling under the same aliases on the same courier routes from Montreal and New York to Richmond. They were similar in age and size. Both were attractive, had black hair and dark eyes, and both spoke French fluently. The definitive evidence that Slater and Brown were different women comes from the diary of British Member of Parliament Thomas Conolly, who visited Richmond in March 1865 just before the fall of the city. While in Virginia, Conolly mixed with an eclectic group of Confederates that included blockade runners and secret service agents.[69]

Thomas Conolly was a bachelor with an eye for the ladies and he soon took a fancy to "pretty" Mrs. Josephine Brown, who had arrived in Richmond carrying dispatches for Clement C. Clay. "Breakfast by invitation with Mr. and Mrs. Pratt, Mrs. Helme sis to Abe Lincoln and Mrs. Brown, Pretty Mrs. Brown...Go to St. Paul's Church with Mrs. Brown and another pretty woman Mrs. Clay."[70] It is certain that the Mrs. Brown in Richmond in March 1865, socializing with Conolly, was Josephine L. Brown. He identifies her as the daughter-in-law of John Potts Brown of New York.[71]

Josephine was in Richmond carrying dispatches for Clement Clay. She wrote to him on 18 March 1865, saying that a draft for $6,000 in Confederate money could not be negotiated because the bank was "dead broke." She told Clay that $275 in Greenbacks from a St. Albans bank—presumably part of the booty from the St. Albans raid in October 1864—had been accepted and the various things Clay had requested purchased.[72]

With money short and Union armies closing in, Brown decided to head back to Canada. Accompanied by Confederate blockade runner Isaac Sterrett, Brown left Richmond heading north to Fredericksburg and New York. Conolly's diary for 22 March 1865, records the following: "Up at 5.30 Sterrett & dear Mrs. Brown go away to try the Fredericksburg route to New York..." Josephine Brown was heading north with dispatches from Judah Benjamin. Three days later, on 25 March, Sarah Slater, under the alias Mrs. Brown and escorted by John Surratt, was on her way south from Maryland to the Confederate capital.[73]

Conolly's diary not only provides proof that Brown and Slater were two different people but it also explains why they were so often confused with one another. Just consider the incredible chronology and coincidence in March 1865.

Josephine Brown left Richmond with Isaac Sterrett on 22 March to "try the Fredericksburg route to New York," from where she would take the train to Montreal.[74] Meanwhile, three days later Sarah Slater, identified as Mrs. Brown, was traveling south to Richmond with John Surratt.[75] The two couriers were in effect traveling the same courier routes but in opposite directions—one accompanied by Isaac Sterrett and the other by John Surratt, and both carrying messages to or from Judah Benjamin. Josephine traveled under her own name, Mrs. Brown, while Slater adopted the alias Mrs. Brown.[76] The coincidences are stunning. No wonder these two women have confounded historians.

After Josephine Brown left Richmond and the city fell to Federal forces, Conolly followed her north to New York, where he hoped to rekindle their budding relationship, but upon arriving in New York he was told by her father-in-law, John Potts Brown, that Josephine had gone on to Canada.[77] Conolly was disappointed and remarked in his diary that he "smelled a rat."[78] The meaning here is unclear. It may imply that her father-in-law packed the attractive, married Mrs. Brown off to Canada to get her away from Conolly or it may be that the British MP finally understood that the "pretty Mrs. Brown" had a serious side to her and was engaged in espionage.

ST. LAWRENCE HALL AND ST. CATHARINES

Finally, there is the question of the St. Lawrence Hall Guest Book where we find both Brown and Slater registered throughout 1864 and 1865. Sarah Slater registered several times in the six months from October 1864 to April 1865. The most significant and legible registration was on 15 February 1865, when she arrived from New York at 3 a.m.[79] Possibly registering right behind her was Walter Pollack, a National Detective Police agent and brother-in-law to Police Chief Lafayette C. Baker.[80] This indicates that she was perhaps being 'tailed' by Pollack. Alternatively, Pollack may have been in Montreal to attend to his brother-in-law's extensive cotton interests, which involved interaction with the Confederate Secret Service.

It is intriguing to find Confederate courier Sarah Slater, who was close to both John Surratt and John Wilkes Booth, traveling on the same train from New York with a senior member of Lafayette Baker's National Detective Police and then checking in to St. Lawrence Hall beside him. But then Pollack appears again in St. Lawrence Hall. For example, his name turns up with John Wilkes Booth and Confederate Commissioner Dr. Luke Blackburn in October 1864, and Thomas Jones in May 1864.[81] There is an intriguing note in St. Lawrence Hall's Departure Book for 2 May 1864, in which Jones' departure is accompanied by a margin note with the name Pollack. This indicates some affiliation between the two. Perhaps Pollack was tailing Jones and the hotel staff knew about it or there was some other affiliation between these two men. What's indisputable, given the margin note, is that Jones and Pollack were associated in some way.[82]

There is also a tantalizing reference to "Miss Slater" scribbled into the margin of the Guest Book for 10 January 1865, staying in room 101 with someone whose name is illegible but whose initials appear to be J.F.H.[83] This is very likely John Harrison Surratt, alias John Harrison.[84] Slater's final registration appears alongside that of John Surratt on 18 April 1865, four days following the Lincoln assassination.[85] This implicates Slater in the conspiracy against Lincoln, at least to the extent that John Surratt was involved.[86]

Surratt would soon go into hiding and flee to Europe. With Surratt gone, Sarah Slater may have taken the enormous risk of traveling to Baltimore in early May when Edwin Stanton's post-assassination dragnet was sweeping up hundreds of suspects. A "Mrs. Slater," was arrested by Provost Marshal James McPhail in late April 1864. McPhail sent Slater to Washington for questioning by Judge Advocate General Prosecutor H. Burnett.

> *"Sir,*
> *Upon telegram order from the Provost Marshal Gen L.J. McPhail for State of Maryland, I had arrested Mrs. Slater and send her to you by the hand of William Parker of the force.*
> *Your servant,*
> *Wn. McPhail in absence of Marl"*[87]

Her interrogator, Judge Advocate General H.L. Burnett, was a tough, ambitious prosecutor. The interrogation revealed little of consequence, at least not on the record.[88] She did acknowledge running the blockade and knowing blockade runners. By this point in the investigation Burnett was in receipt of testimony from George Atzerodt and Louis Weichmann, implicating Slater in the conspiracy.[89] New to the file, Burnett may not have connected Slater with this earlier testimony. Alternatively, she may not have been the infamous Sarah Slater but one of the Baltimore Slaters. Her quick release was certainly out of the ordinary, given that the Judge Advocate General's office was then arresting and holding people without charges for weeks and even months on the slightest suspicion.[90] Just knowing Booth was reason enough to be arrested. John Ford was imprisoned for having known the Booth brothers and hiring them to perform on his stage; he also had the misfortune of owning the theater where Lincoln was assassinated.

Her quick release raises the possibility she was a double agent. It is unusual that at some point in her dangerous travels from Montreal to Richmond she had been captured and turned. Recall her unusual registration with senior federal National Detective Police detective Walter Pollack 15 February 1865. We will never know the truth, except that we are certain Slater was released almost immediately after her arrest and slipped into the ether.

Early on in the Lincoln assassination trial, it became clear how central Slater, Kate Thompson, and Mrs. Brown were to the plot. Secretary of War Stanton issued orders to find and re-arrest Slater, but by then it was too late—Sarah Slater had vanished.[91] Given the formidable reach of the Federal Detective Police and Federal authorities in 1865, it seems strange that Sarah Antoinette Slater, a woman without apparent resources, could not have been tracked down by the vaunted National Detective Police had they wanted to find her.

Slater may have laid low in the post-assassination period but she did not entirely disappear as legend has it. She moved to New York and in 1866 publicly divorced her husband, Rowan

Slater.[92] The associated legal documents were in the public domain. If the National Detective Police had wanted to locate Sarah Slater, here was their chance. Yet apparently nothing was done.[93]

As for Josephine Brown, she was registered at St. Lawrence Hall on a number of occasions from September through December 1864 and through April 1865. On 15 October and 4 November 1864, she was there when the hotel was full of Confederate Commissioners, American cotton speculators, and Northern bankers, as well as senior members of the Republican and Democratic Parties. Many of these guests were there working on a large cotton-for-contraband deal.[94] Others were there laying plans to get Lincoln off the presidential ticket or, in the case of the Democrats, to defeat him at the polls. Lincoln had few friends in Montreal that season.

Brown registered at the hotel on 12 December 1864, arriving from St. Catharines, Ontario (Canada West). St. Catharines was the forward headquarters of the Confederate Secret Service; Clement Clay and Beverley Tucker stayed there often.[95] Robert E. Cox, a cotton speculator with close ties to Republican powerbroker Orville Browning, provided the house for them. Cox may also have had ties to John Wilkes Booth.[96] He was briefly arrested in the aftermath of the Lincoln assassination but released after Orville Browning intervened on his behalf.[97]

Cox was almost certainly a Confederate operative and Josephine Brown carried messages from him to Clement Clay.[98] For a time, she stayed at the Cox family home in Poughkeepsie, New York, awaiting dispatches from Clement Clay.[99] Lincoln

Confederate agent Robert Cox was close to Republican powerbroker and Lincoln friend Orville Browning. Cox was a cotton speculator, Confederate sympathizer, and very likely a Confederate agent. Cox registered at Barnett's Niagara Museum on 20 June 1864. Robert E. Cox. McCord Museum, Notman Collection, Montreal, QC, 1864. I-11517.1

historian William Tidwell suspects that John Wilkes Booth stopped at Cox's Poughkeepsie home on his way either to or from Montreal in October 1864.[100] So we have Josephine Brown and John Wilkes Booth staying at or visiting Cox's house in Poughkeepsie. At the same time, we have Cox, Clay, Tucker, and other Confederate agents sharing a safe house in St. Catharines, not a stone's throw from the vital rail lines to the United States at Niagara.[101]

Confederate couriers and agents who crossed into Canada on the Niagara suspension bridge often spent the night in St. Catharines before

Table Rock Hotel and Barnett's Museum, Niagara, Canada West, where Confederate agents entered their names in the register to show those following who was then already "in country." Table Rock, Niagara, ON. McCord Museum, Notman Collection, Montreal QC, copied 1863. I-6711.0.1

proceeding to Montreal or Toronto.[102] They frequently registered at the Table Rock House and signed the Guest Book at the nearby Barnett's Museum, which was open seven days a week. This Guest Book served to signal the arrival in Canada of an agent who was "in country." Those following would then know who had already arrived in Canada or who had left to go back to the United States.[103] Cox's name is found in the register among those of other Confederate agents.[104]

Republican powerbroker and Lincoln friend Orville Browning crossed into Canada at Niagara on 28 September and returned on 29 September 1864.[105] The purpose of his trip is not recorded in his diary but it is unlikely Browning traveled all the way from Washington to Niagara to see the Falls. His overnight stay in Canada took place during the height of the cotton-for-contraband negotiations and the man in charge of those negotiations, Confederate Commissioner Beverley

Tucker, was then in nearby St. Catharines. Shortly after Browning's visit, Tucker left for Montreal to take up residence at St. Lawrence Hall, where the billion-dollar cotton-for-contraband deal was to be finalized.[106]

Three days after Josephine Brown registered at St. Lawrence Hall on 12 December 1864, courier and agent S.F. Cameron arrived from Buffalo and checked into the hotel on 15 December. We know that Sarah Slater and S.F. Cameron were the two couriers tasked with carrying the legal records proving the St. Albans Raiders were *bona-fide* Confederate officers and enlisted men acting on orders. These documents were essential to the legal strategies of the St. Albans Raiders, proving they were not brigands but soldiers acting under orders and engaging in acts of war on U.S. soil.[107] The British government recognized both warring parties as legal belligerents under the rules of war recently agreed upon in Geneva, i.e., the Geneva Convention.

In the first 1864 trial of the raiders in Montreal, this newly arrived documentation meant the court saw the matter as beyond its jurisdiction, resulting in their release. In the second trial in 1865 in Toronto, the Crown found that it could not successfully prosecute legitimate belligerents for committing acts of war against an enemy on foreign soil. The Crown could concern itself only with what happened on Canadian sovereign territory. Ultimately, the Canadian government made it illegal to plan acts of war from Canadian soil, but these laws could not be applied retroactively.[108] Thus the brave couriers who smuggled these documents to Canada greatly influenced the outcome of the trials and, by extension, Canadian jurisprudence.

The records show that Cameron and Slater left Richmond one day apart and traveled intentionally by different routes. John Headley remembered they had arrived in Montreal at about the same time.[109] And here we have Brown and Cameron registering in St. Lawrence Hall only seventy-two hours apart with Josephine arriving on the courier line from St. Catharines.[110] As for Sarah Slater, she does not appear in the register but may have stayed at another Confederate-friendly hotel like the Donegana.[111] Again we see Sarah Slater's story intertwined with that of Josephine Brown.

While in Montreal, Slater or Brown apparently went to visit the St. Albans Raiders in the "Old Jail," an enormous castle-like structure that still stands brooding today on the eastern end of Old Montreal. Here she left them with a not-too-clear *carte de visite* that featured a photograph. This photograph was reproduced in John Headley's 1906 book about the Confederate Secret Service in Canada.[112]

Four days after Lincoln's assassination, John Surratt made it across the border and safely to Montreal, on 18 April 1865.[113] He reported to General Edwin Lee, now head of the Confederate Secret Service following Jacob Thompson's departure for Europe. Here for the first time we see the two Surratt signatures entered together side by side in the Guest Book. The first is a highly stylized J. Surratt, the second is John Harrison, an alias he acknowledged using. Surratt rented two rooms, 121 and Suite QB, but may have stayed

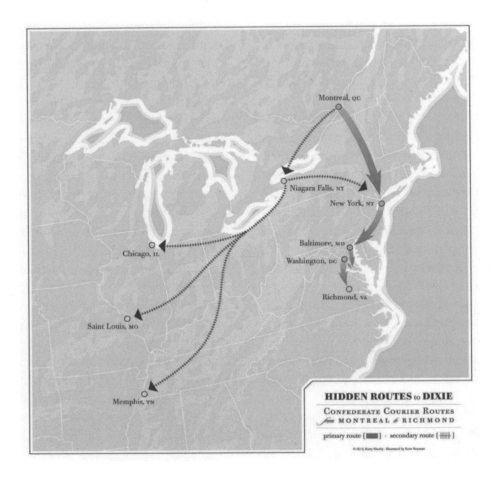

HIDDEN ROUTES to DIXIE

CONFEDERATE COURIER ROUTES *from* MONTREAL *to* RICHMOND

primary route [■■■] · secondary route [||||||]

in neither since Sarah Slater checked in just ahead of Surratt and occupied room 114 or 714, (the number appears intentionally altered in the Guest Book).

Lee knew U.S. and Canadian authorities were hot on Surratt's trail and would soon arrive at St. Lawrence Hall. He gave Surratt some money and a new alias as Charlie Armstrong. Interestingly he tore the page for 18 April from his diary but

the following day recorded "gave messenger $40 for expenses and $100 services (Charley)."[114] It appears Slater may have traveled to Montreal with Surratt. She certainly turned up at the hotel and registered alongside Surratt at 12:30 p.m. on 18 April. When U.S. detectives and Canadian authorities landed at the hotel looking for Surratt, he was quickly spirited out the back door and into a waiting carriage that took him to John Porterfield's townhouse on Sherbrooke Street near McGill University. From there he would go into hiding and eventually, with the help of the Confederate Secret Service, escape to Europe.

With Surratt in hiding, Sarah Slater took the extraordinary risk of returning to the U.S. at the height of the dragnet for suspects in the assassination. Someone by the name of Mrs. Slater was arrested in Baltimore and sent to Washington for questioning by Judge Advocate General Burnett, who was one of the three prosecutors in charge of the investigation. Slater was held overnight, interrogated, and released. She revealed little except that she was familiar with blockade runners and had run the blockade herself. She was then inexplicably let go. It's possible she was not Sarah Slater the Confederate courier, for there was a large Slater family in Baltimore at the time. But given her last name alone, Slater's quick release remains an anomaly.

Josephine and Robert Brown stayed on in Montreal through 1866 and possibly into 1867, and thus witnessed the birth of Canada's own Confederation. If the Civil War did not lead to the creation of a new country in the South, it certainly accelerated the creation of a new nation in the North.

Having served briefly on staff at Andersonville Prison Camp under Henry Wirz, Robert Brown wanted to avoid his commander's fate at the gallows. As for Josephine, she would have been privy to the plots against Lincoln and this represented a liability. Excepting those still at risk of arrest, most Confederate exiles drifted home by 1866, but Robert and Josephine played it safe. With

Josephine Brown's burial site, Camden, S.C. In the burial book, she is recorded as a spy for the Confederacy. (Possessed by Josephine Brown's family in Camden, S.C.)

the War Department busy looking for the ethereal Sarah Slater, Josephine and Robert hunkered down in Montreal to wait out the storm. How they sustained themselves during this extended period of exile is unclear. It must, however, have been a difficult time as Robert began drinking heavily.[115]

We have very little knowledge of Josephine's activities once she returned to the United States. She ultimately divorced Robert in 1873, after making a valiant effort to save their marriage in the

St. James and McGill Streets at Victoria Square, Montreal, QC. McCord Museum, Notman Collection, Montreal, QC, 1858. N-1980.47.2

face of his drinking.[116] The following year, 1874, she married Charles Emile Noel of Riverdale, New York.[117] He died some years later and Josephine took up housekeeping at a resort hotel in the Adirondacks.[118] She spent her declining years living with her daughter in South Carolina. Josephine Brown died on 5 December 1915 and is buried in the Quaker, Beth El and Cedar Cemeteries in Camden under the name Josephine Lovett, Ritter, Brown, Noel.[119] The cemetery records list her clearly and presumably proudly, as a "Spy" for the Confederacy. ∾

CHAPTER 4

American Power Comes to Montreal

A HOST OF IMPORTANT American politicians, radical abolitionists, bankers, newspaper editors, treasury agents, arms manufacturers, and Federal secret service agents (National Detective Police) appeared in a growing wave throughout the summer and fall of 1864, before finally receding during the run up to the 1864 election and declining further in the first quarter of 1865. Montreal's St. Lawrence Hall and nearby Donegana and Ottawa hotels were, at the time, full of Confederate operatives. This remarkable cohabitation of belligerents from each side and every partisan stripe made for an astonishing gathering.

Why did so many diverse, influential, and nominally loyal American political and commercial players gravitate to Montreal in the midst of a savage Civil War? Never before, and certainly not since, has there been such a concentration of American political and financial influence in Montreal or anywhere else outside the United States.

We know some were there to conduct business with the Confederacy. Northern bankers, businessmen, and arms manufacturers did a brisk business trading with the enemy throughout the war. Northern industry ramped up production to equip their enormous new military machine, while also providing considerable materiel to the Confederacy. By the end of the war, western meat-packing plants were feeding not one army but two.[1] Northern money meanwhile found its way into consortia that bought cargoes and ships to run the blockade.[2] This willingness to trade with the enemy was driven by the South's near monopoly on the world's most valuable commodity: cotton. It was the oil of its day. Everyone coveted a piece of this trade including, as events proved, the White House. European markets were hungry for cotton and willing to pay huge premiums for the product. Prices rose a thousand percent during the war. Concurrently, the South was desperately short of almost everything needed to

While the Ottawa Hotel welcomed U.S. Federal operatives, the same was not true of the Donegana a few blocks away on Notre Dame Street EaSt. This was a favorite of the Confederate community and Federal agents found it nearly impossible to get a room. Donegana Hotel, Notre Dame Street. McCord Museum, Notman Collection, Montreal, QC, about 1860. VIEW-7463.1

fight a war: weapons, munitions, uniforms, boots, buckles, medicine, tents, wagons, and especially food for its hard-pressed armies in the field. And the Confederates were also willing to pay a premium for these badly needed supplies. Huge profits were thus made at both ends of the transaction. This set the stage for significant "cotton-for-contraband" trade, culminating in what was probably the largest cotton deal of all time, and orchestrated out of Montreal in late 1864. This trade involved somewhere in the area of one to two million bales of Southern cotton, worth between half a billion and a billion dollars in American currency of 1864.[3]

Montreal in 1864 was a busy inland port and a powerful financial and banking center. Its location just across the border, a twelve-hour train ride from New York, put it out of reach of U.S. authorities. This was the ideal place to negotiate illicit trade deals and blockade running. The only way to buy or sell cotton in large quantities was by dealing with the Confederacy, which was represented in Montreal by a large Secret Service establishment. Getting to Montreal by train was infinitely easier than crossing red-hot battle lines outside Richmond, and far more discreet. Montreal had a well-earned reputation for respecting the privacy of foreign guests. This discretion was exercised by both hotels and local newspapers. For example, General James Singleton was in Montreal at least twice in the summer and fall of 1864, buying cotton with permits signed by Abraham Lincoln himself![4] While in Montreal, Singleton's anonymity was carefully protected but when he later took his prized presidential cotton permits to Richmond, he quickly found himself to be front-page news, making it impossible to do business.[5]

Blockade runners and arms manufacturers used the cover of Montreal's neutrality and the strength of its banking system to finance cargoes and buy vessels insured by Lloyd's as British "bottoms." Various consortia of individuals and banks funded round-trip passages through the blockade, returning enormous profits. When Secretary of State Seward or Secretary of War Stanton wanted to open secret talks with the Confederacy, they did not send their special envoys to Richmond but rather to Montreal.[6] Stanton's representative, Judge Jeremiah Black, arrived in Canada about the same time that unofficial peace negotiations were taking place: from early July through the first week of August 1864 at the Clifton House in Niagara Falls. Black checked in to Barnett's Niagara Museum on 1 July 1864 along with J. Thompson, Senior Confederate Commissioner in Canada.[7] He remained in the Niagara area and was back at Barnett's Museum on 22 July 1864.[8]

Stanton feared that defeat in the November 1864 elections would result in his being treated "with contumely and violence." A consummate bully, Stanton feared the shoe being on the other foot. Judge Jeremiah Black was sent by Stanton to Canada to discuss possible peace terms in advance of the election. Jeremiah Black, a Democrat, served in the Buchanan Cabinet with the senior Confederate Commissioner in Canada, Jacob Thompson, and knew him well. Black had a sterling reputation for integrity and was trusted by the Confederates. When scapegoated by Stanton for going to Canada, Black was furious and made it clear he had been sent there at the behest of the Secretary of War. This betrayal by Stanton effectively ended their friendship.

As for Seward, he sent Halmar Emmons, a Detroit district attorney, as his representative. Emmons' negotiations were supposed to have taken place in early 1865, but he was registered at St. Lawrence Hall as early as 4 November 1864. Emmons appears to have been up to more than simply acting as Seward's emissary in Montreal. He was a regular guest at the hotel until just before Lincoln's assassination. He had ties to Confederate banker, blockade runner, and cotton magnate and slave trader Gazaway Lamar, through Lamar's agent Nelson Trowbridge.[9] This suggests an interest in cotton, which Lamar was then desperately trying to get out of Georgia.

By 1864, all sides in the conflict were using Montreal as a safe place to conduct business and diplomacy. Here enemies could talk with one another off the record, arrange trade deals, or negotiate possible ceasefires, without the press looking over their shoulder. Even the White House and Treasury Department used Montreal as a venue for organizing cotton-for-contraband trading. White House participation in the cotton trade is well documented but remains a subject that has not garnered sufficient historical attention.[10]

Trading with the enemy was not altogether illegal during the Civil War. The law was ambiguous regarding goods crossing state lines. In contrast, it was clearly illegal to break the Union Naval blockade at sea unless approved by the White House or the Treasury Department. Thus trading cotton for bacon across the Tennessee-Georgia frontier was legal, but the same exchange by sea was prohibited. It was all very murky, but the profits were clear as a bell and breathtakingly high. Given murky rules on the one hand and the prospect of high profits on the other, the outcome was never really in doubt. Large-scale trade involving cotton for contraband became the norm as the U.S. war effort became increasingly corrupted. Port cities like New York and rail hubs such as Memphis did a roaring business with the Confederacy throughout the war.[11] Fortunes were made, and the groundwork was laid for the notorious post-war Gilded Age.

POWERBROKERS

Among the many important business leaders at the St. Lawrence Hall during this period was William Fargo, founder of Wells Fargo and American Express.[12] Also there was James Brown of Brown Brothers (today Brown Brothers, Harriman).[13] John D. Rockefeller was at the hotel twice in September 1864.[14] Charles Barney (ante-cedent of today's Smith Barney), A.S. Hatch, Harvey Fisk, and George Bliss, all bankers representing *Jay Cooke and Company* were on hand.[15] Robber baron Jay Gould, James (Diamond Jim) Fisk, Louis Kuhn (Kuhn, Loeb & Co., later part of Lehman Brothers), and banker Russell Sage were all in Montreal.[16] There are several hotel Guest Book registrations under the name Ward arriving from New York. These registrations include one that clearly reads Samuel Ward.[17] Samuel Ward was a Democrat, banker, and lobbyist who served as the U.S. representative for Barings Brothers Bank in London. E.L. Oppenheim, a British banking house with offices in New York, are also found at St. Lawrence Hall.[18]

On 25 October 1864, there was a registration at the hotel for what appears to be a Jay (J.) Cooke and wife, precisely when John Wilkes Booth was a guest at the hotel.[19] We know Cooke's family was in Canada during the summer and fall of 1864. They registered at Barnett's Museum on 22 June.[20] Cooke was close to his family and we can assume Jay Cooke was not far away. There

Signature of Jay Cooke Jr. and other members of the Cooke Family, Barnett's Museum, Niagara Falls 22 June 1864. Cooke was close to his family and it is unlikely they would have vacationed in Niagara without him. Cooke appears to be back in Canada in October 1864. Cooke had been sent two personal invitations from the President which he coldly ignored. He did not even bother to respond with even so much as an explanation.

is a Cooke registration at St. Lawrence Hall a few days later, on 25 June, arriving from what appears to be *N...Falls US*.[21] Earlier in the month a J. Cook (no E,) along with J.L. Clark and R.E. Hatch register together. Clark and Hatch were bankers with a long association with Jay Cooke.[22]

If Cooke found the time to visit Canada during that summer of 1864, he did so at the expense of President Lincoln, who sent him two invitations to visit the White House. These invitations, signed by the President himself, went unacknowledged and unanswered. The affront was intentional and reflected the nadir of Lincoln's presidency when everyone, including the President himself, expected a defeat in November. Serious efforts were already underway within the Republican Party to push Lincoln off the ticket.

If it is indeed Jay Cooke, his presence in Canada crowns a veritable *Who's Who* of American Civil War financiers in the city.[23] Many of these people would later emerge as important participants in the post-war Gilded Age which was characterized by unprecedented corruption and excess. There is no question that the culture of corruption associated with the post-war years took root during the Civil War when power, influence, and money were being concentrated in Washington on an unprecedented scale. The convergence of power and money in the nation's capital quickly attracted a small army of lobbyists seeking deals, preferential arrangements, tax deferrals, protective tariffs, special subsidies, and outright sinecures.

There is an intriguing 22 August registration at St. Lawrence Hall for (E.)J. Dix and son, sug-gesting Union General John Dix may have been in Montreal. Dix was involved in cotton trading out of Norfolk, and in league with corrupt Union General Ben Butler.[24] Although nominally a general, Dix was not a soldier, but a businessman with close ties to both General Benjamin Butler and the equally corrupt, Thomas C. "Doc" Durant of New York. The latter was deeply involved in trading cotton with the Confederacy and had ties to Confederates in Montreal, especially Beverley Tucker. Durant was the driving force behind the Union Pacific Railroad, an institution that came to epitomize post-war corruption. After the war, John Dix became president of the Union Pacific.

Joining American bankers and businessmen in Montreal were many of America's leading arms manufacturers and military suppliers. As discussed in Trading with the Enemy, the names Parker, Stone, Remington, Whitney, Burnside, Snow, Hotchkiss, and Savage (all of whom were associated with arms manufacturing) turn up in Montreal during this period.[25] They were joined in Montreal by Joseph Garneau, the leading producer of hardtack and bread for the Union Army, and Francis Whitaker, the chief meat packer for the Union Army.[26]

The Civil War saw the birth of both modern-day Wall Street and America's military-industrial complex. Both institutions were present in Montreal in 1864 and early 1865.

POLITICIANS

During this period, a small army of American politicians and newspaper editors descended on Montreal. Some were there to trade in cotton, but others were motivated by politics. Some wanted Lincoln off the Republican ticket because he was not prosecuting the war successfully in their view. Some, especially Radical Republicans, were convinced that Lincoln's plans for reconstructing a defeated South were hopelessly weak. Others feared Lincoln would lose the upcoming election in November. By the summer of 1864, the war had become increasingly unpopular. Grant was stalled outside Richmond and taking the highest casualties of the war; Sherman had been bloodily repulsed at Kennesaw Mountain, west of Atlanta. Men were being lost at such a murderous rate that a new draft of 500,000 men was proposed. Conscription was already unpopular and this latest proposal to draft half a million additional men was not welcomed by a nation weary of war. Amidst all this bad news, Confederate General Jubal Early and his small army from the Shenandoah Valley appeared out of nowhere and laid siege to Washington, sending the city into a panic. Gideon Wells called it a national "humiliation."[27] Confidence in Lincoln, particularly among the Republican elite, plummeted. The President looked like a sure loser in November.

In this desperate environment, a powerful conspiracy took root, aimed at forcing Lincoln off the ballot. The conspiracy was initially centered in New York but soon achieved national proportions and very nearly succeeded. Some of those involved in the August Conspiracy turn up in Montreal in the summer and fall of 1864. This list included Jeremiah Black, Parke Godwin, newspaper editors Manton Marble and George Wilkes, New York customs collector Simeon Draper, Philadelphia District Attorney James Van Dyck and, possibly, Congressman Henry Winter Davis.[28]

The Radical Republicans were very much a part of this "dump Lincoln" effort. They wanted Lincoln gone because he stood in the way of their plans to impose a harsh reconstruction regime on the South. So ardently were they committed to this Radical agenda that many ultimately welcomed the President's assassination.[29] Still others, primarily Democrats, looked to the Confederate Secret Service for help in defeating Lincoln at the polls in November. Just as in politics today, this involved money. Among the "Copperheads" in Montreal were Congressmen Fernando and Benjamin Wood, who hated Lincoln and would have welcomed his removal from office by any means. Both were regulars at the hotel and Benjamin was in receipt of large amounts of money from the Confederate Secret Service that had been laundered through the Ontario Bank on Place d'Armes.[30]

Also on hand were key members of Salmon Chase's presidential committee.[31] This included Senator S.C. Pomeroy, Congressman E.G. Spaulding, George S. Hale, and Rhode Island Governor William Sprague, Chase's son-in-law, married to the beautiful and highly-political Kate Chase.[32] Other Chase supporters in Montreal included: John Bingham, William C. Noyes, and John Murray Forbes and Charles Barney.[33]

Radical Republicans like Thaddeus Stevens, James Wilson, James Harlan, and possibly Henry Wilson also appear to have been in Montreal.[34] Radicals John Sherman and James Ashley of Ohio were also in Canada that decisive summer, August 1864, registering at Barnett's Museum in

Niagara, close to St. Catharines and a few hours by train from Montreal.[35] (See *Appendix B*.)

Alexander R. Shepard, a Radical Republican and Washington powerbroker, was in the city in August, listing his point of departure as Washington, D.C.[36] Shepard was a vocal abolitionist and friend of Frederick Douglass. There is no mistaking his bold signature. Republican George S. Hale arrived from Boston on 12 August, the same day as Thaddeus Stevens. Hale was close to Salmon P. Chase and the Radicals. Also on 12 August, E.C. Ketchum registered at the hotel with his wife.[37] We believe this to be Edgar Ketchum, a powerful member of New York's Republican Party. Fellow New Yorker and Radical Republican J. Churchill registered in the Guest Book just after Ketchum.[38] Both Ketchum and Churchill would play prominent roles in the impeachment proceedings against President Johnson.

Union General Benjamin Butler's aide, Lieutenant Colonel H.S. Wade, also arrived in August from New Orleans. Butler was a fierce war Democrat, a failed field commander, and a notoriously corrupt official. He was heavily involved in illegal cotton trading and his nickname "spoons," deserved or otherwise, referred to his seizing the silverware of homes he occupied. Butler was unapologetic about making money from the war.[39] Despite being a Democrat, Butler was a supporter of the Radical Republican agenda.

On 13 August 1864, Republican Congressman, George A. Halsey, of New Jersey, a noted Radical, arrived in Montreal. So it appears the Radicals and their supporters were well represented in the city at this time.[40]

Meanwhile, former Republican Congressman George Ashmun registered at the hotel in July. Ashmun was the last person to see President Lincoln at the White House before he left for Ford's Theatre.[41] Not surprisingly, Ashmun was seeking a cotton license signed by the President. Lincoln asked him to come back the next morning. Ashmun was shortly to be made a Director of the notoriously corrupt Union Pacific Railroad.

W.B. Foulke registered with his son Joseph on 12 August 1864.[42] This was almost certainly former Republican Congressman, P.B. Foulke, who was involved in trading cotton for contraband with the Confederacy. His son was back at the hotel the following month at the same time as Congressman Fernando Wood, twice Mayor of New York and a notorious Lincoln hater.

Republicans such as Thurlow Weed, Orville Browning, and Governor Edwin Morgan (NY) also came to Canada at this time. All were involved in cotton trading. Browning's friend and collaborator in the cotton trade was James Singleton, who was also in Montreal.[43] Republican conservative Joseph Doolittle of Wisconsin arrived with Radical James Harlan on 16 September 1864. Doolittle was likely involved in cotton trading. Precisely why Harlan was in Montreal remains unclear but he was certainly surrounded by a number of Radical Republicans.

Horatio Seymour, Governor of New York and a strident peace Democrat, was another regular at St. Lawrence Hall.[44] He was considered a prime candidate for the Democratic Party's presidential nomination and had the full support of the Confederate Secret Service.

Post Office, St. James Street, Montreal, QC, 1859-60 near St. Lawrence Hall. McCord Museum, Notman Photographic Archives, Montreal, QC, 1859-1860. N-1975.32.8

Jacob Thompson, senior Confederate Commissioner serving in Canada, reported to Confederate Secretary of State Judah Benjamin: "I saw during the course of the summer (1864), in some instances repeatedly, Governor Seymour and Benjamin Wood..."[45] Democrat R. Underwood of Lexington, Kentucky, appeared in the register several times in August and September. James R. Underwood was a Democrat and strong supporter of the Union.[46] Nevertheless, he considered Lincoln a tyrant, imposing what amounted to a military dictatorship on the United States. He backed General George McClellan as the Democratic Party's nominee at the 1864 Democratic Convention in Chicago.[47]

One of the first Democrats to arrive in Montreal was William H. Taylor, a Congressman from Nebraska, who signed the St. Lawrence Hall register on 2 August 1864.[48] He was followed the very next day by Congressman Samuel "Sunset" Cox of Ohio, a determined "Peace Democrat." Cox deeply resented Lincoln's portrayal of all those who opposed the war as traitors.[49] As was true of so many others in Montreal, Cox appears to have had ties to super banker, Jay Cooke.[50]

The Hon. J.S. Phelps of Missouri stayed at St. Lawrence Hall on three occasions in August and September under the names G.R. Phelps and H.E. Phelps, and then, one final time, under his own name: J.S. Phelps.[51] The last registration by Phelps is dated 15 October, only days before John Wilkes Booth registered at St. Lawrence Hall.

Democratic Congressman C. Eldridge registered on 21 August. Eldridge would later be involved in both Andrew Johnson's impeachment and the controversial perjury trial of Charles Dunham in 1868.[52]

Democratic Congressman William Radford of New York, who had voted for the 13th Amendment, also registered at St. Lawrence Hall in August 1864.[53] With so many of his fellow legislators surrounding him, Radford may well have experienced the momentary impression that he had never left his office in Washington, D.C.

The Honorable Amos Kendall, a former U.S. Postmaster General, and W. Stickney registered at St. Lawrence Hall on 9 August 1864.[54] A noted Copperhead, Amos Kendall was vociferously opposed to both Lincoln and the war. He frequently submitted scathing, anti-Lincoln letters to the *Washington Globe*. More importantly, he presided over the 1864 Democratic Convention that the Confederate Secret Service sought so desperately to influence.

It was a centerpiece of Confederate Secret Service strategy to influence the Democratic Convention in Chicago to nominate a peace candidate or, at the very least, a candidate amenable to peace negotiations. Governor Seymour of New York was favored by the Confederacy over the unpredictable and imperious McClellan, but either of these men was preferable to the incumbent, Lincoln. The South was now desperate to negotiate an end to the war but they could not stomach outright surrender. If a negotiated peace could not be had, then the South seemed determined to go down fighting and the cost to the nation would be high. The election in November had thus become a make-or-break event for both sides.

NO QUESTIONS ASKED

No one registering at St. Lawrence Hall, or indeed any hotel in Montreal at that time, was required to show identification or to be truthful about themselves, their business, their destination, or their point of departure. When dealing with Americans in the midst of a terrible civil war, setting brother against brother, hotel staff were particularly circumspect in handling American guests. No one was to be pressed for personal details. Henry Hogan, proprietor of St. Lawrence Hall, understood that discretion was a central attraction of his hotel's value proposition and the war represented a financial windfall to his and other Montreal hotels. Indeed, St. Lawrence Hall's excellent reputation was as much rooted in its policy of complete privacy as its luxurious amenities. If a guest's initials were altered from one visit to the next, no member of the hotel staff would take notice.[55] If a guest claimed to be arriving from New York, London, Havana, Honolulu, Peru, or the moon, no one batted an eye. Given this environment, St. Lawrence Hall's Guest Book reflects a good deal of subtle signature subterfuges, especially involving American guests. When outright aliases were not employed, last names were sometimes accompanied by altered initials or modified by fraudulent points of origin. Sometimes such prefixes as "Dr." or "Rev." or suffixes such as "Jr." were added. Middle names became last names and wives or daughters registered for their husbands or fathers.[56] If Confederate spy John Harrison Surratt, could transform himself into John Harrison, then surely Radical Republican Congressman Henry Winter Davis could become Henry Winter or the Rev. H.W. Davis. Both names appear in the St. Lawrence Hall guest register in 1864 arriving from the U.S.[57] Sometimes a false initial would be inserted in front, so J. Holt becomes A.J. Holt. A quick thumbnail review of names in the register reveals dozens of easily identifiable examples of the use of altered initials or middle name substitutions, suggesting the practice was rather common among American guests both Confederate and Union.[58] These persistent patterns of alteration, noticeable especially at critical times and events during the Civil War, provided just enough of a screen to generate reasonable deniability.

INTO THE ETHER

Following Lincoln's assassination on 14 April 1865, it wasn't long before the Civil War drama in Montreal faded into the ether like a ghost, as if it had never happened. Confederates with knowledge of Booth's kidnapping plan lay low, many of them staying in Canada. Federal officials who had dealings with Confederate Secret Service agents involving cotton did not want this to become public knowledge. The American politicians who had been in Montreal did not want to explain what they had been doing in Canada and in such close proximity to the Confederate Secret Service. The bankers and businessmen who had been doing business with the Confederacy through Montreal laid low. The post-assassination hysteria whipped up by Edwin Stanton and the Radicals turned dangerous, even for them. No one wanted to have to explain why they had been in Montreal rubbing elbows with the Confederate Secret Service.

With so many prominent individuals potentially implicated, a conspiracy of silence took hold. Some even left the country. Fernando Wood of New York went to Europe for an extended stay. Some hoped the whole matter would blow over and be settled with a quick military trial and an equally quick execution of the Lincoln conspirators. Stanton had been quoted as having said he wanted the conspirators found guilty to be dead and buried before Lincoln's funeral train even reached Illinois.

Jacob Thompson, the senior Confederate Commissioner in Canada, wrote in his final report to Judah Benjamin about having destroyed most of his papers and records to protect powerful Northern interests who had collaborated with the Confederacy.[59] Canadian and British authorities were equally squeamish about discussing the goings-on in Montreal, which they had winked at. They faced an entirely different world in 1865, with a powerful, militarized, and belligerent neighbor to the south.

With the war over, Confederate and Federal agents disappeared from the smoking rooms, bars, and restaurants of St. Lawrence Hall, as well as the Donegana and Ottawa Hotels. But they did not disappear without a trace. Their footsteps can be found, if intermittently, in period newspapers, books, and photographic imagery, as well as in the juxtaposition of remarkable surviving records: an unusual collection of more than two dozen large, leather-bound guest registries from St. Lawrence Hall, carefully preserved in the atmosphere-controlled vaults of the Canadian National Archives in Ottawa, Ontario; the massive collection of glass negatives and photographic prints from one of Montreal's finest early photographic studios, William Notman & Sons (1840-1935), now preserved as the Notman Photographic Collection at the McCord Museum in Montreal; and the Visitors' Books from Thomas Barnett's Museum in the Niagara Falls Museum collection. Finally, a few of the St. Lawrence Hall`s "departure" registers have survived at the McCord Museum. There are other sources such as Rev. Stephen Cameron`s diary at the Civil War Museum in Richmond and the Clay family papers at Duke University Library. Together with newly published memoirs and biographies, these constitute "reservoirs of history," unlocking for the first time a window into the clandestine activities and actions of the American Civil War. It is a ghostly world of politics, high finance, tactical initiatives of war, and criminal plans that take the historical researcher on a journey purposefully intended, from its earliest days, to obscure, hide, and confuse. Yet the sheer weight of evidence points to something powerful and unusual occurring in Montreal from the summer and fall of 1864 through the spring of 1865.

A further frustration is manifest in the Montreal social environment of the American Civil War years. Henry Hogan, the proprietor of St. Lawrence Hall, was forever discreet and said little about the goings-on at his hotel during the war except to remember it as an exciting time. He protected the privacy of his guests to the end. He did let slip that he recalled John Wilkes Booth being at the hotel not just in October 1864 but, again in 1865, prior to the assassination.[60] As for

Custom House, Montreal, QC, about 1875. This beautiful and still-standing structure is seen in Notman photographs from the Civil War period. The original Custom House was nearby in the classic Pointe-à-Callière building, which is now a museum for Old Montreal. Meanwhile, this magnificent corner structure has served many commercial roles over the years. It still graces Old Montreal's skyline and is now an upscale club and office complex facing the harbor. McCord Museum, Notman Collection, Montreal, QC, about 1865. VIEW-955.A.0

the other secrets of St. Lawrence Hall, Hogan took them to the grave. In the early twentieth century, the grand hotel was torn down, as was the venerable Donegana. Only the Ottawa Hotel remains standing today on St. James/St. Jacques Street, near McGill Avenue. The building shell has been saved, but its original interiors were gutted. It stands today only a few blocks from the former site of the St. Lawrence Hall. The walk from the Ottawa Hotel to St. Lawrence Hall takes only a few minutes. This was exactly the journey taken by Confederate agent George Sanders, life-long advocate of political assassination, who moved from the Ottawa to the "Hall" in October 1864, likely to be nearer John Wilkes Booth and the Confederates then gathering there. He appears to have checked in with famed Confederate spy, Belle Boyd. Sanders boldly declared in the Guest Book that he was from "Dixie." While the list of names here can be overwhelming, those familiar with the era will recognize their historical significance. For example, the names imply that commercial intercourse between Northern industry and the Confederacy was widespread and involved key suppliers to the U.S. Army. A portion of this illicit trade, especially involving cotton, had the apparent support of the White House and the Treasury Department. It is also clear that opposition to Lincoln was deeper and more ubiquitous than allowed for in the existing Civil War historical narrative. This opposition crossed party lines and involved both Democrats and Republicans. Whatever their reasons for being in the city, both parties were present in Montreal, in a hotel full of Confederate operatives. The presence in Montreal of the key War Department personnel, including the Chief Telegraph Officer, Thomas Eckert, soon to be Assistant Secretary of War under Stanton, senior members of the Judge Advocate General's Office, and the National Detective Police, raises unanswered and unsettling questions. ❧

CHAPTER 5

Trading with the Enemy

IN THE SUMMER AND FALL OF 1864, Beverley Tucker, one of the senior Confederate Commissioners in Canada, was empowered by a reluctant but desperate government in Richmond to release millions of bales of cotton to world markets. A Union blockade declared by Lincoln on 19 April 1861 and enforced by the U.S. Navy had severely reduced the availability of cotton. In a short time, prices had soared to breathtaking levels, rising by over a thousand percent from ten cents a pound to almost a $1.90 a pound.[1] The South was awash in cotton but only a fraction of this supply was making it to market. Meanwhile, the Confederacy was desperately short of foodstuffs (especially meat), for its armies in the field.

The value of the cotton to be released by Tucker, about two million bales (based on an average price of $500-$700 a bale), was *worth as much as a billion dollars* in 1864-1865 currency. This was arguably the largest single cotton deal ever proposed up to that time. The cotton was to be paid for with meat and other contraband goods and U.S. currency (which had been promptly dubbed "Greenbacks" when first introduced in 1862). Most senior Union army and naval officers and many in Congress bitterly opposed this or any other commercial intercourse with the enemy.

Despite powerful opposition to Tucker's plan, both in Washington and among the leadership of the armed forces, the scheme went ahead, with the approval of the White House.[2]

The U.S. Treasury Department was charged with overseeing this massive exchange of cotton for contraband. Special cotton agents were appointed to issue licenses to any loyal citizen claiming "control" of Southern cotton. Lincoln may have thought that by placing this inter-belligerent trade in the hands of the Treasury Department, it somehow could be controlled or sanitized. Instead, it unleashed a wave of corruption that surged all the way to the White House.

Before the war, the South had provided the bulk of American exports and was a large importer of manufactured goods, having little industrial base of its own. This trade paid for much of the Federal budget and kept the U.S. balance of payments in

Senior Confederate Commissioner Beverley Tucker was charged with orchestrating the largest cotton-for-contraband deal of the war. The cotton to be exchanged was valued at over a billion dollars in 1864 currency. Mr. Beverley Tucker. McCord Museum, Notman Collection, Montreal, QC, 1865. I-14269.1

reasonable equilibrium. The war shattered this economic order. The Union naval blockade succeeded in isolating the South and stifling import and export trade. This, however, had the perverse effect of pushing the U.S. balance of trade and balance of payments into deficit. Despite very high tariffs to protect Northern industry, the Union needed to import many of the implements of war, especially from Great Britain. The Confederacy and the government in Washington found themselves competing to buy arms and military materiel in Europe. The South could pay for these imports with cotton that seeped through the blockade; the North had no comparable exports to offset needed imports. Borrowing abroad could have made up the difference, but European credit markets were wary of U.S. debt backed by a brand-new paper currency. The Confederacy had far better luck raising money in Europe with bonds backed by future deliveries of cotton, which was in high demand. Southern bond issues were usually oversubscribed. Thus the payments deficit could only be made up with gold, which depleted Federal reserves and put downward pressure on the Greenback. By 1864 the U.S. was almost out of gold and this, in turn, put downward pressure on the Greenback.

Lincoln saw cotton exports as a means of righting the balance of trade, replenishing the nation's supply of gold, and boosting confidence in America's new fiat currency. When pressed on the matter, Lincoln further suggested that opening the cotton trade would reward nominally loyal Southerners. This was a specious argument, as there was no way of knowing whether the cotton involved came from loyal Southerners or ardent secessionists.

Finally, Lincoln recognized the scheme's potential to create a vast pool of patronage. In the end, the prospect of patronage and profit was at the heart of this risky economic and political gambit. Cotton licenses represented an opportunity to dispense largesse to friends and supporters. Those close to Lincoln and the Republican Party received the bulk of these newly-issued permits.

Lincoln confidant Orville Browning was an intermediary for many of those seeking cotton permits. He wrote in his diary about speaking with Lincoln regarding a scheme to trade Southern cotton, "out of which he (Lincoln), (James) Singleton, Judge (James) Hughes, Senator (Edwin) Morgan, myself and some others hope to make some money, and do the country some service." Lincoln approved of the plan and said, "He wanted to get out all (the cotton) he could and send in greenbacks in exchange."[3] Everyone, including Lincoln, knew the South needed food, not paper money. Greenbacks would figure in the trading equation but food for cotton would be the key driver of this deal.

LINCOLN AND PATRONAGE

Long before he became a Republican, Lincoln had been a member of the Whig Party, whose economic policies, sometimes called the American System, called for high tariffs to protect American industry from competition. In turn, tariffs and excise taxes funded the government and raised revenues for internal improvements.[4] These internal improvements took the form of railroads, canals, and harbors. These projects provided a deep trough from which patronage could be ladled out to friends and supporters.[5]

Rather than shying away from patronage, Lincoln showed himself a master at dispensing it.[6] It was impossible to become President of the United States in this era without some control over the government's vast patronage apparatus, so it's not surprising to find Lincoln's friends, supporters, and even family members receiving special Treasury Department cotton licenses. Among these were Ward Lamon, James

Singleton, Orville Browning, Leonard Swett, and Robert Cox.[7] Singleton, Lamon, Browning, and Cox all visited Canada in the fall and summer of 1864, and all but Browning and Cox are found in St. Lawrence Hall's Guest Book. In Montreal, Cox took the time to pose for a set of photographs at Notman's Studio on Bleury Street.[8]

The connections of Cox and Singleton to Lincoln are interesting. James Singleton had a brother who served in the Confederate Congress. Singleton's loyalty, despite holding a Commission in the Union Army, was doubted in some circles. Whatever his politics, Singleton's primary commitment was to his pocketbook. In a world starved of cotton, special licenses to trade in the commodity were a fast way of getting rich. As a friend of the influential Orville Browning, Singleton was able to obtain licenses signed by the President himself. These presidential licenses were more useful than those procured through the Treasury Department because Lincoln's signature expedited the movement of goods both ways through Union lines.

Robert E. Cox provides yet another example of access to Lincoln procuring special cotton licenses. Facilitated by Browning, Cox was able to obtain cotton licenses signed by the President even though he was a Southerner and almost certainly a Confederate agent.[9] Cox appears to have had ties also to John Wilkes Booth, as well as to Confederate Commissioners Clement Clay and Beverley Tucker, who were posted in Canada in 1864.[10] Cox provided Clay and Tucker with their forward operating base in St. Catharines, Ontario, located near the U.S. border crossing at Niagara.[11]

Robert E. Cox. McCord Museum, Notman Collection, Montreal, QC, 1864. I-11518.1

Senator James Doolittle; Indiana Judge James Hughes; former Illinois Congressmen P.B. Foulke; and Kentucky cotton speculator S.L. Casey. This partial list represents just the tip of the iceberg when it comes to those who sought to participate in Tucker's cotton deal.[15] Some, like Singleton, Doolittle, and Foulke, can be found at St. Lawrence Hall.[16]

Democratic Congressman William Radford of New York was also at the hotel in August 1864. Radford would be one of the few Democrats to vote for Lincoln's proposed 13th Amendment to the Constitution.[17] Lincoln needed every vote; perhaps a cotton license was his payoff?

Confederate courier Josephine Brown carried messages from Cox to Clement Clay and stayed for a time at his house in Poughkeepsie, New York, awaiting dispatches from Clay (see Chapter 3, Confederate Couriers).[12] This was the same house John Wilkes Booth was said to have visited in the fall of 1864 while en route to Montreal.[13] Cox was arrested and held briefly in the wake of Lincoln's assassination but was released following the intervention of Orville Browning.[14]

The list of other powerful and influential people associated with Tucker's cotton trade is extensive. Among them were: U.S. Assistant Secretary of War, Charles Dana; Edward Atkinson, a prominent businessman from New England; Republican powerbroker Thurlow Weed; New York Senator Edwin Morgan; Wisconsin

A FAUSTIAN BARGAIN

Tucker's billion-dollar cotton deal promised to make a small number of people very rich but it was politically risky for Lincoln and his administration. The deal, if it went wrong, could easily have exploded on the eve of the 1864 election. If details about this plan to trade with the enemy leaked, it could easily have brought down the Lincoln administration. Senator (and former New York Governor) Edwin Morgan, who participated in Tucker's scheme, recognized the risks. He warned that the proposed deal and other schemes involving trading with the enemy were sufficiently fraudulent "to destroy any administration at any other time."[18] Thus, Tucker's cotton deal had to be kept secret and executed discreetly.

Montreal's St. Lawrence Hall was an ideal location for such cloak-and-dagger work. It was Montreal's finest hotel and large enough to accommodate the number of expected players.

Perhaps most importantly, it was located outside the United States and beyond the reach of American authorities.

Cotton was the oil of its day. With the prices wildly inflated, the prospect of gaining access to millions of bales of cotton set off a feeding frenzy among speculators. As Lincoln himself observed, "The temptation is so great that nearly everybody wishes to be in it; and when in, the question of profit controls all..."[19]

The truth was that both sides in the war needed cotton back on the market. The U.S. needed at least a partial resumption of the cotton trade as a means to support its new currency, correct its trade imbalance, and stem the outflow of gold. The Confederacy, with its back to the wall, needed to sell cotton to feed and supply its armies in the field.

There is not much doubt that Northerners involved in trading with the enemy knew these transactions would lengthen the war at a time when casualties were at appalling levels. The very idea of enemies at war cooperating to subvert a trade embargo while thousands died in the field is difficult to fathom, but even the President supported some inter-belligerent trade. The hard truth is that fabulous fortunes were made during the war. Some of this wealth represented profits from war-time commerce but some of it came from cotton trading and inter-belligerent commerce. The war launched a great many fortunes. It is no accident that many great commercial dynasties of the late nineteenth and early twentieth centuries date back to this period: Rockefeller, Morgan, Gould, Fargo, Whitney, Vanderbilt,

The rear of St. Lawrence Hall on Rue des Fortifications, from which John Surratt fled as U.S. detectives and Canadian authorities entered from St. James Street one floor up on the opposite side of the building. Note the large Union Jack flying above the hotel. It was precisely because St. Lawrence Hall was in British North America, outside the reach of U.S. authorities, that it was chosen as the site for Beverley Tucker's cotton-for-contraband negotiations. McCord Museum, Notman Collection, Montreal, QC, 1866. I-21896.1

The front of St. Lawrence Hall on St. James Street (now known as St. Jacques Street), just west of the Bank of Montreal and Place d'Armes. This was the unofficial headquarters of the Confederate Secret Service in Montreal. St. Lawrence Hall, St. James Street, Montreal, QC. McCord Museum, Notman Collection, Montreal, QC, about 1890. VIEW-1876

Marsh, Barney, Bliss, Fisk, Hatch, Cooke, Kuhn, Singer, Drexel, Kidder Peabody, Lehman, DuPont, Corning, Farrington and others got their start, or were certainly enriched, during the Civil War. Not surprisingly, many of these names are found in the Guest Book of St. Lawrence Hall or Barnett's Niagara Museum. Lincoln's support of inter-belligerent trade is an inescapable part of this conflicted story. His reasons for supporting cotton-for-contraband commerce had nothing to do with individual gain. He sought to combat a weak currency, balance of payments deficit, and a drain on gold reserves. These were all very real economic problems. But cotton-for-contraband trading involved an appalling Faustian bargain at the height of the war when men were dying on the field in unprecedented numbers. While Lincoln rationalized the trade-off, he never seemed entirely comfortable with it.[20]

THE FRENZY IN MONTREAL

From the summer of 1864 until the assassination of Lincoln in April 1865, everyone interested in cotton trading was at Montreal's St. Lawrence Hall, a Mecca for investment bankers, cotton speculators, blockade runners, and U.S. Treasury agents. For example, James and William Brown of Brown Brothers were on hand—their New York financial house had strong ties to pre-war cotton trading.[21] Their agent, J.V. Barnes, was at the hotel on a number of occasions.[22] Financing the "triangular" cotton trade between the Southern states, New York, and Europe was their specialty, and they did a booming business before the war.[23]

Dooley's Bar in St. Lawrence Hall, where Mint Juleps were always available. George Sanders and John Wilkes Booth engaged in whispered conversations here over drinks. Next door was the billiard room where John Wilkes Booth played Canadian champion Joe Dion in October 1864. It was here that Booth made his chilling prediction that no matter what the outcome of the election *"old Abe's contract is nearly up…his goose is cooked."* Bar room, St. Lawrence Hall, Montreal, QC. McCord Museum, Notman Collection, Montreal, QC, about 1890. VIEW-1882

There are several registrations for the name Ward arriving from New York, including one that clearly reads Samuel Ward.[24] Ward was a Democrat, banker, lobbyist, and the U.S. representative for Barings Brothers Bank in London.

Louis Kuhn, a member of the Kuhn family of New York, was at the hotel on 12 August 1864. The Kuhns would shortly form one of New York's premier financial houses Kuhn, Loeb and Co. In the 20th century, Kuhn, Loeb would be merged with Lehman Brothers, another company involved in cotton trading during the Civil War. They would eventually be absorbed by American Express, yet another firm with roots dating back to the Civil War.

On 18 August 1864, W. Farrington arrived in Montreal from Nassau, the chief transshipment point for contraband cargoes bound for Confederate ports. William Farrington was a successful cotton trader and Memphis banker. He would later found the Union and Planters Bank, which still operates today across the southern United States after being merged with Regions Bank, which itself still uses the Planter's logo depicting a young cotton plant.[25] Arriving with Farrington was A.(R.) Butler, who represented his brother, the thoroughly corrupt Benjamin Butler, in the cotton trade. Also traveling with them was a Mr. A. Burnside. Based on the signature in the Guest Book, this is very likely Union General Ambrose Burnside, who had taken a leave from the army on 13 August 1864, following a disastrous defeat at the so-called "Battle of the Crater" during the siege of Petersburg. What brought him to Montreal we can only guess, but he was the designer of the Burnside rifle, which was being made under contract in Providence, Rhode Island. The Canadian government was apparently a buyer of Burnside rifles.[26]

Registered in mid-August, E.L. Oppenheim was a partner in a London-based banking house with offices in New York.[27] A key banking player of the era is missing from our list: J.P. Morgan, but he or his agents were almost certainly in Montreal.[28] There are more than a dozen Morgan registrations with U.S. points of departure, especially from New York, found in the hotel register. We also know Morgan was involved in orchestrating an assault on the U.S. currency with the American speculators and Canadian Banks in 1863-1864. He made a good deal of money in the process.

Thomas C. "Doc" Durant, the driving force behind the corrupt Union Pacific Railroad, had a deep interest in Tucker's proposed cotton-for-contraband exchange. He does not appear in the hotel register, but his agents were in the city.[29] Durant even invited the U.S. government's chief detective, Lafayette Baker, to participate in his cotton play.[30] Little did he know that thanks to the ubiquitous Orville Browning, Baker and his cotton-trading partner, Roswell Goodell, were already deeply involved in Tucker's cotton deal.[31] Baker, Goodell, and Baker's brother-in-law, Walter Pollack, were soon regulars at St. Lawrence Hall.[32] Since Durant was involved with Tucker, it is very likely that his close associate Union General John Dix was also in the loop. There is an intriguing registration for (E.)J. Dix and son on 22 August 1864. Dix was involved in cotton trading out of Norfolk in league with General Ben Butler.[33] So too, it appears, was Durant's favorite banker, Jay Cooke, of Cooke Brothers Bank.[34] The Cookes were certainly deeply involved in Canadian finance, as seen immediately after the war in the infamous "Pacific Scandal," which brought down the Conservative government of Sir John A. Macdonald. The scandal had to do with secret bank payments and involved many of the same players who had been active during the Confederate heyday in Montreal—including Henry Starnes of the Ontario Bank and Cooke Brothers Bank.[35] Interestingly, John Wilkes Booth kept accounts at both the Ontario Bank in Montreal and Cooke Brother's Bank in Washington.[36] These accounts were set up during, or immediately after, Booth's trip to Montreal in October 1864.[37]

Another financier at St. Lawrence Hall who would later be involved in the Pacific Scandal was the notorious James "Diamond Jim" Fisk, one of the great robber barons of the nineteenth century. He arrived at the hotel on 5 December from Boston, accompanied by a member of the Cheney family.[38] The two occupied parlor suites A & B, suggesting business was to be conducted. The Cheneys were textile magnates in the Northeast and had a factory in Boston that produced Spencer Carbines.[39] Fisk had a well-earned reputation for sharp dealing and, along with his father James Fisk Sr., was known to be active in cotton smuggling.[40]

William Fargo, founder of Wells Fargo and later American Express, was at the hotel in early December. He may have been there on business,

or in his capacity as Mayor of Buffalo. Either way, Confederate agents and operatives surrounded him during his stay. One of Fargo's financial partners was banker Jay Cooke.

Two other "express" men were in Canada at this time: Benjamin Ficklin and W.W. Finney. Both were hardcore Confederates. Ficklin and Finney were graduates of Virginia Military Institute (VMI) and had helped procure the highly successful blockade runner and sea raider, *Robert E. Lee,* for the State of Virginia. Finney had also taken part in the abortive 1863 effort to free Confederate prisoners of war imprisoned on Johnson's Island in Ohio. As with so many other Confederates in Montreal at the time, his photograph can be found in the Notman Collection.[41] Before the war, Ficklin and Finney founded the famous Pony Express.[42] Ficklin was heavily involved in Beverley Tucker's cotton-for-contraband scheme and admitted to Federal authorities that he was in Montreal to meet with Tucker to discuss cotton licenses in 1864.[43] Ficklin had ties to Brown Brothers Bank, which specialized in cotton trading.[44] Early in Lincoln's first term, Ficklin had been identified by an informer as a potential assassin. But Lincoln, as he tended to do, dismissed the threat.[45] Interestingly, Ficklin traveled from Richmond to Washington in April 1865 and was in the Capital on the day Lincoln was assassinated. He was soon arrested as a suspect, but like Robert Cox, Ficklin was protected by Orville Browning and ultimately released.[46]

Another visitor to Montreal was R.R. Wade, financier, railroader, and one of the founders of Western Union. He arrived on 11 August, probably on telegraph business, but Wade, like everyone at the hotel during this period, found himself at dinner surrounded by Republican and Democratic politicians, Treasury agents, cotton speculators, American bankers, blockade runners, and Confederate agents. It must have made for interesting conversation at Dooley's Bar. Only a month earlier, Jay Gould, another of the great robber barons of the Gilded Age, was at the hotel. Gould denied being involved in cotton trading, but his presence in Montreal indicates otherwise.[47] Gould would one day engineer the takeover of Western Union. Wade was an early patron of Thomas T. Eckert, the head of the War Department's Telegraph office and a confidant of Edwin Stanton. Wade, and later Gould, would champion Eckert's career, which culminated in his becoming Chairman of Western Union. Eckert registered in July at both St. Lawrence Hall and Barnett's Museum.[48]

Memphis cotton merchants in Montreal included W.A. Goodwyn and John Leech.[49] Also from Memphis, we find W.A. Miller and A.E. Gibson who, like Goodwyn and Leech, were likely there on cotton business.[50]

J. Van Buren arrived at the hotel from Albany in the fall of 1864. This is almost certainly John Van Buren, someone with close ties to Senator Edwin Morgan and Tucker's cotton-for-contraband scheme.[51] Van Buren was also close to fellow Democrat and cotton speculator, General Benjamin Butler.

George Saunders, of *George Saunders and Son*, which was an important shipping concern in Nassau, was at the hotel in early 1865. Nassau was the primary transshipment center for vessels running the blockade.[52]

BROKERS, AGENTS AND SPECULATORS

During the period from August 1864 to April 1865, notoriously corrupt Treasury Department agent Hanson Risley alone issued special Treasury permits for nearly a million bales of Southern cotton. Risley was one of several Treasury agents with close ties to General Benjamin Butler.[53]

Permits for at least another million bales were issued by other Treasury agents such as New York's Thomas Connatty, by a Nashville agent named Adams, and G.H. Ellery in Memphis and G. M. Lane (who also had ties to General Butler in New Orleans and Norfolk).[54] Risley, Ellery, and Lane were among the Treasury Agents sent to Montreal in 1864-1865 presumably to facilitate Tucker's cotton-for-contraband trade and their names are in the St. Lawrence Hall Guest Book.

Another Republican associated with the Treasury Department in Montreal was H. Van Dyck from Albany who arrived on 14 June 1864. He was then Assistant Treasurer for the United States at New York.[55] In that capacity he played a role in issuing America's new paper currency, the Greenback. He was one of several senior Treasury officials in the city and may have been there to facilitate cotton-for-contraband trading. Van Dyck had close ties to super banker Jay Cooke, the chief financier of the Civil War Union effort and a strong supporter of Treasury Secretary Salmon P. Chase.

The prospect of fabulous profits brought an army of speculators to Montreal, but these poten-

Drawing Room St. Lawrence Hall. Drawing room, St. Lawrence Hall, Montreal, QC. McCord Museum, Notman Collection, Montreal, QC, about 1890. VIEW-1879

tial profits could be realized only if the cotton could first be secured inside the Confederacy and safely transported beyond Union lines. This was Beverley Tucker's job. Armed with a mandate from Richmond to ensure reliable access to Southern cotton in return for meat and other goods, he hammered together this mega-deal as best he could from St. Lawrence Hall in Montreal. His authority, however, was as shaky as the government he represented.

For the cotton to be extracted safely, Richmond would have to hold Union General Grant at bay. It wasn't just Confederates in Montreal who prayed for Richmond's safety in the spring of 1865; in places like New York and Memphis a host of Northern bankers and speculators likewise hoped Lee could hang on as long as possible.[56]

To understand the frenzy that went on in St. Lawrence Hall in the fall of 1864, as speculators, traders, and suppliers went from room-to-room doing deals, we need only read Lafayette Baker's account of the follow-up meetings that took place at the Astor House in New York City.

Although it is likely National Detective Police Chief Lafayette Baker and his partners were themselves involved in cotton speculations, he writes about events at the Astor House as a detective observing a white-collar crime unfolding. The atmosphere was tense and frenetic with speculators racing from room to room, sometimes to buy a license or sell one. They sought financial partners and influence peddlers. Names on contracts were scratched out and replaced with other names. The number of bales was sometimes changed, always upward. Food and champagne were ordered up to the rooms, as no one had time for formal dining.[57] Astonishingly, the Astor House was the headquarters of General John Dix, who commanded the Eastern Department for the Union, which encompassed the entire region. Had he wished, Dix could have had everyone involved arrested and thrown into the dungeons of Fort Lafayette. Yet he did nothing but look on, or more accurately, "away." Why? Perhaps because he was a partner with railway magnate and cotton speculator Thomas Durant, who was at the very center of the cotton-for-contraband free-for-all at the Astor House.[58]

HOW MUCH COTTON?

It's unclear just how much of Tucker's billion dollars in cotton was ever retrieved from the South. By the time the cotton licenses were issued, the war was winding down, the price of cotton was dropping, and the South was in chaos. Some cotton was burned by retreating Confederates or by Union generals set on retribution. But, just as most of the gold ever produced is still in circulation because man understands its intrinsic value, we can assume that much of the South's cotton ultimately found its way to market, though it was too late to save the South. Prices may have dropped with the defeat of the Confederacy, but the fundamental demand for cotton was still strong. Of course, the value of Lincoln's cotton licenses died with him and the much feared "trading with the enemy" scandal ultimately burst publicly with the Washburne hearings in 1865, but by then it was no longer news.[59]

Compared to the surrender of Savannah, the burning of Columbia, or the capture of Wilmington, a Congressional investigation into cotton corruption and war profiteering seemed boring stuff.[60] With the President's assassination, no one was anxious to pursue a story that did not put Lincoln in a positive light.

While we know that some of Tucker's cotton was certainly exchanged for contraband as planned, the chaotic conditions prevailing inside the dying Confederacy make an accurate accounting of goods exchanged impossible. As for the well-connected men at the center of this illicit trade in the North, they landed on their feet and went on to play roles in the post-war Gilded Age, which was characterized by unprecedented opulence and corruption. Some, like Durant, the Cooke Brothers, and James Fisk, would move on to other skullduggery involving railroads and crooked politics. Their Confederate counterparts were not so lucky. Many found themselves homeless, destitute, fugitives living in exile, while others were prisoners. For most of the Confederate residents of St. Lawrence Hall, the war had cost them everything. ∾

Blockade runner and Captain in the Confederate Navy J. Taylor Wood. Museum, Notman Collection, Montreal, QC, 1864. I-17208.1

CHAPTER 6

Montreal, Halifax, Matamoros, and New York

N EW YORK PLAYED an interesting role in the Confederate Secret Service story. America's largest city was generally opposed to both the Civil War and the Lincoln Administration. Before the war, New York benefited immensely from trading with the South. It was the middleman in the triangular cotton trade running from the cotton states through New York and then on to Europe. Cotton was king and, along with the steam engine, the driving force behind the Industrial Revolution. The cotton trade represented the most valuable flow of commerce in the world, and New York was the central *entrepôt*, providing shipping, warehousing, and most especially financing. Lincoln's blockade of the South hurt New York as much as it did Wilmington, Charleston, or Savannah. Early on in the conflict, Mayor Fernando Wood suggested that New York declare itself a sovereign city-state and continue business as usual with the Confederacy.[1] Mayor Wood, a Democrat, distrusted Republicans in

both Albany and Washington. The war and the accompanying military draft were viscerally opposed in New York City. In 1863, street protests turned into the worst, bloodiest rioting in the city's history.

Blockade runner and banker Gazaway Lamar of Savannah knew New York City well. He had done business there as a banker for many years prior to the Civil War. He knew Mayor Fernando Wood and his brother Benjamin Wood, owner of the *New York Daily News*. Both Wood brothers despised Lincoln and wanted the war to end so business could return to normal. Benjamin Wood was actually on the payroll of the Confederate Secret Service in Montreal, receiving a payment of $25,000 in 1864 from the Confederate-controlled Montreal branch of the Ontario Bank.[2] During the war, Gazaway Lamar wrote to Fernando Wood to propose a cotton-for-contraband scheme that closely resembled the plan later adopted by Lincoln and the Treasury Department. (See

Chapter 4, Trading with the Enemy and Beverley Tucker.) His letter to the Mayor was intercepted and published in the *New York Times*, making it impossible to move forward with the plan. It's clear, however, from Lamar's letter that he fully expected Wood to be an enthusiastic partner. Had the scheme not been exposed, it might very well have succeeded; it certainly resembled closely the plan ultimately adopted by the Lincoln administration to get Southern cotton back onto world markets.[3] Gazaway Lamar's life-long track record of business success points to very few losing bets.

NEW YORK'S DIRTY LITTLE SECRET

New York was an old hand at breaking the law in the interests of maritime and banking profits. In the years leading up to the Civil War, it was New York, not Charleston, Savannah, or New Orleans, that was the center of America's participation in the global slave trade. Since the early part of the nineteenth century, it had been illegal to import African slaves into the United States, but in the 1850's, Cuba and much of South America were still importing slaves in large numbers. So there was a lot of money still to be had in "slaving" and New York shipping and banking elements soon specialized in this unsavory trade. Along the Hudson, ships were regularly outfitted to carry slaves. Vessels fitted out for the slave trade were easy to spot; they had unusual requirements for fresh water storage and food preparation, not to mention layer upon layer of cramped accommodations where Africans were "spooned" together in spaces so cramped they could not sit up and were allocated less space than is found in a coffin.[4] It was all thoroughly illegal but for the right price local authorities turned a blind eye. Not only were slave ships outfitted in New York, the city provided much of the cash to finance the trade. On the eve of the Civil War, at least two ships a month were being outfitted as slavers along New York's docks.[5] Gazaway Lamar's son, Charles, who was involved in the last importation of African slaves into the United States, used New York to outfit his infamous slave ship *Wanderer*.[6]

It is not surprising that with the advent of Civil War, New York became pretty much an open city for blockade runners and Confederate agents, who had no difficulty coming and going. They arrived by train, carriage, and especially by ship, and took up residence at New York's many fine hotels and ate at their favorite restaurant, Delmonico's.[7] Confederate agents ran blockade runners in and out of New York regularly, taking cargoes of food, uniforms, and arms to Halifax for transshipment or directly to Nassau or Bermuda.[8] Even the signal rockets used by famous blockade runners like John Wilkinson came from the same New York firm that supplied the U.S. Navy.[9]

The *New York Times* reported in early 1864 on just how open blockade running was in the city and on its corrupting influences: "How is it that those WOLFS (Confederate agent in Nassau) take here their orders from the Government agents of the Confederacy, send them to New York, and receive the goods by the return steamer. Mr. WOLF says every shipment stands him in £500, as bribery for New-York Custom-house officers...Among the goods imported under my name have been, 1,200

Benjamin Wier was a pronounced Confederate sympathizer who flew a Confederate flag over his warehouse entrance. Both Wier and Dr. William Almon received letters of thanks from Judah Benjamin and President Jefferson Davis. B. Weir [sic] and dog. McCord Museum, Notman Collection, Montreal, QC, copied 1870. I-49191.0.1

Dr. William Almon helped found Halifax's first hospital and was three times elected President of the Medical Society of Nova Scotia. A Confederate supporter, he was active in politics and played an important role in the establishment of Canada's Confederation in 1867. Dr. William Almon. McCord Museum, Notman Collection, Montreal, QC, 1864. I-12016-1

Colt's revolvers, 2,000 badges, made of velvet, for Confederate officers, with a small golden palmetto, 13,000 pairs army shoes and 1,200 blankets. Are these contrabands of war or not? The New-York Custom-house is only laughed at here, and it is certainly painful for everybody whose sympathies are with the North, to see how cargo after cargo arrives to supply the rebels."[10]

Confederate mail was given to the purser on board Cunard vessels, like the *S.S. Corsica*, who delivered it to the Cunard Company office in Lower Manhattan. From there the mail was sent on through the U.S. mail or transported by Cunard vessels to Europe. Cunard's ships were also known to carry contraband cargoes on their regular runs from New York to Nassau.

HALIFAX, NEW YORK, AND THE MONTREAL CONNECTION

Benjamin Wier's firm in Halifax acted as agents for the Confederacy and regularly received shipments from New York destined for the Confederacy.[11] Wier and a clutch of Confederate supporters in the city, like Dr. William Almon, played an indispensable role in moving goods and people in and out of Halifax in support of the Southern cause. One of Wier's employees, Alexander "Sandy" Keith, acted as the Halifax agent for a number of blockade-running enterprises including the Importing and Exporting Company of Georgia owned by Gazaway Lamar and his son Charles Augustus Lamar.[12] Keith was involved in Lamar's efforts to smuggle money and bond printing presses from New York, through Halifax, to the Confederacy. Prior to the war, the South's currency was printed in New York and they lacked the wherewithal to produce quality currency and bonds. Lamar was asked by Richmond to remedy the problem. The new printing presses were to be transported to Halifax where Keith would arrange transshipment to Florida. In the interim Lamar was to contract with local agents in New York to print $100,000,000 in Confederate currency and bonds. Much of this money arrived safely in the South but the illicit printing ring was eventually betrayed when a ciphered letter was intercepted by an alert postmaster.[13]

The encrypted letter required the attention of the best code breakers in the Federal government, but the contents proved especially interesting. The letters revealed a large network of agents operating in New York City, many of them Northerners, taking orders from Richmond. At about this same time a letter book of Charles Lamar's was found on a captured blockade runner.[14] It too pointed to a large network of agents operating in New York.

One of the letters from New York, dated 18 December 1863, was addressed to Confederate Secretary of State, Judah Benjamin, who oversaw Secret Service activities.

"Willis is here. Two steamers will leave about Christmas. Lamar and Bowers left here via Bermuda two weeks ago. 12,000 rifles came duly to hand and were shipped to Halifax as instructed. We will be able to seize the other two steamers as per program. Trowbridge has followed the President's orders...We want more money. How shall we draw? ...JHC"[15]

"JHC" was J.H. Cammock, a Confederate agent sent to New York to facilitate the money-printing operation. The reference to seizing ships was no idle threat. It referred to a plan to seize Federal vessels sailing near Canadian waters and then bring them to Nova Scotia to be fitted out with wartime cargoes to be sent on to Wilmington, NC. The *USS Chesapeake* was seized in exactly this way in December 1863 and ultimately ended up in Halifax, creating an international incident that severely strained British-American relations.[16] Benjamin Wier, Alexander Keith, Dr. William Almon, and others were at the center of this scheme. Almon arranged for most of the perpetrators, who were Canadians and British subjects, to go into hiding before they could be arrested, but one of the ringleaders, George Wade, was captured and prosecuted. Almon and

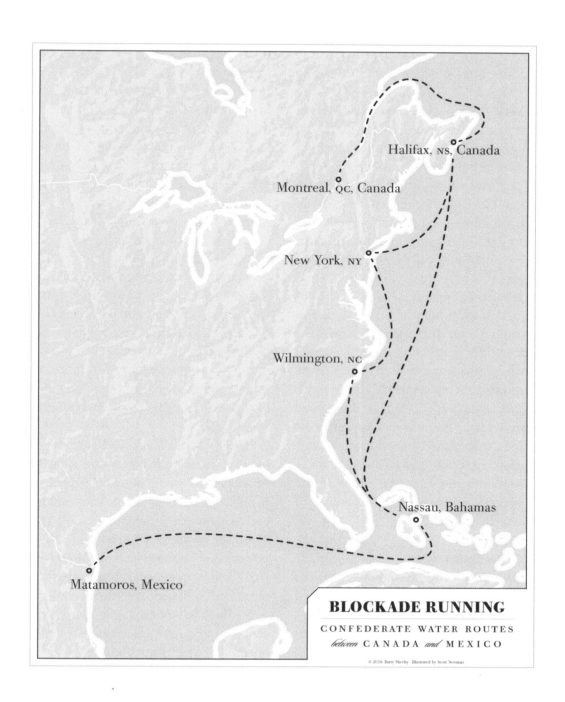

BLOCKADE RUNNING

CONFEDERATE WATER ROUTES
between CANADA *and* MEXICO

© 2016 Barry Sheehy. Illustrated by Scott Newman

Keith then orchestrated his escape from police in broad daylight during a prisoner transfer on the docks of Halifax, after which he went into hiding and was apparently never recaptured.[17]

In New York, Cammock worked with Nelson Trowbridge, a long time agent of the Lamars who had been involved in Charles Lamar's infamous slave importation scheme involving the ship *Wanderer* just prior to the war.[18] The ease with which a noted blockade runner like Lamar and his agents could breeze in and out of New York is astonishing.[19] Shortly after one such visit, Trowbridge wrote admiringly to his friend and employer Lamar, "There are devilishly few rebels these days who come rigged out in your style."[20] Trowbridge also commented on Cammock's infatuation with a beautiful Virginia widow, "She is a stunner, and for fear you won't believe me I will enclose her *carte de visite*. Send it back to me without fail. She spent last winter in Havana with a sick husband, since dead. CAM is having a good time, and so did your humble servant before he got here. 'He that is robbed, not wanting what is stolen, or knowing it not, is not robbed at all.'... Of course he thinks her virtuous, and as it will do him no good to inform him to the contrary, I keep shady on the subject."[21]

MATAMOROS AND NEW YORK

The sleepy Mexican port of Matamoros near the Texas border had almost no traffic from New York before the war. Nobody knew Matamoros even existed but it soon became a vital transfer point for outbound cotton and inbound war supplies. Almost no ships were cleared to sail from New York to Matamoros in the years leading up to the Civil War but in the thirty-six months from 1862 to 1864, 152 ships cleared New York for the Mexican port, which is a stone's throw from Brownsville, Texas. The traffic was so heavy it overwhelmed the small port, which at one point had eighty-two vessels lying offshore waiting to unload their cargoes.[22] The Captain of the *USS Monongahela* reported in December 1863, "Only a few days ago a cargo of army wagons was landed there (Matamoros) direct from New York and cleared from the custom-house at New York."[23] It was reported that, "Pistols, ammunition, musket caps, medicines, shoes, and a variety of other goods were brought in from New York on speculation, and a great amount of cotton brought out." Northern shoes were being issued to Confederate troops, again coming from New York.[24] Not surprisingly, visitors from Matamoros turned up at St. Lawrence Hall in Montreal, the unofficial headquarters of the Confederate Secret Service in Canada.[25]

If one stands back and takes in the whole picture, the vista is pretty stunning. Thousands of rifles were being shipped from New York to Halifax for transshipment south and nobody in authority seemed to notice or care. Confederate blockade runners entered and left New York pretty much as they pleased, with no interference from customs officials, apparently thanks to the placement of judicious bribes.

Meanwhile, much of the Confederacy's currency and bonds were being printed under the noses of Federal authorities in the middle of America's largest city. Armed with the information in Lamar's captured letters, Federal authorities would ultimately break up the money-printing operation, but not until millions of dollars in currency and bonds had been printed and shipped south. Lamar's agent, N.C. Trowbridge, a Northerner, operated openly in the city, and it was only toward the war's end that he was arrested and charged with treason.[26] Sentenced to hang, he was pardoned and fled to the Confederate-friendly Eastern Townships south of Montreal just across the border, and from there ultimately turned up at St. Lawrence Hall.[27] Another agent of the Lamar family operating out of New York and Montreal was the mysterious "Mr. Powell" who specialized in gold and currency transactions.[28] And we do indeed have a "Mr. Powell" (no initials) arriving from New York at St. Lawrence Hall in August and October 1864 and then again in March 1865.[29]

There is clearly more to be learned about these various clandestine activities, but what we do know raises the obvious question: What else was going on in New York that the Federal government didn't know about or couldn't control? It was an open secret that Union and Confederate troops were largely eating meat processed from the same Northern slaughterhouses in the Midwest.[30] The truth is that little was done to effectively combat trading with the enemy during the war. Important bankers, politicians, and powerbrokers were all implicated—even the White House was involved. In New York, such nominally illegal activities had developed into a near art form. No wonder Lincoln's scheme for trading cotton for contraband started in Montreal but was carried forward in New York City.[31] (See Chapter 5, Trading with the Enemy.)

CHAPTER 7

The Hidden Hand — John Wilkes Booth in Montreal

THE RARE BOOK DEPARTMENT of the Free Library of Philadelphia has in its collection a fragment torn from the guest book of Montreal's St. Lawrence Hall dated 18 October 1864.[1] The fragment provides incontrovertible evidence that John Wilkes Booth was in Montreal in the fall of 1864. His signature is clear and bold.

The fragment was part of an entire two-sided page torn from the Montreal St. Lawrence Hall guest book register for 18 October 1864. It contains three names of significance: John Wilkes Booth, Rev. (Dr.) Luke Blackburn, and Walter Pollack.

These names are significant because they are tied to several parallel plots that developed in

John Wilkes Booth[2]

John Wilkes Booth signature fragment. (Rare Books Department; Free Library of Philadelphia, PA; part of an entire page torn from the Montreal St. Lawrence Hall Hotel Arrival Book October 18, 1864)

Canada almost simultaneously from the summer of 1864 through April 1865. The first plot involved a Confederate Secret Service plan to kidnap President Lincoln in order to force the North to resume prisoner exchanges. The South at this stage of the war had been bled white of manpower and desperately needed these POW's, now veterans, back in the line. The North, in contrast, had access to almost unlimited manpower. Consider that General Ulysses S. Grant sustained nearly sixty thousand casualties during the short period from the Battle of the Wilderness through the Petersburg campaign. This was more men than General Robert E. Lee had in his whole army, but despite the casualties Grant continued to advance. Lincoln once commented that Grant understood the "terrible mathematics of the war"—the South would bleed to death long before the North.

In that fateful fall of 1864, a number of plots were afoot in Montreal. The city was bubbling with plots, counterplots, and conspiracies. The Civil War had reached its height, casualties soared to sickening levels, and everyone sensed the deciding crisis was near. Among the Confederates there was a rising sense of desperation but not defeatism; in its place was a fatalistic and bloody-minded determination to fight it out to the end.

In addition to plans for kidnapping Lincoln, there were discussions about unilaterally releasing Northern POW's because the South simply could not afford to feed and house them any longer. Meanwhile, Beverley Tucker, one of the most senior Confederate Commissioners in Canada, was empowered by a reluctant but desperate government in Richmond to release millions of bales of cotton into world markets that had been starved of it by the Federal Blockade.

Signing in with Booth are senior Confederate operative Dr. Luke Blackburn and Federal National Detective Police detective Walter Pollack. Note they have side-by-side rooms 158 and159. Booth is just a few doors away in room 150. John Wilkes Booth signature fragment. (Rare Books Department; Free Library of Philadelphia, PA)

Cotton was then the most important commodity in the world and in short supply. The value of the cotton Tucker would release—about two million bales—was worth a billion dollars in 1864-1865 currency. It was arguably the largest single cotton trade ever conceived up to that time. The cotton was to be paid for with meat, contraband, and Greenbacks. Senior army and naval officers, along with much of Congress, including the Radical Republicans who already despised Lincoln, were bitterly opposed to trading with the enemy. Despite this opposition, the cotton-for-meat scheme had the tacit approval of the White House and went ahead. Perhaps not surprisingly, many of those receiving special cotton permits under this scheme were friends, relatives, and political backers of the president.

The whole plan was politically loaded. The affair had to be kept as quiet as possible lest the resulting scandal bring down the Lincoln administration. Against this backdrop of intrigue and corruption, the Confederate Secret Service in Canada went about its normal business of inciting mayhem, including blockade running, spying, arson, undermining the U.S. currency, and conducting armed incursions into the United States—such as the St. Albans attack in October 1864. What is astonishing is that all of these parallel and sometimes overlapping schemes were centered in one place: St. Lawrence Hall in Montreal. The people involved in these various plots dutifully registered in the hotel guest book, albeit sometimes under an alias or with slightly altered initials, and many took the short walk to Notman's Photographic Studio on Bleury Street

St. James Street, now rue Saint-Jacques. McCord Museum, Notman Collection, Montreal, QC, about 1860. N-0000.193.31.1

to have their photos taken. Through a miracle of historic preservation, historians have access to this precious material, including the hotel guest books, Notman's extensive photographic collection, the Barnett's Museum visitors' books, as well as memoirs, diaries, letters, and court testimony.

Booth was identified as being in the city by a number of witnesses, including the U.S. Consul in Montreal, John Potter.[3] There is reason to believe he was possibly there again in 1865.[4] Booth was supposedly in Montreal to ship his wardrobe through the blockade to the South, but this would hardly have justified his ten-day stay in the city, and he may well have been in the city for several days before registering at St. Lawrence Hall. In a letter to his friend Dr. G.T. Collins on 28 October 1864 he wrote, "I have been in Montreal for the last three or four weeks and no one (not even myself) knew when I would return."[5]

It is likely Booth was in Montreal to meet with members of the Confederate Secret Service and senior Confederate Commissioners to discuss a plan for kidnapping President Lincoln.[6] The genesis of the Lincoln assassination can be traced directly to these meetings. Booth's own diary points to this fact with the words, "for six months we had worked to capture."[7] Written in April 1865, this places the beginning of the plot back to the fall of 1864, precisely when Booth was in Montreal.

The presence of Booth in Montreal is well established but remains a murky part of Civil War history. Why was he there? His explanation for shipping his wardrobe through the blockade is rather thin. Booth did not have to travel to Montreal personally to make such arrangements, nor would this have required such an extended stay. More to the point, the arrangements to ship the wardrobe were made through Captain P.C. Martin, one of the most senior Confederate Secret Service operatives in Montreal. Martin provided Booth with letters of introduction to the courier lines though southern Maryland. This included the "Doctors' Line" made up of doctors who used the cover of their profession to move people and letters through southern Maryland to Virginia.[8] Drs. W. Queen and Samuel Mudd, who both met with Booth in Maryland, were almost certainly part of the "Doctors' Line."[9]

Mudd would later be arrested and charged in connection with the Lincoln assassination. Martin provided similar letters of introduction to numerous British officers traveling secretly south to liaise with the Army of Northern Virginia. In many ways P.C. Martin provides a useful template for examining Booth's visit to Montreal. It is people like Martin who surrounded Booth, rather than the actor himself, who provide a glimpse of what was really happening in Montreal in the fall of 1864.

Booth's companions in Canada, as well as those associated with him in Washington and New York, tell us a lot about the man. Rather than being a deranged assassin alienated from society, the Booth that emerges in Montreal is socially adept, worldly, and a charmer. Rather than being isolated and introverted, Booth appears to have connections to a number of powerful American constituencies. The Confederate Secret Service stands out as the most prominent of these but it was not the only one. Montreal had by 1864 become a safe haven for hundreds of Confederate exiles but it was also a safe place for American officials, bankers, and politicians to do business. These players are also to be found registered at St. Lawrence Hall, especially in the short period from the summer of 1864 to the spring of 1865, and they also make up the milieu in which Booth was circulating.

That Booth pulled the trigger ending Abraham Lincoln's life is not in question; he admits in his diary the fatal decision was made only days before the event. George Atzerodt confirmed this fatal last-minute judgment in his confession.[10] But the idea of murder, as an alternative to the original plan of kidnapping, may well have been planted by people surrounding Booth months earlier in Montreal. There is ample evidence that Booth spent time in Montreal with individuals like Confederate Commissioner George Sanders, who was a life-long advocate of assassinating tyrants, loudly calling for Lincoln's murder.[11]

The names revealed in this and other chapters, as well as the appendices, are sufficiently important to stun anyone familiar with the era. This list includes Democrats, Republicans (some of them Radicals), bankers, business leaders, arms dealers, Treasury Department officials, and War Department agents, including Edwin Stanton's top spies; there was even a governor or two involved. Some of these individuals were in Montreal to trade cotton for contraband, but this put them in direct contact with senior members of the Confederate Secret Service. Others were in Montreal selling arms and food to the Confederacy or laying plans to defeat Lincoln at the polls. Some even wanted to displace him as the Republican nominee. All these powerful Northerners were at St. Lawrence Hall rubbing elbows with Confederates who used the hotel as an unofficial headquarters. This was the universe in which John Wilkes Booth circulated in Canada, and this circle is more interesting and eclectic than one would normally associate with a lone, brooding assassin.

KIDNAPPING THE PRESIDENT

It was at the Parker House in Boston in late July 1864 that Booth was most likely recruited for the Lincoln kidnapping scheme. Here, four men, three of them claiming to be from Canada, visited him. All used aliases. One of these aliases belonged to H.V. Clinton, who would later turn up at St. Lawrence Hall in Montreal in connection with the Confederate Secret Service.[12] Clinton registers at the hotel several times in the four months from May through August 1864.[13] On 24 August, he registered the same day as Canada's senior Confederate Commissioner, Jacob Thompson.

The Boston meeting set the stage for a follow-up session in Montreal in October, presumably to coordinate logistics and financing. It was in Montreal that Booth obtained money and letters of introduction to the courier lines running through southern Maryland, routes he followed during his abortive escape following the assassination.[14]

On the face of it, the idea of kidnapping the President of the United States seems outlandish, but it was a viable operational concept in 1864. The Gray Ghost, John Singleton Mosby, proved that Union generals and their entire staffs could be scooped up and captured deep behind enemy lines.[15] Thanks to Mosby, the concept of capturing an important military or political leader was no longer just a fanciful theory. The concept gained traction after the failed Dahlgren raid in early March 1864. The leader of the raid, Colonel Ulric Dahlgren, was killed but orders were found on his body instructing the raiders to kill Jefferson Davis and his cabinet. The authenticity of the orders was denied by Washington, but in the South they were believed. This hardened attitudes toward striking back at Lincoln.[16]

After the war, Confederate Colonels James Gordon and Robert Martin, rebel agents known to frequent St. Lawrence Hall, admitted possessing advance knowledge of Booth's kidnapping plans.[17] They claimed, however, that the plan they heard about in Canada involved kidnapping, not murder. Gordon's and Martin's advance knowledge of Booth's scheme suggests it was hardly a secret among senior Confederates in Canada.[18]

Lincoln's habit of traveling around Washington accompanied by only a single driver made him an inviting target.[19] In the hot sultry summer and fall when old "foggy bottom" became intolerable, Lincoln often slept at the Old Soldiers' Home on the outskirts of the city, traveling daily to and from the White House by buggy, usually unescorted.[20] So the possibility of five or six well-armed men capturing Lincoln and spiriting him south through Maryland to Virginia was not far-fetched. Maryland was, after all, right next door and the kidnapped President could have been bundled out of the city into Confederate-friendly territory in a matter of hours. It was a daring, dangerous plan—but not impossible.

Lincoln's security throughout the war was incredibly lax. When in evidence at all, his security detail often appeared inept. This was confirmed the night of the assassination, when the lone guard protecting the President at Ford's Theatre went off to have a drink at a tavern next door.[21] Given this lax security, the Confederate kidnapping plan might well have worked. Famed Confederate scout Thomas Conrad, a daring soldier, ordained minister, and a desperado of sorts, was among the first to conceive of such a kidnapping scheme. Conrad had gone so far as to take an experienced team of cavalrymen with him to Washington to carry it out. In his memoirs he wrote, "We had agreed that Lincoln could be kidnapped (and) safely conveyed to Richmond without let or hindrance, and the more we thought on it the more practical it became."[22] Conrad only abandoned the scheme when Lincoln suddenly began traveling accompanied by a troop of cavalry. After the war, Conrad never acknowledged any contact with Booth, who was planning an identical kidnapping, but by then anyone who admitted having dealings with Booth was putting their life at risk.[23]

Perhaps the deadliest plot against Lincoln involved Thomas Harney of the Confederate Torpedo (explosives) Bureau, the South's most skilled bomb maker. Harney had been involved in the deadly City Point explosion in August 1864, which devastated General Grant's most important supply depot. The plan was to blow up the White House during a meeting of Lincoln's Cabinet. Harney's bomb team was on its way to Washington when it ran into a Federal patrol. Some of the Confederates were captured, including Harney, but none were thoroughly questioned.[24] It was only after the war that the details of the bomb plot were revealed.

In comparison to Conrad and Harney, Booth was an odd candidate for such a dangerous mission. He was a fine actor but no soldier. Conrad and Harney were veterans with a proven capacity to organize and kill.[25] In Booth's circle only Lewis Powell (Payne) met this "stone killer" description. Powell had been a member of Colonel J.S. Mosby's raiders, a famed cavalry unit in Virginia whose exploits were legendary. Operating behind Union lines they risked everything. It was they who proved, with Mosby the Gray Ghost, that Union Generals could be captured behind enemy lines and taken prisoner. Powell supposedly deserted in January 1865 but that may well have been a subterfuge to get him across Union lines.[26] If Powell deserted to avoid danger, joining Booth's high-risk scheme was hardly the way to do it.

There was a fourth scheme targeting Lincoln, the most mysterious of all, and it was centered in New York City. Those behind this latter conspiracy remain in the shadows even today. Booth was in contact with them and expressed concern to George Atzerodt that they might get to Lincoln first.[27] Booth spent considerable time in New York in the summer of 1864 and again in early 1865. He boasted to George Atzerodt of dining in the finest mansion in New York but never revealed the name of his host.[28] This was precisely the time when a powerful movement was afoot to force Lincoln off the Republican ticket.[29] This movement may have begun in New York but it soon developed national reach.[30] It also crossed party lines, involving powerful Republicans and War Democrats. A number of influential newspaper editors were also involved. Meetings were held in private homes rather than hotels to avoid publicity. New York Mayor George Opdyke and businessman David D. Field hosted two such meetings; there may have been more. According to Thurlow Weed, who attended these clandestine sessions, the conspiracy was "vicious and powerful ...involving more leading men than I would have thought possible."[31] Security was tight. Even today, a century and a half later, we know the names of only about a dozen of the fifty or more people involved. The ones we can identify include Mayor George Opdyke, businessman D.D. Field, Hon. Henry Winter Davis, Senator Benjamin Wade, Senator Charles Sumner, James Van Dyck, George Wilkes, newspaper editor Parke Godwin, newspaper editor Theodore Tilton, Lewis Parsons, Governor J. Andrew, Governor William Dennison, newspaper editor Manton Marble, and former Attorney General Jeremiah Black.[32] Salmon Chase, forever ambitious for the presidency, sent an observer.[33] The original participants were instructed to reach out by letter to at least three other public officials across the country. One copy of these outreach letters has survived and was signed by former Attorney General Jeremiah Black.[34] Black was a Democrat and friend of Edwin Stanton, the Secretary of War. Stanton sent Black to Canada in the summer of 1864 to open back door negotiations with Confederate Commissioner Jacob Thompson regarding a possible peace settlement.[35] Republicans and War Democrats were nervous about the upcoming November elections

The beautiful Bank of Montreal building on Place d'Armes. The Bank of Ontario is on the left. Both institutions held Confederate Secret Service deposits but the Bank of Ontario, under the leadership of Henry Starnes—soon to be Mayor of Montreal—was the Confederate's favorite bank in Canada. They also kept large deposits at the Niagara and District Bank in St. Catharines. Bank of Montreal, Place d'Armes. McCord Museum, Notman Collection, Montreal, QC, 1871-1872. [lot number]

and confidence in Lincoln was low. Even Lincoln admitted he was likely to be beaten.[36]

The New York anti-Lincoln movement very nearly succeeded in replacing the President as the Republican nominee. Many of those involved in this anti-Lincoln scheme turn up in Montreal in late 1864 and early 1865. This includes Jeremiah Black, Parke Godwin, newspaper editors Manton Marble and George Wilkes, New York customs collector Simeon Draper, and possibly Congressman Henry Winter Davis and James Van Dyck.[37]

The New York Conspiracy apparently collapsed after Sherman's capture of Atlanta and the nomination of George McClellan as the Democratic presidential nominee but did it disappear entirely? Some of those violently opposed to Lincoln may well have carried on. We know that some sort of illicit activity, centered on 178½ Water Street in New York, was still going on as late as March 1865. This is when John Surratt received a letter inviting him to come to New York on urgent business and to send his answer to this address. The letter came from R.D. Watson, a meat supplier, businessman, and Confederate sympathizer who had earlier taken out a certificate of deposit for nearly $13,000 at the Bank of Montreal and who registered at St. Lawrence Hall in October 1864.[38]

A "SECESH" TOWN

When Booth arrived in Montreal in October 1864, he would have quickly recognized this was a "Secesh" friendly town with strong pro-Southern leanings. Most of the city's senior officials and commercial elite were on good terms with the Confederate exile community. A few locals may even have received gratuities or other favors.[39] The Confederates had plenty of money with which to buy influence and the Confederacy's friends in the city included judges, attorneys, bankers, politicians, soldiers, and senior policemen.

British Army officers in Canada also looked favorably on the Confederates. The same could not be said of the reception many Northerners received. American newspapers and politicians, including members of Lincoln's own administration, talked loosely about absorbing British North America, and this aggressive posturing did little to make friends in Canada or Great Britain. The Trent Crisis, in early 1862, further damaged relations.

It was a common diversion for British officers to take extended leave to visit the American front, where battles were being waged on a scale not seen since the Napoleonic Wars. If lots were drawn in the officers' mess at Victoria Barracks, the overstaffed Army of the Potomac, plagued by political interference from Washington, was usually a second choice. Lee's smaller army was the real attraction. But getting there across battle lines wasn't easy. Officers visiting Lee had first to see senior Confederate agent P.C. Martin on St. Jean Street below Notre Dame Basilica to obtain letters of introduction. This ensured safe passage along well-established courier and smuggling lines through southern Maryland and into Virginia.

While in Montreal, Booth spent considerable time with P.C. Martin and his family. Martin's wife was already a Confederate courier and spy. Captain Martin was not only a senior Confederate agent but also a blockade runner who fled Baltimore for Canada early in the war. Martin owned two blockade-running vessels and may have held an interest in others.[40] He also operated a liquor importing business in partnership with Confederate General William H. Carroll of Tennessee. Living in Montreal with Martin and his family was George Kane, a one-time Provost Marshal of Baltimore, who was accused in 1861 of trying to apprehend or even to murder Lincoln while the President was en route to his first inauguration.[41] In late 1864, Kane was working with General John H. Winder on secret operations in northern Virginia and southern Maryland. This coincided with Booth's trip to the area to solidify plans for his escape from Washington, presumably with a kidnapped Lincoln in tow.[42]

By now the Civil War was reaching its murderous height. West of Atlanta at Kennesaw Mountain, Sherman had been bloodily repulsed and outside of Richmond, General Grant was incurring the highest casualties of the war. A hugely unpopular new draft of half-a-million men was proposed. The flood of bad news undermined Lincoln's standing. It was against this background that the "dump Lincoln" movement gained momentum.

By October, however, the tide had turned. The mood in the nation had been reversed with the fall of Atlanta. Suddenly, the political momentum turned back in favor of the President and it now seemed likely Lincoln would win re-election after all.

By this point, Confederate operations targeting Lincoln had taken on a life of their own. In October, Booth arrived in Montreal to arrange financing and coordinate his escape after capturing the President. The President was to be held hostage in order to force an exchange of prisoners-of-war. The South was starved of manpower and exchanged prisoners provided the only ready source of badly needed veterans.[43]

THE NAMES SURROUNDING BOOTH

The key to understanding Booth's visits to Montreal is to examine those around him during his time there, beginning with the Confederates. Booth was surrounded in Montreal by dozens of ardent Confederates, including Captain P.C. Martin, General Carroll of Tennessee, General William Preston, Senior Confederate Commissioner Jacob Thompson, George Cleary, George Sanders (life-long advocate of assassinating tyrants), Beverley Tucker, and Dr. Luke Blackburn, who checked into St. Lawrence Hall on the same day as Booth. John Surratt and courier Sarah Slater were also in the city, as was Reverend Kinsey Stewart, an early champion of kidnapping Lincoln.[44] (For a complete list see *Appendix A*.)

One of the most interesting and intriguing characters at the hotel during this period was James W. Wallis (Wallace). He was almost certainly a double agent and would later be a key witness at the trial of the Lincoln conspirators. Wallis, whose real name was Charles Dunham, had pre-war ties to Edwin Stanton and worked closely with prosecutors Joseph Holt and John

Bingham. Wallis registered at least three times from August through October and November 1864.[45]

The presence of so many powerful Confederates at St. Lawrence Hall immediately before, during, and after Booth's stay is part of the historical record. The evidence pointing to Confederate involvement in Booth's kidnapping plot is compelling, indeed almost overwhelming. We know, for example, that Patrick Martin provided Booth with letters of introduction to the courier lines in southern Maryland. Martin was with Booth at the Bank of Ontario a dozen times during his ten-day stay in the city.[46] If the testimony of the bank's chief teller, given under oath, is to be believed, Booth and Martin were in the bank once a day or more during the actor's stay in the city.[47] Booth was clearly doing more on those visits than managing his savings account, which held less than $500. The bank was known to launder money for the Confederate Secret Service by making out cashier's checks to employees who then endorsed them to the real recipients.[48] Congressman Benjamin Wood, who was at St. Lawrence Hall during this period, was the recipient of $25,000 in this manner.[49] Was this the reason for Booth's numerous visits to the bank?

Among other transactions, we know that Booth deposited a check from a Mr. Davis who was a Confederate currency broker with an office at 12 St. James Street, directly across from St. Lawrence Hall, and next to the city's telegraph office. We know that Davis' office was sometimes used for meetings by the Confederate Secret Service.[50]

Robert Campbell (and Lady), chief teller at the Bank of Ontario on Place d'Armes in Montreal, who testified before the military commission that investigated the assassination of Abraham Lincoln. Henry Starnes, president of the bank, and the real keeper of the bank's secrets, was careful not to appear in Washington where he would have had to testify under oath. Campbell's testimony about hidden drafts for tens-of-thousands of dollars going to American politicians like Benjamin Wood provided an insight into how covert monies were funneled through the Confederate bank accounts in Montreal. Campbell testified that Booth was in the bank a dozen times during his ten-day stay in Montreal. R.A. Campbell and Lady. McCord Museum, Notman Collection, Montreal, QC, 1864. I-13693.1

Henry Starnes, branch manager, Bank of Ontario in Montreal. (He preferred the title 'president'). He was the Confederate Secret Service's favorite banker in Canada. The Confederates effectively controlled the Montreal branch of the bank by virtue of the size of their deposits. When Booth was killed at the Garrett Farm in Virginia on 26 April 1865, he was carrying a draft from the Bank of Ontario signed by "Manager Starnes." U.S. authorities misinterpreted the signature as "Stanus."[53] Starnes also served as Mayor of Montreal both before and immediately after the American Civil War. In summary, a bank draft signed by a Mayor of Montreal was found on John Wilkes Booth's body after he was killed. Surprisingly, none of Starnes's activities with the Confederate Secret Service are mentioned in the Dictionary of Canadian Biography entry for him. Henry Starnes. McCord Museum, Notman Collection, Montreal, QC, 1871. I-67709.

Upon returning to Washington, Booth deposited a $1,500 check in Cooke Brothers Bank.[51] Jay Cooke was in Canada in the summer and fall of 1864. (See *Appendices A* and *B*.) Where Booth got the money is unclear. When Booth was killed, he had on him a cashier's check from the Bank of Ontario signed by Henry Starnes.[52] The signature was misinterpreted as "Stanus" which is how it appears in the Lincoln trial transcript. Starnes was not only a Canadian bank president and a Confederate supporter, but also a former and future Mayor of Montreal. Booth's Bank of Ontario bank book was found in George Atzerodt's hotel room in Washington.

Finally, Booth was seen in Montreal conversing with Confederate Commissioner George Sanders, a strident advocate of political assassination. English author and London *Daily Telegraph* correspondent, George Augustus Sala, was at St. Lawrence Hall during Booth's stay. Confederate George Sanders told Sala that the Confederate Secret Service was going to execute operations that "would make the world shudder."[54] This was reported in the *New York Times* on 6 May 1865, but Sala was never called to testify before the military commission then assessing the guilt or innocence of the Lincoln conspirators; he was not even asked to submit a deposition.[55]

THE MYSTERIOUS SARAH SLATER

The name J.L. or J.R. McPhail appears in the hotel guest book on 7 October 1864. If the signature is indeed J.L. McPhail's then it is important because he was the Provost Marshal of Baltimore and an employee of the War Department–an extension of the Judge Advocate General's Office.[56] When Confederate spy Sarah Slater was captured in Baltimore in the weeks following Lincoln's assassination, it was Provost Marshal McPhail who arrested her. He sent Slater to Washington to be interrogated by Judge Advocate General prosecutor H.L. Burnett. Next to John Surratt, Slater knew more about the plot against Lincoln than any living person. Incredibly, Burnett released Slater almost immediately, after which she utterly disappeared. Conspirator George Atzerodt suggested Slater was intimate with Booth and it certainly appears she and John Surratt were lovers.[57] Slater kept interesting company. On one occasion she appears to check into St. Lawrence Hall with, or at the same time as, senior National Detective Police detective Walter Pollack.[58] On another occasion she checked in on the same day as Copperhead and Lincoln hater Benjamin Wood.[59]

Slater traveled back to Canada with Surratt immediately after the assassination and checked into St. Lawrence Hall on 18 April 1865.[60] Slater certainly knew more about the plot against Lincoln than the hapless Mary Surratt, who was hanged for her involvement. Why Slater was so quickly released by Burnett remains inexplicable. At the time, hundreds of innocent people were being held in prison without charge on the slightest suspicion of involvement with the assassination. Individuals could be arrested for simply having known Booth. Once released, Slater walked off the pages of history and disappeared.[61]

AMERICAN POLITICIANS AND NEWSPAPER MEN

In October, a C.W. Noyes registered at the hotel. This is very likely attorney W.C. Noyes (initials reversed) who was a Radical abolitionist, Lincoln hater, and supporter of Salmon P. Chase. Noyes worked all that summer and fall to have Lincoln removed from the ballot as the Republican nominee.[62] William Sprague, the Governor of Rhode Island, also arrived in October. He was part of the team established to displace Lincoln on the Republican ticket and was a member of Salmon Chase's presidential committee. Sprague was accompanied by a lady, presumably his wife, the politically astute Kate Chase (daughter of Salmon Chase).[63] Senator S. Pomeroy of Kansas, a Radical who headed up Chase's presidential bid, registered at St. Lawrence Hall shortly after Booth's visit to Montreal.[64] Republican A. Pond of Saratoga Springs, New York signed in on 7 October.

W.D. Wallach, editor of the *Washington Evening Star,* registered early in the month. His brother, Richard Wallach, was Mayor of Washington and a Whig turned Republican. Despite being a newspaperman, Wallach produced no stories for publication concerning the machinations in Montreal. Another anti-Lincoln newspaper correspondent who appears to have been in Montreal during Booth's stay was George Townsend of the *New York World.* He registers as George E. Townsend from New York on 21 October 1864. Earlier in the month, we find a registration for J. Gath. "Gath" was Townsend's nom de plume.[65] The two names Gath and Townsend registered so closely together could be mere coincidence but is still striking. Townsend would go on to cover Lincoln's assassination in detail for the *New York World*. He also wrote the first book about the assassination, *The Life, Crime, and Capture of John Wilkes Booth*.[66] W.B. Shaw, the Washington correspondent for the *New York Herald*, was at the hotel in September.[67] Only a month earlier his publisher James Gordon Bennett had written about Lincoln, "As President...he has been an egregious failure...under no circumstances can he hope to be the next President of the United States."[68]

The bankers registered during this Booth period included James Brown of Brown Brothers of New York and London, specializing in funding the triangular cotton trade between the South, New York, and Great Britain,[69] Jay Cooke of Cooke Brothers Bank, Hiram Barney (antecedent of Smith Barney), as well as A.S. Hatch, and George Bliss, who both had close ties to Cooke Brothers Bank. Barney, Cooke, Hatch, and Bliss were all known supporters of Salmon Chase.[70]

Democrats were another important constituency present at St. Lawrence Hall that October. For example, Mr. and Mrs. John S. Phelps of Missouri checked in on 15 October, just days ahead of Booth. The names Chandler and Billings are also in the guest book. Both were prominent delegates at the 1864 Democratic Convention. On 5 October, C.S. Marshall arrived from the U.S. This was almost certainly S.S. Marshall, a prominent Democrat from Illinois and a delegate to the 1864 Chicago convention.

On 24 October, right in the middle of Booth's stay in Montreal, Dr. B. Wood registered at the hotel. This was New York Congressman Benjamin Wood, who was also the editor of the *New York Daily News*. He and his brother Fernando Wood were regulars at St. Lawrence Hall and both had close ties to the Confederate Secret Service. Benjamin Wood was on the Confederate payroll. The Wood brothers hated Lincoln intensely. When registering at the hotel, Wood sometimes used the alias Dr. Wood.[71] In testimony offered at the Lincoln assassination trial, Hosea Carter recounted being introduced to a "Dr. Wood" at St. Lawrence Hall in the company of many of the most senior Confederates in Canada.[72] From July 1864 through March 1865, Ben Wood and his brother Fernando Wood were at St. Lawrence Hall a half dozen times.[73] Fernando Wood would leave for an extended stay in Europe shortly before the Lincoln assassination. In his final report to Judah Benjamin, Jacob Thompson would acknowledge being in regular contact with Wood and New York Governor Horatio Seymour. Finally, John Van Buren, a Free Soil Democrat from New York, signed the St. Lawrence Hall register later that same month.[74] Van Buren was deeply involved in the presidential campaign of General George McClellan.

DOUBLE-CAROM

While in Montreal, Booth played pool with Canadian billiards champion Joe Dion at Dooley's Bar in St. Lawrence Hall. Dion soon cleared the table, and Booth, by now well into his cups, told the champion he might have to learn to dress in "Canuck" style, implying he might someday have to come to Canada to live. He also called on Dion to remember him, because he was going to perform a "double-carom...and bag the biggest game this side of hell." In billiards, the term "carom" refers to the act of sinking more than one ball simultaneously.

When talk turned to the upcoming election and Lincoln's prospects, Booth said, "It makes damn little difference who wins, heads or tails. Abe's contract is nearly up, and whether he is re-elected or not, his goose is cooked."[75] Dion thought this was just boozy bravado until he heard the news of Lincoln's assassination six months later, in April 1865.

During Booth's stay in Montreal, a young messenger named George Iles, formed a friendship with the actor—hero worship might be a better description of their relationship. Iles delivered messages for a number of locals, including John Buckland, owner of Montreal's Royal Theatre and a friend of Booth's. The impressionable young man remembered Booth brandishing a large knife, (very possibly the same knife used to slash Major H. Rathbone in Lincoln's box at Ford's Theatre) while promising to make short work of the President.[76] Kidnapping may have been Booth's original aim but his behavior and choice of words in Montreal suggests that he was contemplating a more lethal outcome.

Finally, we know that key members of Edwin Stanton's National Detective Police were in Montreal. Stanton's chief spy, Lafayette Baker, was a regular at St. Lawrence Hall, as was his brother-in-law, Walter Pollack, who was also a National Detective Police detective. Pollack checked into the hotel the same day as John Wilkes Booth, on 18 October 1864.[77] Baker

Joseph Dion, taken shortly after the Civil War at *Notman's Studio*. Like Booth, Dion was a handsome man with a reputation as a womanizer. While playing pool with Booth at St. Lawrence Hall, he heard the actor say that it didn't matter who got elected in November, "Abe's contract is nearly up." J. Dion. McCord Museum, Notman Collection, Montreal, QC, 1866-67. I-24397.1

checked in a few days earlier as John. L. Baker; no point of departure or room number is given.[78]

A hotel, much like a ship, is a small place, where gossip and rumors flourish. Booth made little attempt to disguise his violent intentions toward Lincoln, especially when he was drinking. That no one at the hotel overheard and reported these threats, not even the National Detective Police present, remains astonishing.

While in Montreal, Booth was surrounded by a diverse and sometimes incongruent set of constituencies. Rather than being a lone wolf alienated from society, Booth was in the company of a powerful network of people. At the center of this cabal was certainly the Confederate Secret Service. Many of them appear to have known about Booth's plans, which were pretty much an open secret within Confederate circles in Canada, but beyond the Confederates there were other anti-Lincoln elements.

THE HIDDEN HAND

What are we to make of it all? The swirling mix of powerful Union and leading Confederate players in Montreal during this period was certainly unusual and has never been adequately explored or explained. There is an enormous weight of circumstantial and substantive evidence pointing to Montreal and especially to St. Lawrence Hall as the place where the Booth plot against the President was coordinated and financed. Of all the schemes targeting Lincoln, Booth's was arguably the least likely to succeed, yet it was he who fired the fatal shot.

In October 1864, when Booth visited Montreal, the theatrical season was just winding up. Booth called on John Buckland and his wife, actress Kate Horn, who were owners of the Theatre Royal, as well as personal friends of the Booth family. That season, the Bucklands' Theatre Royal, located a few blocks from St. Lawrence Hall, featured a dark drama entitled *The Hidden Hand*. It starred legendary actor and Booth friend, John McCullough. (Because of his association with Booth, McCullough would be forced to go into voluntary exile in Montreal in the immedi-

ate aftermath of the assassination.)[79] Given the real-life drama playing out in Montreal at the time, the dark theme of the play seems chillingly appropriate. Also that autumn, the Bucklands' Theatre Royal staged *Our American Cousin,* an otherwise forgettable play, which would later gain notoriety when it was staged at Ford's Theatre in Washington on the night of 14 April 1865.[80]

It is not hard to discern that malevolent and powerful anti-Lincoln forces were at work in Montreal. These forces included, most obviously, the Confederate Secret Service, but other anti-Lincoln elements were also present. Republicans opposed to the President were there, as were senior Democrats and Copperheads. A number of bankers were present, many of whom had ties to Salmon Chase. Members of the National Detective Police, the Judge Advocate General's Office, and the War Department were on hand. A number of newspapermen were present in the city. Booth clearly had dealings with the Confederates in Montreal but did he also interact with other American constituencies on the scene? Who can say? But their proximity in the same city and in the same hotel, cannot be ignored.

The Montreal story challenges the Lincoln narrative born in the immediate aftermath of his death. This narrative began as an unabashed propaganda campaign seeking to politicize the President's violent death to the advantage of the Radical Republicans. Ironically, many of those behind this propaganda had welcomed Lincoln's murder.[82] Soon, the notion of Lincoln as the perfect man and the perfect President took root in the American psyche. The war was drained of all its inherent complexity and contradictions and reduced to a simple battle between good and evil.

The war was certainly ennobled by emancipation, but this was not one of Lincoln's original goals in going to war, as he made perfectly clear in his first inaugural address. What is clear is that the Northern effort by 1864 was characterized by breathtaking corruption, to which Montreal was just one of many hosts. Can both narratives be simultaneously true? Is it possible, as F. Scott Fitzgerald once queried, for two irreconcilable truths to be considered dispassionately, factually, without producing intellectual paralysis?[83]

Montreal Harbour from Custom House, QC. McCord Museum, Notman Collection, Montreal, QC, about 1872. MP-0000.1452.53

CHAPTER 8

Leaks, Anomalies, and Questions

INCONSISTENCIES AND CONTRADICTORY evidence frustrate historians and readers alike, but the questions most difficult to answer may prove the most important in the long run. The anomalies and questions in this story may not be answered any time soon, but they are now at least in the record for historians to pursue. Some will, over time, be run to ground.

The first of these anomalies is found in the people surrounding John Wilkes Booth in Montreal. The Confederate Secret Service is the most prominent of these constituencies, but it is not the only one. In addition to Confederates, St. Lawrence Hall was full of influential American businessmen and politicians, including many opposed to Lincoln. Much of the American banking community was present, as was Edwin Stanton's War Department. Much of Samuel Chase's presidential committee was in the city, as well a number of Chase's Treasury Department agents.

After 150 years, the information is murky, but the names are there in the hotel guest book and Barnett's Niagara Falls Museum registry, as are the associated photographs taken at Notman's Studio, all clearly indicating the physical presence of the people behind the names. Booth's links to the Confederate Secret Service were aggressively pursued by Judge Advocate Joseph Holt and the War Department in the post-assassination trial until perjured testimony imploded the case. There was far less appetite, however, for investigating others who might have been in Montreal in the summer and fall of 1864. Even among historians, who should always be hungry for new information, there has been little interest in discovering who else, in addition to John Wilkes Booth and the Confederate Secret Service, turns up in Montreal during this period.

A second interesting piece of information is that John Wilkes Booth's kidnapping plans were well known to key insiders in the Confederate

Secret Service in Canada; these plans were more or less an open secret.[1] Operational security among Confederates in Montreal was surprisingly loose. This cavalier approach to operational security may explain the number of Confederates who went to Notman's Studio and had their photographs taken using their real names. They clearly felt safe in Montreal. Finally, we know Booth's kidnapping plot was only one of several operations targeting Lincoln in 1864-1865.

Since Confederate operational security was loose, it should have been easy for the National Detective Police, represented in Montreal by Chief Lafayette Baker, his brother-in-law Walter Pollack, and possibly others, to hear rumors about plots and Confederate plans. But there appear to be no reports highlighting the threat.[2] Yet reporting hearsay was an essential part of the National Detective Police's job. When in his cups at Dooley's Bar and billiards room in St. Lawrence Hall, John Wilkes Booth loudly proclaimed his violent intentions regarding Lincoln. All of this was apparently missed by the National Detective Police, whom we know to have been present in the hotel.

Despite the Confederate Secret Service's operational carelessness, there appears to have been only one public leak regarding the plots against Lincoln, and this came not from the National Detective Police but from freelance journalist and double agent, Sanford Conover, who was in Montreal in 1864-1865. His article in the *New York Tribune*, which appeared in early January and again in March 1864, outlined a deadly plot against Lincoln and appeared under Conover's

byline. His real name was Charles A. Dunham, but he operated under multiple aliases and was almost certainly a double agent.[3] He wrote and filed several stories from Montreal about plots to kidnap Lincoln and related subjects.[4] Dunham stayed at St. Lawrence Hall under such aliases as J. Wallace, J.W. Wallis, and James Watson Wallace.[5] While in Montreal he hobnobbed with the large Confederate exile community. Always short of money, he and his wife lived in Canada on a tight budget yet stayed at Montreal's most expensive hotel. He was arrested in 1865 on charges of unpaid bills. Who paid for his expensive stays at St. Lawrence Hall is unknown.

On 22 July, Dunham registered at St. Lawrence Hall as J.W. Wallis. On 8 August, Wallis checked in again, this time just ahead of R.A. Clark, who identified himself as a member of the CSA (Confederates States Army or Confederate States of America.)[6] On 24 August, J.W. Wallis registered the same day as senior Confederate Commissioner J. Thompson and Confederate agent H.V. Clinton.[7] The name Clinton is important because it was an alias used by a Confederate operative in Canada who had early contact with J.W. Booth. Clinton, with other colleagues from Canada, visited John Wilkes Booth at the Parker House in Boston. It has been suggested that this meeting was where Booth was recruited into the plot to kidnap Lincoln.[8]

While Conover's articles in the *New York Tribune* involved some flights of fancy, he did get the essentials of the Lincoln plot right.[9] He is the only one to have published an account that predicted the tragic events that unfolded in April

McGill Street. McCord Museum, Notman Collection, Montreal, QC, about 1869. MP-0000.1828.20

1865. According to Conover's article, Lincoln was to be kidnapped by a team of determined, well-armed men and quickly dispatched through southern Maryland and safely into Virginia. Of even more ominous portent, Conover's article stated that, should the kidnapping plot go awry, a contingency plan was in place for Lincoln's assassination.[10] That Conover's article predated Booth's visit to Canada in October 1864 indicates the plot had been incubating inside the Confederate Secret Service before Booth entered the picture.

Conover's dispatches suggested powerful Northern interests were involved, although he did not point a finger at who they might be, leaving us guessing to this day.[11] We know from the names of American politicians, bankers, military suppliers, and newspaper editors found in the pages of Montreal's St. Lawrence Hall guest book and Barnett's Museum register in Niagara, that Dunham's assertions are credible. Montreal and Niagara were indeed full of powerful Northerners in the summer and fall of 1864. And many of these powerbrokers were keeping close company with the Confederate Secret Service, and among these were many of Lincoln's political enemies.

After the war, Confederate agents like Colonel Robert Martin and Lieutenant Colonel James Gordon admitted to having heard about Booth's plans while they were in Canada.[12] Gordon traveled with Captain Robert Brown and registered with him at St. Lawrence Hall.[13] Brown was married to Confederate courier Josephine Brown, who traveled the same courier routes as John Surratt and mysterious Confederate operative Sarah Slater. (See Chapter 2.) If Gordon and Martin heard rumors of the plot against Lincoln, then why not Dunham, who was mixing with the same Confederate crowd? His articles in the *New York Tribune* reflected at least some inside knowledge. Even if his articles were based on nothing more than rumors heard in Dooley's Bar at St. Lawrence Hall, he still provided more advance warning of the threat against Lincoln than Lafayette Baker's well-funded National Detective Police.[14]

Conover's articles in the *Tribune* claimed that the Confederacy possessed a large, highly-successful courier network allowing information to pass readily from Canada, New York, and Washington through Maryland and across Union–Confederate lines to Richmond. This was certainly an accurate assessment of the courier

network Conover saw operating out of Canada in 1864-1865.

Conover was a slippery character, a gifted storyteller, and sometimes a near-pathological liar. But he was no fool, and it's clear he traveled in the same circles as key Confederates from the summer of 1864 and through the spring of 1865. Senior Confederate Commissioner J. Thompson may not have formally met Conover/Wallis/Wallace but they were in close proximity when both registered at the same hotel.[15] This was just days before John Wilkes Booth arrived at St. Lawrence Hall 18 October 1864.

As for Wallace (Charles Dunham), he was a consummate con man: cool, calculating, and utterly without conscience. He operated under a dozen aliases and was sublimely clever. He managed to enthrall everyone he came in contact with, from the Confederate Secret Service to Lincoln's Secretary of War Edwin Stanton and Judge Advocate General Joseph Holt. During the post-war impeachment battle, which pitted President Andrew Johnson against his old allies the Radical Republicans, Dunham managed to manipulate both sides to his purpose. It was an astonishing performance. He could not have pulled it off, however, if he had not had information, real or implied, that threatened all sides. This was his specialty.

Dunham's ties to Secretary of War Edwin Stanton date back to before the war when Dunham assisted Stanton in his defense of Dan Sickles, who killed his wife's lover in a fit of rage.[16] Stanton was a talented lawyer and his defense, based on the first-ever plea of temporary insanity, was successful. Stanton recognized Dunham as a man who could be counted on to discover evidence or, for the right price, create it. It was almost certainly Stanton who introduced the unscrupulous Dunham to Judge Advocate General Joseph Holt, the lead prosecutor on the Military Commission that tried the Lincoln conspirators. Holt was determined to prove Jefferson Davis and other senior Confederates were involved in Lincoln's death, but evidence was needed, and Dunham was just the man to procure it. Under the alias Sanford Conover, Dunham became a key witness at the trial of the Lincoln conspirators.[17]

The trial of the Lincoln conspirators was controversial from the start. It took place before a military commission, which operated with a far lower threshold of protections for a defendant's rights than a civilian court, especially regarding due process, rules of evidence, and the power to convict. Given that the war was over, many legal and political authorities thought convictions obtained under such circumstances would be tainted, but it was clear Edwin Stanton was in a hurry. Two original members of the Commission, General Cyrus B. Comstock and Colonel Horace Porter, who expressed reservations about employing a Military Commission instead of a civilian court, were quickly replaced. One of the defense attorneys, Brigadier General William Doster, described the affair as an unequal contest between a few disparate, under-resourced attorneys and the whole power of the United States government. According to Doster, "The verdict was known beforehand."[18] The transcripts show that every objection raised by the prosecution was sustained, while almost every objection raised by the defense was overruled.[19]

The military tribunal proceedings took place in the very jail where the prisoners were being held and where they would later be executed. The whole process of incarceration, adjudication, conviction, execution, and burial took place within an enclosure encompassing just a few hundred square yards and all within a short period of sixty days.

With the exception of Mary Surratt and possibly Dr. Samuel Mudd, the prisoners were kept almost constantly in heavy, padded canvas hoods with no eye slits and only a narrow opening for eating. When brought to the courtroom, the hoods were removed and the prisoners appeared dazed and half-blinded. General Lew Wallace, a member of the tribunal, sketched the prisoners during the trial. One of his sketches shows the swollen and distorted face of Lewis Powell after his tight-fitting hood was removed.[20] All except Mary Surratt were handcuffed and shackled, making it difficult to walk. They were allowed to talk to no one except their interrogators and their attorneys, and even the latter's access was controlled by Secretary Stanton.[21] The prisoners were quarantined from the press and the outside world. The thick hoods created acute sensory deprivation and some of the prisoners became mentally disoriented. Stanton's orders to General Winfield Scott Hancock and General J.F. Hartranft, who were charged with overseeing the incarceration of the prisoners, were that they be allowed no communications with anyone—not the press, not the guards, and not with each other. They were to be completely isolated except for strictly controlled access to attorneys and a few family members. Stanton cautioned Hancock not to let them cheat the gallows.[22] Stanton's reference to the gallows before the trial even began points to certainty about the outcome. In addition, Stanton, Holt, and Bingham fully expected the stacked tribunal to order the execution of all the prisoners.[23] Some members of the tribunal, however, proved more independent than expected; they ordered four of the conspirators to life imprisonment in the Dry Tortugas. The other four prisoners, Mary Surratt, Lewis Powell, George Atzerodt, and David Herold, were condemned to death. Holt, Bingham, and Stanton were apparently incensed that four prisoners had escaped the noose.[24]

Several of the tribunal members would only agree to the death sentence for Mary Surratt if it were to be accompanied by a recommendation for clemency. President Johnson later claimed the clemency request for Mary Surratt was not shown to him. Lead prosecutor Joseph Holt, who reported to Edwin Stanton, denied the President's assertion that the President was ill during this period and Holt took the Commission's verdict to his room in the White House, indicating where the President's signature was needed. It was Holt's responsibility to present requests for clemency from the tribunal. Whether he did so is unclear.

The clemency request was kept under wraps until it emerged during the trial of John Surratt two years later, when Surratt's prosecutor, Edwards Pierrepont, slapped the execution order down on the desk of the defense in a flourish of courtroom drama. President Johnson received the news about a clemency request with fury. He told his assistant Colonel William Moore that he had never seen any such request. He ordered Pierrepont, who was a friend and supporter of Stanton, to send the document to the White House immediately.[25]

This incident finished an already strained relationship between Stanton and Johnson. The President ultimately fired the Secretary of War, only to find that he refused to go. Supported by the Radicals in Congress, Stanton proposed to remain in office and in the cabinet, with or without the approval of the President. It turned the American Constitution on its head and ignited the great impeachment battle between the Radical Republicans and Johnson that came within one vote of ousting the President and putting the Radical Republicans in charge of the country.

On his last days in office, President Johnson pardoned the surviving conspirators imprisoned on the Dry Tortugas. This was a clear repudiation of Stanton and the War Department's military tribunal. It was also a slap at Holt, Bingham, and the Radicals who supported them.

OVERLOOKED FOOTNOTE IN HISTORY

A sometimes-overlooked footnote in the trial of the Lincoln Conspirators is that Louis Weichmann was himself an employee of the War Department. He told his colleague, Major D. Gleason at the War Department, details of the plot to kidnap the President. He identified Surratt, Booth, Atzerodt, Powell, and a French-speaking woman from Montreal, later identified as courier Sarah Slater, as being involved. Gleason may have provided his roommate Lieutenant Joshua Sharp the details of Weichmann's report. Like Weichmann and Gleason, Sharp worked for the War Department. Whether he passed this information on within the War Department is unclear.[26] There were, no doubt, many rumors regarding threats against Lincoln pouring into the War Department. Yet this plot was afoot in Washington right under their noses and no action was taken to interdict it. Perhaps it was a question of not connecting the dots in a frenzied environment, but the bottom line was that Weichmann and Gleason were employees of the War Department and Weichmann's testimony establishes that somewhere inside Stanton's War Department there was information regarding the Booth plot by March 1865. It may have lain dormant and ignored but it was there. This might explain why authorities zeroed in so quickly on the Surratt boarding house following Lincoln's murder.[27]

With the trial over and the conspirators dead or jailed, Judge Holt continued his pursuit of Jefferson Davis as a party to the assassination. This became for him a mission, even an obsession. Holt turned once again to the unscrupulous Sanford Conover (Charles Dunham), requesting that he obtain the necessary evidence to convict Davis. The relationship between the Judge Advocate General's office and their prize witness appeared to some to be unusually close and almost complicit. At the original trial, Defendant Samuel Arnold claimed that prosecutor John Bingham was overly friendly with Conover (a.k.a. Charles Dunham). Arnold recalled: "I saw him in the witness room approach Conover, button-hole him with his right hand and placing his left upon his shoulder, enter into earnest conversation with him for some time only to return again with startling disclosures collected on his visit to Canada."[28]

By this point, however, Dunham's credibility was fraying. Letters written from British North America indicated that at least one of his coached witnesses, Richard Montgomery, was involved in skullduggeries in Canada.[29] This was to be the first of many cracks in Dunham's orchestrated testimony. Holt had chosen the wrong man on whom to anchor his case against Davis and other Confederate leaders.

Dunham may have been a paid liar but he clearly knew something about the nefarious goings on in Canada during the war. The record shows he was in Montreal and at St. Lawrence Hall while it was full of Confederate agents, but where the truth left off and the lies began is difficult to ascertain. Like all gifted con men, Dunham liberally mixed fact with fiction. Thus, some of his testimony was likely rooted in fact, but which part?

Dunham's perjury created a public scandal, putting enormous pressure on lead prosecutor Holt. There was no time for investigators to sort the wheat from the chaff of Dunham's claims. The aggressive, prosecutorial atmosphere fed by a near-hysterical national reaction to Lincoln's murder, had begun to wane. Holt and his team found themselves under increasing and uncomfortable public scrutiny.

As for Dunham and his coached witnesses, they acknowledged one absolute truth: they had been handsomely paid by officials of the War Department and the Judge Advocate General's office to perjure themselves.[30] Perjury is a crime, but then so is subornation of perjury. In a civilian court these actions would have resulted in a mistrial, and charges would very likely have been laid against the prosecutors and possibly even the Secretary of War. But this was not a civilian court; it was a military tribunal where the Judge Advocate General's office could pretty much make up the rules as they went along. Hence, the entire blame for Dunham's orchestrated perjury was laid at his feet alone. The case against Confederate President Jefferson Davis, and the Confederate Commissioners in Canada—Jacob Thompson, George Sanders, Clement Clay, and others—quickly collapsed. The scandal cast a pall over the controversial execution of Mary Surratt. It was a prosecutorial debacle.

The question for the War Department was what to do with their bought and paid-for witness, Sanford Conover? The answer was to silence him judicially. Conover/Dunham was charged with perjury and sentenced to ten years in prison. It was assumed that, once locked away in a distant penitentiary, he would be silenced for enough years to erase the whole ugly business from public consciousness. He may well have been quietly promised a pardon if he cooperated; this contingency of a Presidential pardon was certainly on his mind during his subsequent efforts to extricate himself. Those in Washington who were thinking that Dunham's imprisonment would silence him were in for a shock. He proved a hard man to bury. Dunham was unwilling to be served

up as a lone scapegoat. If he was going down, he was going to take a lot of powerful people with him and he let that be known.

PERJURY THE NORM?

The use of perjured, untruthful, or incomplete testimony by the Judge Advocate General's prosecutors and the Secretary of War during the trial of the Lincoln conspirators was more the rule than the exception. Consider the case of Booth's diary, which detectives found on his dead body. This was taken to Edwin Stanton, who quickly had Major Thomas Eckert lock it away. If it had been introduced as evidence at the trial it would have shown that those defendants who claimed they were participating in a kidnapping plot rather than a murder, were telling the truth. The diary said as much: "For six months we sought to capture..." Whatever his reasons, Stanton wanted the existence of the diary suppressed. The detectives who searched Booth's body testified under oath regarding the items they found. These were listed in extraordinary detail but there was no mention of the diary. The decision to withhold this key piece of evidence could only have been made by Edwin Stanton. The Judge Advocate General prosecutors knew about the diary but were careful not to ask about it. The detectives who testified under oath and left out this important piece of material evidence were as guilty of perjury as Sanford Conover/Charles Dunham.

Lafayette Baker later made the existence of the diary public in his memoirs, and it was subpoenaed during the post-war trial of John Surratt. An incensed President Johnson, who knew nothing of the diary, asked Stanton for a detailed report on the handling of this missing piece of evidence. Johnson's request rattled Stanton, who drafted several possible replies, sending all of them to Joseph Holt for comment.[31] Eventually, and reluctantly, Stanton handed over the diary, which was missing as many as eighteen pages. Baker swore under oath the diary he handed to Stanton was not missing pages.[32] Other witnesses, who still worked for the War Department, rebutted his testimony, so the truth is impossible to discern. Both Baker and Stanton had proven adept dissemblers, if not outright liars, so who can say? Baker and Stanton were also involved at this time in a very public spat, further clouding the issue.

Dunham's perjury and Booth's diary remain shrouded in controversy, but one indisputable fact remains: the Secretary of War and Judge Advocate General officials were prepared to break the law in pursuit of their aims.

DUNHAM AND THE SECRETARY OF WAR

We know Dunham had prewar ties to Edwin Stanton, and the Secretary of War clearly intended Dunham to play an important part in the post-war trial of the Lincoln conspirators. When Dunham was arrested in Canada on a charge of unpaid bills, the Secretary reacted with genuine alarm. He sent the highest-ranking military officer in New England, Major General John A. Dix, to Canada to gain his immediate release. The tone of Stanton's note to Dix reflects real urgency: "The President desires me to instruct you upon receipt of this telegram to proceed in person and in haste to Montreal...and use every lawful means to procure his release...if Conover is held under any criminal or civil proceeding you will cause bail to be entered into...the government will hereby indemnify you as to all costs...Time is important. You will telegraph the receipt of this telegram, the time of your start and your arrival and address in Montreal..."[33]

Here we see the newly sworn-in President of the United States and the Secretary of War sending the most senior officer in the northeastern United States on a rescue mission to Montreal, with an open checkbook, to retrieve a single witness of dubious character. Stanton's response to Conover's difficulties in Canada appears, at the least, disproportionate.

Dix spent time in both Quebec City and Montreal. After Dunham's debts had been settled, he was released to Dix's custody, whereupon he was escorted back to Washington to be available to support Holt and his Judge Advocate General prosecutors.[34] No comparable effort was made on behalf of any other witnesses at the trial of the Lincoln conspirators.

In the end, Stanton and Holt might well have wished they had left Dunham in a Canadian jail. His perjured testimony proved the undoing of Holt's plan to blame the assassination on the Confederates. The discredited testimony of Dunham and his coached witnesses brought into question the legitimacy of the trial of the original Lincoln conspirators. The Republican-dominated Senate Judiciary Committee, headed by Radical George Boutwell, tried to cover up the scandal, but the whole performance was so shabby and

St. Paul Street near Bonsecours Market. McCord Museum, Notman Collection, Montreal, QC, 1859. N-0000.193.7.2

transparent, it could not be swept under the rug. Congressman A.J. Rogers of New Jersey had only two days to prepare a minority report, but his assessment of Boutwell, Holt, Bingham, and the whole of the proceedings amounted to a scathing moral indictment. The facts indicated that Holt, Stanton, Bingham, and others had suborned perjury and had paid handsomely for it.[35] Congressman Rogers wrote: "The cool turpitude of the whole crew sickened me with shame and made sorrow over the fact that such people could claim the name of American."[36] It was, in the end, a tawdry and shameful performance by the War Department and Judge Advocate General's Office.

There was no recourse now but to silence Dunham by shutting him away in a penitentiary, but Dunham was not about to go silently into some dark corner of the American penal system. He let it be known, through his indefatigable wife, Phele, who had been with him in Montreal, that he would fight back and, "if he could not have a pardon then he would have revenge."[37] He threatened the release of information that would, like the biblical Samson, bring the temple down around everyone's ears. No one would be safe. Dunham let it be known that he had been in contact with Radical Republicans Thaddeus Stevens and Benjamin Wade, along with Holt, Congressman James Ashley, and others in the course of his orchestrated perjury.[38] He hinted there were other people to be named and more facts to be uncovered. Suddenly, Dunham had everyone's attention.

Having worked both for and against Radical Republicans and the White House during the Johnson impeachment battle, Dunham now played both sides against the middle. His thinly veiled threat to tell all rattled everyone. No one knew what he might say about subornation of perjury, collusion with the Judge Advocate General's Office, or Montreal.[39] Almost overnight, Democrats, Republicans, and the White House wanted him out of jail and out of town. It was an astonishing turn of events. President Johnson quickly signed the requisite pardon issued by Judge Advocate Holt. Dunham walked out of jail a free man and disappeared, to everyone's apparent relief.[40]

JOHN SURRATT AND SARAH SLATER

A similar pattern repeated itself at the trial of Lincoln co-conspirator John Surratt, where a hung jury should have triggered an immediate retrial. There was a feeble attempt to retry him on lesser charges of conspiracy but the presiding judge was not about to allow such an egregious exercise in double jeopardy. After this setback, Federal prosecutors dropped the case, letting Surratt leave the country for Mexico.[41] Who paid Surratt's $25,000 bail, his legal fees, or his travel expenses has never been revealed.

All this fits a disturbing and recurring pattern. When the American consul in Liverpool discovered in late September 1865 that Surratt was hiding in that city, he requested permission to have him taken into custody by British authorities. The response from the Secretary of War and the acting Secretary of State was baffling. The consul was told to take no action against Surratt.[42] This decision allowed him to slip out of the city and make his way to Rome. Lest there be any confusion regarding Washington's policy toward Surratt, the War Department immediately withdrew the $25,000 reward on his head.

Congress later censured the White House for its lackadaisical pursuit of Surratt. When he was finally arrested in Alexandria, Egypt and brought home for trial, no prosecutor wanted to touch the case, especially those who had prosecuted his mother and sent her to the gallows. Edwards Pierrepont, a friend and supporter of Stanton, was finally dragooned into taking the case.[43] He made such a botch of the prosecution that the trial ended in a hung jury. Ultimately, Surratt was released and allowed to go free.

Finally, Montreal-based Confederate spy and courier, Sarah Antoinette Slater, who was intimate with both Booth and John Surratt, had arrived in Montreal with Surratt on 18 April 1865 and checked into St. Lawrence Hall with him at 12:30 p.m.[44] Slater and Surratt were apparently lovers. Surratt was soon forced into hiding and would only resurface later that year in Europe. Consequently, Slater was left on her own. It is a mystery why she did not simply remain in Montreal along with other Confederates who had inside knowledge of the plot. Perhaps General Edwin Lee, then the leading Confederate Commissioner in Canada, had given her one last courier assignment. Alternatively, some reports have it that Lee disapproved of her relationship with Surratt. With the war over, perhaps there was simply no money to support her in Montreal. Whatever the case, she left Montreal forever and moved to New York City to be with her family. In 1866 she divorced her husband and the records

were in the public domain. We also know that a Mrs. Slater was arrested in Baltimore following Edwin Stanton's nationwide dragnet in late April and early May 1865. Mrs. Slater, whoever she was, was turned over to Provost Marshal James McPhail, who sent her to be interviewed by Judge Advocate General prosecutor H. Burnett in Washington; Burnett was then the lead investigator in the case.[45] The interview was brief. Slater revealed nothing of any significance except that she had run the blockade several times and knew at least one other blockade runner. Slater was quickly released by Burnett.[46]

It is unclear whether the Mrs. Slater questioned by Burnett was Confederate courier Sarah Slater. There was a large Slater clan in Baltimore at the time. Perhaps Burnett had not had time to connect the French-speaking courier from Montreal, identified by George Atzerodt, with Sarah Slater? Events were unfolding quickly and this was an age when notes were mostly taken longhand. Nevertheless, her quick release is anomalous.

The policy at the time was to arrest and hold anyone on the slightest suspicion. Stanton's prosecutors—Burnett, Bingham, and Holt—were holding people in jail for weeks and even months without charges. Simply having the misfortune of knowing Booth or his family was sufficient to get one arrested. Slater's release took place well after the testimony of Weichmann and Atzerodt placed Slater at the very center of the cloak-and-dagger activities at the Surratt boarding house in Washington.[47]

Always a shadowy figure, Sarah Antoinette Slater stepped off the pages of history forever in 1865 but she did not entirely disappear. She moved to New York City to live with her family and soon divorced her husband. The divorce was public, so the National Detective Police could presumably have found her had they wanted to. For her part, Sarah Slater remarried twice but never discussed her life as a Confederate Courier with anyone.[48]

LINKS AND LINKAGES

It is curious to note how many of those who appear to have been at St. Lawrence Hall during 1864 and early 1865 would later become involved in the post-war trials of the Lincoln conspirators, as well as the trials of Charles Dunham and John Surratt and the impeachment trial of Andrew Johnson. The list is extensive and includes: John Bingham, Thaddeus Stevens, William Radford, Jeremiah Black, W.B. Matchett, Charles Dunham, John Surratt, possibly Edwards Pierrepont, Henry Wilson, J.R. Doolittle, J. Harlan, Orville Browning, J. Churchill, Edgar Ketchum, George Halsey, James Wilson, C. Eldridge, James Ashley, Preston King, Thomas Eckert and possibly even George Boutwell.[49]

John Bingham, who prosecuted the Lincoln conspirators, appears a number of times at St. Lawrence Hall as John Bingham and J. Bingham. One of them was in October 1864 when Booth was at the hotel.[50] But if that seems a strange coincidence, consider that the name Holt also appears in the guest book of the hotel twice. The first time was on 16 July 1864 when (O.H.) Holt registered, accompanied by Republican Congressman George Ashmun.[51] Ashmun was the last person to see Abraham Lincoln alive at the White House. He stopped in to see the President in search of a "cotton license" on 14 April 1865. Lincoln was just leaving for Ford's Theatre and asked Ashmun to come back in the morning.[52] The name Holt appears again on 3 February 1865, accompanied by H.H. Emmons, William Seward's unofficial ambassador to the Confederates in Canada. Emmons was then conducting back-door peace negotiations with the Confederates on behalf of Seward.[53] Whoever Holt was with in Montreal, he was traveling in interesting and important company. Holt's name also appears in Barnett's Museum in Niagara as A.J. Holt on 17 October 1864.[54]

Another interesting name found in the guest book is "Eckert," arriving from Cincinnati on 27 July 1864 just as many powerful Americans, including some of Lincoln's enemies, were gathering in Montreal.[55] He had registered earlier at Barnett's Museum at Niagara's Table Rock on 22 July 1864. Although the initials are slightly altered, there is no doubt both signatures are made by the same man and are a good match with Eckert's surviving autographs.[56] More importantly, he registers with his son and namesake, Master Thomas, both arriving from Cincinnati, Ohio. This makes the identification near certain.[57] Thomas Eckert was the Chief Telegrapher for the War Department and worked directly for Edwin Stanton. In the six months following Lincoln's assassination, Eckert was promoted from Major to Colonel, then to General, and finally to Assistant Secretary of War. This was a meteoric rise. Also at the hotel at this time was

Albert Building, St. James Street. McCord Museum, Notman Collection, Montreal, QC, 1868. I-32362.1

Thomas Eckert's friend and later benefactor, the notorious robber baron Jay Gould.[58] Gould would help Eckert rise to the top of both *American Union Telegraph* and *Western Union*.[59] We also find the ubiquitous National Detective Police Chief Lafayette Baker registered at the hotel the day before Eckert's arrival.

T.T. Eckert of Ohio reported directly to Secretary of War Stanton. He would take charge of interviewing Lincoln conspirator Lewis Payne/

Powell, who apparently revealed little during his long, difficult interrogation.[60] This role as an interrogator seems an odd one for a telegraph operator but may reflect Edwin Stanton's particular confidence in Eckert. On 14 April 1865, President Lincoln invited Eckert, a strong, powerful man, to attend Ford's Theatre with him on the night of the assassination—perhaps as a surrogate bodyguard. He first asked Stanton if he could spare Eckert and the Secretary of War, in his typically rude and disrespectful tone, refused the President. Lincoln then went to Eckert himself with the invitation and was again turned down, allegedly because the telegraph operator was too busy. Perhaps Eckert was reluctant to contradict his fierce and always angry superior, but it remains a stunning rejection of an invitation from the President of the United States to an employee of the War Department. General and Mrs. Grant had already turned down the President's offer as they were leaving town. The whole scene is rather pathetic. The President of the United States could not get anyone on his payroll to go with him to the theater either as security or simply for company.

Despite Eckert's claim of overwork, he went home for dinner as usual that evening and was there when news of Lincoln's assassination arrived. John Parker, the single guard assigned to protect the door to the presidential box, apparently left his post and went next door for a drink. This allowed Booth to enter the box from the rear unhindered. Booth was armed with a single-shot derringer and a knife, indicating foolhardiness or considerable confidence about gaining access to the President's box. Parker was apparently charged with negligence but the charges were quickly dismissed.[61]

STANTON'S DETECTIVES IN MONTREAL

The presence at St. Lawrence Hall and Barnett's Niagara Museum of Lafayette Baker, the leader of the National Detective Police, and his brother-in-law detective Walter Pollack, also raises questions. They also signed in at Barnett's Museum in Niagara on several occasions, from the summer of 1864 through the spring of 1865. Pollack signed in at St. Lawrence Hall on 18 October 1864, the same day as John Wilkes Booth. On that day, Pollack registered alongside senior Confederate agent Dr. Luke Blackburn. Later, Pollack would sign in either with, or directly alongside, noted Confederate spy Sarah Slater.[62] In the hotel "departure" book for 2 May 1864, Pollack's name is associated with T. Jones in a margin note placed by hotel staff. Pollack was not a guest at St. Lawrence Hall at the time but T. Jones, listed as Coln (Colonel) T. Jones, registers that day. We know that Thomas Jones was a senior signals officer for the confederacy in southern Maryland and a key link in the courier routes through that state. He played an important role in John Wilkes Booth's escape from Washington following Lincoln's assassination. Whether the T. Jones in the St. Lawrence Hall register is the same man cannot be established definitively but the association with Pollack is intriguing. It's clear that senior National Detective Police detective W. Pollack had some interest in or affiliation with T. Jones at St. Lawrence Hall in May 1864.

In early April, Baker was scheduled to meet Nelson Trowbridge in Montreal. Trowbridge was a slave trader and agent for the powerful Lamar family of Savannah, Georgia. Baker missed the meeting but we can assume they were planning to discuss Lamar's stores of cotton in Savannah. Like his earlier dealings with Beverley Tucker, this places Baker and the National Detective Police in direct contact with Confederate agents in Canada.

One thing is clear: Baker and Pollack were in Montreal, in a foreign country outside their jurisdiction, and in a hotel full of Confederate agents. If they were there to discover sedition, it was all around them in plain view. They may have been there to participate in cotton-for-contraband trading, but if so, breaking the blockade by trading with the enemy was certainly an illicit business and would have involved close interaction with the Confederate Secret Service. This was odd company for the leader of the National Detective Police to be keeping.

Again, much like a ship, a hotel is a small place. During this period, there were rumors about plots and raids aplenty at St. Lawrence Hall.[63] Booth openly bragged about his violent intentions. How did America's chief detective and his agents miss all this?

The hotel also played host to a number of important American newspaper editors and journalists. Their job was to report news. Surely sedition against the United States, planned and financed in a foreign country, qualified as news? But they issued no stories or reports from Montreal. It was as if they had never been there,

St. Lawrence Hall.

yet there is no mistaking their registrations in the hotel guest book.[64]

UNANSWERED QUESTIONS

Some of the names, photographs, and historical details highlighted in this book may be written off to coincidence, but where does coincidence leave off and serious historical skepticism take hold? There are questions here that may never be adequately answered but that does not mean they should not be asked. The names in the surviving St. Lawrence Hall guest books at the National Archives of Canada and Barnett's Museum cannot be ignored simply because the implications are unsettling to the existing American Civil War narrative.

Any of the anomalies highlighted in this book, when viewed as discrete events, could be mere accidents. But when viewed cumulatively, especially given the known interrelationships among many of these people, the picture becomes clearer...and unnerving. The suggestion of corruption at the highest levels of the American government is certainly here and so is the possibility of outright sedition, at least by some. The implication that American military suppliers sold to both sides at the height of the bloodletting is hardly consistent with historical narratives which picture the Civil War as a conflict between good and evil, between slavery and freedom.

The level of opposition to Lincoln in 1864 was clearly deeper and more vociferous than the existing historical narrative allows for. This surely challenges many bedrock assumptions about the conduct and conclusion of the war. Long cherished myths, be they American and Canadian or British, will be bruised by a hard examination of the facts. At the very least this new information demands attention by historians studying the Civil War and seeking to understand Montreal's role in that calamity.

Finally, in thinking about St. Lawrence Hall, remember that the names in the hotel do not originate from some widely circulated source, such as the New York or Philadelphia city directories, but rather from the guest books of a single hotel in Montreal over a short time period. Even allowing for obfuscation of initials and instances of mistaken identity, the distilled list of guests remains extraordinary. As for the Notman Collection, it contains the greatest concentration of Confederate Secret Service photos, including their Canadian and British cohorts, in existence. The historical significance of these photographs has long gone unrecognized.

Clearly something unusual, powerful, and malevolent was afoot in the city during the summer and fall of 1864 and remains, even today, part of Montreal's secret history. ~

CHAPTER 9

The British Players and Their Stories

LIEUTENANT COLONEL GARNET WOLSELEY VISITS ROBERT E. LEE

In the wake of the Trent Crisis, Lieutenant Colonel Garnet J. Wolseley was posted to Canada as assistant quartermaster general. He was then not only a combat veteran but also, at twenty-eight, the youngest lieutenant colonel in the British Army. By 1861, he had served in Crimea, India, and China.

The British had learned the hard way in Crimea how important sound logistics were to military success. These bitter lessons were still fresh in the minds of the British military establishment when Wolseley was sent to Canada to make preparation for the arrival of eleven thousand British Regulars, the first contingent of a proposed army of seventy thousand men.

Lt. Col. Wolseley landed in Halifax in December 1861 as part of the quartermaster and army train staff charged with making preparations to receive the British Expeditionary Force and move it over-land from Halifax to Montreal, all in the midst of a frigid Canadian winter.

Wolseley led an advance team which attempted to reach Bic, near Rivière-du-Loup on the St. Lawrence River, which was a critical way station on the army's planned transit route. The weather in the Gulf of St. Lawrence that December was horrible. Despite their best efforts, they could not make headway in the face of a winter storm and heavy seas. Their vessel ultimately turned about and, seeking a safe port, limped into Sydney Harbour on Cape Breton Island. Wolseley and his comrades passed a cold, miserable Christmas in Sydney, sleeping on tables as icy green seawater sloshed about in what they described as the "cuddy cabin" (most likely a small cabin in the stern below the poop deck).[1]

As a soldier with a trained eye, Wolseley immediately saw that the absence of east-west rail lines represented a huge strategic liability for British North America. Reinforcing his opinion,

Wolseley's advance party, having failed to reach Rivière-du-Loup via the St. Lawrence, instead had to make their way to Boston and ultimately reached Montreal on the Grand Trunk Railroad via Portland, Maine. It must have been a touch humiliating, but they decided to "brass it out," wearing their full red serge uniforms the whole time they were in the United States. They were

Lieutenant Colonel Garnet Wolseley. McCord Museum, Notman Collection, Montreal, QC, 1862. I-13559.1

not about to skulk through Boston and Portland like spies, and according to Wolseley, they were generally well received.[2] An east-west Railroad between Halifax, Montreal, and points to the west would have made such a circuitous route through the U.S. unnecessary. During the Trent Crisis, British authorities even contemplated seizing Portland to secure access to the Grand Trunk Railroad. The importance of railroads linking the disparate parts of Canada would become an enduring theme in the early development of the nation.

Wolseley's first assignment was to set up a camp and transfer station at Rivière-du-Loup to support the thousands of British Regulars who would be making the frigid overland trip from Halifax to Montreal in the winter of 1862. Wolseley's preparations and those of other competent logisticians ensured that no casualties were incurred during this incredible overland march in the dead of winter, across a landscape as harsh as any in the Northern hemisphere.[3]

In August 1862, with the Trent Crisis past, Wolseley requested six weeks' leave to visit the front lines of the Civil War in Virginia. He was accompanied by *London Times* special correspondent Frank Lawley. Before leaving Canada, Wolseley reached out to important Confederate operatives in Montreal, seeking letters of introduction to the Marylanders who, at great risk, organized the courier lines which smuggled dispatches, covert operatives, and contraband goods between Richmond and Canada.[4] Among the Confederates likely approached were Captain P.C. Martin and George Kane. Martin was the senior

Confederate representative in Montreal at the time and well liked in British military circles. He provided similar letters of introduction to John Wilkes Booth when the actor traveled to Montreal in October 1864. Armed with these letters, it is likely that Wolseley was introduced to some of the same people who would later play important roles in Booth's escape from Washington through southern Maryland and into Virginia. In his writings after the war, Wolseley was careful never to reveal the names of his benefactors in either Montreal or southern Maryland.

Once in Maryland, after darkness fell, Wolseley and his companion traveled from safe-house to safe-house along well-established courier routes, hospitably welcomed wherever they spent the night. They eventually arrived in Virginia and made their way to Richmond, where, upon arrival, they presented their credentials to Confederate authorities, including Secretary of State Judah Benjamin. The Confederate Congress was in session and lodging was nearly impossible to come by. In any case, Wolseley and Lawley had not come to see politicians—they had come to see Robert E. Lee and the Army of Northern Virginia. In his memoirs, Wolseley admitted to being intrigued, even fascinated, by this outnumbered, ragged Southern army that seemed for a time invincible.[5]

The two Englishmen soon joined Lee's Army near Winchester, Virginia, shortly after the bloody battle of Sharpsburg-Antietam. Here they met with Generals Lee, Longstreet, Jackson, and Stuart, all of whom impressed Wolseley, but none so much as the gentlemanly Lee. He noted that the Confederate army was dressed in an irregular and haphazard manner. Most of their equipment had U.S. markings and many of their weapons had been captured in the field. Lee seemed to sense what Wolseley was thinking and said to his guest, "There is one attitude in which I would never be ashamed for you to see my men; that is to say, when they fight."[6] It was a statement Wolseley would never forget.

Wolseley observed that both American armies, North and South, were made up of trained civilians led by brave junior officers and non-commissioned officers; but very few were professional soldiers. Brave to a fault, Lee's army was not always capable of realizing their general's bold strategic and tactical conceptions. Nowhere was this clearer than the following summer at Gettysburg, when Lee asked more of his brave army than it could do.[7] How could it be otherwise? The Confederacy went from having no army or navy at all to having three-quarters-of-a-million men under arms, and all in just two years. Ultimately, close to a million would serve the South representing much of the serving-age population. Close to half of these would be killed, wounded, sickened, or otherwise debilitated by the war. A whole generation disappeared. Wolseley observed that the British Army faced the same problem in finding enough competent officers to support the newly-expanded Canadian Militia: "Those who know how difficult it is to supply our own militia and volunteer forces with efficient officers can appreciate what difficulties General Lee had to overcome in the formation of the army he so often led to victory."[8]

After the Civil War, Wolseley wrote a number of insightful treatises and articles about the conduct of operations by both armies in the Civil War. His observations were always balanced; he was the consummate third-party professional observing a runaway American tragedy as it unfolded, but his quiet admiration for what Robert E. Lee and his outnumbered army managed to accomplish can be read between the lines. In theory and on paper, Lee and his Army of Northern Virginia had no chance of success. Yet they achieved one stunning victory after another in the early years of the war. Five years after the war, Wolseley wrote a moving tribute to General Lee upon the general's death in which he acknowledged that Lee had a "genius for war" but also a remarkable character as a man. In his tribute to Lee he wrote, "I have met with many of the great men of my time, but Lee alone impressed me with the feeling that I was in the presence of a man who was cast in a grander mould and made of different and finer metal ..."

Wolseley remained in Canada after the Civil War and helped defend the country against the Fenian Raiders in 1866. He led the Red River Expedition in 1870. Again, the absence of east-west railroads proved a hindrance. Like the great march from Halifax to Montreal in 1862, the Red River Expedition was a logistical tour de force.

After leaving Canada, Wolseley would go on to fight battles in the Ashanti, Zulu, Egyptian, and South African campaigns, emerging as the most-decorated soldier of the Victorian age. He retired in 1900, holding the rank of field marshal, a rare honor in the British Army.[9]

LT. COLONEL A.E. CLARK-KENNEDY AND THE GREAT MARCH ACROSS CANADA

Lt. Col. Clark-Kennedy commanded the British "Army Train," providing the army with vitally needed logistics and transportation. This was the giant logistical tail that enabled the army to move and fight. It provided food, medicine, tents, boots, weapons, water, and ammunition the army needed. Without it, operations defensive or offensive, were impossible. Without the "Train," the Army went nowhere.

In this role, Colonel Clark-Kennedy served with Quartermaster-General Garnet Wolseley and oversaw the transfer of thousands of British regulars, part of a force of eleven thousand troops landed in Halifax in the immediate aftermath of the RMS Trent crisis. They discovered the only train line to Montreal (The Grand Trunk) began in Portland, Maine. For a time they considered capturing Portland and seizing the line but war had not yet been declared, so the British hesitated. They opted instead to send the army cross-country from Nova Scotia through New Brunswick and Quebec in the dead of winter. They carried with them all their equipment, including three batteries of artillery and ammunition. This is arguably the greatest overland troop movement in Canadian history prior to the massive mobilizations of the First and Second World Wars.

In the face of every obstacle, these men traveled by sleigh through snow, with temperatures plunging as low as minus twenty-five degrees Fahrenheit, but pushed on. They traveled more than four hundred miles across some of the most inhospitable landscape on earth, following a route pretty much parallel to today's Trans-Canada Highway. Their destination was a train depot near Quebec City, from which they could reach Montreal by rail. Each man was equipped with special cold weather gear, including a fur cap with flaps, woolen sweaters, long underwear, sheepskin coats, mittens, heavy woolen socks, and moccasins (lined mukluks). Each sleigh was provided with thick Buffalo hide blankets and the troops were regularly ordered out to run beside the sleigh to maintain circulation. For British soldiers from Yorkshire, Wales, or Ireland, this must have seemed like a trip across the far side of the moon. Desertions were surprisingly few given the awful conditions. At the time, Union recruiters, "crimps," were everywhere in Canada, offering large signing bonuses and immediate promotion for experienced British soldiers.

A medical team accompanied each convoy, and others were stationed at each stop. Hot meals were provided at specific stations for breakfast, lunch, and dinner. Rough but warm sleeping accommodations were ready on each of the ten nights of the overland journey. The advance preparations necessary to support this massive movement of men and materiel in the dead of winter were prodigious, and Clark-Kennedy and Garnet Wolseley were at the center of it all.

The experience of moving this mass of troops with all their accoutrements and equipment across half a continent in the dead of winter left a lasting impression on everyone involved. The experience convinced John A. Macdonald, the Minister of Militia and later Canada's first

Lt. Col. Clark-Kennedy, M.T. McCord Museum, Notman Collection, Montreal, QC, 1862. 1-2049.1

Prime Minister, that an east-west rail network was essential to Canada's survival as a nation. This east-west railroad theme would dominate the early decades of Confederation as the Macdonald government championed first a rail link to Halifax and later a trans-continental railroad from coast to coast.

Once the British troops arrived in Montreal, they were stationed at the newly completed Victoria Barracks on Royer Street and at other locations across the city. They settled into a regular garrison

Victoria Barracks and Parade Ground. This beautiful and historic structure still stands on Le Royer Street in the shadow of Notre Dame Basilica. Note that the Regiment is in column as if for a parade. In the background are guests and onlookers in the windows. No marker or sign recognizes the unique role in Canadian and indeed in Montreal's military history the building played. Highland Regiment at Barracks. McCord Museum, Notman Collection, Montreal, QC, about 1870. MP-0000.2915

routine involving drills, inspections, parades, field maneuvers, and nightly social life.

Like many of his brother officers, Clark-Kennedy was awed by the scale and bloodiness of the American Civil War raging to the south. Although leaders on both sides of the U.S. conflict were generally professional soldiers, their armies were made up of civilian volunteers, whom the British Regulars regarded with a degree of con-tempt. Yet these volunteer armies clashed on a gargantuan scale. Robert E. Lee's outnumbered and under-equipped Army of Northern Virginia seemed to perform miracles on the battlefield. Professional British soldiers were keen to have a first-hand look. Like most British officers, Clark-Kennedy wanted to travel south to Dixie but, in the end, received permission to visit the Army of the Potomac. This was not without purpose. Northern U.S. armies would be the enemy in the event of an invasion of Canada. So Clark-Kennedy was as much a spy as a military observer.

Lt. Col. Garnet J. Wolseley, already a veteran of the Crimean War and Indian Mutiny would go on to become the greatest soldier of the Victorian age.

BRITISH CAPTAINS L.G. PHILLIPS AND E. WYNNE AT THE BATTLE OF FREDERICKSBURG

Captain Lewis Guy Phillips was an interesting and adventurous character. Stationed in Montreal during the Civil War, he was educated at Eton and Oxford and spoke several languages, including Greek, German, French, and Italian.[10] He was commissioned in 1859 in the elite Grenadier Guards as an Ensign/Lieutenant. His battalion was dispatched to Canada during the RMS Trent crisis in 1861, when Great Britain and the United States came to the brink of war. During the crisis, Britain sent forty steam-powered, heavily-armed, iron-clad cruisers to Halifax. In addition, eleven thousand British regulars arrived in Canada as the first installment of a build-up to a force of seventy thousand troops. Among the first units to arrive were the Grenadier Guards and the regiments of the Rifle Brigade. The Rifles were stationed in Hamilton and the Grenadier Guards in Montreal.

The officers of these units understood that their job was to protect British North America from the threat of invasion by the United States. This is what they planned and practiced for daily. It was the topic of conversation over dinner in the Officers' Mess and afterwards over drinks. Thus the succession of victories achieved by the outnumbered Confederates early in the war were generally welcomed in Canada—at least in military circles. Contemporary records show that sentiment in the army was generally sympathetic to the South, in accordance with the ancient axiom "the enemy of my enemy ..."

The fighting then raging in Virginia and Tennessee represented the future of modern warfare. There was a natural professional curiosity about what was happening in the field. British officers wanted to have a first-hand look at the strategy, tactics, new doctrines and technologies coming out of the American Civil War. The intrepid Captain Phillips and his friend Captain Edward Wynne were among the most eager to see it all first-hand.

Bored with garrison life, they sought and received an extended leave of absence, allowing them to travel south to see the war up close.

They were given letters of introduction to Confederate agent William Glenn, who ran a courier line through Maryland to Virginia. These letters of introduction came most likely from Captain P.C. Martin, the senior Confederate Secret Service

Captain Lewis Guy Phillips. McCord Museum, Notman Collection, Montreal, QC, 1864. I-10531.1

agent in Montreal at the time. Martin would later provide John Wilkes Booth with similar letters of introduction to Confederate agents in southern Maryland, including Dr. William King and Dr. Samuel Mudd. Captain Martin appears to have counted among his best friends a large coterie of British officers in Montreal that likely included Phillips and Wynne.

The two British officers left Montreal by train on 27 October 1862, heading south first to New

Captain Wynne, 1862. Both Wynne and Phillips are found in the surviving hotel registry of St. Lawrence Hall, Montreal's finest hotel and the unofficial headquarters of the Confederate Secret Service in Canada. (See Chapter 1.) McCord Museum, Notman Collection, Montreal, QC, 1862. I-3387.1

York and then on to Washington. From the capital they traveled to southern Maryland where William Glenn smuggled them across the Potomac to Virginia just as he would any Confederate courier heading to Richmond. (See Chapter 2.) After a nine-day overland journey through wartorn Virginia, they arrived in Richmond on 26 November. They presented their credentials, including letters of introduction from Glenn and likely P.C. Martin and other Confederate agents in Montreal. They were sent on to General Robert E. Lee's headquarters at Fredericksburg where a major battle was soon expected. Federal commander General Ambrose Burnside was positioning his large, well-equipped army to cross the Rappahannock on pontoon bridges in anticipation of capturing Fredericksburg and invading Virginia.

The British Officers received a friendly reception at General Lee's headquarters and were invited to become temporarily attached to the Army of Northern Virginia. This was more than just a professional courtesy for the British Officers—it was a sign of respect. Phillips was a soldier who thoroughly enjoyed camp life and soon became friends with a number of Confederate Officers including Major John Pelham, commander of J.E.B. Stuart's horse artillery. Pelham was a West Point graduate whose photographs show him as young and boyish in appearance. Despite his youth, Pelham earned for himself a formidable reputation as a leader and gunner. While not reckless, he was certainly fearless. General Stonewall Jackson wrote of Pelham: *"It is extraordinary to see such courage in a mere boy. With Pelham on each flank I believe I could whip the world."* Coming from Jackson, who had a reputation as a demanding and often hypercritical commanding officer, this was mighty praise indeed.[11] By the time of the Battle of Fredericksburg, Pelham had already distinguished himself in the great clashes of 1861-1862 between the Army of the Potomac and The Army of Northern Virginia.

He was soon promoted to the rank of Major and given command of J.E.B. Stuart's artillery.

On the night of 12-13 December 1862, with the Battle of Fredericksburg expected to commence the next morning, Phillips and Pelham spent the evening with friends around a campfire in J.E.B Stuart's Cavalry Division camp. The evening was raw and snow swept across the field on which so many men would die the following day. The air was cold and filled with anticipation. A veteran of many battles, Pelham was under no illusions as to what the morrow would bring. Phillips, the older man and a well-trained professional soldier, had but a fraction of the combat experience of his younger friend. He noted that Pelham possessed a calm, steely determination to see his duty through.

As dawn approached, Phillips offered Pelham his most prized possession, a Regimental Grenadier Guards tie, as a good luck talisman. Pelham accepted the memento, calmly assuring Phillips he would return it in the evening. The truth was that neither of them knew if Pelham would be alive that evening.[12]

During the battle, Stuart's cavalry, along with Pelham's artillery, was posted to the right flank of the army, downriver from Fredericksburg to guard the flank. When a Division of Federal troops crossed the Rappahannock in an attempt to turn the right flank of the Confederate Army, Stuart's cavalry blocked their advance. Seeing an opportunity to enfilade the advancing Federals, Pelham raced forward with a small battery of 12-pound Napoleons and caissons. He took a position on the flank and rear of the Federals, from

Captain E. Wynne. McCord Museum, Notman Collection, Montreal, 1863. I-5781.1

which he could deliver enfilading fire. This was his signature maneuver. His guns were soon firing solid shot down the rows of advancing infantry. Pelham's firing position was so far to their flank and rear that the initial Federal assumption was that the artillery fire was coming from their own guns on the heights across the river but as Pelham's guns took an ever-greater toll, the Federals responded by bringing up their own artillery to return fire. Heavy guns on the Stafford Heights on the far side of the Rappahannock also let loose on Pelham, but still he held his ground.

Union counter-battery fire was soon taking its toll, and Pelham was down to a single gun, but by now the entire Federal advance was in disarray. Eleven of Pelham's twelve horses were dead, his single caisson was smashed, and most of his gunners were wounded or dead. One of the few men still standing was Pelham himself, who helped service the single remaining gun. Three times he was ordered by J.E.B Stuart to withdraw, but replied that he could hold his ground. This extraordinary performance was being witnessed not only by Stuart but also by Stonewall Jackson and Robert E. Lee. Through binoculars, Pelham could be seen wearing an odd, striped, red-and-blue favor tied around his cap. The third and last order to withdraw was scribbled by J.E.B. Stuart and read: "Stop firing and withdraw your guns you crazy gallant Pelham."[13] After two hours under fire and with the Federal flank attack defeated, Pelham and the surviving members of his gun crew withdrew.

Fredericksburg turned into yet another stunning defeat for the Army of the Potomac at the hands of the smaller but better-led Army of Northern Virginia. Pelham emerged as one of the heroes of the battle. He returned to camp that night and gave Phillips back his tie with a quiet thank you. Phillips would return to Canada with it. As for the gallant Pelham, he would be dead in a few weeks, struck down leading a cavalry assault at Kelly Ford, not far from Fredericksburg.

Following the battle, Phillips and Wynne made their way back to Canada along the same Confederate courier line that carried agents and correspondence between Richmond and Montreal. On the last leg of the trip, they traveled separately. Phillips arrived safely, but Wynne was captured by Federal authorities in Maryland and imprisoned in Washington. The fact that he was carrying Confederate correspondence did not help support his story of being a neutral officer on leave, traveling home to his unit in Canada. Not persuaded by Wynne's explanation, American authorities charged him with spying. The British Ambassador in Washington, Lord Lyons, intervened on his behalf, claiming that Wynne was protected from imprisonment as a neutral. Wynne did not wait to see how the diplomatic tug of war would end. He used a hidden breakfast knife to cut through a door panel and made his way onto an adjoining prison roof. From there he jumped to the ground and eventually made it to the house of William Glenn in Baltimore. Glenn arranged for his return to Canada by a circuitous route that took him by train through Ohio. In Montreal, Wynne and Phillips made the local papers and were toasted by their brother officers in the Mess where they were pressed for details of the great battle. Glenn kept a diary and notes of the whole affair, which eventually found their way into the hands of historians early in the 21st century.[14] Whatever became of the Grenadier Guards Regimental tie worn by the gallant Pelham during the battle is not known.

Phillips and Wynne left Canada in 1864 when the 1st Battalion Grenadier Guards were posted back to Great Britain. Phillips stayed in the army and rose to the rank of Colonel before retiring in 1885.[15] ∾

Two photos of the St. Albans raiders posing for the camera outside the gate of the Montreal jail. Both the jail and the gate can still be seen today on the eastern edge of Old Montreal. In the shot on the right, Bennett Young, Commander of the raid, stands to the left of the group in a "Garibaldi" jacket. The men to his immediate right are William Hutchinson, Charles Moore Swager, Lewis Sanders, and likely Squire Turner Teavis. The clean-shaven man on the right in front is General Edwin Lee. In the second photo (on the left) we see the same group joined by Confederate Commissioner George Sanders (back row), who stands beside his son Lewis, who was responsible for supplying the Raiders with necessities in prison. George Sanders assembled the raiders' defense dream team of Abbott, Kerr and Laflamme. St. Albans raiders at the jail door. McCord Museum, Notman Collection, Montreal, QC, 1864. 14018.1, 1-14017.1

CHAPTER 10

St. Albans Raid

THE ST. ALBANS RAID resulted in the most northerly engagement of the Civil War. The leader of the operation was Kentucky cavalryman Bennett Young, a veteran of John Hunt Morgan's famous raid into Ohio. The other twenty-three Raiders were also mostly veterans of Morgan's command. The purpose of the raid, which had been planned and financed by the Confederate Secret Service in Canada, was to force the redeployment of Federal troops to guard the northern border, thereby taking pressure off of hard-pressed Confederate armies in the South. There was also a retaliatory motive behind the raid. Northern armies were increasingly turning their firepower on Southern civilians and civilian infrastructure, in an effort to break the South's will to resist. Whole swaths of Virginia, Tennessee, and Georgia were laid to waste in actions that were contrary to United States Army regulations regarding the treatment of civilians and private property and also contrary to the newly-signed Geneva Convention on the conduct of war. The senseless burning of the defenseless town of Darien, Georgia by Federal troops was one of the acts the raiders cited as an example of why the attack on St. Albans was necessary. If Federal troops could burn Southern towns and villages, why not give Northern civilians a taste of the same medicine?

Prior to the raid, most of Bennett Young's command holed up in the Donegana Hotel near the corner of Notre-Dame and Bonsecours Streets. This whole hotel was often booked out by the Confederate Secret Service and was one of the establishments in the city where Federal agents could not get a room at any price. Since all of Bennett's men knew each other, security was tight and no one was talking. The financing for the raid came from Confederate Commissioner Clement Clay, assisted by George Sanders and Confederate bankers John Porterfield and Hezekiah Payne. Expecting an angry response from British and Canadian authorities, Jacob Thompson, the senior Confederate Commissioner in Canada was kept deliberately out of the planning loop so that he would have plausible deniability.

Bennett's men infiltrated St. Albans over several days leading up to market day, which was on

Tuesday, 18 October. Young knew that the following day, 19 October, St. Albans banks would be flush with cash. At about three o' clock in the afternoon of 19 October, Young's men took to the main street in St. Albans armed with Colt Navy pistols. Designated teams raced for the banks and were soon in possession of more than $200,000 in cash. The civilian population was herded into the main square as Bennett's men raced up and down the street throwing containers of "Greek Fire" at buildings. The containers were supposed to combust spontaneously. Fortunately for St. Albans, the Greek Fire mostly failed to ignite. There was some exchange of gunfire in the streets and several people were wounded. One man would later die of his wounds.

It all ended in a little over an hour, and Young and his men, mounted on stolen horses, crossed the border into Canada where they assumed they were safe, but a posse was right behind them. Several of the raiders were captured at Frelighsburg and Phillipsburg, across the border in the Eastern Townships. They were about to be taken back to St. Albans when a British Major came onto the scene and reminded the Americans they were on the wrong side of the border and in violation of British neutrality laws. He demanded the prisoners be turned over to him. There were a few tense moments as rifles were leveled and curses flew, but in the end cooler heads prevailed and the prisoners were surrendered to Canadian authorities. They were then taken to the military barracks at St. Jean where there was a sufficient garrison to protect them in the event the Americans changed their minds.

Squire Turner Teavis. McCord Museum, Notman Collection, Montreal, QC, 1866. I-20325.1

The trial of the captured raiders in Montreal would make more than headlines; it would also make Canadian legal history. The trial pitted Montreal's generally pro-Southern establishment against the Canadian government, which wanted the raiders extradited to avoid an international incident. In Montreal, the captured raiders were treated like celebrities and their trial before Judge Charles Coursol was followed closely in the press.

Here we see Marcus Spurr, one of the St. Albans raiders, in a Kentucky-style belted jacket favored by their commander, Bennett Young. This was sometimes referred to as a Garibaldi jacket. Along with Thomas Collins, Squire T. Teavis, and Louis S. Price, Spurr was assigned the job of plundering the St. Albans Bank. When the bank manager, Martin A. Seymour, resisted handing over his gold deposits, Spurr put a Navy Colt pistol to his skull and proclaimed he would "put a bullet through his head." Mr. Marcus Spurr. McCord Museum, Notman Collection, Montreal, QC, copied 1865. I-15007.0.1

Charles Moore Swager was a Kentucky cavalryman and another veteran of John Hunt Morgan's raid into Ohio. Many of the cavalrymen who evaded capture or escaped imprisonment made their way to Canada, where they put themselves at the service of Confederate authorities. Swager was part of Bennett Young's command, which captured and plundered the banks of St. Albans, Vermont, in October 1864. The raid was in part staged in retaliation for what the Confederates saw as wanton vandalism and savagery practiced by Union Armies against Southern civilians in Virginia, Tennessee, and Georgia. During the trial, their Canadian lawyers cited the needless burning of Darien, Georgia as an example of these crimes. It is likely this photograph was taken before the raid and subsequent arrest of the raiders in Montreal. Like many other Confederate exiles, Swager never returned to the United States after the war. He studied law in Canada and then went to Europe to study medicine. He was in France during the Franco-Prussian War and served as a surgeon in the French Army, where he was killed by artillery fire. Mr. Charles Swager. McCord Museum, Notman Collection, Montreal, QC, copied 1865. I-15666.1

Samuel E. Lackey was part of Bennett Young's command that, in the fall of 1864, staged the northernmost engagement of the Civil War. Like most of the raiders, Lackey was a Kentucky cavalryman and a veteran of John Hunt Morgan's raid into Ohio. Following the St. Albans Raid he was captured in Canada at East Stanbridge, not far from the Vermont border. Samuel E. Lackey. McCord Museum, Notman Collection, Montreal, QC, 1865. 1-18795.1

Alamanda Pope Bruce was a Kentucky Cavalryman and veteran of John Hunt Morgan's famous raid into Ohio. He and a number of Morgan's men were captured but later escaped and fled to Canada. There, they became an armed wing of the Confederate Secret Service. Bruce served as one of the volunteers sent ahead to reconnoiter the Federal POW camp on Johnson's Island, Ohio in anticipation of an assault on the facility. During the raid on St. Albans, Bruce, James Doty, Joseph McGrorty, and Caleb M. Wallace robbed the First National Bank of $55,000. Eighty-two-year-old General John Nason was parked in his usual chair in the corner of the bank when the raiders burst in carrying Navy Colt revolvers. Quite deaf and a little senile, Nason was known to sometimes spend the whole day sitting in the corner of the bank reading the newspaper. He took no notice of the raiders and continued to read his paper even as the robbery took place around him. He ignored orders from the raiders to go to the back of the room and one of them threatened to "shoot the old cuss" but the others would not have it, so he was left unmolested and completely oblivious to the robbery.[2] On trial in Montreal, Bruce explained that his actions were in retaliation for the cruelty Federal armies were visiting upon innocent civilians in the South. He also told the court about a cousin who was brutally murdered in Camp Douglas, a Federal POW Camp. He stated clearly, "Yankee plundering and cruel atrocities without parallel provoked the attack on St. Albans as a mild retaliation."[3] A.P. Bruce. McCord Museum, Notman Collection, Montreal, QC, 1865. I-18781.1

LEGAL DREAM TEAM

The Confederate Secret Service provided money for a powerful defense dream team consisting of Sir John Abbott, William Kerr, Rodolphe Laflamme, and J.G. Houghton. Abbott was the Dean of McGill's Law School and Canada's senior jurist. He would later serve as Solicitor General and eventually become Prime Minister of Canada. Confederate Commissioner George Sanders and his son Lewis were charged with overseeing legal and other expenses associated with the trial and seeing to the comfort of the raiders in custody. The Crown, the Vermont Banks, and the United States government were represented by Bernard Devlin, the Honorable John Rose, George Edmonds, Edward Carter, and F.G. Johnson.

The case would be determined largely on jurisdictional grounds based on the legal status of the raiders as either Confederate soldiers or brigands. Had ordinary bank robbers taken refuge in Canada, British authorities in Canada would have been obligated to extradite them back to the United States. If, however, the raiders were Confederate soldiers acting on orders, then extradition would be subject to dispute. Britain had officially recognized the Confederacy as one of two legal "belligerents" in the American Civil War. The act of war against St. Albans had been carried out in the United States, not in Canada. Yes, the planning and financing of the attack had clearly taken place in Montreal but at the time there was no law against this. Canada would later adopt a neutrality law making it illegal to use Canadian soil as a base for planning or executing acts of war but this law was not in effect in 1864 when the St. Albans Raid was conducted. And laws cannot be applied retroactively. So the status of the raiders was of paramount importance in the trial.

The defense team maintained that the raiders were commissioned and non-commissioned officers in the Confederate States Army. They requested a pass from the United States for one of the attorneys to visit Richmond and determine the facts but the White House refused. Richmond responded by issuing a memorandum confirming the status of the raiders as bona fide members of the Confederate States Army acting on orders, although the raiders apparently wore civilian clothing. This and other supporting documents were given to two experienced couriers, the mysterious Sarah Slater and Reverend Stephen Cameron. Each traveled to Montreal by a different route and they arrived safely in the city only 24 hours apart.

Meanwhile, Canadian and British authorities were anxious to have the raiders extradited to avoid an international incident, but the Confederates were very popular locally. And all politics is local. While imprisoned in Montreal's grim jail on the eastern outskirts of the city they were granted every reasonable courtesy by Gaoler Louis Payette. They took their meals in Payette's house outside the jail, which still stands, isolated and somber, under the Jacques Cartier Bridge. The best foods and wines were provided thanks to Lewis Sanders. They had a string of visitors, including some of Montreal's belles, and posed for countless photographs. When couriers Sarah Slater and Stephen Cameron arrived in Montreal

Sir John Abbott, lead member of the St. Albans raiders' defense dream team. He was Dean of McGill's Law School and the senior jurist in Canada. He would go on to become Solicitor General and eventually Prime Minister. Sir John Abbott. McCord Museum, Notman Collection, Montreal, QC, 1863. I-6498.1

William Kerr was the most active member of the raiders' legal dream team. If Abbott conceived the strategy, it was Kerr who carried it out on a day-to-day basis. He was well known and respected within the Confederate exile community in Montreal. William Kerr. McCord Museum, Notman Collection, Montreal, QC, 1864. I-13145.1

Montreal Gaol-keeper Louis Payette, who provided the raiders with every reasonable courtesy. They took meals and met visitors in his house outside the jail. Bennett Young, the leader of the raiders, liked to refer to the Montreal jail as "Payette's hotel." Louis Payette. McCord Museum, Notman Collection, Montreal, QC, 1866. I-21667.1

J.G. Driscoll. It was Driscoll who prepared the brief Judge Coursol used as the basis for his decision to release the St. Albans raiders because the matter was beyond his jurisdiction. J.G.R. Driscoll. McCord Museum, Notman Collection, Montreal, QC, 1863. I-7774.1

This is the old Court House where the trial took place and which still graces Old Montreal today. The Court House, Notre Dame Street. McCord Museum, Notman Collection, Montreal, QC, 1866. I-20774.1

with the documents that would clinch the case, they too went to visit the raiders in jail. Slater apparently left a *carte de visite*, which provides the only likeness of the mysterious spy.

Behind-the-scenes efforts were being made to secure the raiders' early release in anticipation of the arrival of supporting documentation from Richmond. Defense attorney William Kerr asked his friend J.G. Driscoll to prepare a brief for Judge Coursol outlining the jurisdictional grounds on which the raiders could be released as legitimate belligerents acting on orders who thus had broken no laws in Canada. The brief provided grounds for the return of the money seized from the raiders upon capture, which amounted to some $80,000. One hundred and twenty thousand dollars was still missing and presumably in the hands of the Confederate Secret Service. So sure were Kerr, Abbott, and the rest of the defense team of the outcome of the trial that they arranged a meeting between Confederate Commissioner George Sanders and Montreal Police Chief Guillaume Lamothe to discuss details of the money handover. The meeting, which took place at the Donegana Hotel, was highly irregular and Lamothe was later censured for his role in the affair.

As if on cue, the raiders appeared in court on 13 December 1864 ready to travel, with bags, winter coats, and all. Judge Coursol immediately dismissed the case on jurisdictional grounds and the audience broke into applause. Bernard Devlin, representing the U.S. government, objected strenuously and asked that the prisoners be held over pending additional charges, but it was too late. The raiders made for waiting sleighs and were soon out of the city. Confederate banker John Porterfield went immediately to the Bank of Ontario on Place d'Armes, which was opened after hours, to allow Police Chief Lamothe to retrieve the $80,000 dollars in stolen money. The money was handed over to Porterfield in a carpetbag. Both the money and the raiders were soon safely in hiding.

Washington was naturally furious and so was Ottawa. Some of the raiders were recaptured the following year and put on trial in front of a new judge in Toronto, a less friendly venue. The trial ended in the same way, with the raiders being released on the grounds that they were legal

Jefferson Davis. McCord Museum, Notman Collection, Montreal, QC, copied 1863. I-6438.0.1

belligerents who had broken no laws in Canada. Embarrassed by the whole mess, Canadian and British authorities quickly passed new neutrality laws, making the planning and execution of hostile action from Canadian soil illegal. But the damage had been done. Canada also reimbursed St. Albans for the $80,000 dollars handed over by Police Chief Lamothe.

Relations with America, already tenuous following the Trent Crisis, were shattered by the St. Albans Raid. One effect was to accelerate the Confederation of Canadian Provinces into a single country. ᘒ

CHAPTER 11

Jefferson Davis in Montreal

VARINA DAVIS, wife of imprisoned Confederate President Jefferson Davis, was released from virtual house arrest at the Pulaski Hotel in Savannah, Georgia in the summer of 1865. She was not permitted to visit her husband who was being held in close confinement and under harsh conditions at Fortress Monroe in Virginia.

Fearing for the safety of her four children, Varina had earlier sent them with her mother, Margaret Howell, to seek refuge in Montreal. Still unable to visit her husband, she soon followed her children north.[1] Here, local businessmen, including publishing magnate John Lovell, a supporter of the Confederacy, sponsored the Davis family. Lovell later opened his home, a large townhouse near Union Square, to them. This support allowed Varina to send her daughters to Convent School in the city while young William and Jefferson Davis Jr. were educated southeast of Montreal in Lennoxville. Varina and her mother did their best to provide the nearly destitute family with a sense of security and normalcy, but living as exiles was not easy. Later in life, Varina Davis would comment on the support provided by the Catholic community both in the South and in Montreal. "These good people were the first come to offer me help. I will forever be grateful..."[2]

When, as a result of public pressure, Varina was ultimately allowed to visit her husband in prison, she was appalled by his poor health and living conditions. She started a letter-writing campaign and sought the help of powerful Americans like Horace Greeley and Cornelius Vanderbilt. After nearly two years in confinement, Davis still had not been brought to trial. The government sidestepped a public trial in part because it was concerned he would be acquitted if he came before a Virginia jury. With civilian rule and the writ of *habeas corpus* restored and no trial in sight, Davis was ultimately freed on $100,000 bail posted by Greeley, Vanderbilt, and others.

His health broken, Davis went to Montreal but vowed to return for trial if the government proceeded against him. Davis welcomed the opportunity to defend the constitutional right of states to secede from the Union. He was convinced he would win this legal battle and be

John Lovell, successful publisher and a sponsor of the Davis family in Montreal, 1865, McCord Museum, Notman Collection, Montreal, QC, John Lovell, Montreal, QC, 1865. I-19133.1

Ad for Lovell Printing, which still operates on St. Nicholas Street in Old Montreal. John Lovell & Son. McCord Museum, Notman Collection, Montreal, QC, 1850-1885. M930.50.1.114

vindicated. He joined his family at the Lovell residence. The townhouse must have been a busy place, accommodating two large families with small children. Davis' correspondence was forwarded to Lovell's printing house on Rue St. Nicholas, probably for reasons of security. Lovell Printing still operates from this location in Old Montreal, probably the oldest continuously operating family business in Canada. The Davis family attended services every Sunday at beautiful Christ Cathedral directly across the street from the Lovell townhouse.

Lovell's townhouse was just around the corner from Robert Reid's sculpting studio, The Montreal Marble Works. Reid would likely have been a parishioner of Christ Church along with the Davis family. It was Reid who designed and built the Confederate monument in Savannah, the largest in the South. He also sculpted the haunting statues of "Silence" and "Judgement," which stand guard over Confederate graves at Laurel Grove Cemetery in Savannah and nearby Thomasville Cemetery. It was these mysterious works of art that first awakened the author's interest in Montreal's ties to the Confederacy.

Varina Davis smuggled Jefferson Davis' papers to Canada and deposited them in the vault of the Bank of Montreal on Place d'Armes. During the war, the bank, along with other Canadian financial institutions, held large deposits of money for the Confederate Secret Service. The impressive bank building, with its beautiful interiors and hardened vault, still graces Place d'Armes.

In Montreal, President Davis was reclusive, politely refusing almost every dinner invitation.

Jefferson Davis' Children in Montreal 1867. McCord Museum, Notman Collection, Montreal, QC, 1867. I-28153.1

Jefferson and Varina Davis in Montreal 1867. McCord Museum, Notman Collection, Montreal, QC, 1867. I-28149.1

All the signs of deep depression were evident. Noting his despondency, Varina suggested he begin work on his memoirs, but Davis was not ready. The carnage in which he and Lincoln had played a part still weighed heavily on him. Davis remarked "I cannot speak of my dead so soon."[3] It would be almost fifteen years before he could bring himself to begin this work and it would require Varina, a natural writer and journalist, to bring it to fruition.

Shortly after arriving in Montreal, Confederate statesman James Mason, who had been at the center of the infamous RMS Trent crisis, invited Davis to visit the small Confederate colony taking root at idyllic Niagara-on-the-Lake. Davis traveled by ship from Montreal to Toronto and from there to Niagara. On the trip, they sailed by *Fort Niagara* with its fluttering Stars and Stripes. On seeing the flag, Davis remarked to Mason, with perhaps a touch of bitterness: "Look Mason, there is the gridiron on which we have been fricasseed"[4]

Upon his arrival in both Toronto and Niagara-on-the-Lake, large welcoming crowds and bands received him. In Niagara, he emerged from Mason's house to say a few words to Canada, which was then a brand new nation only days old. "I thank you most kindly for this hearty reception, which I take as a manifestation of your sympathy and goodwill for one in misfortune." He wished Canada to hold fast to British principles and "ever remain as free a people as you are now."[5]

Davis spent a week in Niagara surrounded by other prominent Confederate exiles and then returned to Montreal. John Lovell made arrangements for the Davis family to occupy a townhouse at 1181 Mountain Street, which still stands today, its historical significance unrecognized.

President Davis generally shunned public appearances, but a showing of *The Rivals* at the Theatre Royal in support of Southern hospitals and wounded veterans brought him out of seclusion. Following the second act, his presence in the balcony was noticed. The orchestra played 'Dixie' and the crowd rose in a standing ovation. Davis rose reluctantly from his chair and returned the salutation.

Later, in 1867, the Davis family moved to Lennoxville in the Eastern Townships, southeast of the city, to be near William and Jeff Jr. who were attending Bishop's Grammar School and a local school run by a Mrs. Clark. They took up residence at Clark's Hotel, now the Lennoxville Public Library. Davis described Lennoxville thus:

A pretty little place with the Massawippi River winding between the village and Bishop's College. On the heights less than a mile away one could see the surrounding town, green hills, sleek cattle, wheat fields and appealing bucolic vistas.

The Eastern Townships had been largely settled by United Empire Loyalists who distrusted Washington and were generally sympathetic to the Confederacy. Money was tight but Varina retained fond memories of Lennoxville. Years later she wrote "The old days in Lennoxville return to my memory. I wonder if I shall wake up as if from a dream and find my husband and children nearby. I suppose Lennoxville has changed very much since Mr. Redpath's servant at Clark's Hotel used to prod us on the ribs and ask (before dinner) 'beef or beans, pudding or pie.'"[6]

Eventually the Davis family traveled to Europe and later returned to the United States after President Johnson issued a general amnesty in December 1868. Jefferson and Varina ultimately settled in Beauvoir House in Biloxi, Mississippi.

St. Urbain Street. Montreal, McCord Museum, Notman Collection, Montreal, QC, [year].N-0000.193.76.2.

Aside from the Confederate colony at Niagara-on-the-Lake, Davis' departure from Canada marked the last act in Montreal's incredible Confederate story. All that remains are historic buildings with forgotten ties to the Confederacy and Civil War, old photographs in the McCord Museum, faded hotel registrations in the National Archives, and signatures in Barnett's Museum Visitors' Books as the Niagara Falls Museums. All of them hiding in plain sight for a century-and-a-half. ༄

Characters in Montreal: Ten months from June 1864-April 1865 St. Lawrence Hall Guest Book and Notman Collection of Photographs, McCord Museum

INTRODUCTION

The entries in St. Lawrence Hall's guest registers contain numerous examples of aliases and subtly disguised signatures, especially in 1864-1865. The prefixes Rev., Dr., and Judge were common (e.g., Rev. H.W. Davis and Judge Beverley Tucker). Initials were sometimes reversed or a false initial added in front of the real one. This was a technique used by cryptographers well into the Second World War, adding initials or words at the front and back of every encrypted message. Sometimes, as with John Harrison Surratt, a middle name became a last name, for example, John Harrison Surratt became John Harrison and Henry Winter Davis became Henry Winter or Rev H.W. Davis—both names appear in St. Lawrence Hall's Guest Book. The practice was common enough in 1864 and early 1865, primarily among American guests who far outnumbered Canadian or British residents at the hotel. During the Civil War, Montreal was a city awash in intrigue with Federal and Confederate spies operating from hotels a few blocks apart on St. James Street. Fast money was being made in trading cotton for contraband and running the blockade. The presence of Confederate money and influence was felt everywhere in the city. Large Confederate accounts were held at The Bank of Ontario on Place d'Armes and the Niagara and District Bank in St. Catharines. The Confederates were funded with a million dollars in gold and hard currencies like British pounds. These funds had been appropriated by the Confederate Congress and approved by President Jefferson Davis and Secretary of State Judah Benjamin. The Confederates in Canada also had access to funds from blockade running, the sale of cotton, and robbing Northern banks; for example, more than $200,000 was stolen from banks in St. Albans and brought back to Canada. The Confederate Secret Service in Canada faced many challenges but lack of money was not one of them.

Given the times, it's not surprising that some guests sought to disguise their identities or at least blur them. The times were dangerous. The writ of *Habeas Corpus* had been suspended in the U.S. and thousands were arrested and held without trial. Newspapers were closed and state legislatures intimidated or arrested whole scale. It is not surprising then that initials were sometimes changed, reversed, or disguised. Wives and daughters sometimes registered for husbands and fathers. Middle names became last names. In his memoirs, National Detective Police Chief Detective, Lafayette Baker, admitted to registering at St. Lawrence Hall using an alias, and sure enough, the name Baker, with altered initials, appears several times in the hotel guest book. Confederate leader Dr. Luke Blackburn registered as Josiah Blackburn and Senior Confederate Commissioner Jacob Thompson used any number of different initials and points of arrival. Blockade runner and slave trader Charles Lamar registers as Charles de Lamar. Former Governor E.D. Morgan of New York registers as D. Morgan. Hon S. Pomeroy registers as J.S. Pomeroy and A. Pomeroy. New York bankers W.T. Hatch and G. Bliss sign in as C.W. Hatch and W.R Bliss. In fact, Hatch and Bliss, who were regulars at St. Lawrence Hall, use a number of different initials. W.H. Stanton (whoever he is) registers on 13 August 1864 as W.H. Stanton but changes his initials to H.M. the very next day. The reversing of initials was a common practice. An early example of its employment was when Confederate agent George Sanders crossed into Canada at Niagara in 1864 and registered at Clifton House using the reversed initials S.N.G.[1] Another common subterfuge was to place a false initial at the front of the registration. For example, S. Draper becomes H.S. Draper or S. Pomeroy becomes J.S. Pomeroy

Jacob Thompson wrote in his final report to Confederate Secretary of State Judah Benjamin, that Congressman and New York newspaper publisher Benjamin Wood, as well as New York Governor Horatio Seymour, had visited him a number of times in the summer and fall of 1864. Seymour registers as Jas Seymour, and Benjamin Wood only subtly alters his name to read Mr. Wood, H. Wood, B. Wood or Dr. Wood. The use of prefixes and suffixes like Rev., Dr., Judge, and Jr. was common. These subtle subterfuges provided a shadow of plausible deniability. Like their Confederate counterparts, American politicians, both Democratic and Republican, often employed altered initials or used middle names as last names. British bankers and businessmen, as well as military suppliers and American newspapermen, were generally less shy about using their full names, but even here we find initials occasionally altered. It is impossible to make sense of St. Lawrence Hall's registry without understanding this phenomenon. The fact is, many American guests at St. Lawrence Hall, both Confederate and Federal, altered their names or initials subtly to provide a degree of deniability. It was a sensible precaution given the times and the erosion of civil liberties in the United States, which resembled a nascent military dictatorship by 1864.[2]

In deciphering the hotel registry, it is important to link last names with affiliations. For example, the arrival of (J.)S. Pomeroy becomes more compelling when linked to the registrations of E. Spaulding and W. Sprague, who, like Pomeroy, were leaders of Salmon Chase's presidential committee. Another example is the August 1864 registration of Radical Republican Tha(d) Stevens that is accompanied by the names Sprague, Pomeroy, Churchill, Halsey, Hale, and a number of other Radicals. We can more easily identify Jacob Thompson when his registration is accompanied by his personal secretary, William Cleary. There are dozens of such confirmatory cross references found in the guest book.

Remember, this extraordinary list was not derived from some mass document like the New York or Boston City Directory but from the guest book of a single one hundred room hotel, in a foreign country, over a very short period of time. What are the odds?

So what are we to make of this avalanche of powerful Americans in Montreal in 1864-1865? The statistical likelihood of so many American powerbrokers in one setting being a coincidence is so remote as to be almost incalculable. Something extraordinary was clearly afoot in Montreal from June 1864 through April 1865. Nothing like it had ever happened before and would never be repeated. It remains an historical anomaly never adequately explained.

This extraordinary gathering included bankers, treasury agents, military suppliers, newspaper editors, spies, Democratic and Republican politicians, with a number of anti-Lincoln Radicals, and important members of Salmon Chase's presidential committee. What would have brought all these powerful Americans to Montreal?

One reason is that the largest single cotton deal ever conceived was being negotiated in Montreal in 1864.

Valued at between half a billion and a billion dollars in 1864 currency, the economic stakes were enormous. This cotton, warehoused in the South, was to be traded for U.S. Greenbacks and contraband, especially food. This was a clear breaking of the blockade, involving trading with the enemy.

Montreal was the perfect setting for this illicit trade. It was located far enough away in British sovereign territory, making it a safe, discreet venue for this shady business. What is extraordinary is that this trade deal had the tacit support of both Jefferson Davis and Abraham Lincoln. Such a gigantic exercise in trading with the enemy faced considerable opposition in Congress and the armed forces. To oversee this trade, the Treasury Department was placed in charge, and this explains the large number of Treasury Department officials in Montreal. They were accompanied by cotton brokers, speculators, and bankers. Trading with the enemy had by this late stage of the war become more the rule than the exception. This also explains the large number of U.S. military suppliers in the city.

On the political side, the many Democratic politicians in the city were there to collect money and lay plans for defeating Abraham Lincoln in the upcoming election. The presence of large numbers of Republicans, including Radicals and supporters of Salmon Chase, is harder to explain, but we can assume they were in Montreal trying to unseat Lincoln as the Republican nominee. Various names were proposed to replace Lincoln, including Butler, Rosecrans, Grant, and Chase.

Another mysterious constituency in the city consisted of the National Detective Police, Judge Advocate General's Office, and the War Department. All worked for Secretary of War Edwin Stanton, who supported the Radical Republican agenda, especially regarding reconstruction. If these War Department employees were in Montreal spying on the Confederate Secret Service, there are precious few surviving reports to indicate this. The same holds true for the large number of newspaper editors, both Republican and Democratic, who were in the city. Surely, trading with the enemy, plots against Lincoln, and attacks on Northern cities represented newsworthy sedition. Yet none of it was reported.

So what conclusions can we draw? An obvious one is that the Northern war effort had, by 1864, become thoroughly corrupted. For many powerful individuals, the war was about making money. Trading with the enemy was a common practice, approved in some cases even by Lincoln himself. Not surprisingly, many of the robber barons of the notoriously corrupt post-war Gilded Age turned up in Montreal. The level of corruption implied by the names in Montreal is far greater than is acknowledged in America's mainstream Civil War narrative. Another conclusion hard to escape is that opposition to Lincoln in 1864 was far deeper, more widespread, and better organized than acknowledged within accepted Lincoln lore. The names in Montreal pose a challenge to America's mainstream and fiercely-protected historical narrative surrounding both Lincoln and the Civil War. Lincoln's near canonization in the months following his assassination has calcified into a dogma that inhibits needed historical debate. It is ironic that the authors of this "Lincoln as Saint" narrative were, for the most part, Radical Republicans who hated the President and celebrated his death.

CONFEDERATE AGENTS AND SYMPATHIZERS

- **Dr. William J. Almon:** prominent physician in Halifax in the 1860's who pioneered the use of chloroform as an anesthetic in British North America. His son, Dr. William Bruce Almon, served in the Confederate Army as a surgeon. Almon had ties to the Confederate Secret Service through Dr. Luke Blackburn and Confederate Commissioner Beverley Tucker. He treated Tucker for an infected wound which involved the removal of part of his thumb.[3] Almon was charged for his involvement in forcibly freeing the Canadian sailors involved in the seizure of the *USS Chesapeake* in 1864.[4]

Dr. Almon helped found Halifax's first hospital and was three times elected President of the Medical

Society of Nova Scotia. He was a courageous pioneer in the use of chloroform as an anesthetic. He was active in politics and played an important role in the establishment of Canada's Confederation in 1867. He served as a Member of Parliament and later as a Canadian Senator. Both Dr. Almon and Benjamin Wier, another Halifax Confederate supporter, are considered Fathers of Confederation. Almon's and Wier's photographs were taken at Notman's Studio in 1864.

- **John Yates Beall:** swashbuckling Confederate agent who was up for any assignment. He led an unsuccessful raid on the POW camp in Johnson's Island, Ohio. He participated in efforts to burn 12 major hotels in New York City. He was later captured trying to highjack a train carrying Confederate Generals to POW camps. Beall was executed at Fort Lafayette in New York Harbor just prior to war's end. (His photograph is found in McCord Museum, Notman Collection.)

- **Dr. Luke Blackburn:** senior Confederate Commissioner, courageous yellow fever doctor, implicated in plans to use yellow fever as a 'germ warfare' agent. His hatred of the Union was visceral. His brother once wrote that *"He held every Northern traitor as his enemy."* Blackburn later served as Governor of Kentucky. (31 August and 18 October 1864)

- **Belle Boyd:** famed Confederate spy and author. (12 June, 25 October, 5 November, 25 December 1864, and 18 April 1865)

- **Josephine and Robert Brown:** along with Sarah Slater, one of the Confederacy's most successful couriers. She and her husband stayed in Montreal for a year in the immediate aftermath of the Lincoln assassination. (21 June, 15 October, 12 December 1864)

- **Rev S. Cameron:** Confederate spy who was one of two couriers delivering the documents from Richmond needed for the defense of the St. Albans Raiders in Montreal. The other courier was Sarah Slater. They traveled by different routes and arrived in Montreal only a day or so apart. This documentation resulted in the release of the Raiders and the return to them

of the money robbed from St. Albans' banks. See Mr. Cameron's group photo of key Confederates, Notman Collection, McCord Museum, Notman Collection. (24 August, 15 December 1864, and 20 March 1865)

- **General William Carroll:** Tennessee. Business partner of P.C. Martin. (7 August and 24 October 1864)

- **John B. Castleman:** Confederate agent, part of the Secret Service in Canada. Registered as Louis Castleman, Kentucky. There is a photograph featured in Tidwell's *Come Retribution* that features Confederates George N. Sanders, Raider Thomas Hines, Col. George St. Leger Grenfell, and John B. Castleman at Niagara Falls on 7 July 1864. This establishes that Castleman was in Canada and in the company of key Secret Service operatives, even though his operations took him to Missouri and the Mississippi River region. Grenfell was later captured and imprisoned along with Samuel A. Mudd, Edmund Spangler, Samuel Arnold, and Michael O'Laughlen on Dry Tortugas. (1 March 1865; also Barnett's Museum 1 July 1864)

- **C.C. Clay:** former Senator from Alabama and close friend of President Franklin Pierce. He was a Confederate Commissioner in Canada in 1864. Clay orchestrated the St. Albans Raid in October 1864. Clay had close ties to Confederate spy and courier Josephine Brown. (6 November 1864 arriving from St. Catharines)

- **William Cleary:** secretary and assistant to Jacob Thompson, Senior Confederate Commissioner in Canada. Cleary had exiled in Canada earlier in the war and his familiarity with the country would have been an asset to Thompson. He checks in with Thompson on a number of occasions, including 14 June and 3 October 1864.

- **Clinton Clinebell:** graduate of the University of Virginia, a deserter from the Union Army. His purpose in Montreal is unclear. His name is mentioned as giving testimony in the impeachment trial of Andrew Johnson. He registers 4 June 1864 and identifies himself as being from CSA (Confederate States Army), Virginia.

- **H.V. Clinton:** St. Louis. Clinton was an alias for a Confederate operative who had earlier made contact with John Wilkes Booth at the Parker House in Boston. This is presumed to be where Booth was recruited for the Lincoln kidnapping plot. (28 May, 8 July, and 24 August 1864; also as Mr. V. Clinton at Barnett's Niagara Museum on 28 May 1864.)

- **W. Corse:** CSA, checked in with H.V. Clinton. Corse had been a broker in Alexandria, Virginia and served as a conduit for Confederate correspondence moving north and south. In that role he would have been familiar with Sarah Slater, Josephine Brown, and John Surratt. He was close to General Edwin Lee. (8 November, 20 December 1864)

- **Robert Cox:** cotton trader and Confederate sympathizer who provided Clement C. Clay and Beverley Tucker with their forward headquarters at St. Catharines, Ontario. This safe house was located near the train station on the Niagara rail line between Montreal and Toronto. Cox apparently knew Booth. (His photograph was taken at Notman's Studio in 1864, McCord Museum, Notman Collection.) He registers at Barnett's Niagara Museum on 20 June 1864.

- **B.A. Davis (alternatively H. Davis):** currency broker with offices across from St. Lawrence Hall on Greater St. James Street. The Confederate Secret Service used his office for clandestine meetings. He had dealings with John Wilkes Booth during his visit to Montreal in October 1864 and advanced him money. The Davis who gave Booth money was referred to in the Lincoln Conspiracy Trial as a "broker," most likely from Virginia. Both B.A. Davis and H. Davis fit this description. B.A. Davis registers arriving from Petersburg on 13 February 1865. Both B.A. Davis and H. Davis had their photographs taken at Notman's Studio. (15 February 1865)

- **Jefferson Davis and Varina Davis:** President of the Confederate States of America fled to Montreal after being released from Fortress Monroe. The Davis and Howell families lived in exile in Montreal during 1866. They were supported by publisher John Lovell and other Confederate sympathizers in the city. Davis' personal papers were smuggled into Canada by Varina Davis and stored in the vault of the Bank of Montreal on Place d'Armes. (See McCord Museum, Notman Collection.)

- **Sam Davis:** Confederate courier, captured and sentenced to hang. The sentence was commuted by President Lincoln on receiving a note from Jacob Thompson swearing that Davis, while a courier, was not a spy. (5 November 1864)

- **James Donnelly:** soldier and strong-arm man for the Confederate Secret Service. A ready man with a pistol. (8 June, 24 October 1864, and 4, 14 February 1865)

- **Benjamin Ficklin** and **W.W. Finney:** Confederate agents involved in cotton trading. Ficklin had contact with Brown Brothers Bank and with former Congressman Orville H. Browning. Like Finney, Ficklin was in Canada during the war. He was also in Washington on the day of Lincoln's assassination. He was arrested but never charged, having been vouched for by Orville H. Browning. Ficklin admitted under questioning to having been in Canada and in contact with Beverley Tucker. His partner in founding the *Pony Express*, W.W. Finney, became an active agent for the Confederacy operating out of Halifax and Montreal. He registered at St. Lawrence Hall on 11 August, 8 October 1864. His photograph, taken during the war at Notman's studio, is found in McCord Museum, Notman Collection.

- **General D. M. Frost:** Missouri. Photo in McCord Museum, Notman Collection. (10 October 1864)

- **Colonel James Gordon CSA:** Gordon and Col. Robert Martin were active in Secret Service operations in Canada. Both acknowledged after the war that they heard about Booth's kidnapping plot in Canada. It appears Booth's plans were somewhat of an open secret among Confederates in the country. (Barnett's Niagara Museum on 21, 22 July 1864 and St. Lawrence Hall on 8 March 1865)

- **J.M. Griffiths:** registered as CSA. His role as a Confederate operative is murky but he is definitely at St. Lawrence Hall on 14 October 1864 when important meetings were being held at the hotel.

- **J.W. Headley:** Confederate soldier and active Secret Service operative in Canada. He wrote a very readable account of his service in Canada entitled *Confederate Operations in Canada and New York*, (Neale Publishing: New York, 1906). Like John Yates Beall, Headley was a swashbuckler willing to undertake just about any mission. He registers at St. Lawrence Hall on 17 July 1864.
- **Captain Bennett Hornsby:** native of Kentucky and a successful lawyer. He raised a company of volunteer infantry during the Mexican War. During the Civil War, he was an officer in the CSA. He resigned his commission, perhaps as a result of wounds suffered, and moved to Halifax in 1863 where he became a successful land speculator. He built the famous Tower House on Edinburgh Street and developed the Willow Park area. He was part of the pro-Confederate cabal in Halifax that included Dr. William Almon, Benjamin Wier, and the Catholic Archbishop of Halifax, Thomas Connolly. Hornsby visited Montreal during the war and registered at St. Lawrence Hall. Hornsby, Wier, and Almon all had their photos taken at Notman's Studio in 1864 and 1865. Hornsby was at St. Lawrence Hall 10 November 1864 and 13 February 1865. He became a Canadian citizen after the Civil War.
- **Joseph Hyams:** Confederate agent turned informer. Hyams testified at the trial of Lincoln conspirators regarding attempts by Dr. Luke Blackburn to use yellow fever as a biological agent during the war. Blackburn signed into St. Lawrence Hall in the same timeframe as Major J. Hyams CSA. (31 August 1864)
- **William "Colorado" Jewett:** Confederate agent and business speculator. Participated in the ill-fated Niagara Falls peace talks in 1864. Accompanied John Surratt on his flight to Europe following the Lincoln assassination. (31 August 1864)
- **Robert Cobb Kennedy:** Confederate agent who participated in efforts to burn major hotels in New York City. Captured and executed at Fort Lafayette in New York Harbor just prior to the end of the war. There are a number of Kennedy registrations at St. Lawrence Hall

in the fall of 1864, including one on 1 November 1864 for J.R. Kennedy.
- **Charles Lamar:** blockade runner and slave trader. He orchestrated the arrival of the last slave ship to America just prior to the Civil War. The importation of slaves was illegal but no jury in Savannah was prepared to convict him. He and his father, banker Gazaway Lamar, were both active in blockade running and selling cotton for contraband. Lamar arrived at St. Lawrence Hall on 21 August 1864, the same day as Lafayette C. Baker, head of the National Detective Police. Baker signed in as L.E. Baker and Lamar as Charles de Lamar. Baker had ties to the Lamars through the latter's agent Nelson C. Trowbridge who was in Montreal just prior to the assassination.

Trowbridge told American Consul John F. Potter that he had an appointment to meet Baker in Montreal, but the latter did not show up. This was on 8 April 1865, only seven days before Lincoln's assassination. Nelson C. Trowbridge was an agent for the Lamar family in New York during much of the war. Before the war, he had been a slave trader in league with Charles Lamar and was a part owner of the slave ship *Wanderer*. The Lamars were shipping contraband out of New York Harbor regularly on ships like the *Wild Pigeon*. Trowbridge's correspondence with Gazaway Lamar in April 1865 indicates his business in Canada had to do with selling cotton. He confirmed with U.S. Consul John Potter that he was in Montreal to meet Lafayette Baker. (8 April 1865)
- **Edwin Lee:** Confederate General and veteran Cavalry officer who replaced Jacob Thompson as the Senior Confederate Commissioner in Canada at the end of 1864. Lee was an early advocate of assembling a "destructionist" cadre to operate behind enemy lines. In this strategy, he worked with John Yates Beall while both were convalescing from wounds. They would work together again in Canada. (10 March 1865) (McCord Museum, Notman Collection. Lee's photograph is taken with Bennett Young and key leaders of the St. Albans Raid.)

- **Daniel B. Lucas:** cousin to General Edwin Gray Lee, posted to Canada in 1864 to assist Jacob Thompson with Secret Service operations. Lucas had begun his service in paramilitary operations and privateering in the Chesapeake Bay area. There, he worked closely with John Yates Beall, another agent who would play an important role in Confederate Secret Service operations in Canada. Lucas interviewed Union prisoners captured during the infamous Dahlgren affair to authenticate orders found on Dahlgren's body calling for the assassination of Jefferson Davis and his cabinet. These orders were believed authentic in Richmond and hardened Confederate attitudes toward striking back at Lincoln. It was in this vengeful environment that plans for kidnapping Lincoln were set in motion. When General E.G. Lee was assigned to Canada by Jefferson Davis, Lucas accompanied him as his secretary. Lucas' role in interrogating Federal prisoners establishes him as a Secret Service operative even before his arrival in Montreal. He wrote a biography of John Yates Beall following the latter's execution. The book was published by John Lovell, who sponsored Jefferson Davis and his family in Montreal. *The Montreal Gazette* published a poem by Lucas following the Civil War, entitled "*The Land Where We Were Dreaming*." This became part of the South's "*Lost Cause*" lore. (See photos of both Lucas and Beall, McCord Museum, Notman Collection.)
- **Minor Major CSA:** active agent in the Confederate Secret Service. He was implicated in plots to load explosives, disguised as pieces of coal, onto Federal ships on the Mississippi. Some suspected this ordinance was used to sink the *S.S. Sultana* along with 1,800 POW's from Andersonville Prison Camp returning home in April 1865. (26 January 1864)
- **Captain P.C. Martin:** senior Confederate in Montreal until the arrival of Jacob Thompson, provided Booth with letters of introduction to the "Doctors' Courier Line" in southern Maryland, a group which included Dr. Samuel Mudd. He had a home with his wife and family in Montreal near Union Square. George Kane was a house guest for a time and John Wilkes Booth also visited. Martin was lost at sea, blockade running under mysterious circumstances. At the time, he was transporting contraband, including John Wilkes Booth's wardrobe, to Nassau. He had business ties to the unsavory "Sandy Keith" of Halifax. Keith became an expert in timed explosives during the war and used these skills to commit murder and insurance fraud in the post-war years. (Photograph in the Notman Collection)
- **Col. Robert Martin:** active member of the Confederate Secret Service in Canada. Took part in the attempt to burn New York City's leading hotels. He is found at Barnett's Niagara Museum as L. or R. Martin. (Barnett's Niagara Museum, 26 June 1864)
- **R.G. McCulloch:** (speculative: the evidence is credible but not conclusive). We suspect the registration for J. G. McCulloch on 15 August 1864, arriving from Louisville, Kentucky, may well be R.G. McCulloch, who was an active Confederate Secret Service agent. (Louisville was a common arrival point of convenience used by both sides.) McCulloch was involved with the Torpedo Bureau in employing explosives disguised as lumps of coal to sink Union shipping. He was captured off the Florida coast trying to escape the country on 17 May 1865. The arresting officer wrote to Edwin Stanton that McCulloch was part of the "Poison and Dagger Service of the Confederacy."
- **Dr. M.A. Pallen:** Confederate agent charged with inspecting (and spying on) Federal prison camps. An active member of the Confederate Secret Service. (7, 12, 15 October 1864)
- **George Payne** and **Hezekiah Payne:** Confederate bankers with ties to the Bank of Ontario. Payne checks in a day ahead of Confederate agent "Colorado" Jewett who would accompany John Surratt on his escape to Europe following the Lincoln assassination. (31 August and 1 September 1864) (Photographs in the McCord Museum, Notman Collection.)
- **John Porterfield:** banker who hid John Surratt in his home near McGill University following the Lincoln

assassination. Porterfield had ties to the Bank of Ontario. Porterfield's townhouse was in Prince of Wales Terrace, at the corner of McTavish and Sherbrooke Streets. Porterfield played an important role in orchestrating the Confederate assault on the U.S. currency, the "Greenback." He founded a Confederate colony at Niagara-on-the-Lake after the war and never returned to the United States. (Photo taken at Notman's Studio, McCord Museum, Notman Collection.)

- **General William Preston:** Kentuckian, originally a Confederate Commissioner in Europe. His wife and children lived in Montreal during the war. He was in Montreal during the busy month of October 1864 when much of the senior echelon of the Confederate Secret Service was at St. Lawrence Hall. John Wilkes Booth was also present at the hotel at this time. (6, 30 September 1864)

- **George Sanders:** lifelong advocate of assassinating tyrants, he spent considerable time with Booth during the actor's stay in Montreal in October 1864. When it became known that Booth was staying at St. Lawrence Hall, Sanders checked out of the Ottawa Hotel and moved two blocks east to register at St. Lawrence Hall. Here, he checked in along with Confederate spy, Belle Boyd, and identified himself as being from "Dixie." (25 October 1864)

- **Sarah Slater:** courier, spy, consort of John Surratt and probably John Wilkes Booth as well. Given her intimacy with Surratt and Booth, Sarah Slater was almost certainly an insider in the plot against Lincoln. She checks into St. Lawrence Hall with interesting company, including her lover, John Surratt, but also with Copperhead B. Wood and possibly National Detective Police leader Walter Pollack. (13 September 1864, 10 January, 15 February, and 18 April 1865)

- **Colonel L.R. Smart:** active Confederate operative in Hamilton area. Signed in as J. Smart from Hamilton. Checked in with General D.M. Frost CSA. (10 October 1864 as Major John Smart.) (24 August 1864) (Photo in McCord Museum, Notman Collection.)

- **J.S. Snyder:** arrived with Confederate Commissioner Beverley Tucker 11 November 1864 from the forward Confederate operating base in St. Catharines. Who Snyder was remains unclear but he was certainly traveling in Confederate circles.

- **Rev. John Kinsey Stewart:** active Confederate agent in Canada and an early advocate of kidnapping Lincoln. His original scheme for kidnapping the president was presented to Jefferson Davis, who thought the plan impractical. Following the infamous Dahlgren Raid on Richmond, where orders for the murder of Davis and his cabinet were recovered, Confederate attitudes toward Lincoln hardened. Stewart met Colonel Edwin Lee (later Brigadier General) before the latter took up his post in Canada. Stewart was at St. Lawrence Hall during Booth's stay at the hotel. (25 October 1864)

- **Benjamin Stringfellow:** Confederate agent and would-be assassin. He shares a suite of rooms with another suspected Confederate R./D./C./ Watson. (14, 30 August, 13 September, 8 October, and 3 November 1864)

- **John Harrison Surratt:** John Wilkes Booth's most trusted lieutenant. On 5 November, Surratt checked in with fellow Confederates Josephine and Robert Brown, J.(H.) Thompson, William (J.) Cleary, Sam Davis, and Geo Payne. Also checking in were Confederate agents J. Corse and Col. J. Gordon CSA, and Copperhead Benjamin Wood (Mr. Wood). Surratt registers more than a dozen times at St. Lawrence Hall, sometimes as J. Harrison and other times using a highly calligraphic J. Surratt. On 18 April 1865, following the Lincoln assassination, he uses both aliases side by side.

- **Jacob Thompson:** Senior Confederate Commissioner in Canada prior to the arrival in late 1864 of General Edwin Lee. Thompson has multiple registrations at St. Lawrence Hall, sometimes altering his initials. (2 June, 24 August, 4 September, 14 and 20 October 1864, and 20 March 1865.) Photograph in McCord Museum, Notman Collection, under file *Mr. Cameron's Group.*

- **Beverley Tucker:** charged with orchestrating a huge cotton-for-contraband deal out of Montreal. In these efforts, he had the support of the U.S. Treasury Department and the White House. The value of the cotton exceeded half a billion dollars in 1864 currency, a staggering sum for the era. We know from Lafayette Baker and O.H. Browning's diary that Tucker was also in Montreal earlier in September and October of 1864. (10 November 1864)
- **Mr. and Mrs. Watson:** very likely R.D. Watson, who was involved in trading contraband for cotton. He took out an account at the Bank of Montreal for just under $13,000, which was a substantial sum at that time. A field grade officer in the Confederate army earned $100 a month. Watson's money was released to his heirs after the war. R.D. Watson wrote John Surratt on 19 March 1865, asking him to come to New York on urgent business. This was just a month before the assassination. Surratt was instructed to answer by telegraph to 178½ Water Street in New York City. This address has remained a source of mystery since it was first mentioned in the trial of the Lincoln conspirators. On 18 June, 14 August, 17 and 25 October 1864, W. Watson registered as Mr. and Mrs. Watson, Liverpool; B. Watson, London; and later, Dr. Baron C. Watson.
- **Benjamin Wier:** successful merchant and shipping magnate in Halifax. He owned warehouses along the harbor and became a force in civic and, later, national politics. He was a pronounced Confederate sympathizer who flew a Confederate flag over his warehouse entrance and accepted Confederate currency. Both Wier and Dr. William Almon received letters of thanks from Judah Benjamin and President Jefferson Davis.[5] Whenever a Confederate vessel visited the city, its officers would be hosted by Wier, Almon, and other prominent Confederate sympathizers such as Archbishop Thomas Connolly. Wier was active in blockade running and his business often took him to Montreal where he had his photograph taken at Notman's Studio in 1864. Following the collapse of the Confederacy, Wier, like many pro-Southern Canadians, turned his energies toward building Canada's own Confederation and later served in the Canadian Senate. (Photographs of Hornsby, Wier, and Bishop Connolly are found in the Notman Collection 1864-1865)
- **Bennett Young:** Commander of the St. Albans Raiders, registered with his brother 26 July 1864. A number of St. Albans Raiders turned up at St. Lawrence Hall both before and after the assault in October 1864. Many had their photographs taken at Notman's.

REPUBLICANS

- **George Ashmun:** former Congressman from Massachusetts who had ties to Canada through his legal work for the Grand Trunk Railway. Early in the war, he was sent by U.S. Secretary of State William Seward as a spokesman to Canada, but the mission was cancelled when Lord Lyons, the British Ambassador to the United States, protested. Ashmun was involved in cotton trading during the war. He approached President Lincoln for a special cotton license the evening of 14 April 1865, just as Lincoln was about to leave for Ford's Theatre. Lincoln asked Ashmun to come back in the morning. Ashmun's name appears several times in the St. Lawrence Hall register. After the war, he served on the board of Thomas Durant's notoriously corrupt Union Pacific Railway. Durant was deeply involved with efforts to exchange Confederate cotton for contraband. A number of important people in this story appearing at St. Lawrence Hall in 1864-1865 had ties to Durant and the corrupt Union Pacific Railroad. (16 June, 27 September 1864)
- **J.F. Benjamin:** Republican delegate to the 1864 convention from Missouri. Benjamin was born in New York but educated in Texas and Missouri. (15 August 1864)
- **John Bingham:** Radical Republican and a member of Salmon Chase's presidential committee, which was well represented in Montreal in the summer and fall of 1864. Bingham was a lead prosecutor under Joseph Holt in the military commission that tried the Lincoln

conspirators. Both he and Holt worked closely with his superior, Secretary of War Edwin Stanton. John Bingham registers at St. Lawrence Hall from a number of locations, including London and Philadelphia. Bingham's law office was in New Philadelphia, Ohio. After the war, Bingham would become involved with the notoriously corrupt Thomas C. Durant and the Union Pacific Railroad. He was implicated in receiving bribes from Durant. It is noteworthy that in the fall of 1864, Durant was involved in Confederate Beverley Tucker's cotton-for-contraband scheme centered in Montreal. Durant's Union Pacific runs like a thread through this story, touching a number of Republicans who were in Montreal.

- **Crawford, Smead, and Dickinson:** (speculative) These names appeared on 11 August 1864 as a party arriving from the U.S. All three names match those of Republican delegates to the 1864 Republican convention. Tha(d) Stevens from Philadelphia registered the next day.
- **J. Churchill:** registered just after Republican **E. (Edgar) Ketchum** in the guest book.[6] Both Ketchum and Churchill would play prominent roles in the impeachment proceedings against President Johnson. (Coincidently, John Surratt registered at St. Lawrence Hall during this period using his regular alias J. Harrison.) The next day, on 13 August, Republican Congressman **George A. Halsey** of New Jersey, a noted Radical, arrived in Montreal, listing New York as his point of departure. (12, 13 August 1864)
- **John Cochrane:** New York war Democrat turned Republican who supported the Radical Republican agenda and opposed Lincoln's war and Reconstruction policies as too moderate. He was nominated as Vice President under John Fremont in a rogue convention in 1864 designed to unseat Lincoln. The movement failed, but Cochrane's opposition to Lincoln continued. (9 August 1864)
- **Schuyler Colfax:** (speculative) Colfax signed in as Wm. Colfax from New York on 25 July 1864. Colfax was the grandson of a Revolutionary War hero who

commanded Washington's Life Guards. Colfax was born in New York but later settled in Indiana where he was elected to Congress. He founded the South Bend *Register,* a pro-Republican newspaper that he ran for three decades. In 1863, he was elected Speaker of the House and aligned himself with the Radical wing of the Republican Party. (25 July 1864. See also Barnett's Niagara Museum, 20 June 1864.)

- **Henry Winter Davis:** (speculative) A Radical Republican Congressman who never forgave President Lincoln for pocket vetoing the Wade-Davis Bill that would have placed post-war Reconstruction of the South under Congressional and, by extension, Radical control. This pocket veto is viewed as the final break between Lincoln and the Radicals. Davis attended meetings in New York during the summer of 1864 aimed at denying Lincoln the Republican nomination. A number of those involved in this plot turned up in Montreal in the summer and fall of 1864. On 19 November 1864, we see a registration for *Henry Winter,* one day after Salmon Chase's presidential committee members *Pomeroy* and *Spaulding* register at the hotel. John Harrison Surratt used his middle name as his last name in registering at St. Lawrence Hall. If John Harrison Surratt could become John Harrison, why could Henry Winter Davis not become Henry Winter? There are registrations for both Henry Winter and Rev. H.W. Davis at St. Lawrence Hall. Aliases, altered initials, the use of prefixes such as Dr., Rev., or Judge were not uncommon at St. Lawrence Hall in 1864 and early 1865.
- **Simeon Draper:** (speculative) Republican, corrupt collector of revenue from the New York Custom House. Involved with Edwin Stanton in shipping large amounts of cotton out of Savannah after the fall of the city. Registered as H.S. Draper from New York. (26 June 1864)
- **W.B. Foulke:** registered with his son Joseph on 12 August, arriving from the U.S.[7] This was almost certainly former Republican Congressman P.B. Foulke, who was involved in trading cotton for contraband with

the Confederacy. His son Joseph Foulke was back at the hotel the following month on 24 September 1864 at the same time as Congressman Fernando Wood, twice Mayor of New York and a notorious Lincoln hater.

- **George S. Hale:** Republican delegate from Massachusetts and a supporter of Salmon Chase and the Radicals. He checked in the same day as Radical Congressman Tha(d) Stevens. (12 August 1864)
- **George A. Halsey:** of New Jersey, a noted Radical, arrived in Montreal, listing New York as his point of departure. (12-13 August 1864). Tha(d) Stevens also registered at this time.
- **Hon. James Harlan:** Radical Republican and Lincoln opponent checks in with **Hon. J. Doolittle**, conservative Republican. Doolittle was probably there on cotton business but what Harlan, a die-hard anti-Lincoln Radical, was doing in Montreal is unclear. (16 August 1865)
- **Jonathan Harvey:** Republican from Indiana. Registered as J. Harvey. (27 July, 3 August 1864) On 27 July, he arrives from Washington, DC. Registers at Barnett's Niagara Museum on 1 July 1864.
- **E. Ketchum:** We believe this to be Edgar Ketchum, a powerful member of New York's Republican Party.
- **A.A. Lawrence:** Free Soil advocate who was an early financial supporter of John Brown. Over time, as Brown's violent tactics became known, Lawrence sought to distance himself from the massacres committed in Kansas. Lawrence is an enigma. While working to keep Kansas a slave-free state, Lawrence was the leader of the New England Textile industry, which depended on Southern cotton for manufacturing. Lawrence and a delegation of Boston Brahmins, including names like Appleton and Amory, were in Montreal at St. Lawrence Hall on 14 April 1865, the day Lincoln was assassinated.
- **Gov. E.D. Morgan:** New York. Governor Morgan was deeply involved in cotton trading. There are more than a dozen Morgan registrations in the summer and fall of 1864. The initials are altered but Morgan's role in cotton trading is well documented. One of the most interesting is for D. Morgan. Typical of these regis-

trations were C.E. Morgan and D. Morgan. (28 July, 2 August, 16 September 1864, and 11 March 1865)

- **W.C. Noyes:** stalwart supporter of the Radical Republican agenda and Salmon P. Chase. An ardent foe of Lincoln, he, along with **John M. Forbes**, worked to stage a new "Union" convention to dump Lincoln from the Republican ticket. These efforts continued through the summer and fall of 1864. Both Noyes and Forbes appear in the St. Lawrence Hall register. Noyes from New York, with initials reversed as C.W. Noyes, and Forbes registered as J.M. Forbes. (4 July, 6, 7 August, 3 October 1864)
- **George Palmer:** Republican, New York (12 October 1864) A Democrat turned Republican, a founding member of the Free Soil Party. Served in Congress 1857-1861. He was a delegate at the Baltimore 1864 Republican Convention.
- **R. Peck:** Republican delegate from New York. (29 July 1864)
- **S. Pomeroy:** Republican from Kansas and the head of Salmon Chase's presidential committee. He checked in with E. Spaulding; both were involved in Salmon Chase's presidential run. Registering the next day was Henry Winter (Davis). In November, Pomeroy registered as J.S. Pomeroy. He did so only days before William Sprague, another Chase supporter and then Governor of Rhode Island, who arrived on November 24, 1864, traveling with a lady. (26 August, 18 November 1864)
- **A. Pond:** Republican, Saratoga Springs, New York (7 October 1864)
- **John F. Potter:** U.S. Consul in Montreal and Congressman from Wisconsin, considered a Radical. Potter led what amounted to a witch hunt to rid the Federal bureaucracy of clerks thought to have Confederate sympathies. As a result of his McCarthy-like investigation, hundreds were purged from the government. This investigation of disloyalty would have brought Potter into close contact with Lafayette Baker of the National Detective Police and by extension Baker's boss, Edwin Stanton. Potter was in Montreal during Booth's visit in the fall of 1864

and into 1865. He observed that Booth may have been in Montreal again in 1865. (17 July 1864)

- **Sherman S. Rogers:** successful lawyer from Bath, New York and an active Republican. May have had ties to Governor and later Senator E.D. Morgan who was active in trading contraband for cotton. (27 August 1864)
- **John Sanford:** Republican, Massachusetts. Sanford had close ties to General Benjamin Butler. After the war, he and Butler became involved in the infamous "Sanford" tax collection scandal. Sanford registered a number of times during the summer and fall of 1864 using various initials, sometimes arriving from Boston and sometimes Chicago. (11 August 1864)
- **Alexander Shepard:** Radical Republican and Washington powerbroker, was in Montreal in August, listing his home as Washington, D.C. Shepard was a vocal abolitionist and friend of Frederick Douglass; he was closely allied with the Radical Republicans. (17 August 1864)
- **E.G. Spaulding:** Radical Republican and Congressman from New York, checked in at that same time as Samuel Pomeroy. Both were key players in Salmon Chase's presidential campaign. Spaulding played an important role in the introduction of the new American fiat national currency. Sometimes called the father of the "Greenback," Spaulding registered as R.E. Spaulding, Syracuse (26 August 1864)
- **Gov. William Sprague:** Salmon Chase's son-in-law. Married to highly-political Kate Chase. Was a key member of Chase's presidential committee and heavily involved in cotton trading. (25 October, 14 November 1864) **T. Howe,** Republican delegate from Wisconsin, supportive of the Radical agenda, checked in with William Sprague who, in addition to supporting Salmon Chase, was also deeply involved in cotton trading.
- **Thaddeus Stevens:** Radical Republican and Lincoln opponent from Pennsylvania registers as Tha(d) Stevens from a roughly-scribbled "USA" in July 1864 and from Philadelphia in August 1864. (11 July, 12 August

1864) Note the concentration of Radical Republicans arriving in mid-August 1864 that includes E. Ketchum, J. Churchill, George Hale, William Sprague, Alexander Shepard, J. Wilson, George Halsey, and others.

- **H.H. Van Dyck:** newspaperman, financier, senior official in the Treasury Department, and Republican delegate from Albany. He checked in with Mr. and Mrs. Ramsey and Kelly. Both Ramsey and Kelly were also Republican delegates, Ramsey from Minnesota and Kelly from New York. (14 June 1864, and 23, 30 March 1865)
- **J.A. Wilson:** (speculative) arrived on 19 August 1864 from Washington D.C. when St. Lawrence Hall was full of Republican and Democratic politicians, including some Radicals. Wilson arrives with (D.M.S.) Ford, also of Washington, D.C. We believe this is Radical Republican J.F. Wilson. In October, he checked in with D.S. Skinner and Charles Abbot from Rhode Island as well as newspaperman W.B. Shaw, *New York Herald*. (19 August, 27 October 1864)
- **W.W. Wilson** and **Mr. and Mrs. Goodrich:** (speculative) arrived on 10 August 1864. We believe this may have been Henry Wilson and John Goodrich who belonged to the Radical wing of the Massachusetts Republican Party.
- **J.S. Wright:** Republican delegate from Ohio (22 June 1864)

NEWSPAPERMEN

Newspapers were deeply political and closely aligned with one party or the other. The concept of balanced, unbiased reporting was largely alien to this era.

- **A.G. Boynton:** *Detroit Free Press* (6 July 1864)
- **M.M. Davis:** *Portage City Recorder* Wisconsin. Had ties to Radical Republican John F. Potter, American Consul in Montreal. (19 September 1864)
- **J.R. Elder:** editor of the Democratic *Indiana Sentinel*. Elder had openly opposed the Emancipation Proclamation. (7 August 1864) Elder arrived with **W. D. Bickham** editor of the *Dayton Journal*. Bickham was

close to General Rosecrans who was then being touted as a replacement for Lincoln on the Republican or Union ticket. On the same day that Elder and Bickham registered at St. Lawrence Hall, so did Gov. Horatio Seymour of New York.

- **R. Huddock:** *New York Tribune* (24 June 1864) Huddock checked in with robber baron J. Gould. (24, 29 June 1864)
- **W.H. Kent:** *New York Tribune* (30 August 1864)
- **Manton Marble:** editor of the *New York World* and a key participant in the New York-centered "August" anti-Lincoln scheme to force Lincoln off the 1864 ticket. There is a registration in July 1864 for a Miss Marble who booked two rooms. Having wives or children take the lead in registering at St. Lawrence Hall was not uncommon.
- **S.B. McCracken:** *Detroit Free Press* (24 June 1864)
- **W.B. Shaw:** senior Washington correspondent for the *New York Herald*. (22 September 1864)
- **George Townsend:** (speculative) George A. Townsend was a newspaperman and journalist from New York City. He wrote the first account of Lincoln's assassination and the subsequent execution of the conspirators. He signs in as George (E.) Townsend from NYC on 21 October. Earlier, on 12 October, we find a registration for J. Gath; "Gath" was Townsend's legendary nom de plume. Townsend ran into Booth at the Pennsylvania Hotel in Washington on 26 March 1865, only two weeks before the assassination. While he was talking with Booth, a group of men arrived, presumably his co-conspirators, and they adjourned to a private room.[8] Townsend had just returned from Europe and was, at the time, a correspondent for the Democratic-leaning *New York World*.[9] "*By mid-1864, Townsend returned to America and took up editing and writing for a collection of New York papers...*"[10] He wrote under pseudonyms for the Republican *New York Times* and other publications like *The New York World*. He would spend a lifetime studying and writing about the assassination, beginning with his 1866 account: *The Life, Crime and Capture of John Wilkes Booth*. Townsend was a friend and contemporary of Mark Twain and a prolific author and journalist. It was Townsend who provided the first report that the telegraph wires out of Washington went down for a time on the evening of 14 April immediately following Lincoln's assassination. He never elaborated on this assertion or speculated as to why it might have occurred.

- **W.D. Wallach:** newspaperman, Washington, D.C. His brother was Richard Wallach, Republican Mayor of Washington, D.C. W.D. Wallach, owner and editor of the *Washington Star*, arrived at the hotel on 1 October. Richard Wallach was a strong Union man but he adamantly opposed emancipation and universal suffrage. He got the job of mayor because the previous mayor had been arrested for failing to take the Loyalty Oath. One might imagine this would have made both brothers cautious in discussing their politics. (1 October 1864)
- **W.H.L. Whitman:** *Boston Journal* (30 August 1864)
- **George Wilkes:** New York, *Spirit of the Times*, was part of the August Conspiracy to dump Lincoln from the Republican 1864 ticket. (13 August 1864)

DEMOCRATS

- **Jeremiah Black:** sent by Edwin Stanton as his representative to open secret discussions with the Confederates in the summer and early fall of 1864, when it appeared Lincoln would lose the election. Black, a Democrat and friend of Stanton, served with Confederate Canadian Commissioner Jacob Thompson in the Buchanan administration and knew him well. Black was already involved with the New York "August Conspiracy" to dump Lincoln from the Republican ticket. Stanton must have known this, which suggests that his own position regarding Lincoln's 1864 candidacy was in doubt. As always, Stanton was looking to his own interests. There are a number of Black registrations at St. Lawrence Hall, including one for J.S. Black on 24 April 1865, but none specifically for Jeremiah Black. But the historical record is clear that Black went to Canada before the 1864 election to negotiate a deal to protect Edwin Stanton in the event that Lincoln would lose in November. There is a registration for J. Black at Barnett's Museum in Niagara for 1 July 1864 and his name appears alongside J. Thompson.

- **Hon. S. (Sunset) Cox:** Ohio. Resented the Lincoln Administration suggestion that anyone opposed to their war policies was disloyal. Cox appears to have ties to super banker Jay Cooke. (3 August 1864)
- **John Dana:** Maine. Democratic delegate 1864 convention. (3 September 1864)
- **E.J. Dix:** (speculative) John Dix was a political general closely associated with Thomas Durant and the corrupt Union Pacific Railroad. Durant was involved in trading cotton for contraband with the Confederacy. (13 August 1864)
- **Cyrus Field:** brother of anti-Lincoln conspirator and New York businessman W.D. Field. Field was one of the prime movers behind the Atlantic Cable that connected North America to Europe by telegraph. (15, 22 September 1864)
- **James D. Field:** (speculative) registered as J., D., or C. Field arriving from Hamilton, and in August as J.J. Field. Field was one of the leaders of the dump Lincoln movement (or "August Conspiracy") centered in New York City but with national reach. His brother, Cyrus Field, checked into St. Lawrence Hall two days earlier on 15 September 1864. (10 August, 17 September 1864.)
- **S.R. Lyman:** Democratic delegate for Maine (3 September 1864)
- **W.B. Matchett:** defrocked minister and Democratic political fixer. He operated in the murky periphery of Democratic politics. He would become involved in efforts to support Sanford Conover/Charles Dunham during the Andrew Johnson impeachment trial. (23 September 1864)
- **S.S. Marshall:** Democrat from Illinois signed in as C.S. Marshall (24, 27 August 1864)
- **Hon. John S. Phelps:** Democrat from Missouri (16 July, 24 August, and 15 October 1864).
- **William Radford:** Democratic Congressman from New York who voted for the 13th Amendment, registered at St. Lawrence Hall on 20 August 1864.
- **E.J. Riley:** Adjutant General for New York who had, for a time, commanded the 40th Infantry. This regiment was raised out of New York City's Mozart Hall, a stronghold of Mayor, and later Congressman, Fernando Wood. Riley was named Adjutant General for New York. (18 October 1864)
- **Gov. H. Seymour:** New York, peace candidate seeking to become the Democratic Party's presidential nominee. Heavily backed by the Confederate Secret Service, he was a regular at St. Lawrence Hall. Jacob Thompson, head of the Confederate Secret Service in Canada, in his final report to Secretary of State Judah Benjamin, stated that he met Gov. Seymour and Congressman Benjamin Wood a number of times in the summer and fall of 1864. Seymour often used the alias Jas Seymour or William Seymour. On 7 August and 11 August 1864, Seymour arrives from St. Catharines, the forward operating base of Confederates. Seymour was also at St. Lawrence Hall in October 1864 when John Wilkes Booth was at the hotel. (11 July, 16 October, 27 November 1864)
- **James Singleton:** associate of Republican powerbroker and former Senator O.H. Browning, who was deeply involved in illicit cotton trading. In possession of cotton licenses signed by Lincoln himself. (2 August 1864)
- **R. Underwood:** Lexington, Kentucky. Pro-Union Democrat who considered Lincoln a tyrant. (18 August 1864)
- **John Van Buren:** Free Soil, War Democrat from New York registered 28 October 1864. Van Buren was deeply involved in the presidential campaign of General George McClellan. (28 October 1864)
- **Fernando and Benjamin Wood:** Fernando Wood was the former Mayor of New York City. Benjamin Wood was editor of the *New York Herald*. Both were New York congressmen and virulent Lincoln haters. Benjamin appears to have been on the Confederate payroll and registered along with Confederates Luke

Blackburn and Sarah Slater. (2, 10, 11 July; 24 October; 5, 15, 27 November 1864; and 28 February 1865)

NATIONAL DETECTIVE POLICE (U.S. SECRET SERVICE AND JUDGE ADVOCATE GENERAL'S OFFICE)

- **Lafayette C. Baker:** head of the National Detective Police, who worked for Secretary of War Edwin Stanton. The National Detective Police was the antecedent of the modern-day Secret Service and the FBI. He registered a number of times from June 1864 through March 1865 (21 August, 20 September, 13 October 1864, and 16, 20 March 1865)

- **John Bingham:** Judge Advocate General. See Bingham under Republicans.

- **T.T. Eckert:** Chief of Telegraphy for the War Department, reported directly to Secretary of War Edwin Stanton. Lincoln asked Eckert to accompany him to Ford's Theatre on 14 April, remarking on his great physical strength, but he begged off because of work. Eckert's boss, Edwin Stanton, had already refused Lincoln Eckert's attendance, again because of his workload. Eckert became one of the key interrogators of the Lincoln assassins. He was charged with interrogating the mysterious and stoic Lewis Payne. The registration for 27 July appeared to be for G.G., G.T., or T.T. Eckert Ohio, which was Eckert's home state. Registering nearby was robber baron Jay Gould, who would later be involved with Eckert at Western Union. (27 July 1864) A few days earlier, on 22 July 1864, what appears to be T.T. or Y.F. Eckert from Cincinnati, Ohio registers at Barnett's Niagara Museum. The two signatures are clearly made by the same man. Eckert's writing style made his T's sometimes appear to be Y's, F's, or even elaborate G's. He was traveling with his son and namesake, Master Thomas (T. Eckert), making the ID nearly certain. Finally, these two signatures are a good match with Eckert's surviving autographs.

- **Joseph Holt:** Judge Advocate General responsible for prosecuting the Lincoln conspirators. The name

Holt appears twice in the St. Lawrence Hall register as O.H. Holt and J.L. Holt on 16 July 1864 and 3 February 1865. On 3 September, he registers as J. Holt at Barnett's Niagara Falls Museum. In July, Holt arrived at St. Lawrence Hall in the company of Francis Whitaker, a major meat supplier to the U.S. Army from St Louis. Also in the party was former Republican Congressman George Ashmun, who was involved in cotton trading. On 3 February, J. Holt arrived with H.H. Emmons, who was involved in cotton trading and was William Seward's unofficial liaison with the Confederate Secret Service in Canada. Emmons also had ties to N.C. Trowbridge, who represented Savannah's powerful Lamar family in New York and Montreal, especially in cotton trading and blockade running. Trowbridge also had business ties to National Detective Police Chief Lafayette Baker. (16 July 1864, 3 February 1865) (Also A.J. Holt Barnett's Museum 17 September 1864)

- **J.L. McPhail:** (speculative) Provost Marshal of Baltimore who would arrest Confederate potential spy Mrs. Slater or someone by that name in May 1865.[11] He sent her as a prisoner to Judge Advocate General Prosecutor Burnett, who promptly released her. (7 October 1864)

- **Edwards Pierrepont:** This is speculative, but the hotel registration of 27 October 1864 is intriguing. Pierrepont Edwards (first and last names reversed) registered on that day. Edwards Pierrepont was a member of the Lincoln Administration and attached to Edwin Stanton's Judge Advocate General's office. He was a strong supporter of Stanton, Chase, and the Radical Republicans. (27 October 1864)

- **Walter Pollack:** senior detective, National Detective Police, worked for Secretary Edwin Stanton. Like Baker, he was in Montreal frequently. Pollack checked in with John Wilkes Booth and Confederate agent Dr. Luke Blackburn on 18 October 1864. He checked in with a (P.) H. Ballantine on 3 September 1865, arriving from New York. Perhaps Ballantine was another member of the National Detective Police. Pollack checked in with or alongside Confederate spy and courier Sarah Slater on 15 February 1865. He checked in again on 23 February 1865. In the St. Lawrence Hall Departure Book, Pollack is noted in a margin note next to the name T. Jones. This implies an affiliation between Jones and Pollack. Perhaps Pollack was tailing Jones or had some other affiliation that the hotel staff noted. 2 May 1864.

DOUBLE AGENTS

- **Charles A. Dunham:** a.k.a. Sanford Conover, James Watson Wallace, J. Wallace, and J. Wallis. Dunham was at St. Lawrence Hall several times during the summer and fall of 1864 and well into 1865. He was the star witness against the Lincoln conspirators, but some of his testimony proved to be perjury. He carefully mixed facts with lies, so it is difficult to tease out the truth in his testimony, but he appeared to be close enough to events in Montreal to have some inkling of Confederate plans.

    Dunham had a long association with Edwin Stanton and was being paid handsomely for his testimony by Judge Advocate General Holt and John A. Bingham. This amounted to suborning perjury, which is a serious crime. When arrested in Montreal for bad debts, just before the trial of the Lincoln conspirators, the Secretary of War went to *extraordinary* lengths to have him released from jail and returned to Washington. (20 September, 3, 14 October 1864.)

- **Richard Montgomery:** There are several registrations for the name Montgomery at St. Lawrence Hall. He appears to have been a double agent who funneled Confederate correspondence to Edwin Stanton. He also turns up as one of Charles Dunham's perjured witnesses in the trial of the Lincoln Conspirators. (18 July, 24 August, 1 September 1864.)

BANKERS AND BUSINESSMEN

- **J. Barnes:** agent for Brown Brothers Bank and dry goods king A.T. Stewart. Stewart profited from wartime contracts and was a regular contributor to the Republican Party. Mrs. Lincoln borrowed money from Stewart. (4 November 1864) Mrs. Lincoln owed considerable money to Stewart because of her obsessive shopping. In all, her debts were said to total $27,000 most of which was owed to Stewart.

- **Charles Barney:** (antecedent of *Smith Barney*) registered the day after banker Jay Cooke. Barney had close ties to both Cooke and Salmon Chase. His registrations coincided with other names associated with Salmon Chase's presidential committee, such as Spaulding, Pomeroy, Sprague, and his own brother, Hiram Barney. (12 September, 26 October 1864)

- **H. Barney:** close to Secretary of the Treasury Salmon Chase and under his patronage was made Collector of Revenues at the notoriously corrupt New York Custom House. His subordinates at the Custom House, including Henry Stanton, became entangled in numerous scandals involving contraband shipments to the Confederacy in return for fat bribes. When Chase left the cabinet in 1864 and renewed his ambitions to become President, Barney was soon replaced. He continued to support Chase's presidential campaign and was known to have loaned the former Secretary money that apparently was never repaid. Barney was also close to William Sprague, the former Governor of Rhode Island who married the beautiful and highly political Kate Chase. Both Barney and Sprague were senior members of Chase's presidential committee. William Sprague, Hiram Barney, and Charles Barney all turned up in Montreal in the summer and fall of 1864. (12 August, 12 September, 25 October 1864)

- **James Brown:** *Brown Brothers* London & New York. Specialized in financing the three-way cotton trade between the South, New York, and England. Brown Brothers had links to Confederate agent Benjamin Ficklin in cotton trading. Ficklin was in Canada during the war and was in Washington the day of the assassination. He was arrested but never charged, having been vouched for by former Congressman Orville H. Browning. Ficklin admitted under questioning to having been in Canada on cotton business and having been in contact with Beverley Tucker. His partner in founding the *Pony Express*, W.W. Finney, became an active agent for the Confederacy operating out Halifax and Montreal. Finney registered at St. Lawrence Hall on 11 August and 8 October 1864. His photograph, taken during the war years, is in the McCord Museum, Notman Collection.

- **Jay Cooke:** super banker, strong supporter of Salmon Chase, registered on 25 October 1864 when Booth and Surratt were at St. Lawrence Hall. Earlier that summer, his family registered at Barnett's Museum in Niagara on 22 June 1864. Cooke was close to his family so it is likely he was vacationing with them. Four days later, he registers at St. Lawrence Hall on 27 July, arriving from "N Falls, US." This suggests that he and his family may have been staying at the famous Cataract Hotel on the American side of the Falls. In November 1864, following his sojourn in Montreal, Booth deposited a $1,500 check in Cooke Brothers Bank in Washington.

- **William Fargo:** founder of Wells Fargo and American Express, in Montreal several times that summer and fall. (6 December 1864, 14 March 1865)

- **W. Farrington:** founder of the Union and Planters Bank in Memphis. Farrington made his fortune during the war presumably trading in cotton. (18 August 1864)

- **R.B. Forbes:** regular at St. Lawrence Hall in 1864. He was a famous seafarer and shipbuilder who made his fortune in the Opium Wars in China. He offered to intercept blockade runners if allowed to keep the prize, but the Navy Department under Gideon Wells was not keen on privateers doing the Navy's work. He undertook to build gunboats for sale directly to Congress. What he was doing in Montreal is unclear but it likely touched on blockade running. (22 July, 23 August 1864)

- **W.A. Goodwyn** and **John Leech:** appear to have been involved in the cotton trade.[12] Also from Memphis, we find **W.A. Miller** and **A.E. Gibson** who, like Goodwyn and Leech, were likely there on cotton business.[13] (12 November, 26 December 1864, and 25 February 1865)

- **Jay Gould:** noted robber baron, sometimes referred to as the dark genius of Wall Street. Involved in cotton trading. Gould had close ties to T.T. Eckert. (24, 29 June, 15 July, 13 August 1864) Eckert claimed that he did not meet Gould, who became his business patron at Western Union, until the early 1870's, but their paths appear to cross at St. Lawrence Hall in the summer of 1864.

- **A.S. Hatch, Harvey Fisk,** and **George Bliss:** bankers representing Jay Cooke and Company were in Montreal. Also there were **James (Diamond Jim) Fisk, Louis Kuhn (Kuhn, Loeb & Co., later part of Lehman Brothers)** and also possibly banker **Russell Sage**. (3 July 1864) James Fisk began his career as a sales agent for **Jordan Marsh** in Washington, where his liberal wining, dining, and bribes produced a steady stream of orders for army uniforms and coats. All of the above were likely involved in cotton trading with the Confederacy. (9, 17 June; 12 August; 5, 7 September; 25, 26 October; 5 December 1864; 30 March 1865)

- **E.M. Hotchkiss:** New Haven, Connecticut. We presume this was someone associated with Hotchkiss and Sons artillery shell makers. 2, 7 September 1864. Other names associated with arms manufacturing that turned up in Montreal include Snow, Parker, Savage, Stone, Whitney, Remington, Spencer, and Fulsom.

- **Henry (C.W./C.H.) Starnes:** President of the Bank of Ontario branch on Place d'Armes. Because of their large deposits, the Confederates effectively controlled this institution and used it for money laundering. After Booth was killed at Garrett's farm, soldiers found on his person a Bank of Ontario money order signed by Starnes, misinterpreted as Stanus in the trial records of the Lincoln conspirators. Starnes went on to become Mayor of Montreal. After the war he became involved in the 'Pacific Railroad' scandal that brought down the MacDonald government in Canada. Many of the American bankers and politicians hovering around Montreal in 1864-1865 would have known Starnes and many were also involved in this ugly scandal. (4 June 1864)

- **L./J.A. Milbank:** J. Milbank funded Borden's canned and condensed milk in the years leading up to the war.

With the start of the Civil War, canned and condensed milk became staple rations for Federal troops. (29 July 1864, New York)

- **E.L. Oppenheim:** partner of a London-based banking house with operations in New York (16 August 1864)
- **C.R. Otis:** registered as a "Boston Traveler," indicating he was one of Jay Cooke's salesmen for Union bonds. (14 August 1864)
- **John D. Rockefeller:** founder of Standard Oil and a major supplier of goods to the U.S. Army, in Montreal in September 1864. Ostensibly on his honeymoon in Niagara, Rockefeller found time for two trips to Montreal in the fall of 1864. (14, 20 September 1864)
- **Samuel Ward:** There were several 'Ward' registrations during this period but one in particular reads Samuel Ward who was a Democrat, banker, and lobbyist for **Barings Brothers** Bank of London.[14]
- **Eli Whitney Jr.:** son of the inventor of the cotton gin, an arms manufacturer from New Haven, Connecticut. (17 September 1864)

U.S. TREASURY DEPARTMENT OFFICIALS (LOYAL TO SALMON CHASE)

- **G.M. Lane and G.H. Ellery:** Treasury agents stationed in Memphis, Tennessee. Their corrupt operations extended as far east as New York City, where most cotton buyers were located. Lane had close ties to General Benjamin Butler, who had a notorious reputation for corrupt dealings, especially in cotton. (3, 6, 24 October 1864)
- **Hanson Risley:** Treasury agent responsible for the issuance of licenses for 900,000 bales of Southern cotton to friends of the administration and those who provided the right gratuities. Each bale was worth $500-$700. More than half a dozen senior Treasury agents were at St. Lawrence Hall from July 1864 through early 1865. Risley was close to William Seward, and his 20-year-old daughter traveled with Seward around the world following the war. To squelch ugly rumors, Seward ultimately adopted Risley's daughter. (18 March 1865)

- **H. Van Dyck:** Albany. Arrived on 14 June 1864. He was then Assistant Treasurer for the United States at New York.

POW CONDITIONS AND SANITARY COMMISSIONS

In the summer of 1864, the Confederate and Federal Sanitary Commissions responsible for improving POW conditions met in Montreal. The purpose of these meetings is unclear but there was talk at the time of reopening exchanges. The Confederacy was even musing about the possibility of releasing prisoners unilaterally because they could not feed them. Dr. Luke Blackburn may have been involved in these negotiations.

- **Geo Elliot and Alfred Bloor:** U.S. Sanitary Commission (20 August 1864) and **Gen. and Mrs. Beale CSA,** prisoner welfare (27 August 1864).

INTERESTING OUTLIERS

- **W.A. Burnett:** Republican from Vermont with apparent ties to the War Department. Played a part in Lincoln's funeral. These funeral arrangements were handled tightly by Edwin Stanton and anyone involved would have had ties to the Radical Republicans and/or the War Department. (1 July 1864)
- **J.B. Brigham:** commission merchant in Boston at 38 Central Street and a regular visitor at St. Lawrence Hall in the summer and fall of 1864. (10, 31 May, 6 June 1864)
- **Sam DeBow:** (arriving from New Orleans) He was a member of the powerful DeBow family of New Orleans who were involved in publishing and cotton trading. J.D.B. DeBow made a good deal of money during the war trading cotton across enemy lines and through Mexico. He established bank accounts in the UK and purchased a number of valuable properties across the south. It seems certain that DeBow would have had dealings with General Butler and his corrupt brother Andrew after the fall of New Orleans to Federal forces in 1862. DeBow's visit to Montreal in August 1864 was likely tied

to Beverley Tucker's cotton for contraband mega-deal then being orchestrated in the city. (9 August 1864)[15]

- **Martin Duggan:** merchant from Savannah. His purpose in being in Montreal is unclear but likely had to do with Gazaway Lamar's cotton sitting in warehouses in Savannah. (24 February 1865, Savannah)

- **H.H. Emmons:** district attorney from Detroit. He represented William Seward in backdoor peace negotiations held with Confederates in Canada at a time when it appeared Lincoln was going to lose the November 1864 election. Emmons also had ties to the Lamar family of Savannah (blockade running and cotton) through their agent Nelson Trowbridge in New York and Montreal. Trowbridge was a slave trader closely associated with the infamous *Wanderer,* the last ship to import slaves to the United States. There were multiple registrations for Emmons from the fall of 1864 through the early spring of 1865. (4 November 1864, 28 February, 22 March, 8 April 1865)

- **Henry Finnegass:** witness at the trial of the Lincoln Conspirators whose testimony touched on events in Montreal. (6 February 1865)

- **Joseph Garneau:** leading producer of hardtack and bread for the Union Army and **Francis Whitaker,** the chief meat packer for the Union Army, were both in Montreal. The Confederacy was in desperate need of food for its hard-pressed armies in the field and was willing to pay premium prices, presumably in cotton. (8, 16, 28 July 1864)

- **R.E. Goodell:** partner with Lafayette Baker in the cotton business. Checked in with Lafayette Baker 11 August 1864. Both Baker and Goodell had ties to former Congressman O.H. Browning, who lobbied on their behalf in relation to cotton transactions.

- **Count Georgi Austrian Ambassador to the U.S. from Austria:** Count Georgi arrives in Montreal in mid-October when St. Lawrence Hall was full of senior Confederates and when John Wilkes Booth was in town. This may well be coincidence but it is nevertheless intriguing. (13, 20 October 1864)

- **John McCullough:** actor and friend of John Wilkes Booth. Was in Montreal for a Theatre Royal appearance during the 1864 theatrical season. Tainted by his association with Booth, McCullough went into voluntary exile in Montreal in 1865 and 1866. (27 June 1864)

- **Herman Melville:** author of "Moby Dick" and numerous books, and published poetry. In 1864, he was a Customs Officer in the New York Custom House. (13 August 1864)

- **J.W. Myers:** border broker, Rouses Point, New York. He is one of the most interesting characters found in St. Lawrence Hall. He cleared merchandise and packages moving north and south on the rail line between Montreal and New York. Myers was the *most frequent guest* at the luxurious St. Lawrence Hall during the 10 months from June 1864 until April 1865. He was there sometimes twice a week. A border broker's job is normally at the crossing point but Myers' frequent presence in Montreal indicates that he was doing more than just clearing merchandise at Rouses Point. He was carrying packages, correspondence, and perhaps sometimes even people across the border.

Being a successful border broker was certainly a solid profession but it would hardly qualify one as being wealthy—then or today. Yet J.W. Myers was the *most frequent guest* at Montreal's most expensive hotel. St. Lawrence Hall was no ordinary hotel; it played host to the Confederate Secret Service, members of the Canadian government, including two future Prime Ministers, British Army generals, ambassadors, and even British royalty. At the time, Montreal was full of first class, comfortable, affordable hotels, yet Myers stayed exclusively at the luxurious St. Lawrence Hall. For a border broker he was living well. While Myers was St. Lawrence Hall's most frequent guest, the Confederate Secret Service was arguably at the same time the hotel's biggest customer.

Having a broker at the Canada/U.S. border able to clear packages, correspondence, and merchandise would have been of immense value to the Confederate courier system and they had more than enough money on hand to buy such services. The courier network operating out of Montreal to New York and Washington, and through southern Maryland to Virginia, was acknowledged to be efficient and effective, with Rouses Point as the first way station and crossing point.

It's difficult to imagine an American from Rouses Point having pro-Southern sympathizes, but consider that nearly all his Canadian neighbors would have been United Empire Loyalists who distrusted the U.S. central government. In 1861 Myers married a Canadian girl from New Brunswick, Margaret Rossitter, whose family appears to have had United Empire Loyalists roots. One thing is certain, a border broker at Rouses Point, sitting astride the courier line between Montreal, New York, Washington, and Richmond, was well positioned to solicit business and make money.

Myers' travel patterns are certainly unusual for a border broker. While most of his hotel registrations list Rouses Point as his point of departure, he also claimed to have been arriving from Brockville, New York City, England, and even Montreal, and all this in a relatively short time period spanning a few months.

We find him registering with the likes of Confederate spy and courier Sarah Slater, Confederate sympathizer and English writer Augustus Sala, as well as notorious Confederate spy, Benjamin Stringfellow.[16] He also registered with one or both of the Wood Brothers (Benjamin and Fernando Wood), Congressmen from New York both violently opposed to Lincoln.[17] Myers also checked in with W.C. Noyes, a powerful Chase supporter and Radical Republican.[18] During this same period, Myers registered with J.S. Pomeroy, almost certainly Senator Samuel Pomeroy, a Radical Republican in charge of former Secretary of the Treasury Salmon Chase's presidential bid in 1864.[19] Pomeroy was an ardent Lincoln opponent and was joined in Montreal by nearly a dozen politicians and bankers backing Chase's run for the White House.[20] Was Myers on the Confederate payroll? His travel habits and company certainly suggest he was not a run-of-the-mill border broker.

- **David Ogden:** businessman and cotton speculator from New York, had business ties to New York Governor E. Morgan and friendly ties to the Confederates in Montreal. He was a regular at St. Lawrence Hall. It was he who remarked on hearing of the assassination that it was the work of "Sanders and Co." (16 September 1864, 3 February 1865) On 28 July, Ogden signed in as Dr. Ogden.
- **George Augustus Sala:** English author and newspaper personality. He became a close friend of Confederate spy Belle Boyd and helped her write her autobiography. (16 September, 8 October 1864)
- **A.R. Suter:** cotton factor, planter, and wheeler-dealer from New Orleans. To survive in the cotton business in New Orleans, he had to be in the pocket of corrupt General Benjamin Butler. The general and his brother (who fronted for his illicit businesses) arrived in New Orleans with a limited net worth. Within 18 months, they had amassed a fortune of several million dollars. From New Orleans, they transferred to the port of Norfolk where they accumulated an even greater fortune selling contraband for cotton to the Confederacy.[21]
- **James Van Dyck:** Philadelphia District Attorney involved in the August 1864 conspiracy to force Lincoln off the Republican ticket. St. Lawrence Hall 23 March 1865.
- **Hon. R.J. Walker:** Southerner who supported the union during the Civil War. He was instrumental in helping the U.S. government raise money in Europe where there was considerable distrust of America's new fiat currency known as the "Greenback." In 1865, he spent an extended period in Montreal negotiating with Confederate Commissioners, especially George Sanders, on the terms of a compromise peace. (McCord Museum, Notman Collection.)

BRITISH PLAYERS OF NOTE
- **Col. Clark-Kennedy:** commanded the British "Army Train" providing the army with vitally needed logistics and transportation. This was the giant logistical train

that enabled the army to move and fight. It provided food, medicine, tents, boots, weapons, water, and ammunition the army needed. Without it, operations—defensive or offensive—were impossible. Without the "Train," the British Army went nowhere. Along with Colonel Garnet Wolseley, Clark-Kennedy played a central role in moving 12,000 British troops from Halifax to Montreal overland during the winter of 1862. It was one of the great logistical feats in Canadian military history. See photograph, McCord Museum, Notman Collection.

- **Lord Lyons:** British Ambassador to the United States. Lord Lyons was in Montreal at St. Lawrence Hall in the fall of 1864. The purpose of his visit is unknown. (15 September 1864; 5 October 1864)
- **Captain Lewis Guy Phillips:** interesting and adventurous character. Stationed in Montreal during the Civil War, he was educated at Eton and Oxford, and spoke several languages including Greek, German, French, and Italian.[22] He was commissioned in 1859 in the elite Grenadier Guards as an Ensign/Lieutenant. His battalion was dispatched to Canada during the RMS Trent crisis in 1861.

In 1862, he and Captain E. Wynne took leave to visit the Army of Northern Virginia. They were present at the Battle of Fredericksburg. Wynne was arrested as he returned north to Canada and accused of being a spy. The fact that he was carrying Confederate correspondence at the time did not help his case. Lord Lyons, the British ambassador to the United States, intervened on his behalf. Rather than wait to see how this diplomatic tug of war would turn out, Wynne made good his escape from the Old Capital Prison in Washington. With the help of Confederate sympathizers, he returned to Canada via Niagara. His story made the local press in Montreal. Both Phillips and Wynne are found registered at St. Lawrence Hall and their photographs are in the McCord Museum, Notman Collection.

- **Lieutenant Colonel Garnet Wolseley:** In the wake of the RMS Trent crisis, Lieutenant Colonel Garnet J. Wolseley was posted to Canada as assistant quarter-master general. He was then not only a combat veteran but, at 28, the youngest lieutenant colonel in the British Army. By 1861, he had served in the Crimea, India, and China. Wolseley would go on to become the greatest British soldier of the Victorian age. In Canada he played a vital role in moving 12,000 British infantry overland from Halifax to Montreal in the winter of 1862. It was one of the great logistical feats in Canadian military history. He visited with General Lee and his officers in the field and wrote a number of papers and articles about his impressions. He was certainly an admirer of Lee as a soldier.

INTERESTING BUT UNIDENTIFIED REGISTRATIONS

- **Charles Blanchard:** Boston (16 August 1864)
- **H.S. Booth:** New York (26 January 1865). The initials H.S. are obscured and appear to have been erased and replaced. The day before, we find a G./L.L. Hale and a Miss Hale registering from New York. Lucy Lambert Hale had a relationship with John Wilkes Booth. Before dismissing this registration, consider the following: Henry Hogan, proprietor of St. Lawrence Hall and John Potter, U.S. Consul General in Montreal, stated that Booth was in Montreal in 1865. Arthur Loux in *Booth Day by Day* places Booth in New York in early February only a train ride from Montreal. As for the dates 24-27 January 1865, Loux admits the placement of Booth is murky, as the evidence is based on recollections and testimony two years after the fact. He confirms that the events described clearly happened but the dates in late January are uncertain.
- **J.M. Boutwell or Bouttlet:** (17 September 1864) The signature bears a strong resemblance to Radical Congressman George S. Boutwell's distinctive autograph.
- **A.R. Burnside:** arriving from Nassau on 18 August 1864. The signature is a good match with General A.R. Burnside who had just been cashiered from the Army of the Potomac following the disastrous "Battle of the Crater" near Petersburg, Virginia in July 1864.

He arrives with an R. or A. Butler. The latter may be General Benjamin Butler's brother who managed his cotton-for-contraband business. The third member of the party was banker W. Farrington, founder of the Union Planters Bank of Memphis. They arrived from Nassau on 18 August 1864. Burnside was a rifle manufacturer who sold some of his "Burnside Rifles" to the Canadian military.[23]

- **H.S. Chase:** Boston (20 August 1864)
- **A.K. Curtis:** San Francisco (6 August 1864)
- **D. Dodge and R.D. Dodge:** (21 September 1864, 3 April 1865)
- **Rob Forsyth:** Chicago (17 August 1864)
- **D.B. Goodwin/Godwin:** New York (17 August 1864)
- **Geo Hancock and family:** Register shows them staying at the Donegana Hotel, arriving from Louisville, Kentucky. (28 July 1864)
- **W. Hunter, R.B. Hunter, R.J. Hunter:** New York and Philadelphia. (15 June, 30 July, 10 September 1864)
- **Charles E. Noble:** (New York, 27 July 1864)
- **J.D. Raymond:** New York and Washington D.C. (27 July 1864)
- **Mathew Riddell:** checked in with Republican politician Joseph Doolittle 28 August 1864. Riddell claimed to be arriving from Glasgow and Doolittle from Grafton. Doolittle was a Republican Congressman who later registered with his full name and designation; the references to Glasgow and Grafton are likely bogus. (18, 28 August 1864)
- **Edgar Stanton, Geo Stanton:** (New York, 16 September 1864)
- **J.L. Stanton:** (26 October 1864)
- **W.H. Stanton:** (13 August 1864)
- **R.Y. Townsend:** (Philadelphia 16 August 1864)
- **W. Townsend:** (St. Catharines 9 January 1865) He arrived with James Taylor. Taylor arrived again from St. Catharines on 4 April 1865. St, Catharines was the Confederate Secret Service's forward operating base near the Niagara border crossing. C.C. Clay, Beverley Tucker and James Holcombe operated from here and Clay kept nearly $100,000 in hard currency, most likely British pounds and gold, in the local Niagara and District Bank. This gave the Confederates enormous leverage, if not outright control, of the institution. The Confederates operated from a house directly across from the bank, provided to them by Confederate sympathizer Robert Cox. (9 January, 4 April 1865)

NAMES DROPPED

- **Caleb Cushing** provides an illustration of the challenge of identifying individuals when initials are tampered with: Cushing of Massachusetts was Attorney General of the United States in the cabinet of Franklin Pierce. He was sympathetic to Southern interests but supported the preservation of the Union. He fit exactly the profile the Confederacy sought in building a "peace" party in the North. The registration for S. Cushing from Boston 14 June 1864 offers an interesting example of the dilemma presented by subtle changes to initials. There are a number of Samuel or S. Cushing's in the Boston City Directory but all have mid-ranking positions (clerk, bookbinder, shoemaker, etc.) making it unlikely they would have been in Montreal. Caleb Cushing, on the other hand, would have been a prime candidate for the "peace party" the Confederacy was trying to build. He is listed in the Boston directory as Caleb Cushing, counsellor, 27 Tremont Row, House at Newburyport. We did not include Cushing in the text because the case was unclear. There are dozens of similar tantalizing suspect registrations that, while credible, were uncertain and thus left out of the text.

Thomas Barnett's Museum Visitors' Book Listings June-November 1864

In 1831, Thomas Barnett established his first museum of curiosities and natural history in Niagara Falls (then Clifton) near Table Rock, in an abandoned building on the north side of Murray Hill. He was born in 1799 in England and emigrated to North America in 1824. By the end of that decade, Barnett had moved to his second location, also along Table Rock, an area referred to as "the Front." His attractions included a zoological annex and a winding stairway that descended to the floor of the gorge near the base of the Horseshoe Falls.

Mentioned in Niagara's earliest publications and actually marked by some of the first mapmakers, Thomas Barnett's museum was billed second only to the Falls themselves. Barnett would enjoy growth and success along with the industry of tourism for many years and in 1858 he notified the public that there was a new museum soon to adorn their streets. This was a grand building, one of the grandest on either side of the River, and is said to have cost $150,000.

His museum was the quintessential cabinet of curiosities, and by the mid-nineteenth century, he was displaying thousands of specimens, both foreign and domestic. As a trained taxidermist, he collected and displayed everything he could. He was known to mount the creatures that the local people brought him, including their beloved pets and any other beastly oddities they might encounter. All who visited Barnett's museum will forever remember both the three-eyed pig and the two-headed calf. Mr. Barnett even stuffed and displayed his own cherished companion, Skipper, a small dog born with only two hind legs. Mr. Barnett had built Skipper a wheeled contraption that allowed the dog his own freedom and mobility and it was a common sight to see Mr. Barnett and Skipper out for their daily walk.

The Front continued to gain both fame and notoriety in this early incarnation of Niagara Falls tourism. It was only a quarter of a mile long and three hundred yards wide, but here on the banks of the great cataract, every type of huckster and cheat could soon be found. During this time, when the Front resembled Canada's own Wild West, Barnett was certainly not an innocent. Always a businessman needing to turn a profit, he shared in the growing and often disheartening spectacle that the people came to see. However, Thomas Barnett was thought of as a respectable man who was genuinely committed to his collection. Known to offer half-price admission to his visitors and even to let teachers and students in for free, he was a genuine collector who took pride in his museum. Barnett was committed to preserving a record of the visitors who passed through his doors by keeping a series of guest registers that included the signatures of not only the everyday tourist but also famous names like Abraham Lincoln, General Ulysses S. Grant, P.T. Barnum, and the Prince of Wales (later King Edward VII).

In 1852 the *Boston Journal* printed that "few people visit Niagara Falls without calling at Barnett's Museum and few are disappointed." Like the great Falls themselves, Mr. Barnett's museum was a place where people could marvel and learn and never forget their experience. At a time when literacy rates were low and access to resources limited, he was a man seeking to provide truth and understanding to his visitors. His specimens were proof that these marvels did exist and that they were not just something learned about through lore or stories. His desire seemed to be to provide his audience with a twinkling of wonder, moments that would illuminate a truth or provide a flash of new knowledge.

Barnett's story is remarkable and, as with so many entrepreneurs, it ends sadly in loss. The fierce competition along the Front left Barnett at the mercy of his creditors and he was forced to sell his building and its contents in 1877. His life's work was given a value of $78,000, and on auction day, sold for only $48,000. Even more disheartening was the fact that the lot was sold to Mr. Saul Davis, Barnett's archenemy and bitter rival for more than twenty-five years.

Davis operated the Museum and Barnett's other concessions for 10 more years until eventually the land along the Front was expropriated by the Queen Victoria Park Commission. In 1888 Davis moved the Museum across the River to Niagara Falls, New York where it operated for the next 70 years. In 1958, the Museum returned to the Canadian side for a further 40 years until the time of its final closing. In 1999 the Niagara Falls Museum collection (more than seven hundred thousand objects) was purchased by a Toronto collector and dealer named William Jamieson. Jamieson would sell off pieces of the collection until the time of his death in 2011. In 2014 the Niagara Falls History Museum(s) became the proud custodian of several objects from Barnett's collection, including fifty-nine guest registers dating back to 1838. This became a treasure trove for historians, as the registers were meticulously maintained and many of the names are historically significant. These objects bear witness to the past and stand not only as examples of this City's history, but also represent the cabinet of curiosities that was so popular and well attended in the mid-nineteenth century.

In reviewing the Visitors' Books from Barnett's Museum, made available thanks to the generous support of *the Niagara Falls Museums,* covering the months from June through November 1864, we have identified a number of names that appear to match registrations at St. Lawrence Hall in Montreal. As at St. Lawrence Hall, there is evidence of some obfuscation using altered initials, middle names as surnames, daughters and wives registering for husbands, and false points of departure. It is clear, nevertheless, that many of the historical characters who turn up at St. Lawrence Hall (Confederates, American politicians, bankers, etc.) are also found in the Barnett's Visitors' Books.

There is also evidence of cryptic messages attached to some registrations, although further research is required to decipher their meaning. For example, on 11 October 1864, for the registration for E.E. Singleton, the point of departure appears to be instructions that say "Go H 26 (last word obscured)." Charles Van Gordon's registration has a cloud with 29 inside it. William S. Adams, Jr.'s registration is followed by a pyramid and an elaborate O headed for Troy, New York. There is some reference to the suspension bridge or symbols indicating the bridge. There is a cryptic message in the margin on 25 August 1864 that is mostly illegible except for the word "downfall." On 30 August, Mrs. Lowe writes in the margin: "Stay by bridge (last word illegible)." On 9 September, J.D. Whitney includes after his signature the Greek letters O.A.X. This was the probably the symbol for the anti-Lincoln Sons of Liberty, a group committed to the reestablishment of American civil and judicial rights that was deeply involved in the Northwest Conspiracy.[1] They worked in close cooperation with the Confederate Secret Service. All in all, these secret signals are intriguing but largely indecipherable, yet the messages were clearly left for someone to read.

In searching through the Museum Register from May through November 1864, a number of names appear in the museum guest book that also turn up in Montreal at St. Lawrence Hall (and a few that do not appear in Montreal but are noteworthy). There are probably many more to be discovered with further research, but the existing list is impressive and historically significant. As at St. Lawrence Hall, we find senior Confederates mixing with American politicians, bankers, and members of the War Department.

- **James Ashley:** Radical Republican, in Niagara in early September. Ashley's wife Emma registers at the Museum on 4 August 1864. An H. Ashley registers a month later on 4 September 1864. Ashley was a fierce opponent of Abraham Lincoln and played a major role in efforts to impeach Andrew Johnson.
- **Belle Boyd:** Famous Confederate Spy Belle Boyd registered on 18 June.
- **Lafayette Baker:** Federal Secret Service Chief, appeared to be at the Museum several times, including 22 June 1864.
- **C.W. and L.D. Beale:** Washington, D.C. Members of the Confederate Sanitary Commission. They raised money by selling cotton and used the funds to buy blankets and other necessities for Confederate POW's. It was suggested by some that they were not above lining their own pockets in the course of their duties. (22 August 1864)
- **James Gordon Bennett**: Editor of the Democratic, anti-Lincoln *New York Herald*, 27 May 1864. He is back as G.G. Bennett on 4 August 1864.
- **Dr. Luke Blackburn:** senior Confederate stationed in Montreal, appears to have been in the Niagara area in early August. His daughter Miss L. Blackburn registers at the Museum on 11 August 1864. He registers earlier as Jn Blackburn from Toronto on 25 May 1864. Blackburn checks into St. Lawrence Hall with John

Wilkes Booth and National Detective Police detective Walter Pollack. The latter was National Detective Police chief Lafayette Baker's brother-in-law. He too turns up in the Museum's Guest Book.

- **Captain John Castleman:** Confederate operative is at the museum on 1 July 1864.
- **Schuyler Colfax:** The signature is obscure but appears to be that of Schuyler Colfax, Republican Speaker of the House 1863-1869, Minnesota Congressman, radical, and opponent of Lincoln. He was later implicated in the Union Pacific scandal where he appears to have accepted bribes. The corrupt Union Pacific was the brainchild of Thomas Durant who was deeply involved in illicit cotton trading with the Confederacy out of Montreal. 20 June 1864
- **Jay Cooke:** Civil War super banker, helped finance the Union effort, is clearly registered 22 June. This is a huge confirmatory find. He appears to return 26 October. He appears to be in Montreal at St. Lawrence Hall in October when John Wilkes Booth was at St. Lawrence Hall. Cooke found the time to visit Canada in the summer of 1864 but ignored two invitations from President Lincoln to visit him at the White House. That summer represented the nadir of Lincoln's Presidency. He was experiencing one setback after another on the battlefield. Casualties had reached sickening levels and a new draft of five hundred thousand men was called for to fill the ranks. Lincoln himself predicted his defeat in November. His invitations to Cooke went unanswered. Not even an explanation was provided by Cooke. It was a studied and intentional insult.
- **(G?)B. Course:** Montreal. Almost certainly Confederate operative W. Corse/Cours/Course, who lived in Montreal and was a friend of Senior Confederate Commissioner Brigadier General Edwin Lee. 31 August 1864.
- **Robert Cox:** registered as R.E. Cox on 20 June 1864. He was involved in cotton trading with Orville Browning. He provided the house which served C.C. Clay and the Confederate Secret Service as a forward operating base in St. Catharines. Confederate courier Josephine Brown

stayed for a time in his house in Poughkeepsie, New York. May have had some ties to John Wilkes Booth.

- **Sam Davis:** Confederate Operative, in the guest book on 14 July 1864. Davis was later captured and sentenced to death. Senior Confederate Commissioner in Canada Jacob Thompson wrote directly to Lincoln explaining that Davis was a courier but not a spy. Lincoln commuted the sentence.

- **T.T. Eckert:** head of the War Department's Telegraph operations and close confidant of Secretary of War Edwin Stanton. He appears to visit both Niagara and Montreal in the summer of 1864. In Montreal, Eckert uses the initials G.G., G.T., or T.T. on 27 July 1864 at St. Lawrence Hall. A few days earlier, on 22 July 1864, he registered in Niagara as T.T. or Y.F. Eckert from Cincinnati, Ohio. The Eckert signatures in both cases were made by the same person and both claim *Ohio* as the point of departure. Eckert was indeed originally from Ohio. Eckert's distinctive signature style sometimes made his T's look like F's or G's. Eckert is traveling with his son and namesake Master Thomas (T. Eckert). This makes the identification almost certain.

  Through robber baron Jay Gould (also in Montreal in July and August 1864), Eckert would one day become chief of Western Union. On the night of Lincoln's assassination, the President asked Edwin Stanton if Eckert, a powerful man, could accompany him to Ford's Theatre as an unofficial body guard. Stanton refused, stating rudely that Eckert was too busy. Lincoln then asked Eckert himself but received the same answer. Despite his apparent workload Eckert went home that night as usual. He was there when the news of Lincoln's assassination reached him. The signatures in St. Lawrence Hall and Barnett's Museum are a good match with Eckert's surviving autographs.

- **H. Emmons:** backdoor peace negotiator sent to Canada in 1864 by Secretary of State William Seward. Emmons had close ties to the Confederate Secret Service. His daughter Ann Emmons registers at the Museum on 2 July 1864.

- **J.H. Farrington:** We suspect this may be William Farrington, a successful cotton broker and banker from Memphis, Tennessee. He lists his point of departure as Saratoga Springs, a popular New York resort for the well-to-do. Farrington founded the Union and Planters Bank which today operates as Regions Bank. The latter still uses the Planters Bank logo depicting a young cotton plant.[2] On 16 September 1864, he arrives with S.H. Pond from Saratoga Springs. A. Pond was a Republican delegate from Saratoga Springs. Both Farrington and Pond are found at St. Lawrence Hall in Montreal.

- **William Finney:** active member of the Confederate Secret Service dividing his time between Halifax and Montreal. He and his cohort Benjamin Ficklin helped found the Pony Express. They also purchased the famous Confederate blockade runner *Giraffe*, later renamed *Robert E. Lee*. Finney was involved with blockade running and efforts to capture Northern POW camps. Ficklin became involved with Confederate Beverley Tucker's cotton-for-contraband schemes. In this, Ficklin worked for Brown Brothers Bank of London and New York. He was captured in Washington the day after Lincoln's assassination but was released at the intercession of former Congressman and Washington power broker Orville Browning, who was likewise involved in cotton trading.

- **James W. Halsey:** (New Jersey, 15 November 1864) We believe this is George Halsey, Radical Republican from New Jersey and present at St. Lawrence Hall.

- **Ja Harlan and Miss Mary Doolittle**: (12 August 1864) This points to the presence of Radical Republican Senator James Harlan from Iowa and Republican Congressman Joseph Doolittle of Wisconsin. Both are also found registered at St. Lawrence Hall in Montreal.

- **J. Harvey:** Radical Republican Congressman who stridently opposed Lincoln, registered on 1 July 1864.

- **E.R. Hatch:** New York. Registered on 1 September 1864. This, we believe, is A.S. Hatch, a banker from New York with ties to Jay Cooke, who was a regular at

St. Lawrence Hall. In Montreal, Hatch and his banking associate G. Bliss usually disguised their initials.

- **A.J. Holt:** Joseph Holt was the Chief Judge Advocate General prosecutor of the Lincoln Conspirators. Registered on 17 September from Buffalo. Holt is found registered at St. Lawrence Hall twice accompanied by powerful Republicans.
- **Mr. and Mrs. Howe:** (Brandon, Wisconsin 24 September 1864) This is likely T. Howe, Republican delegate at the 1864 convention, who also turned up at St. Lawrence Hall. He registered just ahead of L.L. Baker who we believe to be Lafayette Baker, head of the National Detective Police.
- **Mr. A. Oppenheimer:** banker, broker from New York. 26 June 1864.
- **James Pallon/Pallen:** (Montreal, 7 October 1864) Almost certainly Dr. M. Pallen, a senior member of the Confederate Secret Service in Montreal.
- **G.W. Palmer:** Democrat turned Republican, a founding member of the Free Soil Party. Served in Congress from 1857 to 1861. Inclined to support the Radical agenda. He was a delegate at the Baltimore 1864 Republican Convention. (26 May 1864)
- **Hezekiah Payne/Paine:** Montreal-based Confederate Banker present at the museum on 19 June 1864.
- **A.H.M. Pollack:** We suspect this is Walter Pollack, brother-in-law of Lafayette Baker and a senior member of the National Detective Police. (7 July 1864) Pollack was a regular at St. Lawrence Hall. Pollack was back in Niagara as L.C. Pollack from New York on 3 September 1864.
- **W.G. Rattray:** (Nassau, 20 October 1864) Likely a cotton broker. Rattray also turns up at S. Lawrence Hall, arriving from Nassau with a large family and retinue joining him from New York.
- **John Rogers:** We believe this to be New Jersey Democratic Congressman Jack Rogers. He wrote a scathing rebuttal to the finding of the Military Commission that condemned Mary Surratt, Lewis Powell, George Atzerodt, and David Herold to death. (25 August 1864)

- **Mr. and Mrs. J.R. Sage:** Philadelphia. (speculative) This is likely Russell Sage with his first wife. Sage was a successful banker who profited substantially from the war. He had close ties to banker Jay Cooke and through Western Union, to T.T. Eckert.
- **George Augustus Sala:** English author, Confederate sympathizer and friend of spy Belle Boyd. He helped her write her autobiography which was published in England. 30 July 1864.
- **E. Seymour:** very likely Governor Horatio Seymour, a peace Democrat with close ties to the Confederate Secret Service. 26 June. He registered a number of times at St. Lawrence Hall.
- **John Sherman:** Radical Republican, another opponent of Lincoln and brother of General William T. Sherman, registered 22 Aug.
- **John Slaughter:** 6 October 1864, arriving from an obscured location, may be H.C. Slaughter, a member of the Confederate Secret Service who operated out of Montreal and Toronto.
- **W.H. Smart:** (Kentucky, 8 October 1864) Probably Col. Smart CSA from KY, who operated primarily out of Hamilton.
- **W.B. Stickney:** member of the Confederate Signal Corps (an extension of the Confederate Secret Service) is at the Museum 30 July, arriving from New Orleans. As a telegraph operator he played a vital role in the Confederate defense of New Orleans early in the war. Interestingly, L.P. Stickney, a member of the Federal Signal Corps (a brother?), is also in Niagara earlier that month on 3 July 1.
- **Jacob Thompson:** Senior Confederate Commissioner in Canada, appears in the guest book several times including 1 July 1864. He checks in with J.C. (Jeremiah) Black who was a backdoor peace representative sent to Canada by Secretary of War Edwin Stanton in the summer of 1864. On 7 October 1864, he signs in as R.H. Thompson from Liverpool; he used this same registration at St. Lawrence Hall. Note he registers at the museum next to James Pallen who is

almost certainly Dr. M. Pallen, senior Confederate from Montreal. J. Black is back at the museum on 17 July 1864. On 18 August, R. Thompson registers as being from the CSA. A third party inserts the word "Rebel" into the registration.

- **Samuel Tilden:** (speculative) Registered as L.E. Tilden from New York. Tilden was a prominent New York politician who opposed Lincoln's conduct of the war. He rose to become Governor of New York during Reconstruction. Tilden challenged the constitutionality of the draft in 1863. Tilden was part of the anti-Lincoln New York-based "August Conspiracy" aimed at displacing Lincoln as a presidential candidate. (19 July 1864)

- **J.W. Wallace (Sanford Conover, Charles Dunham):** double agent, at the Museum several times during this period. He arrives on 26 June 1864 from the Confederate forward operating base at St. Catharines. He does so again on 1 September, arriving again from St. Catharines. On 9 October, J Wallace registers with his wife from Catchy, Mississippi. Wallace used this same peculiar point of departure at St. Lawrence Hall.

- **J.B. Watson:** (Kentucky, 8 September 1864) This may be the same B. Watson who registered at St. Lawrence Hall and took out a large money order for nearly $13,000 at the Bank of Montreal. It was released to his heirs shortly after the war. Watson, or someone using his name, wrote a telegram to John Surratt, asking him to come to New York on urgent business shortly before Lincoln's assassination.

- **Captain John Wilkinson:** legendary Confederate sea raider/ blockade runner is present on 9 August 1864.

- **B.A. Wood:** We suspect this is Congressman Benjamin Wood, brother of New York Mayor and Congressman Fernando Wood. Benjamin Wood was on the Confederate Secret Service payroll and violently opposed to Lincoln. (4 July 1864)

- **F.E. Wood:** very likely New York Mayor and Congressman Fernando Wood, who despised Lincoln. (30 June 1864)

- **Bennett Young:** leader of the St. Albans Raid, along with a number of his raiders. Turned up at Barnett's Museum on 4 July, 3 August 1864. Raider Doty, on 20, 22 June, 1 July; Raider Deveny, on 20 June; Raider Hutchinson, on 23 June; Raider Price, on 13 September; Raider Swager, on 10 October 1864.

Jacob Thompson Reports to Judah Benjamin on Confederate Secret Service Activities in Canada

TORONTO, CANADA WEST, December 3, 1864.

SIR: Several times have I attempted to send you communications, but I have no assurance that any one of them has been received. I have relaxed no effort to carry out the objects the government had in view in sending me here. I had hoped at different times to have accomplished more, but still I do not think my mission has been altogether fruitless. At all events we have afforded the North Western States the amplest opportunity to throw off the galling dynasty at Washington and openly to take ground in favor of State Rights and Civil Liberty. This fact must satisfy the large class of discontents at home, of the readiness and willingness of the Administration to avail itself of every proffered assistance in our great struggle for independence. On my arrival here, I heard that there was such an organization as the Order of the "Sons of Liberty" in the Northern States, and my first effort was to learn its strength, its principles and its objects, and if possible to put myself in communication with its leading spirits. This was effected without much difficulty or delay. I was received among them with cordiality, and the greatest confidence at once extended to me. The number of its members was large, but not so great as Mr. Holt, in his Official Report represented it to be. Its objects were political– its principles were that the government was based on the consent of the parties to it – that the States were the parties and were sovereign; that there was no authority in the general government to coerce a seced-

ing State. The Resolutions of 1798 and 1799 were set forth as presenting the true theory of the government. Its organization was essentially military – It had its Commanders of Divisions, of Brigades, of Regiments, of Companies. In the month of June last the universal feeling among its members, leaders and privates, was that it was useless to hold a Presidential election; Lincoln had the power and would certainly reelect himself, and there was no hope but in force. The belief was entertained, and freely expressed that by a bold, vigorous, and concerted movement the three great North Western States of Illinois Indiana and Ohio could be seized and held. This being done, the States of Kentucky and Missouri could easily be lifted from their prostrate condition and placed on their feet, and this in sixty days would end the war. While everything was moving on smoothly to a supposed successful consummation, the first interruption in the calculation was the postponement of the meeting of the Democratic Convention from the 4th of July to the 29th of August; but preparations still went on, and in one of the States the 20th of July was fixed as the day for a movement. But before the day arrived a general Council of the order from different States was called, and it was thought the movement on the 20th of July would be premature, and the 16th of August was fixed upon for a general uprising. This postponement was insisted upon on the ground that it was necessary to have a series of public meetings to prepare the public mind, and appointments for public peace meetings were made, one at Peoria, one at

Springfield, and one at Chicago, on the 16th. The first one was at Peoria, and to make it a success I agreed that so much money as was necessary would be furnished by me. It was held, and was a decided success. The vast multitudes who attended seemed to be swayed but by one leading idea - Peace. The friends were encouraged and strengthened, and seemed anxious for the day when they would do something to hasten them to the great goal of peace. About this time that correspondence between our friends and Horace Greeley made its appearance. Lincoln's manifesto shocked the country. The belief in some way prevailed over the North that the South would agree to a reconstruction, and the politicians, especially the leading ones, conceived the idea that on such an issue Lincoln could be beaten at the ballot box. At all events, they argued that the trial of the ballot box should be made before a resort to force, always a dernier resort. The Springfield meeting came off, but it was apparent that the fire exhibited at Peoria had already diminished; the whole tone of the speakers was that the people must rely on the ballot box for redress of grievances. The nerves of the leaders of the order began to relax. About this time a large lot of arms was purchased and sent to Indianapolis, which was discovered, and some of the leading men were charged with the design to arm the members of the order for treasonable purposes. Treachery showed itself at Louisville. Judge Bullitt and Dr. Kalfus were arrested and sent to Memphis. The day on which the great movement was to be made became known to Mr. [J. E.] McDonald, candidate for governor of Indiana, and believing that it would mar his prospects for election unless prevented, he threatened to expose all the parties engaged unless the project was abandoned. Thus the day passed by and nothing was done. The Chicago convention came; the crowd was immense; the feeling was unanimous for peace. A general impression prevailed that a reconstruction could be had, and that it was necessary to so far pander to the military feeling as to take Genl McClellan to secure a certain success.

This nomination, followed as it was by divers disclosures and arrests of persons – prominent members – totally demoralized the "Sons of Liberty". The feeling with the masses is as strong as ever. They are true, brave, and, I believe, willing and ready, but they have no leaders. The vigilance of the Administration, its large detective force, the large bounties paid for treachery, and the respectable men who have yielded to the temptation, added to the large military force stationed in those States, make organization and preparation almost an impossibility. A large sum of money has been expended in fostering and furthering these operations, and it now seems to have been to little profit; but in reviewing the past I do not see how it could have been avoided, nor has it been spent altogether in vain. The apprehensions of the enemy have caused him to bring back and keep from the field in front at least 60,000 to watch and browbeat the people at home. In this view of the subject, the same amount of money has effected so much in no other quarter since the commencement of the war. In July last Capt Chas H. Cole, of Genl Forrest's command, made his escape from prison. He represented to me that he had been appointed a lieutenant in our Navy. I sent him around the Lakes with instructions to go as a lower-deck passenger, to familiarize himself with all the channels and different approaches to the several harbors, the strength of each place, the depositories of coal, and especially to learn all that he could about the war steamer "Michigan", and devise some plan for her capture or destruction. This duty he performed very satisfactorily. He was then instructed to return and put himself in communication with the officers of the "Michigan", and, feeling his way, to endeavor to purchase the Boat from its officers. For a time he thought he would succeed in this if he could give the guaranties of payment of the sums stipulated, but by degrees the question was dropped, and he asked permission to organize a force, board and take her. This was given, and Acting Master John Y. Beall was sent him to aid in the organization and in carrying out the enterprize. Their plan was well conceived and held out the promise of success. It had been previously ascertained from escaped prisoners from Johnson's Island that an organization existed among the prisoners on the Island for the purpose of surprizing the guard and capturing the Island; the presence of the steamer Michigan, which carried 14 guns, was the only obstacle. Secret communications were had by which they were advised that on the night of the 19th of Sept an attempt to seize the Michigan would be made. On that night Capt Cole, who had previously established the friendliest relations with the officers of the steamer, was to have a wine drinking with them on board, and at a given hour Acting Master Beall was to appear, on a Boat to be obtained for that purpose, with a sufficient body of Confederate Soldiers to board and take the steamer. Should they capture the steamer, a cannon shot sent through the officers quarters on Johnson's Island was to signify to the prisoners that the hour for their release had come. Should they take the Island, boats were to be improvised and Sandusky was to be attacked. If taken, the prisoners were to be mounted and make for Cleveland, the boats cooperating; and from Cleveland the prisoners were to make Wheeling and thence to Virginia. The key to the whole movement was the capture of the Michigan. On the evening of the 19th, by some treachery, Cole was arrested, and the messenger who was to meet Acting Master Beall at Kellys Island did not reach him. Disappointed, but nothing daunted Acting Master Beall, having possession of the "Philo Parsons", passenger steamer from Detroit to Sandusky, went on his way towards Johnson's Island. Having landed at Middle Bas Island to secure a supply of wood, the steamer "Island Queen" with a large number of passengers and 32 soldiers, came up alongside and lashed herself to the "Parsons". An attack was at once resolved upon. The passengers and soldiers were soon made prisoners, and the boat delivered up to our men. The soldiers were regularly paroled, the passengers were left on the Island, having given their promise not

to leave for 24 hours, and the boat was towed out into the Lake and sunk. The "Parsons" was then steered directly for the Bay of Sandusky. Here the men, from certain reasons not altogether satisfactory, but possibly fortunately, refused to make the attack on the "Michigan". Beall returned, landed at Sandwich, CW, and the men scattered through the country. Most of them have returned to the Confederate States; but a few days since Acting Master Bennett G. Burley was arrested, and the trial is now going on for his delivery under the extradition treaty. If we had Cole's, Beall's, or his own commission, I should not fear the result; as it is, they will have to prove that they acted under my order, and that will in all probability secure his release; but it may lead to my expulsion from the provinces. At least, I have it from a reliable source that this last proposition has been pressed upon the Canadian Authorities, and they have considered it. Should the course of events take this direction, unadvised by you I shall consider it my duty to remain where I am and abide the issue. I should prefer, if it be possible, to have your views on the subject. Capt Cole is still a prisoner on Johnson's Island. In obedience to your suggestion, as far as it was practicable, soon after my arrival here I urged the people in the North to convert their paper money into gold and withdraw it from the market. I am satisfied this policy was adopted and carried into effect to some extent, but how extensively I am unable to state. What effect it had on the gold market it is impossible to estimate, but certain it is that gold continued to appreciate until it went to 290. The high price may have tempted many to change their policy, because afterwards gold fell in the market to 150. When it was about 180, and exportation of gold was so small that there appeared to be but little or no demand for it, Mr. John Porterfield, formerly a Banker in Nashville, but now a resident of Montreal, was furnished with $100,000, and instructed to proceed to New York to carry out a financial policy of his own conception, which consisted in the purchase of gold and exporting the same, selling it for Sterling

Bills of Exchange, and then again converting his exchange into gold. This process involved a certain loss - the cost of transshipment. He was instructed by Mr. Clay and myself to go on with his policy until he had expended $25,000, with which he supposed he would ship directly $5,000,000, and induce others to ship much more, and then, if the effect upon the gold market was not very perceptible, he was to desist and return to Canada and restore the money unexpended. By his last report he had caused the shipment of more than $2,000,000 of gold at an expense of less than ten thousand dollars, but it seems that a Mr. Lyons, who had been a former partner of Porterfield, was arrested by Genl Butler on the ground that he was exporting gold; and although Mr. Lyons had no connection with Mr. Porterfield in this transaction, yet he thought it prudent to return to Canada, and while he retains the unexpended balance of the $25,000 to carry out his instructions, he has restored $75,000. I must confess that the first shipment had a marked effect on the market. I am inclined to the opinion that his theory will work great damage and distrust to the Federal finances if vigorously followed up, and if no untoward circumstances should interfere with the operation. Soon after I reached Canada, a Mr. Minor Major visited me and represented himself as an accredited agent from the Confederate States to destroy Steam Boats on the Mississippi River, and that his operations were suspended for want of means. I advanced to him $2,000 in Federal currency, and soon afterward several Boats were burned at St. Louis, involving an immense loss of property to the enemy. He became suspected, as he represented to me, of being the author of this burning, and from that time both he and his men have been hiding, and consequently have done nothing. Money has been advanced to Mr. Churchill, of Cincinnati, to organize a corps for the purpose of incendiarism in that city. I consider him a true man, and although as yet he had has effected but little, I am in constant expectation of hearing of effective work in that quarter.

Previous to the arrival of Lt-Col Martin and Lieut Headly, bringing an unsigned note from you, all the different places where our prisoners are confined – Camp Douglas, Rock Island, Camp Morton, Camp Chase, Elmira – had been thoroughly examined, and the conclusion was forced upon us that all efforts to release them without outside cooperation would bring disaster upon the prisoners and result in no good. All projects of that sort were abandoned, except that at Camp Douglas, where Capt Hines still believed he could effect their release. We yielded to his firmness, zeal, and persistence, and his plans were plausible, but treachery defeated him before his well-laid schemes were developed. Having nothing else on hand, Col Martin expressed a wish to organize a corps to burn New York City. He was allowed to do so, and a most daring attempt has been made to fire that city; but their reliance on the Greek fire has proved a misfortune; it cannot be depended on as an agent in such work. I have no faith whatever in it, and no attempt shall hereafter be made under my general directions with any such materials. I knew nothing whatever of the Raid on St. Albans [VT.] until after it transpired. Desiring to have a Boat on whose Captain and crew reliance could be placed, and on board of which arms could be sent to convenient points for arming such vessels as could be seized for operations on the Lakes, I aided Dr. James T. Bates, of Ky, an old Steam Boat Captain, in the purchase of the steamer "Georgian". She had scarcely been transferred when the story went abroad that she had been purchased and armed for the purpose of sinking the "Michigan", releasing the prisoners on Johnson's Island, and destroying the shipping on the lakes and the cities on their margin. The wildest consternation prevailed in all the border cities. At Buffalo two tugs had cannon placed on board; four regiments of soldiers were sent there - two of them represented to have been drawn from the Army of Virginia; bells were rung at Detroit, and churches broken up on Sunday. The whole Lake Shore was a scene of wild excitement. Boats were sent out, which boarded the "Georgian" and found nothing contraband on board, but still the people were incredulous.

The bane and curse of carrying out anything in this country is the surveillance under which we act. Detectives, or those ready to give information, stand at every street corner. Two or three cannot interchange ideas without a reporter.

The Presidential election has so demoralized the leaders of the order of the "Sons of Liberty" that a new organization, under new leaders, has become an absolute necessity. This is now going forward with great vigor and success. The new order is styled the "order of the Star". There is a general expectation that there will soon be a new draft, and the members swear resistance to another draft. It is purely military, wholly independent of politics and politicians. It is given out among members that Stonewall Jackson is the founder of the order, and the name has its significance from the stars on the collars of Southern officers. There is no ground to doubt that the masses, to a large extent, of the North, are brave and true, and believe Lincoln a tyrant and usurper. During my stay in Canada a great amount of property has been destroyed by burning. The information brought me as to the perpetrators is so conflicting and contradictory that I am satisfied that nothing can be certainly known. Should claims be presented at the War Office for payment for this kind of work, not one dollar should be advanced on any proof adduced until all the parties concerned may have an opportunity for making out and presenting proof. Several parties claim to have done the work at St. Louis, New Orleans, Louisville, Brooklyn, Philadelphia, and at Cairo. Within the last few days Dr. K. J. Stewart, of Va, has reached this place, and very mysteriously informs me that he has a plan for the execution of something which has received the sanction of the President. He is in want of money, and states to me that you gave him a draft on me for $20,000 in gold, which has been lost on the way. He has sent back to Richmond for a renewal. He has rented a large house and moved his family into it. I cannot doubt his word, but of course I do not feel authorized to advance him money without your authority or that of the President. I have however been constrained to advance him $500 in gold, on his written statement that unless the money was in hand the lives and liberties of high Confederate officers would be imperilled.

Owing to the health of Mr. Clay, we separated at Halifax, and since then we have not lived together, though we have been in consulting distance. As the money was all in my name, which I supposed to be controlled by us jointly, and as he desired to have a sum placed in his hands, at all times subject to his personal control, I transferred to him $93,614, for which I hold his receipts, and for which he promises to account to the proper authorities at home. Including the money turned over to Mr. Clay, all of which he has not yet expended, the entire expenditures as yet, on all accounts, are about $300,000. I still hold three drafts for $100,000 each, which have not been collected. Should you think it best for me to return, I would be glad to know in what way you think I had best return with the funds remaining on hand. I infer from your "personal" in the New York News that it is your wish I should remain here for the present, and I shall obey your orders. Indeed, I have so many papers in my possession which, in the hands of the enemy, would utterly ruin and destroy very many of the prominent men in the North, that a due sense of my obligation to them will force on me the extremist caution in my movements.

For the future, discarding all dependence on the organizations in the Northern States, our efforts, in my judgment, should be directed to inducing those who are conscripted in the North, and who utterly refuse to join the army to fight against the Confederate States, to make their way South to join our service. It is believed by many that at least a number sufficient to make up a Division may be secured in this way for our service before spring, especially if our army opens up a road to the Ohio. Some are now on their way to Corinth, which at present is the point of rendezvous. Also to operate on their Rail Roads and force the enemy to keep up a guard on all their roads, which will require a large standing army at home, and to burn whenever it is practicable, and thus make the men of property feel their insecurity and tire them out with the war. The attempt on New York has produced a great panic, which will not subside at their bidding. This letter, though long, does not, I am aware, report many things of minor importance which have occurred during my sojourn in Canada; but I shall omit them at present.

Very respectfully, Yr obt servant,
J. THOMPSON.
Hon. J. P. BENJAMIN,
Secretary of State.

Blockade Runners with Ties to Montreal, the St. Lawrence River, and the Great Lakes

A thousand miles up the St. Lawrence River from the Atlantic Ocean, Montreal sustained and financed a number of blockade runners during the war. An examination of these vessels provides unmistakable evidence of the involvement of prominent Montreal businessmen, bankers, and even politicians in this illicit trade. The profits in blockade running were so enormous that *everyone* wanted a piece of the action. Blockade-running money flowed into Canada during the war from nearby New York and from as far away as New Orleans.[1]

The economics of the business were fabulous. You could buy and equip a mid-sized blockade runner for approximately $50,000. This vessel would carry desperately-needed arms, munitions, food, and medicines into the South where they commanded huge price premiums. The ship loaded up on cheap and abundant Southern cotton, which was valued as high as 1000% above pre-war levels. A single round-trip voyage could produce top line revenue of one half to three quarters of a million dollars. Two successful runs through the blockade could produce 300-500% return for investors. Canadian registered vessels were classed as 'British bottoms' and thus eligible for *Lloyd's of London* maritime insurance covering both the vessel and cargo. So, the risk was negligible. Such coverage was not available to vessels registered to either of the belligerent parties and so we find American vessels, backed by American investors, being transferred to Canadian ownership—at least on paper. For example, Confederate banker and blockade runner Gazaway Lamar invested in two

Montreal-based blockade runners with Captain P.C. Martin as his partner. Martin was a senior member of the Confederate Secret Service in the city.[2] One of his vessels was named *Marie Victoria*, and it is believed the second may have carried the name *Lockalva*.[3]

Lamar's reach extended from Montreal to New York, where his vessels *Wild Pigeon* and *Rosalie* sailed regularly from Nassau to New York City to pick up contraband cargoes without ever being challenged by U.S. Customs officials, who were paid to look the other way.[4] One of the men who captained these vessels, William Ross Postell, was a long time Lamar employee and fellow Savannahian.[5] Lamar also had an agent, "Mr. Powell," who traveled regularly between New York and Montreal speculating in currency and gold arbitrage.[6] And sure enough, a mysterious "Mr. Powell" arrived at St. Lawrence Hall on 29 October 1864, just when contraband-for-cotton negotiations were at their peak. (See *Trading with the Enemy.*) Finally, Savannah merchant and Lamar acquaintance Martin (Marty) Duggins turned up at St. Lawrence Hall early in 1865.[7] We can only guess at what business brought him to Canada, but Duggins was certainly a long way from home.

A prominent Canadian who appears to have had ties to blockade running is politician and Member of Parliament the Hon. Joseph-Édouard Cauchon. "*The Evening Times publishes a telegram from Quebec, saying that the steamers Bowmanville and Caledonia are understood to be fitting out at Quebec to run the Southern blockade, and that Hon. Mr. CAUCHEN (sic) is interested in the speculation.*"[8] Other

Canadians who appear to have been involved directly or indirectly with blockade running and blockade-runner vessels include Harrison Stevens, A. Heron, D.T. Leach, Benjamin Wier, J.F. Phalen, E. Chaffey, and banker H. Starnes. When examining Canadian involvement in blockade running, these names represent only the tip of the iceberg. As with so many other characters in this story, photographs of many can be found in the McCord Museum, Notman Collection.

THE SHIPS

Below is a partial list of Canadian ships associated with blockade-running activities that operated in Montreal both during the Civil War and in post-war service.

Acadia– Built at Sorel, Quebec – 738 tons, 211 feet long with 900 horsepower steam engines. Sold September 1864 to U.S. interests for blockade running to Nassau and Havana, lost in the Gulf of Mexico.

Arabian– Owner or investor A. Heron of Montreal. Sold to U.S. interests for blockade running 1862. Destroyed off the coast of Wilmington, North Carolina in 1863 after running aground trying to evade U.S. Naval blockade.

Alliance/Caledonia– Owner J. Wilson of Quebec City. Sold to New York interests and shortly thereafter became a blockade runner. The Hon. Joseph-Édouard Cauchon, a Member of Parliament, Cabinet Minister, and prominent Quebec politician, apparently had a financial interest in this blockade runner.[9]

Blue Bonnet– Paddlewheel steamer built at Sorel, Quebec in 1855. Sold to *DeSalaberry Navigation Company* of Montreal 1859. Sold to U.S. interests in New York for "Civil War" activities, presumably blockade running, in 1862.

Boston– Paddlewheel steamer built for A. Burns of Quebec in 1852. Owned by Chaffey Brothers of

McCord Museum, Notman Collection, M930.50.5.23

Brockville, Ontario in 1861. Transferred to U.S. interests for blockade running in 1863. This appears to have been a paper transaction as the ship's registry was transferred back to Canada the very next day. This legal sleight of hand was a common tactic to shield investors from potential prosecution in the U.S. and to enable the blockade runner to obtain maritime insurance, which was only available to British-registered ships.[10]

Bowmanville– Ownership unclear but she is definitely listed as taking on cargoes at Montreal bound for Nassau, the main transshipment point for blockade runners heading into Wilmington, North Carolina and Charleston, South Carolina. The Canadian politician the Hon. Joseph-Édouard Cauchon is reported to have had an "interest" in the vessel.[11] The *Bowmanville* had to put into New York for emergency repairs and U.S. authorities seized her as her Nassau-bound cargo was deemed suspicious.

British Queen– Paddlewheel steamer, sailed from Montreal to Kingston and later from Montreal to Quebec. Sold to U.S. interests as a blockade runner in 1863. Made at least two runs through the blockade to the Gulf of Mexico, possibly to Matamoros, Mexico.

Clyde– Ownership unknown. "*The steamer Clyde, of 410 tons register, nine years old, left Montreal on the 3d instant for the coast. I have no doubt you will see the three last-named (ships) in New York before they commence operations to and from Nassau.*"[12]

Chicora– Originally named *Let Her Be*, she was one of three sister ships built in Britain for blockade running, the others being *Let Her Go* and *Let Her Rip*. The *Chicora* was a very successful blockade runner, making twelve round trips. Owned by the *Importing and Exporting Company* of Charleston, South Carolina. Sailed out of Halifax during the war carrying cargoes for *Benjamin Wier and Co.* Came into Great Lakes service after the war.[13]

City Of Quebec– Paddlewheel steamer. Built in Liverpool specifically as a blockade runner. Later owned by the *Quebec Steamship Company* in post-war Canadian service.

Commerce– Screw propellers, owner J.F. Phalen of Halifax. The vessel also operated under the name *PET*, making fifteen round trips through the blockade. She appears to have come to Canada after her war service.

Douro– A highly-successful blockade runner. Ownership unclear. This vessel also apparently came to Canada after the war.

Lady Mulgrave– Of Halifax, is associated with Harrison Stevens, a prominent Montreal shipper and businessman. The ship left Montreal in 1863 carrying a number of Confederate officers who had escaped from Johnson's Island or other Federal prisoner-of-war camps. One was said to have been a senior member of J.E.B. Stuart's staff. Interestingly, a newspaper report had Stevens visiting Charleston, South Carolina, which required running the final leg of the blockade from Nassau.[14] The vessel was loaded at Montreal with two hundred tons of anthracite coal, which was highly valued by blockade-runners as it burned extremely hot but emitted almost no smoke. The ship also carried leather boots, shoes, soap, and whiskey. The cargo was to be off-loaded at Nassau.[15]

Georgia– Owned by the *Quebec and Gulf Ports Steamship Company* after the war.

Little Ada– Built in Scotland as a blockade runner and highly successful in this role. Her owners were Gazaway Lamar and the *Importing and Exporting Company of Georgia*. The vessel appears to have come to Canada in the immediate aftermath of the war.

S.S. Luna– A paddle-driven steamer that ran regularly on the St. Lawrence and into Montreal. We find passengers from the vessel registered at St. Lawrence Hall.[16] We also know that a vessel named *S.S. Luna* made two runs through the blockade in 1865.[17] After the war she was purchased for the Australian trade out of Sydney. Her past as a blockade runner and her speed were acknowledged in the local press.[18]

Mary Ellen– A Montreal-based blockade runner captured by the *USS Kanawha* off of Velasco, Texas.[19] Ownership is unclear.

Marie Victoria– One of two blockade-running schooners owned by Montreal-based Confederate agent and blockade runner Captain P.C. Martin, the other possibly being the *Lockalva*.[20] Gazaway Lamar, a Savannah banker, funded the vessels as blockade runners and financed them through the Confederate-controlled *Bank of Ontario* located on Place d'Armes in Montreal. Both of Martin's vessels were lost on the same expedition under suspicious circumstances in separate incidents in 1865; one foundered downriver from Quebec City and the other was lost somewhere between Halifax and Nassau. The first vessel was carrying John Wilkes Booth's theatrical wardrobe, which was later salvaged and sold at auction. The second was lost with all hands, including the intrepid Captain Martin, off the coast of Nova Scotia. Martin's partner, the disreputable "Sandy" Keith of Halifax, absconded with the insurance money, leaving Mrs. Martin and her family in Montreal in dire straits. Keith would eventually be exposed as an insurance fraud and mass murderer who is suspected in the post-war disappearance of many of the Canadian blockade-runner ships he had earlier serviced in Halifax.[21]

Powerful– Paddlewheel steamer built in Levis, Quebec in 1862. E. Gringras of Quebec City was the owner of the vessel and sold it to U.S. interests as a blockade runner in 1863.

Prince Albert– A Mr. Wilson of Quebec City built the 193-ton vessel in 1854 for the Montreal to Quebec run. In 1865, she was sold to U.S. interests as a blockade runner.[22]

Secret– Purchased after the war in Halifax by the *Quebec and Gulf Ports Steamship Company*.

Saint John– Paddlewheel steamer built by H. Irvine in Saint John, New Brunswick in 1847. Employed as a blockade runner. Sank on a voyage from New York to New Orleans in 1863.

Teazer– Operated as a blockade runner under the name *Bat*, owned by the *Quebec and Gulf Ports Steamship Company* after the war.

Pinoro– Outfitted in Montreal to run the blockade. Ownership unclear.

Rothesay Castle formerly *Southern Belle*– Owners A. Heron of Montreal and D.T. Leach of Toronto. Purpose-built blockade runner appears to have come into Canadian service immediately after the war.[23]

Union– Paddlewheel steamer built in New Brunswick, successfully ran the blockade three times before being captured. Ownership unclear.[24]

This partial list does not include vessels that ran the blockade out of Halifax or Saint John, nor is it likely to include all the vessels with ties to Montreal that ran the blockade. In *one week alone* in 1863 a *New York Times* reporter identified no fewer than five ships in Montreal being loaded with cargo to run the blockade.[25] It is a safe assumption that there were other ships engaged in this lucrative business both before and long after this newspaper report. The frequent reference to U.S. and New York ownership should come as no surprise. New York money was heavily involved in blockade running and contraband trading.

Cotton Pass Signed by A. Lincoln

Executive Mansion
January 11, 1865

An authorized agent of the Treasury Department having with the approval of the Secretary of the Treasury contracted for the cotton and other products above mentioned, and the party having agreed to sell and deliver the same to such agent.

It is ordered that the cotton and other products, moving in compliance with, and for fulfillment of said contract, and being transported to said agent, or under his direction, shall be free from seizure or detention by any officer of the government, and, commandants of military Departments, districts, posts and detachments, naval stations, gun boats, flotilla's and floats fleets will observe this order, and give the said Henry J. Eager, his agents and transports, free and unmolested passage for the purpose of getting the said cotton or any part thereof through the lines, other than blockaded lines, and safe conduct within our lines while the same is moving in strict compliance with the regulations of the Secretary of the Treasury, and for fulfilment of said contract with the agent of the government.

Abraham Lincoln

Map of Confederate Montreal Sites

The majority of historic buildings in Old Montreal would be recognized by Confederate agents if they were to return to Montreal today. Below is a list of just some of the buildings that have particular ties to Confederate activities in Montreal during the American Civil War:

1. **Victoria Barracks**—This impressive and imposing structure was completed shortly before the onset of the American Civil War and served as the center of British military activity in central Canada. A number of the British regiments sent to Canada during the crisis were stationed here. This beautiful building has survived intact on Royer Street in the shadow of Notre Dame Basilica but is largely unrecognized and forgotten.

2. **St. Lawrence Hall Hotel**—Built in the early 1850's on St. James Street for Henry Hogan, St. Lawrence Hall was Montreal's finest hotel during the Civil War. It was located across the street from the main telegraph office where war news was readily available—an ancillary telegraph station was set up in the hotel lobby. St. Lawrence Hall became the unofficial headquarters for the Confederate Secret Service during the later years of the war with whole floors being rented out by them. Every important Confederate agent and official in Canada stayed here at one time or another, including Lincoln assassin John Wilkes Booth. The hotel was located within a stone's throw of the Bank of Montreal and the Bank of Ontario, where the Confederate Secret Service kept something near a million dollars in gold and cash on deposit. Mint Juleps were always available in the hotel's bar.

3. **Bank of Montreal**—Confederate Secret Service kept large deposits in both the Bank of Ontario and the Bank of Montreal. When Confederate Raiders were arrested in Ohio they were carrying large money drafts from the Bank of Montreal. When Varina Davis, wife of Confederate President Jefferson Davis, sought a safe place to store her husband's papers, the Bank of Montreal offered its main vault as a repository.

4. **Bank of Ontario**—Facing Place d'Armes, the Montreal Branch of the Bank of Ontario was a favorite with the Confederate Secret Service, which kept deposits on hand in the range of three quarters of a million dollars. The Bank even employed Confederate bankers in senior positions.

5. **Donegana Hotel**—Under proprietor Daniel Gale, the 150-room Donegana Hotel was a favorite with the Confederate Secret Service. Thanks to Confederate business, the hotel went from a seasonal hostelry to a year-round establishment. Originally a male-only hotel, this too changed once the Confederate Secret Service became the hotel's largest customer. This was the one hotel where U.S. Federal agents found it almost impossible to get a room. Many of the St. Albans Raiders stayed here in the run up to the famous raid into Vermont.

6. **Ottawa Hotel**—Still standing on St. James/St. Jacques Street, this was the unofficial headquarters of the U.S. Secret Service in Montreal. One observer wrote that it was one of the few hotels where a loyal American could get a room without being insulted. While U.S. Federal agents found it impossible to get a room at the Confederate-dominated Donegana hotel, rebel agents would sometimes stay at the Ottawa Hotel, presumably to tweak the noses of their Federal counterparts.

7. **Royal Theatre**—The Royal Theatre was originally located on St. Paul Street across from the famous Rasco Hotel. At the time of the American Civil War, the theatre had moved to Côté Street just around the corner from the Bank of Montreal. During his exile in Montreal, President Jefferson Davis attended a benefit playing of "The Rivals" to raise money for Southern hospitals. The crowd recognized him and rose to give Davis a standing ovation. The orchestra immediately struck up "Dixie."

8. **Lovell Printing House**—Located at 423 St. Nicholas Street in the heart of Old Montreal, Lovell printing has been operating since 1835. The founder, John Lovell, sponsored the Davis family when they were in exile in Montreal. They lived at his home facing Phillips Square across the street from Christ Church Cathedral. Later, Lovell arranged for the Davis family to occupy a beautiful townhouse on Mountain Street. For security reasons Lovell had President Davis' mail sent to this office.

9. **Site of Lovell House**—This was the site of the Lovell Townhouse across the street from Christ Church Cathedral. The Davis family lived here during much of their exile in Montreal. The studio of sculptor Robert Reid, who designed the Confederate monument in Savannah's Forsyth Park, was around the corner on St. Alexander Street.

10. **Approximate site of P.C. Martin's house**—One of the earliest Confederate Secret Service agents in Montreal, Martin lived here with his wife and children. John Wilkes Booth stayed with Martin for a time during his stay in Montreal in October 1864. (He later took a room at St. Lawrence Hall.) Martin provided Booth with money and letters of introduction to Confederate sympathizers on the Maryland/Virginia border. These contacts would be indispensable to Booth's plans to either kidnap or kill President Lincoln. Among these contacts was Dr. Samuel Mudd, who was later convicted of involvement in the Lincoln assassination. It seems very likely that the planning and financing of the plan to kidnap or kill Lincoln originated in Montreal. Martin was also an experienced blockade runner with ties to Southern blockade-running tycoons like Gazaway and Charles Lamar. He was lost at sea on his schooner the *Marie Victoria* in the Gulf of St. Lawrence—part of the cargo was John Wilkes Booth's elaborate theatrical wardrobe.

11. **Patrick C. Martin's Office** on St. John/St. Jean Street in the shadow of magnificent Notre Dame Basilica. This was where Martin and his partner, General William Henry Carroll of Tennessee, ran their liquor importation business. Behind this front their real business was blockade running, which produced breathtaking profits. One round trip on a blockade-runner ship able to carry war materials and medicines inbound and 750-1,000 bales of cotton outbound would be worth half to three quarters of a million dollars (in 1860 currency). Building a large, fast blockade runner would cost about forty to sixty thousand dollars. It doesn't take an MBA to do the math. This was the most lucrative trade on the globe. Some ships made as many as a dozen or more successful round trips through the blockade. Someone was clearly making a lot of money and some of these were Canadians in league with their Southern partners. Martin was a well-established figure in Montreal and was particularly well liked by many of the British officers whose units were garrisoning the city. John Wilkes Booth no doubt visited Martin here at his office on St. Jean Street during Booth's stay in the city in the fall of 1864. It was from here they would have walked around the corner to the Bank of Ontario on Place d'Armes were Booth opened an account.

12. **Christ Church**—Located directly across from the Lovell house, Jefferson Davis and his family attended religious services here during their exile in Montreal.

13. **Montreal Harbour**—Montreal's harbor boomed during the war years and was home to at least twenty blockade runners.

14. **Old Montreal Custom House**—Cargoes were cleared here before setting off down the St. Lawrence River. Cargoes cleared in Montreal did not have to stop in Quebec City on their way to the Gulf of St. Lawrence and the Atlantic. Confederate blockade runners would have been familiar figures in the Custom House during the war.

15. **Mountain Street Townhouse**—This beautiful townhouse at 1181 Mountain Street was made available to the Davis family during the latter half of their stay in Montreal

16. **McGill University**—William C. Macdonald founded the Macdonald's Tobacco Company in Montreal just before the American Civil War. Shortages of tobacco in the northern United States afforded Macdonald a market hungry for his product and his business boomed. His product came from the American South, including both Confederate States and other slave-owning states, like Kentucky, that remained nominally loyal to Washington. Macdonald arranged for tobacco to be shipped north to Montreal for processing and then the finished product was shipped into the northern United States. He used his immense wealth to support many public endeavors, including McGill University where he sponsored the building of a number of McGill University's early halls and refectories.

17. **Mount Royal Cemetery**—Margaret Howell, mother of Varina Davis, took ill and died during their years of exile in Montreal. She was buried in Mount Royal Cemetery. A Montreal philanthropist placed a marker on her grave late in the 20th century.

18. **Site of Prince of Wales Terrace**—Located on Sherbrooke and McGregor Streets, this was one of the finest townhouse complexes in Montreal when it was built in the 1850's. Nashville banker and Confederate Secret Service agent John Porterfield had his home here. He sheltered John Surratt, an accomplice in the Lincoln assassination, in this house in 1865 before Surratt was spirited out of the country by Confederate Secret Service operatives.

19. **Old Court House**—Designed by John Ostell in 1856 this was the scene of the trial of Bennett Young and the other St. Albans raiders in 1865. They were eventually released and much of the stolen loot was returned to them by Canadian authorities.

20. **Old Jail and Gaoler's House**—This was where the St. Albans raiders were imprisoned pending trial. They were given a great many privileges by Jailer Louis Payette, including taking their meals and receiving guests in his house. The dashing Bennett Young became an instant hit with the young ladies of Montreal including, apparently, Payette's daughter. Circumstances for the Raiders could not have been all that bad as Young referred to the jail as "Payette's hotel."

21. **Bonsecours Market**—Construction began in the mid 1840's and was completed by architect George Browne in 1860. The building design was influenced by the Dublin Custom House. Part of the building's east wing served as Montreal's City Hall and Police Headquarters in the 1860's. Police Chief Guillaume Lamothe, who was accused of supporting the St. Albans Raiders, had his office here. Following the release of the Raiders and the return of the stolen bank money to them by Lamothe, he was forced to resign.

22. **Notman House**—Designed by John Wells in 1844, it was acquired in 1876 by famed Montreal photographer William Notman, whose studio was nearby on Bleury Street. Notman was the favorite photographer of Confederate agents, commissioners, raiders, soldiers, and spies visiting Montreal.

Another site of importance not on this map.

Lennoxville—(*Not featured on this map—located in the beautiful Eastern Townships south of Montreal*) Bishop's College was where the Davis boys attended school. Varina and Jefferson Davis lived nearby in Lennoxville at Clark's Hotel. A small colony of Confederate exiles made this area of southern Quebec their home in the immediate aftermath of the war. The area was populated by United Empire Loyalists who were instinctively hostile to any strong central government in Washington.

Notes

INTRODUCTION

1. The Barnett Museum registers were recently acquired by the Niagara Falls Museums and are now for the first time available to scholars. See http://niagarafallsmuseums.ca/discover-our-history/barnett-guest-register/default.aspx (Accessed July 2016.)
2. Elizabeth G Muir. *Riverdale: East of the Don*. (Dundurn Books, Toronto, 2014), 89 and http://www.tchevalier.com/background/40-the-underground-railroad. The total number is not measurable, but even at 30,000 it remains an extraordinary achievement. Given the *Fugitive Slave Act,* which required their enforced return to slavery, these refugees had to avoid law enforcement officials, a sometimes-hostile public, and enormous geographic obstacles. (Try swimming the Niagara River in any season.) The overland trip was a thousand miles or more in length. Getting to Canada was an extraordinary achievement.

CHAPTER 1
Montreal and the Confederacy

1. Claire Hoy, *Canadians in the Civil War* (Toronto, McArthur & Company, 2004), 368. There was no legal restriction on Canadian banks dealing with the Confederacy. Early on in the conflict, the Crown recognized both the North and the South as legitimate "belligerents" at war; thus Britain and Canada were free to do business with both sides, which was precisely what they proceeded to do.
2. Hoy, *Canadians in the Civil War.*
3. To grasp the magnitude of the concentration of American power in Montreal, we need only review the St. Lawrence Hall Guest Book for October 1863 or the summer of 1866 for comparison. In the first case, a few Confederates are present but almost no American politicians, War Department officials, Judge Advocate General officers, Treasury agents or newspapermen. The Guest Book for summer of 1866 is even eerier. The Confederates are entirely gone, vanished into thin air as if they had never been there, the one exception being Robert Cox who makes a single, solitary visit on 15 August 1866. Missing almost entirely are the Democratic and Republican politicians who filled the hotel in the summer and fall of 1864. Also missing are representatives of the JAG Office, the War Department, and the Treasury Department and American newspapermen. Gone also are the mysterious visitors from Cuba and Matamoros. One or two recognizable bankers and businessmen are there but then Montreal was still the business and banking Capital of British North America. The Guest Books for the summer of 1866 have an entirely different and more benign aura about them than those in summer and fall of 1864. Guest Books July, August 1866, National Archives. Guest Departure Books October 1863-August 1864 McCord Museum.
4. Donna R. Causey *Historic Montgomery Theatre Partially Collapses.* <http://alabamapioneers.com/historic-montgomery-theatre-partially-collapses/#sthash.nKwk7ywh.dpbs> (Accessed April 2016.) See also: Barry Sheehy and Cindy Wallace, *The Booth Fragment,* (Published for the Free Library of Philadelphia, 2013). This paper provides details of Gazaway and Charles Lamar's blockade-running activities in New York and Montreal. Available from the Free Library of Philadelphia.
5. St. Lawrence Hall Guest Departures Book for October, November, December 1863, McCord Museum. Only two of St. Lawrence Hall's Guest Departure Books have survived and they are found at the McCord Museum in Montreal. Unlike the Guest Registration Book(s), which

were filled out by the guest or someone in the party, the departure records were the work of professional clerks. The period of October-December 1863 illustrates clearly the uniqueness of the American presence in Montreal in the summer and fall of 1864. In the same period, a year earlier, almost no American politicians were present. The exception is former New York senator Preston King, on 19 November 1863, who was affiliated with the New York Custom House. King had just been displaced by E. D. Morgan in the Senate. In 1865, he served as President Johnson's Chief of Staff. King and Senator Lane of Kansas prevented Mary Surratt's daughter from presenting a clemency plea to President Johnson. Coincidentally, both King and Lane later committed suicide. Also missing from the hotel registers are members of the Judge Advocate General's Office, National Detective Police, and Treasury Department. A few bankers like Hatch, Bliss and Fisk are present but nothing like the tidal wave of bankers, brokers, and robber barons who turn up in Montreal in 1864 and early 1865. Confederate operatives are certainly visible in 1863 but again not on the scale of 1864 and early 1865. Missing also is the long list of Lincoln's enemies and opponents that we find in Montreal in 1864-1865. One interesting note is the initials "DH" beside certain names in the Departure Book. The meaning of the initials "DH" is unclear but may indicate guests that proprietor Henry Hogan took a particular interest in.

6. Barry Sheehy and Cindy Wallace with Vaughnette Goode-Walker, "The Montreal Connection." *Savannah—Immortal City*, Civil War Savannah Series, (Austin: Emerald Press, 2010).

7. The total cost of the war has been estimated by economists as at least 1.5 times the GDP of the entire United States in 1860. Roger L. Ransom, *The Economics of the Civil War*, https://eh.net/encyclopedia/the-economics-of-the-civil-war/ (Accessed March 2016.)

CHAPTER 2
Confederate Montreal

1. Hoy, *Canadians in the Civil War*, viii.
2. Ibid., 16.
3. Thomas DiLorenzo, *The Real Lincoln*, (New York: Three Rivers Press, 2002), 35.

4. Lincoln's First Inaugural Address http://www.abrahamlincolnonline.org/lincoln/speeches/1inaug.htm (Accessed January 2016.)
5. Hoy, *Canadians in the Civil War*, 368.
6. Amanda Foreman, *A World on Fire*, (New York: Random House, 2010), 153.
7. Hoy, *Canadians in the Civil War*, 372.
8. My father, Captain Maurice Sheehy, who is buried in the Notre-Dame-des-Neiges Fireman's Cemetery, the oldest in North America, was laid to rest not far from McGee. He often took me to visit McGee's grave and referred to him as an Irish Nationalist and a Canadian Patriot. McGee was an accomplished historian, writer, publisher, poet, political leader, and a man of action. He donated his extensive library to Loyola College in Montreal, now part of Concordia University.
9. William Fong, *Biography of William C. Macdonald*, (Montreal: McGill Queen's University Press, Kingston, 2010), 61-66.
10. Foreman, *A World on Fire*, 210.
11. Foreman, *A World on Fire*, 117
12. Ibid., 177.
13. Foreman, *A World on Fire*, 172-179.
14. Ibid.
15. John Herd Thompson and Stephen J. Randall, *Canada and the United States: Ambivalent Allies*, 37. https://muse.jhu.edu/book/11562 (Accessed October 2011.)
16. Ibid., 37
17. Foreman, 184.
18. Foreman, *A World on Fire*, 194.
19. Ibid., 193.
20. Ibid., 185.
21. Ibid., 189-190.
22. Ibid., 187.
23. Ibid., 193.
24. Mrs. P.C. Martin was arrested at Rouses Point carrying a letter sewn into her clothing, and was taken into custody and questioned. Belle Boyd, who was at St. Lawrence Hall when John Wilkes Booth registered in October 1864, was twice arrested and imprisoned. She was finally forced into exile. (Judge Advocate General Edwards Pierrepont, who may have been at St. Lawrence Hall under the name Pierrepont Edwards in October 1864, was responsible for Boyd's conditional release.) Reid Sanders, son of

Confederate Commissioner George Sanders, was captured carrying dispatches from Montreal to Richmond and died in a Federal Prison Camp. Robert Kennedy and John Yates Beall, who both operated out of Montreal, were captured and executed at Fort Lafayette in New York harbor just prior to the end of the war. Sam Davis, also registered at St. Lawrence Hall, was captured carrying dispatches and likewise sentenced to death. Only the intervention of Jacob Thompson directly with President Lincoln saved his life.

25. Guest Book 16 July 1864 has two side-by-side registrations for a Beall and a Hines arriving from Buffalo and Oswego, NY. These are very likely Confederate agents John Y. Beall and Thomas Hines. Beall would be hanged at Fort Lafayette in New York harbor late in the war and Hines went on to play a major role in the Northwest Conspiracy.

26. Accounts and Papers of the House of Commons 1865, Testimony following President Lincoln's Assassination. See http://bit.ly/2p0O1TZ (Accessed March 2016.) See also Edward Steers and William C. Edwards. *The Lincoln Assassination: The Evidence.* (Chicago: The University of Chicago, 2009), 686.

27. Peter J. Sehlinger, *Kentucky's Last Cavalier: General William Preston 1816-1887*, 183. http://bit.ly/2oBLrrb (Accessed March 2016.)

28. Charles Hawkins, trans., *Blockade and Blockade Running*, 6. http://chab-belgium.com/pdf/english/Blockade%20Runners1.pdf (Accessed March 2016.)

29. Richard Frajola, *Tales of the Blockade*, Exhibit. See http://www.rfrajola.com/blockade/Blockades.pdf (Accessed March 2016.) The Navy had captured 1,149 blockade runners, and burned, run aground, or destroyed a further 355. Clearly, many others got away, indicating that the total fleet must have been near two thousand vessels of all classes. (Accessed March 2016.)

30. Barry Sheehy and Cindy Wallace, *The Booth Fragment*, (Published for the Free Library of Philadelphia, 2013). This paper provides details of Gazaway and Charles Lamar's blockade-running activities in New York and Montreal. Available from the Free Library of Philadelphia.

31. John Bell, *Rebels on the Great Lakes*, (Toronto: Dundurn Group, 2011), 163. Ann Larabee. *The Dynamite Fiend*, (Halifax: Nimbus Publishing, 2005,) 61.

32. Guest Book 21 August 64.

33. James Duffey, *Victim of Honor, The Life and Death of John Yates Beall*, (Westfield Center: Rion Hall Publishing, 2007).

34. Sheehy, *Immortal City*, 420 and Sheehy and Wallace, *The Booth Fragment*.

35. Carman Cumming, *The Devil's Game, the Civil War Intrigues of Charles A. Dunham*, (Chicago: University of Illinois, 2004), 159.

36. Sheehy, *Immortal City*, 420; Barry Sheehy and Cindy Wallace, *Brokers Bankers and Bay Lane*, (Austin: Emerald Books, 2011), 157; Sheehy and Wallace. *The Booth Fragment.* St. Lawrence Hall Guest Book 8 April 1864.

37. *New York Times* 16 January 1864, *New York Times* Archives

38. John Bell, *Rebels on the Great Lakes*, (Toronto: Dundurn Press, 2011), 49-67.

39. John Wilkinson, *The Narrative of a Blockade Runner*, (New York: Sheldon and Co., 1877), 182-184.

40. Adam Mayers, *Dixie and the Dominion*, (Toronto: Dundurn Press, 2003), 88 & Charles Wilson Murray, *Memoirs of a Great Detective* assembled by Victor Speer, 1904-1905, London. William Heinemann, 25. Murray was a gunner on the SS Michigan at Sandusky Ohio during the incident and an eye witness. He appears to be the chief source regarding Captain Coles letters and money. Murray claims Coles had $600 in cash, some letters and a number of money drafts for $5,000 each drawn on the Bank of Montreal. Murray is certainly credible. He went on to become a legendary detective in Canada and is featured in the Ontario Provincial Police Museum. See also: Horan, James David. *Confederate Agent: A Discovery in History.* (Golden Springs Publishing, 2015). In writing about Captain Thomas Hines and the Northwest Conspiracy in his book, James Horan discussed a meeting in Montreal between Senior Confederate Commissioner Jacob Thompson and C.C. Clay witnessed by Captain Hines. Hines noted tension between Thompson and Clay who had only recently arrived in Canada. Clay insisted that he have an independent account to cover his work. Thompson agreed to provide just under $100,000. This was deposited in an account under Clay's name the next morning at the Bank of Montreal. Most of this money would later be transferred to the Niagara and District

Bank in St. Catharine's where Clay set up headquarters. Such a large deposit in a small regional bank gave the Confederates effective control of the institution.

41. Daniel B. Lucas, *Memoir of John Yates Beall*, (Montreal: John Lovell,1865), 38-46. Lovell's printing house still operates on St. Nicolas Street in Old Montreal, probably the oldest continuously operating family business in Canada.

42. John W. Headley, *Confederate Operations in Canada and New York*, (New York: Neale Publishing, 1906), 274-277; Nat Brandt, *The Man Who Tried to Burn New York*, (Syracuse: Syracuse University Press, 1986), 77; Adam Mayers, *Dixie and the Dominion*, (Toronto: Dundurn Press, 2003), 88.

43. Ibid., 292-293. Headley registered at St. Lawrence Hall 17 July 1864 as J.W. Headley/Hedley. R. Kennedy registered 1 November 1864. Jacob Thompson wrote to Secretary of State Judah Benjamin about destroying shipping along the Mississippi in his final report. See Appendix C.

44. Guest Book and Guest Departure books. There are a number of registrations for Morgan from New York in 1864. For example, on 2 June 1864, J.V. Morgan is registered in the hotel's "departure" book preserved at the McCord Museum, Montreal.

45. Mathew Josephson, *The Robber Barons*, (New York: A Harvest Book, 1962), 62. For a discussion of the Bank of Montreal's participation in the New York gold market during the Civil War see Dictionary of Canadian Biography, Vol 12, 486, http://bit.ly/2nK9ccD

46. William Tidwell, *April '65*, (Ohio: Kent State, 1995), 141-146, 171.

47. William Tidwell, James Hall and David Gaddy, *Come Retribution: The Confederate Secret Service and the Assassination of Lincoln*, (Jackson: University Press of Mississippi, 1988) 238.

48. Guest Book 6 August 1864.

49. Larry Tagg, *The Unpopular Mr. Lincoln, The Story of America's Most Reviled President*, (New York: Savas Beatie, 2009), 417.

50. James Conroy, *Our One Common Country. Abraham Lincoln and the Hampton Roads Peace Conference*, (Guilford: Lyons Press, 2014), 273. It is interesting that rumors of Lincoln's possible assassination were already known to some in Congress.

51. Tidwell, *April '65*, 16-18, 21-25, 128. A copy of the original appropriation signed by Jefferson Davis and Judah Benjamin is in the National Archives, Washington. See also Mayers, *Dixie and the Dominion*, 29-30.

52. Mayers, *Dixie and the Dominion*, 88. Confederate raiders arrested prior to attacking Johnson's Island POW camp were found in possession of hundreds of dollars in cash and a batch of cashier's checks for $5,000 drawn on the Bank of Montreal.

53. Benn Pitman, ed., *The Assassination of President Lincoln and the Trial of the Conspirators* (1865), (New York: Moore, Wilstach & Baldwin, 1865), 63.

54. Francess G. Halpenny, *Dictionary of Canadian Biography - Volume 12* (Toronto: University of Toronto Press, 1990), 486. "It was common knowledge that gold was being withdrawn from Upper Canada by the branch (main branch of the Bank of Montreal) and offered in the New York market, where gold prices were high because of the Civil War...Gold could be lent at very high rates of interest (in New York). As security for the gold, current funds were deposited. These funds were employed by Edwin King (GM, Bank of Montreal) in discounting commercial bills." Large profits were made. See also "King, Edwin Henry, Banker Montreal," http://www.biographi.ca/en/bio/king_edwin_henry_12E.html (Accessed March 2016.)

55. Edward Steers, The Assassination of President Lincoln and the Trial of the Conspirators, (Louisville: The University of Kentucky Press, 2003), 401.

56. Tidwell, Hall, and Gaddy. *Come Retribution*, 333-335, 416. Three Confederates, including H.V. Clinton, met with John Wilkes Booth at the Parker House in Boston. Clinton was almost certainly an alias and the name turns up again at St. Lawrence Hall. The Parker House meeting was followed by a larger, longer meeting in Montreal. Thomas Jones was a senior Confederate Signals Officer in southern Maryland. He assisted Confederate couriers traveling north to Canada and south to Richmond. The trip had become almost routine. Whoever he is, the name T.A. Jones appears in the Guest Book on 13 August 1864 arriving from the border state of Tennessee. As for T. Jones he is also found in the St. Lawrence Hall Guest "departure" book on 2 May 1864. Jones registers as Dr. T. Jones accompanied by Conl (Col) Jones room 122; perhaps the two are the same man, i.e., Col T. Jones.

What's intriguing is a margin note which lists "Pollack" and "Jones" as being affiliated or associated in some way, noted by hotel staff or proprietor Henry Hogan. Walter Pollack was a senior National Detective Police detective and brother-in-law to National Detective Police chief Lafayette Baker. Was Pollack tailing Jones or involved with him in some other way? Pollack keeps interesting company in St. Lawrence Hall. He checks in with senior Confederate Commissioner Luke Blackburn 18 October 1864, the same day as John Wilkes Booth. He also registers with or alongside mysterious Confederate courier Sarah Slater. At Barnett's Niagara Museum, he checks in on 3 September 1864, the day before Radical Republican James Ashley. Jones registers again on 13 August 1864. Registering the day after Jones, on 14 August, was Benjamin Stringfellow, a key Confederate operative with a swashbuckling reputation as both a spy and a daring cavalry officer. He served as a scout for both J.E.B. Stuart and the Gray Ghost, Colonel John S. Mosby. This is significant as a detachment of Mosby's Rangers had been sent into the Northern Neck area of northern Virginia where they were to support clandestine crossings of the Potomac. Stringfellow was known to be operating in the North and in Canada from the middle of 1864 through the end of the war. After Lee's surrender, Stringfellow refused to take the oath and lived for a time with his wife in Canada.

57. Alexandra Lee Levin, *This Awful Drama: General Edwin Gray Lee, C.S.A., and His Family,* (New York: Vantage Press, 1987), 174, 177,188,190,192; Duffey, *Victim of Honor.*

58. Daniel Lucas, *The Land Where We Were Dreaming* http://cw.routledge.com/textbooks/9780415537070/data/section5/lucas-in_the_land.pdf (Accessed March 2016.)

59. Colonel Ulric Dahlgren was killed leading a cavalry raid on Richmond on 2 March 1864. The nominal mission of the raid was to free prisoners but orders to assassinate Jefferson Davis and members of his cabinet were found on Dahlgren. The orders were disavowed but the authorities in the South were convinced the orders were authentic. Tidwell, Hall, and Gaddy *Come Retribution,* 249.

60. Ibid.

61. Stephen Wise, *Lifeline of the Confederacy: Blockade Running during the Civil War,* (Columbia: University of South Carolina Press, 1989) 139.

62. Wilkinson, *Narrative of a Blockade Runner,* 181-188.

63. http://www.pddoc.com/skedaddle/articles/wilmington_NC_during_blockade%20.htm (Accessed March 2016.)

64. Hoy, *Canadians in the Civil War,* 247-248.

65. Charles Higham, *Murdering Mr. Lincoln,* (Beverly Hills: New Millennium Press, 2004), 195-196, 224.

66. Frank Van Der Linden, *The Dark Intrigue,* (Golden: Fulcrum Publishing, 2007), 158-163.

67. Ibid. He feared the defeated cabinet members would be treated "with contumely and violence." Black had a sterling reputation for integrity and was trusted even by the Confederate Secret Service.

68. Ibid.; Headley, *Operations,* 257; Edward M. Coffman, *CAPTAIN HINES' ADVENTURES IN THE NORTHWEST CONSPIRACY.* The Register of the Kentucky Historical Society Vol. 63, No. 1 (January, 1965), pp. 30-38. https://www.jstor.org/stable/pdf/23375860.pdf?seq=1#page_scan_tab_contents (Accessed 3/12/17.) See also *The Papers of Jefferson Davis,* Jefferson Davis, reprinted by LSU Press, 30; Cumming, *The Devil's Game,* 158, 280. Like so many others in this story, Judge Black would later be involved in the Johnson impeachment. In this case, Black opposed Stanton and supported President Johnson. He also became entangled in the trial of Charles Dunham who was a key witness in the Lincoln Assassination Trial. Cumming, *The Devil's Game,* 158, 252-254.

69. Cumming, *The Devil's Game,* 159, 280.

70. Guest Book 4 November 1864. There is also an intriguing registration at Barnett's Museum at Niagara Falls on **25 Aug**ust 1864 for William Seward. The signature is a good match with examples of Seward's surviving autograph. In the absence of some additional confirmatory evidence, however, we have listed this as speculative. However, it remains intriguing.

71. *MONTREAL, Monday, Feb. 27, 1865.*
DEAR SIR: Upon my urgent request Hon. R.J. WALKER came to Montreal. After nearly a month's conference with myself and the leading Confederates in Canada, and overcoming what appeared to be almost insurmountable obstacles on both sides, Mr. WALKER has created a basis of settlement to be presented to the public over his own signature, that if acted upon in the true spirit of conciliation and compromise in which the Federal Constitution was framed,

will, in my opinion, lead to an adjustment of all difficulties, satisfactory alike to the North and South. The leading feature of this compromise is to prevent the ascendancy of geographical parties, and make the election of a sectional President and Vice-President impossible; also, further guarantees for line protection of the rights of the minority under the constitution, by requiring at least partial concurrent legislative action of the different sections on important subjects; also, a diminution of executive power, Mr. WALKER thinks these would be important provisions for preventing sectional difficulties; and that secession as a constitutional right should be surrendered, leaving that question to stand upon the right revolution, as in other countries.

Mr. WALKER proposes that the constitution shall be so amended as that after the lapse of a reasonable period, to prohibit the levying of all duties upon imports except for revenue.

Mr. WALKER's address will be based upon the principle of perfect constitutional equality of all the States, and the reserved rights of every one of them to be regarded by the general government, to assure Mexico and all other portions of North America of non-intervention in their local affairs should they choose to become members.

It is an essential part of this compromise, with a view to prevent Negro States in the South, that the constitution should be so amended as to forever forbid the interference by Congress with the regulation of the right of suffrage in any State.

The constitutional amendment abolishing slavery having passed Congress, Mr. WALKER says that no agitation in Congress can take place hereafter, all responsibility of the Federal Government having thus ceased on this question.

The North and South agreeing upon the basis of settlement, the war to cease, and a convention of all the States to be held as soon as practicable.

This plan is the result of patient comparison of ideas, and is founded upon that principle of mutual concession, by which both sections, though yielding nothing injurious to their honor or interest, will put an end to the otherwise disastrous warfare. Let me ask you to consider whether such a settlement is not better than an indefinite prolongation of, the present struggle, with all the dangers that are to follow.

If you desire, Mr. WALKER will confer with you on the subject. He leaves here for New-York and Washington

in a few days. I would also be pleased to hear from you myself. Direct under cover to Mr. HENRY HOGAN, proprietor St. Lawrence Hall, Montreal. Respectfully, GEO. N. SANDERS.

EDITOR N.Y. TIMES, N.Y.

72. Who were Mr. Vance and Mr. Stites/Stiles who arrive in Montreal on 28 September or James Taylor who arrives on 12 October or J.S. Snyder who arrives on 11 November 1864?

73. David Surdam, *Traders or Traitors: Northern Cotton Trading During the Civil War*, (Chicago: Dept. Economics, Loyola University, 1999), 307 – quote from Browning Diary, 1933, Vol. 2, 1,5 and *Browning Diary* 24, 26 December 1864, Browning recorded in his diary 5 January 1865: "*I had previously talked with him about permitting Singleton to go South to buy Cotton, tobacco and a scheme out of which he, Singleton, Judge James Hughes of the Court of Claims, Senator Edwin D. Morgan myself and some others hope to make some money, and do the Country some service. He wished to see me upon this subject now. We talked it all over, and before leaving him he gave me two cards of Singleton to pass our lines with ordinary baggage, and go South.*" See quote http://abrahamlincolnsclassroom.org/abraham-lincoln-in-depth/abraham-lincoln-and-cotton/ (Accessed March 2016.)

74. Tidwell, Hall and Gaddy, *Come Retribution*, 188.

75. Ibid.

76. Confederate agents George Kane and Kinsey J. Stewart, both of whom operated in Canada, proposed clandestine operations to Jefferson Davis and Judah Benjamin in 1864. Historian William Tidwell, *Come Retribution*, believes these plans were directed against Lincoln and may have been the antecedents of efforts to kidnap the President, of which John Wilkes Booth's plot was one of several. Stewart asked General Lee his views on the "morality" of his proposed plan, which certainly indicates it was out of the ordinary. Lee did not think much of the plan or Stewart's ability to pull it off but passed him on to Colonel E.G. Lee. He eventually put his plan before Jefferson Davis and Judah Benjamin. Whatever the plan, everyone seemed a little squeamish about it. The failed Dahlgren raid on 2 March 1864, where orders were found calling for the assassination of Jefferson Davis and his cabinet, hardened attitudes considerably in the South. It was in this environment that a number of

operations against Lincoln were set in motion. Tidwell, *Come Retribution*, 274-283

77. See Alabama Claims http://future.state.gov/when/time-line/1861_timeline/alab_claims.html (Accessed March 2016.)

78. William Cooper, *Jefferson Davis, American*, (New York: Random House, 2010), 612.

79. Nicholas Rescher, *Niagara-on-the-Lake as a Confederate Refuge*, (Niagara Historical Society, NAP Publications, 2003.

CHAPTER 3
Confederate Couriers

1. H. Donald Winkler, *Stealing Secrets*, (Naperville: Cumberland House, 2010), 42.

2. Michael W. Kauffman, *American Brutus: John Wilkes Booth and the Lincoln Conspiracies*, (New York: Random House, 2004), 198, 351.

3. Winkler, *Stealing Secrets*, 29.

4. George Atzerodt's Lost Confession. **See** http://rogerjnorton.com/Lincoln82.html (Accessed March 2016.)

5. James O. Hall, *The Saga of Sarah Slater*, (*The Surratt House Society* February 1982).

6. Louis J. Weichmann, *A True History of the Assassination of Abraham Lincoln and the Conspiracy of 1865*, (New York: Alfred A. Knopf, 1979), 385.

7. Ibid., 85. Mary Surratt tells Weichmann that Slater will go to the French Consul for help if arrested. The family of Josephine Brown living in and around Camden, SC were interviewed in October 2012 and one piece of oral history passed down to them was that Josephine spoke French fluently and would seek help from the French Embassy if arrested. The coincidence is eerie. The original family interview notes are in the possession of the author.

8. Notes from *Camden, SC Archives* including a letter from historian James Hall dated 30 August 2012. These notes and photocopies are in the possession of the author.

9. Tidwell, *Come Retribution*, 406.

10. Daniel E. Sutherland, *The Confederate Carpetbaggers* (Baton Rouge: Louisiana State University Press, 1988), 146.

11. Charles Hallock, *The Hidden Way to Dixie, Confederate Veteran*, Vol. XXIV. November 1916, No. 11, 494-497. Note: The address is variously listed as 12 or 93 Beaver Street. Perhaps he was associated with both addresses. Beaver Street was in downtown Manhattan near Wall Street. In Virginia Clay's memoirs, *A Belle of the Fifties*, she quotes a letter which lists Brown's address as 93 Beaver Street, 237: "*To the Honourable H. L. Clay, Richmond, Virginia. I am well. Have written every week, but received no answer later than the 30th of June. Can I return at once? If not, send my wife to me by flag of truce, via Washington, but not by sea. Do write by flag of truce care of John Potts Brown, No. 93 Beaver Street, New York. Answer by personal [advertisement] through Richmond Enquirer and New York News.*" Delmonico's was a favorite of Confederate agents. For example, Nelson Trowbridge, who worked for blockade runners Gazaway and Charles Lamar, frequented Delmonico's. See *New York Times* 1864 article *The Lamar Correspondence; Further Interesting Developments* about intercepted correspondence at http://www.nytimes.com/1864/01/16/news/lamar-correspondence-further-interesting-developments-implications-citizens-new.html?pagewanted=5 (Accessed March 2016.)

12. Tidwell, *Come Retribution*, 406.

13. Sutherland, *Confederate Carpetbaggers*, 146-148. Note: The partnership did not end well, with Cuyler accusing Potts Brown of skimming money off the top.

14. Hoy, *Canadians in the Civil War*, 353. Files for Josephine Brown at Camden archives in possession of the author. The dreadful conditions at Andersonville had to do with insufficient food and poor source water, both of which were largely beyond the control of Captain Wirz. It can be argued the real cause of these unnecessary deaths was the Federal government's unwillingness to exchange prisoners. Confederate POW's tended to return to the front while Federal POW's were usually invalided home. Grant forbade exchanges because he feared a war of "extermination" if Confederate prisoners of war, now veterans, were paroled and returned to reinforce Confederate armies in the field. Lincoln noted that General Grant understood the terrible mathematics of the war, i.e., the South would bleed to death long before the North. Additional note of interest: when stationed in Richmond, Robert was a member of an accomplished theatrical group. Virginia Clay remembers him playing in *The Rivals* to a sell-out crowd. Ironically, this was the

same play Jefferson Davis attended at the *Royal Theatre* in Montreal in 1867 where the crowd acknowledged him as the orchestra played "Dixie." Virginia Clay-Clopton, *A Belle of the Fifties, Memoirs of Mrs. Clay of Alabama, covering social and political life in Washington and the South, 1853-66* (New York: *Doubleday*, 1904), 176.

15. Elizabeth Hough, "*Josephine Noel, Camden's Confederate Spy,*" *UDC Magazine*, August 2007, provided by the Camden Archives and Museum 30 August 2012.

16. *Notes of James Hall*, copied by the Camden Archives and Museum for Barry Sheehy August 2012 and in possession of the author.

17. Ibid.

18. Ibid.

19. Thomas Conolly, *An Irishman in Dixie: Thomas Conolly's Diary of the Fall of the Confederacy,* Edited by Nelson Langford (Columbia: University of South Carolina Press, 1988). 42. Conolly records in his diary "Pretty Mrs. Brown." He spent considerable time with Josephine in Richmond in March 1865 just before the fall of the city.

20. Hallock, *The Hidden Way to Dixie Confederate Veteran,* Vol. XXIV, November 1916, Number 11.

21. *Notes of James Hall* from Camden Archives and Museum, in possession of the author.

22. *Clement C. Clay Papers* H.L. Clay to C.C. Clay, 8 March 1865 and 22 March 1865. Josephine Brown to C.C. Clay as cited in Lankford, Nelson D., ed. *An Irishman in Dixie: Thomas Conolly's Diary of the Fall of the Confederacy.* Columbia: The University of South Carolina Press, 1988.

23. Ibid.

24. Camden Archives and Museum, *Notes of James Hall* in possession of the author. See also Clay-Clopton, *A Belle of the Fifties.*

25. Tidwell, *Come Retribution,* 406 and Footnote 9 on 424.

26. Notes from Camden SC Museum and Archives on Josephine Brown, *UDC Magazine* August 2007, in possession of the author.

27. Ibid.

28. Notes and copies obtained by researcher Tracy Bakic October 2012 in Greenwood SC. Notes are signed and notarized.

29. A possible candidate for the "Yankee" in the story is former president Franklin Pierce. At Clay's request Josephine met with "Mr. Pierce" in New Hampshire on her last trip to Richmond in March 1865. She then carried private correspondence from Pierce to Clay. This is very likely former President Franklin Pierce who retired to New Hampshire. Unfortunately, Clay did not make it to Richmond. His vessel ran aground running the blockade. He survived but failed to make the rendezvous with Brown in Richmond. After waiting for weeks, Josephine, running out of money, headed north to New York and Montreal 18 March 1865. *Clement Clay Papers*, Duke University, collection of letters by Virginia Clay

30. *Clement Clay Papers*, Duke University, collection of letters by Virginia Clay

31. Lankford, *An Irishman in Dixie*, 42-44, 46, 60, 61, 104, 113, 126.

32. Ibid.

33. Ibid.

34. *Clement Clay Papers*, Duke University, Collection of Virginia Clay, 18 March 1865. Brown to C. Clay.

35. Martin was a sort of unofficial Consul for the Confederacy in the city. His role was superseded with the arrival of Commissioner Jacob Thompson in 1864.

36. Wilkinson, Narrative of a Blockade Runner, 183-184.

37. Ibid.

38. Bell, Rebels on the Great lakes, 33-37.

39. Alexander Milton Ross, Recollections and Experience of an Abolitionist, (Toronto: Roswell and Hutchison, 1875), 140-149.

40. Ibid.

41. Ibid.

42. Ann Larabee, The Dynamite Fiend, (Halifax: Nimbus Publishing, 2005), 62-63.

43. Tidwell, *Come Retribution,* 415-416; Weichmann, *A True History,* 85-86; Surratt, *Trial of John H. Surratt in the Criminal Court for the District of Columbia, Hon. George Fisher Presiding* (Washington: *Government Printing Office,* 1867), 1107-1108.

44. Pitman, *The Assassination of President Lincoln and the Trial of the Conspirators,*114.

45. Ibid., 1354.

46. Ibid.

47. Surratt, *Trial of John Surratt 1867,* 1354.

48. Ibid. Note: McMillan could not remember the woman who urged the shooting. When asked by the prosecutor if

her name was "Mrs. Slater" he responded that it sounded like that but he could not be certain.

49. Text of *George Atzerodt's Lost Confession* at http://rogerjnorton.com/Lincoln82.html (Accessed March 2016.)

50. Surratt, *Trial of John Surratt 1867*, 1354.

51. "Hidden Way to Dixie," *Confederate Veteran*.

52. Weichmann, *A True History*, 385.

53. Ibid.

54. *George Atzerodt's Lost Confession* at http://rogerjnorton.com/Lincoln27.html (Accessed April 2016.)

55. Sarah Slater at http://bit.ly/2nDZ988 (Accessed Mar 2016.)

56. Surratt, *Trial of John Surratt 1867*, 467.

57. Ibid., 435. Slater/Thompson/Brown are recorded as being from North Carolina. In *Confederate Operations in Canada and New York*, John Headley reported that she was from Kentucky, 377, and in *George Atzerodt's Lost Confession* he described Thompson/Brown as being a widow from South Carolina.

58. Headley, *Confederate Operations in Canada and New York*, p. 376; *George Atzerodt's Lost Confession*; Weichmann, *True History*; and Surratt, *Trial of John Surratt*. Note: George Atzerodt thought she was about 20, Louis Weichmann about 22, and John Headley about 24 years of age. David Barry thought she was under 30 years of age. All describe her as attractive with black hair and black eyes, generally wearing a veil or "lady's mask" which disguised her identity; she apparently spoke fluent French.

59. Kauffman, *American Brutus*, 192, 193.

60. Surratt, *Trial of John Surratt*, 1876, 1107-1108.

61. Ibid.

62. Higham, *Murdering Mr. Lincoln*, 194, 248; Tidwell, *Come Retribution*, 406-407; MacMillan Publishing, *The Confederacy: Selections from the Four Volume McMillan Encyclopedia of the Confederacy*, (MacMillan Library Reference, 1991), 380. Brown and Slater identified together as couriers.

63. Sheehy, *The Booth Fragment*.

64. Headley, *Confederate Operations*, 376.

65. Headley, *Confederate Operations*, 377.

66. Ibid.

67. Clearly the mouth in the Headley 1906 book photo of Sarah Slater is off center, possibly from an inadvertent movement during the extended photo shoot. Headley, *Confederate Operations in Canada and New York*, 376-377.

68. James Hall notes, *Camden SC Archives and Museum*.

69. Edward Steers, *Blood on the Moon: The Assassination of Abraham Lincoln*, (Lexington: The University Press of Kentucky, 2005), 58-59.

70. Notes from Camden SC Archives and Museum. This may be Mrs. Virginia Clay, wife to former Senator and now senior Confederate Commissioner in Canada Clement C. Clay. She was a close friend of Josephine and Robert Brown. Only ten years older that Brown, who called her "auntie," Clay was a great beauty in her own right. See Clay, *A Belle of the Fifties*. Conolly, *An Irishman in Dixie*, 42.

71. Lankford, *Irishman in Dixie*, 126.

72. Clement Clay Papers, Duke University, Collection of Virginia Clay 18 March 1865, reproduced in notes from Camden SC Archives and Museum. In the possession of the author.

73. Surratt, *Trial of John Surratt*, testimony of David Barry, 1107-1108. Tidwell, *Come Retribution*, 415-416.

74. Lankford, *Irishman in Dixie*, 61, 104, 113, 126.

75. Surratt, *Trial of John Surratt 1867*, 1107-1108.

76. Ibid.

77. Lankford, *Irishman in Dixie*, 42-44, 46, 60, 61, 104, 107-108, 113, 126.

78. Ibid.

79. St. Lawrence Hall Guest Book at the National Archives of Canada 15 February 1865. Mrs. Sarah Slater registers at 3 a.m. in the morning after arriving from New York.

80. St. Lawrence Hall Guest Book 20 December 1864, 15 February 1865. Walter Pollack keeps interesting company in St. Lawrence Hall. He checks in with Dr. Luke Blackburn 18 October 1864, the same day as John Wilkes Booth. His room is next to Blackburn's 158/159. In the "Departure" book for 2 May 1864 Pollack's name appears in the margin notes, put there presumably by hotel staff who note "Pollack, Jones." Pollack was not registered at the hotel at the time but someone noted in the margins an implied relationship or interest between Pollack and Jones. On the same page in the "Departure" register for 2 May 1864, T. Jones and Conl (Col) Jones are in room 122, perhaps the two are the same man, i.e., Thomas Jones and Col T. Jones CSA Signal Corps. Thomas Jones was the Confederacy's chief signals officer in southern

Maryland. He was also a key player in the courier lines running through that part of the state and knew all the key couriers running this line which would have included, among others, Sarah Slater, Josephine Brown, and John Surratt. Jones played a key role in John Wilkes Booth's escape following the Lincoln assassination. Was Pollack tailing Jones or involved with him in some other way?

81. Ibid.

82. St. Lawrence Hall Departure Book 2 May 1864

83. St. Lawrence Hall Guest Book 10 January 1865. Historian John Stanton, who has spent many years investigating Slater, believes she may have also registered at St. Lawrence Hall under her mother's maiden name, A. Renaud; and indeed we find an A. Renaud at St. Lawrence Hall, arriving from New York, on 10, 17 December 1864, as well as 9, 17 March 1865.

84. Guest Book 10 January 1865.

85. Guest Book 18 April 1865.

86. Ibid.

87. Roy Z. Chamlee, *Lincoln's Assassins: A Complete Account of Their Capture, Trial, and Punishment*, (North Carolina: McFarland Publishing, 1990), 198.

88. Ibid., 198.

89. Ibid.

90. Ibid.

91. Donald E. Markle, Spies and Spymasters of the Civil War (New York: Barnes and Noble, 1994), 164-166.

92. James O. Hall, "The Saga of Sarah Slater." Reprinted in *In Pursuit of: Continuing Research in the Field of the Lincoln Assassination* (Surratt Society, 1990). John F. Stanton, "A Mystery No Longer: The Lady in the Veil." Surratt Courier, August 2011 and October 2011. See http://bit.ly/20IBuFk. Sarah Slater is buried next to her mother and sister in Poughkeepsie NY's Rural Cemetery. Despite her extraordinary past and her ties to Booth and Surratt, she does not appear to have discussed these years with her family. She was truly a keeper of secrets.

93. Ibid.

94. St. Lawrence Hall Guest Book 4 November 1864.

95. Tidwell, *Come Retribution*, 192, 194, 265. Confederate couriers and agents regularly checked the register of Barnett's Museum – Niagara Falls Museums to determine which agents were in the area or who had passed north ahead of them.

96. Ibid., 194.

97. Ibid., 265, 175, 192, 194, 195.

98. Clement Clay Papers 1811-1925, *Duke University*, Collection of Virginia Clay. Josephine Brown letters. It is ironic that Brown and Sarah Slater, who were so often confused with one another, should both have ties to Poughkeepsie NY. Brown stayed there for a time at Cox's house awaiting dispatches from Clement Clay.

99. Ibid.

100. Tidwell, *Come Retribution*, 194, 265.

101. In yet another ironic crossing of paths, Brown and Slater both have ties to Poughkeepsie. Brown spent time there at Robert Cox's home awaiting dispatches from Clement Clay. Meanwhile Sarah Slater, as well as mother and sister, spent their last years in Poughkeepsie and appear to be buried in Poughkeepsie's Rural Cemetery. John F. Stanton, "*A Mystery No Longer: The Lady in the Veil.*" Surratt Courier, August 2011 and October 2011

102. Tidwell, *Come Retribution*, 192, 194, 265.

103. Ibid.

104. Ibid.

105. Browning, Orville H. *Diary of Orville Hickman Browning*. Edited by Theodore C. Pease and James G. Randall, (Springfield: Illinois State Historical Library, 1925), 685, entries for 28, 29 September 1864.

106. Sheehy, *The Booth Fragment*.

107. Hoy, *Canadians in the Civil War*, 324-330.

108. The British government urged Canada to strengthen its neutrality laws. With Macdonald leading the way, the Frontier Outrages Bill, later known as the Alien Act, was passed into law on 1 February 1865. On 6 February, the new law was promulgated with the approval of Governor General Monck. Robin Winks, *Civil War years: Canada and the United States*. (Montreal: McGill-Queen's Press,1960), 329.

109. Headley, Confederate Operations, 376.

110. St. Lawrence Hall Guest Book 15 December 1864.

111. There is a registration for A. Reynaud in the hotel on 10, 17 December. Historian John Stanton has suggested Slater sometimes registered under her mother's maiden name A. Renaud. The Renaud signature, however, is bolder than Slater's diminutive hand.

112. Headley, Confederate Operations, 377.

113. Guest Book 18 April 1865

114. Levin, Alexandra Lee. *This Awful Drama.* (New York: Vantage Press, 1987.) 154.

115. Original notes from Camden SC Archives and Museum containing letter from James O. Hall.

116. Ibid.

117. Ibid.

118. Ibid.

119. She is listed in the graveyard records as "Confederate spy Josephine Brown, born in New York 1835, died in Camden SC 1915." Lincoln Assassination Forum http://www.lincoln-assassination.com/bboard/index.php?-topic=43.0 (Accessed Mar 2016.)

CHAPTER 4
American Power Comes to Montreal

1   Bernhard Thuersam. *Wilmington to Canada: Blockade Runners & Secret Agents.* http://www.cfhi.net/Wilmingtons WartimeCanadianConnection.php (Accessed Mar 2016.) In just four months from October 1864 to January 1865, the Port of Wilmington received nearly nine million pounds of meat, almost all of it salted and much of it canned. Most of this meat came from packers in the North. In addition, more foodstuffs were crossing the porous border to the west and from Texas in the south. This inflow of contraband was paid for primarily with cotton.

2. Lawrence Karson, *American Smuggling as a White Collar Crime,* (New York: Routledge, 2014), 72. One of those engaged in cotton trading and blockade running was Governor William Sprague of Rhode Island. Sprague was Salmon Chase's son-in-law and a member of his presidential committee. Sprague was in Montreal at St. Lawrence Hall in October 1864 during John Wilkes Booth's stay in the hotel. Sprague's partners included a number of influential banking houses in Providence and New York. (pp 71,72). As for John D. Rockefeller, his unsavory business practices are discussed in Karson's book (p 6) and Rockefeller is among the influential Americans at St. Lawrence Hall in 1864. Guest Book 14, 20 September 1864.

3. Cotton during the war was trading at $500-$700 per bale with prices, at their peak, rising as high as $1,000. Jay Sexton, *Debtor Diplomacy: Finance and American Foreign Relations in the Civil War,* (Oxford: Oxford University Press, 2005), 165.

4   Guest Book 2 August, 14 September 1864. Singleton is also found at Barnett's Niagara Museum 25 July 1864.

5. *Richmond Sentinel* and *New York Times* stories, see http://www.nytimes.com/1865/01/19/news/gen-singleton-in-richmond.html (Accessed Mar 2016.)

6. Black had been involved in the New York-based August Conspiracy to pressure Lincoln to step down as the Republican nominee. This suggests that Stanton, a supporter of the Radicals, was possibly involved on the periphery of this organized effort to unseat Lincoln or at least knew about the plot. Secretary of State William Seward and Edwin Stanton both sent back-door peace feelers to the Confederate Commissioners in Montreal in 1864. See Carman Cumming, *The Devil's Game,* 159; Frank van der Linden, *Dark Intrigue,* (Colorado: Fulcrum Publishing, 2007) 158-163; Headley, *Confederate Operations,* 257. Hines, *The Northwest Conspiracy,* 501. Also Report of Jacob Thompson in *The Papers of Jefferson Davis,* Jefferson Davis, reprinted Louisiana State University Press, 25-30.

7. Barnett's Niagara Museum Guest Book 1 July, 22 July 1864. Also in Niagara at this time is Lincoln's secretary John Hay who registers at Barnett's Niagara Museum as William J. Hay 7 July 1864. Registering on these same dates is Confederate Operative B. Castleman as J.B. Castleman.

8. Ibid.

9. Cumming, *The Devil's Game,* 159.

10. Charles B. Flood, *1864: Lincoln at the Gates of History,* (New York: Simon & Schuster, 2009), 412.

11. On 19 April 1861, President Lincoln issued the Proclamation of Blockade against Southern Ports. The President's executive order made it illegal to break the Federal blockade of the South. The edict, depending on interpretation, did not restrict neighbors from trading across hostile borders. This gigantic loophole was exploited by everyone, including the White House and Treasury Department, members of Congress, and the great robber barons of the Northeast. The exchange of guns, ammunition, uniforms, medicines, and especially food for cotton was big business from the very first months of the Civil War and continued throughout the conflict. Robert Browning Jr., *Lincoln's Trident: The West Coast Blockading Squadron during the Civil War,*

(Tuscaloosa: University of Alabama Press 2015), 514. Also Ludwell Johnson, *Commerce between Northern Ports and the Confederacy 1851-1865*, *The Journal of American History*, 1967, 34; *Tales from the Blockade* http://www.rfrajola.com/blockade/Blockades.pdf (Accessed March 2016.); Surdam, *Traders or Traitors*.

12. Fargo was also the Mayor of Buffalo at this time but his purpose in Montreal was almost certainly related to his banking and express businesses.

13. Guest Book 10, 16 October 1864.

14. Guest Book 14, 20 September 1864.

15. Guest Book 2 August 1864, 26 October 1864. Hatch and George Bliss, who interchanged their initials: the "G" goes to Hatch and the "R" to Bliss.

16. Guest Book 3, 15 July, 11 August 1864. Both Cooke and Barney appear to have loaned money to Salmon Chase for which there is no evidence of repayment, suggesting a serious conflict of interest for the Secretary of the Treasury. See: Philip Leigh *Trading with the Enemy*, (Philadelphia: Westholme Publishing, 2014), 95; Russell F. Weigley, *A Great Civil War: A Military and Political History, 1861-1865*, (Bloomington: Indiana University Press, 2000), 208; Guest Book J. Fisk and Col. J. Fisk 22 June 1864, 30 March 1865, Jay Gould 13 August 1864.

17. Guest Book 24 June 1864; 2, 3 Jul; 1, 4 August 1864; April 26, 1865.

18. Guest Book 16 August, 1864.

19. Guest Book 16 August 1864.

20. Guest Book 25 October 1864. The distinctive "J" which looks almost like an "E" was common on Cooke's less formal surviving signature samples. The signature reads J. (L) Cooke and wife. There were several Cooke registrations during the summer and fall of 1864. That summer President Lincoln invited Jay Cooke to visit him at the White House. These invitations were extended to Cooke not once but several times. Astonishingly, Cooke did not respond, not even to offer the courtesy of an explanation. Cooke's effrontery in the face of a presidential invitation is shocking. This reflected either arrogance and self-assurance or indicates the depth to which Lincoln's stature had fallen in the summer of 1864. It was during this period that the New York centered August Conspiracy, aimed at forcing Lincoln off the November ballot, gained momentum. Ellis Oberholtzer,

Jay Cooke: Financier of the Civil War, (Philadelphia: George W. Jacobs and Co., 1907), 434. Some of those involved in the August Conspiracy, like Salmon Chase and banker and Mayor of New York George Opdycke, were close to Cooke, indeed obligated to him. Cooke was a backer of Chase's run for president and Opdycke ran a branch of the Cooke-Clarke Bank in New York.

21. St. Lawrence Hall Guest Book 25 June 1864. This may point to the Cataract Hotel on the American side of the falls as the hotel where the family stayed in Niagara.

22. St. Lawrence Hall Guest Book 6 June 1864.

23. There are about a dozen registrations for the name Morgan from New York from June through December 1864. Some of these were likely Governor Edwin Morgan who was involved in cotton trading. Cooke—or, at least, his family—is signed in at the Barnett's Museum in Niagara 22 June, 26 October 1864.

24. Guest Book 22 August 1864, Leigh, *Trading with the Enemy*, 94-95.

25. Guest Book 12 January 1865. Stone arrives from Meriden, Connecticut, a major center of arms manufacturing for the U.S. Army. Other names are found on 6, 12, 24, 31 August and 2, 7, 14, 18, 24 September 1864. For example, L.A. Sloan arrives in Montreal in January 1865 from Meriden, Connecticut.

26. Guest Book 8, 16 July 1864 Garneau and Whittaker

27. John Waugh, *Reelecting Lincoln: The Battle for the 1864 Election*, (New York: Da Capo Press, 1997), 244.

28. Guest Book 26 Jun; 22, 27, 28 Jul; 13 Aug, 31 Oct; 1, 3 November 1864; and 18 January 1865. Guest Book 19 November 1864: Mr. and Mrs. Henry Winter arrive with two children and Henry Winter Davis had at this time two daughters. He registered directly after J. Pomeroy (Samuel Pomeroy), campaign manager for Samuel P. Chase, 18 November 1864. In November, Pomeroy registered as J. S. Pomeroy. Henry Winter (Davis) registered only days before William Sprague, another Chase supporter and Governor of Rhode Island, having arrived 24 November 1864. Sprague was traveling with a lady we presume was his wife, the beautiful and very political Kate Chase. On 14 June we also find a listing for "Rev. H.W. Davis." The names of those involved in the Anti-Lincoln Conspiracy who are found in St. Lawrence Hall include Godwin, Tilton, Davis,

Wilkes, Briggs, Parsons, Marble, and Wilson, who turn up at St. Lawrence Hall, arriving from the U.S. during this period. Guest Book (Wilson) 10 August, (Wilkes) 13 August, (Curtis) 30-31 August 1864, 20 September 1864, 8 Nov, (Godwin) 29, 31 October, 2 November 1864, (Dennison) 18 January 1865, (Parsons) 9 November 1864, (Tilton) 9-10 August, 4 November 1864, (Draper) 26 June 1864, 27 March 1865, (James Van Dyck) 23 March 1865.

29. *Diary of George Julian,* Radical Republicans, See archive.org/stream/jstor-27785702/27785702_djvu.txt (Accessed March 2016.)

30. Original transcript of the trial of the Lincoln conspirators, 1865 testimony of Daniel Eastwood of the *Ontario Bank* 16 June 1865. Wood was in receipt of a $25,000 bank draft given him by Jacob Thompson.

31. Guest Book 24, 27 August; 3 25, 26 October; 18 November 1864. The Republican National Executive Committee included Pomeroy, Spaulding, Sprague, Hale, Barney, Forbes, Noyes, and Kate Chase. Another supporter of Chase was J.A. Bingham, who had close ties to both the Radical Republicans and Secretary of War Edwin Stanton. J. Bingham, and John Bingham appear several times in the register during this period. Jay Cooke was a keen supporter of both Chase and his presidential ambitions.

32. Guest Book 25 October 1864. Sprague checks in with Republican Senator T. Howe.

33. Kate Chase or *"a lady"* accompanied (Gov.) W. Sprague to Montreal on 25 October 1864. In addition to supporting Chase for president, Sprague was deeply involved in cotton trading with the Confederacy. See Philip Leigh, *Trading with the Enemy,* (Yardley: Westholme Publishing, 2014), 52-54, 60, 80. There is also an interesting registration for a W.W. Chase and one daughter in parlor suite B, Guest Book 6 August 1864. The politically involved Kate Chase acted as her father's informal campaign manager in his perennial bid for the presidency. J.M. Forbes, another Chase supporter, registered on the same day, 6 August 1864. His friend and fellow Chase supporter, W.C. Noyes, appeared at the hotel on 4 July and again on 3 October 1864. Noyes signed in as Cha. W. Noyes in July and as C.W. Noyes in October; this is a reversal of his initials W.C Noyes. As

for Chase, on leaving the Cabinet, he spent August and early September 1864 visiting his friends J.M. Forbes and W.C. Noyes in northern New England only a few hours' train ride from Montreal. Here they discussed plans for delaying the Republican Convention and making Chase the Republican nominee. John Niven, *Salmon Chase: A Biography,* (New York: Oxford University Press, 1995), 370-371. Guest Book registration for G. Hale, 12 August 1864. Guest Book 26 June 1864, Simeon Draper was in charge of the notoriously corrupt New York Custom House. He went with Edwin Stanton to Savannah after the fall of that city to retrieve tens of thousands of bales of cotton to be taken to New York and sold. Secretary of the Navy Gideon Wells always suspected the transaction was shady and dishonest. Gazaway Lamar later successfully sued for the loss of this cotton. The fact that his agent, N.C. Trowbridge, was in Montreal negotiating with the likes of Lafayette Baker (head of Stanton's National Detective Police) raises the possibility that Lamar made money both coming and going. He may well have sold his cotton in New York at a discount, thus profiting his New York partners, and then successfully sued the U.S. government for the loss of the very same cotton. Whatever happened, Simeon Draper, was in the middle of it.

34. Guest Book 11, 12 August 1864 with Stevens arriving from Philadelphia. Thad Stevens is also found in the Guest Book on 11 July 1864 recording his departure point as a roughly scribbled "USA." W.W. Wilson and Mr. and Mrs. Goodrich arrived just prior to Stevens on 10 August 1864. We believe this is Henry Wilson and John Goodrich who belonged to the Radical wing of the Massachusetts Republican Party. Horatio Seymour (under the alias Jas Seymour), Governor of New York and candidate for the Democratic Party's nomination, registers shortly after, arriving from the Confederate forward operating base at St. Catharines 11 August 1864. Seymour was a regular at St. Lawrence Hall during this period. Jacob Thompson acknowledged in his last report to Judah Benjamin that he had met multiple times with Governor Seymour in Canada in 1864. Guest Book: James Wilson 19 August 1864 and J. Wilson registered 27 October 1864. The authors checked the Philadelphia City Directories for 1863-1865 to see if there was a Thomas

Stevens in Philadelphia and we did find one living in a middle-class neighborhood with tailors, cutters, and laborers. Thomas Stevens served as a 2nd Lieutenant with the 114th Pennsylvania Volunteers through much of the war and in 1864 was fighting outside of Richmond.

35. Barnett's Museum Niagara 4, 22 August, 4 September 1864.

36. Guest Book 7 August 1864.

37. Tidwell, *Come Retribution*, 263. Steers, ed., 38, 39.

38. Guest Book 12 August 1864. Churchill had also signed the Guest Book two days earlier on 10 August.

39. Michael T. Smith, *The Enemy Within: Fears of Corruption in the Civil War North*, (Charlottesville: University of Virginia Press, 2011), 48-49.

40. Guest Book 18 August 1864. Another interesting Republican at St. Lawrence Hall was William D. Bickham, editor of the *Dayton Journal* and someone close to Union General William Rosecrans. General Rosecrans had been proposed as a possible Republican nominee in place of Lincoln.

41. Guest Book 16 July 1864. Ashmun visited the President seeking a special cotton license. Lincoln asked him to come back in the morning. Ashmun had interesting ties to Montreal, having done legal work for the Grand Trunk Railway before the war.

42. Guest Book 25 July, 12 August 1864.

43. Guest Book 2 August, 14 September, 1864 and Pease and Randall, eds., *Diary of Orville H. Browning*, entry for 23 November 1864, 24 and 26 December 1864. See also, Surdam, *Traders or Traitors*. There are a dozen Morgan registrations at St. Lawrence Hall between August and October 1864. Even Lincoln's friend and so-called bodyguard, Ward Lamon, was involved in cotton speculation and appears to have been in Montreal on 10 August 1864 and again on 10 March 1865.

44. Seymour arrived in Montreal regularly via the Confederate Secret Service forward headquarters in St. Catharines, Ontario. He registered under the alias Jas. Seymour. One example of Seymour registering is found on 8 August; Fernando Wood registered on 15 September 1864 and Benjamin Wood on 15 October 1864, under Dr. Wood. Note that Wood's stay overlaps with that of John Wilkes Booth. Benjamin Wood was not only a Congressman but also editor of the *New York Daily News*.

45. Jane Singer, *The Confederate Dirty War*, (Jefferson: McFarland and Co., 2005), 55.

46. Jean Keith, *Underwood Friend of African Colonization.* http://filsonhistorical.org/

47. Proceedings Democratic Convention, Chicago, 1864, J.R. Underwood, 34, "*I came here to unite with everybody who is willing to unite with me, in order to remove from office that misguided and tyrannical man who has brought the nation into its perilous position. (Loud cheers).*"

48. Guest Book 2 August 1864

49. Van Der Linden, *Dark Intrigue*, 42.

50. Oberholtzer, 365.

51. Guest Book 9 August 1864, 9 September 1864, 15 October 1864.

52. Cumming, *The Devil's Game*, 252-53, 255.

53. Guest Book 20 August 1864.

54. Guest Book 9 August 1864. William Stickney was both secretary and son-in-law to Kendall.
Among the last of the Democrats to arrive during this period were John W. Dana and S.R. Lyman of Maine, who registered on 3 September 1864.

55. There are some interesting margin notes in the St. Lawrence Hall Departure Books which, unlike the Arrival Books, were completed by professional clerks. It is likely that few guests ever saw the Departure Ledgers. Unfortunately, only a handful of the latter have survived. They are carefully preserved by the McCord Museum, Montreal.

56. The use of repeating initials (such as R.R., W.W., or M.M.) also indicates attempts to conceal identities, as does the employment of prefixes or suffixes such as Rev., Dr., Judge, or Jr. See also: Horan, *Confederate Agent*. Horan observed that nearly all the characters associated with the Confederate Secret Service used aliases including Hines who posed as a doctor, banker, teacher and French Canadian exporter. To compound matters Hines, with his black curly hair and mustache, was often confused with John Wilkes Booth.

57. Guest Book 19 November 1864. Mr. and Mrs. Henry Winter arrive with two children and Henry Winter Davis had at this time two daughters. He registered the previous day, directly after J. Pomeroy (Samuel Pomeroy), campaign manager for Samuel P. Chase, 18 November 1864. In November, Pomeroy registered as

J.S. Pomeroy. Henry Winter (Davis) registered only days before William Sprague, another Chase supporter and then Governor of Rhode Island, having arrived on 24 November 1864. Sprague was traveling with a lady we presume was his wife, the beautiful and very political Kate Chase. John Harrison Surratt acknowledged after the war that one of his aliases was John Harrison, employing his middle name as his last name. Andrew Jampoler, *The Last Conspirator*, (Annapolis: Naval Institute Press, 2008), 65-66. On 14 June we find a listing for "Rev. H.W. Davis." The use of prefixes and titles such as Dr., Rev. Judge was a common tool employed used in St. Lawrence Hall. Beverley Tucker once registered as "Judge" and Benjamin Wood was sometimes introduced as Dr. Wood.

58. Some of those who altered their names subtly include Luke Blackburn, Jacob Thompson, Henry Starnes, John Surratt, R. Kennedy, Lafayette Baker, Thurlow Weed, Gov. Edwin Morgan, Gov. H. Seymour, J. Singleton, C.W. Noyes, Hon. P.B. Foulkes, Hon. J.S. Phelps, Alfred S. Hatch, George Bliss, Ben Wood, Charles Dunham, R. Underwood, S.S. Marshal, and there are many others. While some important American guests registered with their full names, making them easy to identify, just as many subtly altered their registrations. Understanding this phenomenon is essential to making sense of St. Lawrence Hall's registers.

59. Jacob Thompson to Judah Benjamin 3 December 1864. (For complete letter see *Appendix C*.)

60. Mark Kearney and Randy Ray, *Whatever Happened To? Catching Up with Canadian Icons*, (Toronto: Dundurn, 2006), **84**; and Franklin T. Graham, *Histrionic Montreal* (Toronto, Montreal: *Ayer Publishing*, 1972), 145. Finally, U.S. Consul in Montreal, John Potter, wrote that Booth was in the city in the latter part of October and "probably under an assumed name at a subsequent point." Letter quoted in Mayers, *Dixie and the Dominion*, 209. After the assassination, the *Montreal Gazette* referred to Booth being *"in Montreal last winter"* which would indicate a period beyond October 1864. Mayers, *Dixie and the Dominion*, 208.

CHAPTER 5
Trading with the Enemy

1. See http://civilwartalk.com/threads/cotton-prices.22077/ (Accessed March 2016.)

2. Michael Burlingame and J.R Turner Ettinger, *Inside Lincoln's White House: The Complete Diary of John Hay*, (Carbondale: Southern Illinois University Press, 1999), 217.

3. University of Northern Iowa, The Selected Works of David Surdam, "Traders or Traitors, Northern Cotton Trading During the Civil War." https://works.bepress.com/david_surdam/22/ (Accessed April 2016.); and *Browning Diary* 24 and 26 Dec. This note in Browning's diary appears to be the only reference to Lincoln's having possibly benefited from trading with the Confederacy, but he clearly had no objection to others making money from this trade, whether they were family, friends, supporters, or powerful allies.

4. DiLorenzo, *The Real Lincoln*, 67. See also *Lincoln's Wrath*, Jeffrey Manber and Neil Dahlstrom. (Naperville, Sourcebooks, 2005, Photo Caption opposite 167, "Lincoln appointed more men to patronage positions than any President in history."

5. Michael Holt, *The Rise and Fall of the American Whig Party: Jacksonian Politics and the Onset of the Civil War*, (New York: Oxford University Press, 1999), 57-58

6. John Nicolay and John Hay, *Abraham Lincoln*, (Carbondale: Southern Illinois University Press, reprinted 2007), 35-44

7. Higham, *Murdering Mr. Lincoln*, 57, 61, 168-173, 183, 184, 193, 224, 225.

8. St. Lawrence Hall Guest Book 2 August 1864, R.H. Singleton arrived from Nashville. The use of alternative initials was a common practice among those wanting to remain incognito. Singleton's presence in Canada and his meetings with Beverley Tucker and Clement Clay are recorded in Orville Browning's Diary 24 November 1864. Browning confirms that he (Browning) crossed into Canada at Niagara, no doubt to meet Tucker and Clay, on 28 September 1864. St. Lawrence Hall Guest Book: W. Lamon 10 March 1865 and Diary of Orville Browning entry for 28 September 1864, 24 November 1864. Cox admitted being in Canada fairly regularly from September through November 1864, where he conferred with Clay and Tucker.

9. Tidwell, *Come Retribution*, 194, 265

10. Ibid. 265

11. Ibid.

12. Clement Clay Papers 1811-1925, Duke University, Collection of Virginia Clay.

13. Tidwell, *Come Retribution*, 194,254.

14. Higham, *Murdering Mr. Lincoln*, 224, 226.

15. Surdam, "Traders or Traitors, Northern Cotton Trading During the Civil War." For another source of Surdam's "Traders or Traitors" PDF see http://www.thebhc.org/sites/default/files/beh/BEHprint/v028n2/p0301-p0312.pdf (Accessed April 2016.)

16. Guest Book 2 August 1864, 17 August 1864, 24 September 1864, and 25 September 1864. W.B. Foulke registers with his son J. Foulke on 12 August 1864. Joseph Foulke, from New York, registered at the hotel on 24 September 1864, at a time when St. Lawrence Hall was full of cotton speculators, bankers, and merchants. This could well be Congressman P.B. Foulke who was involved in cotton trading. See "Abraham Lincoln and Cotton." http://www.abrahamlincolnsclassroom.org/abraham-lincoln-in-depth/abraham-lincoln-and-cotton/ (Accessed April 2016.) The use of thinly-veiled aliases with slight changes to initials, spelling or using middle names as last names, was common.

17. Guest Book 20 August 1864.

18. Surdam, "Traders or Traitors," 306. http://www.thebhc.org/sites/default/files/beh/BEHprint/v028n2/p0301-p0312.pdf (Accessed April 2016.)

19. Abraham Lincoln, *Collected Works of Abraham Lincoln*, Vol 6, Wildside Press, 2008, 307.

20. Michael Burlingame, *Abraham Lincoln: A Life*, (Baltimore: Johns Hopkins University Press, 2008), 763.

21. J.T.W. Hubbard, *For Each the Strength of All, A History of Banking in the State of New York* (New York and London: New York University Press, 1995), 103.

22. Guest Book 15 August 1864, 4 November 1864. Barnes remains a murky character about which not a great deal is known. He was said to have been an agent for retailing magnate A.T. Stewart in New York before becoming affiliated with Brown Brothers. He is listed in the 1865 New York City Directory as a banker operating from 53 Wall Street. Brown Brothers Bank was located a few doors away at 59 Wall Street. A.T. Atkinson advanced $20,000 or more in credit to Mary Todd Lincoln to support her extravagant, often obsessive shopping sprees. She once bought 200 pairs of gloves. It is not clear this money was ever repaid. Mrs. Lincoln lived in dread of her frugal husband finding out about her lavish purchases. Elizabeth Keckley *Behind the Scenes: Thirty Years a Slave and Four in the White House.* (New York, G.W. Carleton, 1868), 149.

23. Hubbard, *For Each the Strength of All*, 103.

24. Guest Book 24 Jun; 2-3 Jul; 1, 4 August 1864; 26 April 1865.

25. *Regions Financial* merges with *Union Planters Bank* see http://usatoday30.usatoday.com/money/industries/banking/2004-01-23-up-regions-merger_x.htm (Accessed April 2016.)

26. Burnside Rifles see http://www.victorianwars.com/viewtopic.php?f=21&t=6731

27. Guest Book 16 August 1864. Oppenheim checked in with a colleague, A. Linberger or Lunberger.

28. There are a dozen or more registrations for Morgan during the summer and fall of 1864. Gov. E.D. Morgan, who was involved in Tucker's cotton deal is certainly among these registrations. But given the other bankers at the hotel, it seems likely that J.P. Morgan, possibly with altered initials, is among these registrations. The practice of using aliases or obfuscating initials was common. In his memoirs, John Surratt acknowledged using the alias John Harrison and Lafayette Baker was recorded staying at St. Lawrence Hall under an alias. Confederate Commissioner Jacob Thompson stayed at St. Lawrence Hall on many occasions but his full name is absent from the register. General Edwin Lee and his family lived in St. Lawrence Hall some time in 1865, yet his name appears only once on 10 March 1865. Secret service agent H.V. Clinton is in the hotel in July and August, shortly after visiting with J.W. Booth at the Parker House in Boston, but H.V. Clinton was an alias and his actual identity remains a mystery. The practice of obfuscating initials, using middle names instead of last or resorting to outright aliases appears to have been common among those who wished to remain incognito. (H.) V. Clinton also turns up at Barnett's Niagara Museum on 28 May 1864 and signs in as Mr. V. Clinton.

29. Guest Book 13 August 1864. (R.B.) Latham registered at St. Lawrence Hall. Lafayette Baker points to Latham as

an agent for a "ring" involving cotton-for-contraband trading in which Durant was involved. Baker testified to this before Congressman E.B. Washburne's committee investigating illicit trading with the enemy involving cotton. Ironically, Baker himself was involved in cotton trading. See http://bit.ly/20a3d3T (Accessed April 2016.)

30. Lafayette C. Baker, *History of the United States Secret Service*, (Philadelphia: LC Baker, 1867), 339, 345-361.

31. Guest Book 17-18 November 1864. Note: In his diary Orville Browning acknowledges helping Baker and Goodell to obtain cotton permits. See *Diary of Orville H. Browning*, 24 and 25 October 1863, 23 November 1863, 15 December 1863, and 24 December 1863, which suggests Browning intervened with the President in support of Singleton, Judge Hughes, Browning, Risley, Butler, Baker, and Goodell regarding cotton permits. On 28 and 29 September 1864, Browning records in his diary crossing into Canada at Niagara near St. Catharines where Confederates Beverley Tucker and Clement Clay lived. The house on Park Street was provided for them by Robert Cox, a cotton speculator with ties to John Wilkes Booth.

32. Guest Book 18 August 1864, 17-18 November 1864. In his diary, Orville Browning acknowledges helping Baker and Goodell to obtain cotton permits, reference 24-25 October 1863, 23 November 1863, 15 and 24 December 1863, which suggests Browning intervened with the President in support of Singleton, Judge Hughes, Browning, Risley, Butler, Baker, Goodell in regard to cotton permits.

33. Guest Book 22 August 1864. Philip Leigh, *Trading with the Enemy*, (Philadelphia: Westholme Publishing, 2014), 98-99, 94-95.

34. Guest Book 10 Aug, 26 October 1864.

35. Guest Book 24 December 1864, 18 February 1865.

36. Steers, *Blood on the Moon*, 73.

37. John Bell, *Rebels on the Great Lakes*, 191-192.

38. Guest Book 5 December 1864, 30 March 1865, National Archives of Canada, Ottawa. Note: Fisk made a fortune managing war contracts for the dry goods firm of Jordan Marsh.

39. See http://www.livingplaces.com/CT/Hartford_County/Manchester_Town/Cheney_Brothers_Historic_District.html (Accessed April 2016.)

40. Hubbard, *For Each, the Strength of All*, 127.

41. Capt. Robert D. Minor, *The Plan to Rescue the Johnston's [sic] Island Prisoners*. Southern Historical Society Papers. 1895. http://www.csa-dixie.com/csa/prisoners/t67.htm (Accessed April 2016.)

42. Tidwell, *Come Retribution*, 181.

43. Steers and Edwards, eds., *The Lincoln Assassination: The Evidence*, 495-496. Statement of Benjamin Ficklin given under oath.

44. Ibid.

45. Tidwell, *Come Retribution*, 233.

46. Ibid.

47. Guest Book 24, 29 June, 3, 15 July, 13 August 1864.

48. Guest Book St. Lawrence Hall 27 July 1864 and Barnett's Museum 22 July 1864.

49. Guest Book 12 November 1864.

50. Guest Book 26 December 1864, 25 February 1865.

51. Guest Book 28 October 1864.

52. Guest Book 19 February 1865.

53. Compiled from original sources, *The Record of Benjamin F. Butler* (Boston: 1883), 19.

54. Guest Book 3, 6, 24 October 1864; 18 March 1865; Surdam, "Traders and Traitors"; Johnson, *Contraband Trade during the Last Year of the Civil War, Mississippi Valley Historical Review*, June 1962. Also DeBow letter regarding cotton. See http://docsouth.unc.edu/imls/cotton/cotton.xml (Accessed April 2016.)

55. S.S. Randall, *History of Common School System of the State of New York*, (New York: General Books LLC, 2009), 334.

56. Ludwell Johnson, "Beverley Tucker's Canadian Mission," *Journal of Southern History* 29, no. 1 (1963).

57. Baker, *History of the United States Secret Service*, 340-365.

58. *Official Record of Directors and Officers of the Union Pacific Railroad*, 1863-1889, 4.

59. *New York Times*, 26 January 1865, 2, 9 March 1865, Gen. Washburne has ordered the arrest of the chief clerk in the office of Mr. Ellery, Treasury Agent, for the purchase of cotton. <http://www.nytimes.com/1865/03/02/news/sherman-s-march.html> <http://nyti.ms/203kIlR>

60. Lincoln and Cotton. See http://www.abrahamlincolnsclassroom.org/Library/newsletter.asp?ID=132&CRLI=180 (Accessed April 2016.)

CHAPTER 6
Montreal, Halifax, Matamoros, and New York

1. "Mr. Lincoln and New York City" http://www.mrlincolnandnewyork.org/inside.asp?ID=80&subjectID=3 (Accessed April 2016.)

2. Pitman, *The Assassination of President Lincoln*, 63.

3. http://www.nytimes.com/1863/12/19/news/mr-gb-lamar-blockade-upshot-his-letter-fernando-wood-why-they-plotted-get-vessel.html (Accessed April 2016.)

4. Barry Sheehy, Cindy Wallace, with Vaughnette Goode-Walker, *Civil War Savannah: Brokers, Bankers and Bay Lane*, (Austin: Emerald Book Company, 2012) Chapters One and Two and Wanderer chapter.

5. Phyllis Eckhaus. "New York City and the Slave Trade." *In These Times*. January 6, 2006. http://www.inthesetimes.com/article/2457/the_northern_slave_trade/ (Accessed April 2016.)

6. Tom Henderson, *The Slave Ship Wanderer*, (Athens: University of Georgia Press, 1967), 9-10. Sheehy, *Brokers, Bankers and Bay Lane*, Wanderer chapter.

7. *New York Times* 16 January 1864, http://www.nytimes.com/1864/01/16/news/lamar-correspondence-further-interesting-developments-implications-citizens-new.html?pagewanted=all

8. New York sending ships to Nassau carrying arms and uniforms. See http://www.rfrajola.com/blockade/Blockades.pdf (Accessed Mar 2016.) The two vessels mentioned in the article, *Wild Pigeon* and *Rosalie*, were captained by William Postell of Savannah and belonged to Gazaway and Charles Lamar's Importing and Exporting Company of Georgia. See also Wilkinson, *The Narrative of a Blockade Runner*, 169, 173, 174, 175, 176.

9. Ibid., 156.

10. See http://nyti.ms/2nb2dgm (Accessed April 2016.)

11. Larabee, *Dynamite Fiend*, 43-44.

12. Sheehy, *Brokers, Bankers and Bay Lane*, 141-160.

13. Larabee, *Dynamite Fiend*, 40-47.

14. http://nyti.ms/2o3jsz5 (Accessed April 2016.)

15. Larabee, *Dynamite Fiend*, 40-47.

16. Chesapeake Affair http://en.wikipedia.org/wiki/Chesapeake_Affair (Accessed April 2016.)

17. Larabee, *Dynamite Fiend*, 35.

18. Sheehy, *Brokers, Bankers and Bay Lane*, Wanderer chapter.

19. Larabee, *Dynamite Fiend*, 40-47.

20. *New York Times* 20 August and September 16 1863. http://nyti.ms/2nXR289 (Accessed April 2016.)

21. Lamar correspondence New York Times, 20 August 1863 http://nyti.ms/2nXR289 (Accessed April 2016.)

22. Ludwell Johnson, "Commerce Between Northern Ports and the Confederacy 1851-1865," *The Journal of American History*, (1967), 34. And *Tales from the Blockade* http://www.rfrajola.com/blockade/Blockades.pdf (Accessed April 2016.)

23. C. L. Webster, *Entrepot*, (Minnesota: Edinborough Press, 2010), 206.

24. Ibid.

25. St. Lawrence Hall Guest Book 3 September 1864.

26. *New York Times* 20 January 1865. "Mr. N.C. TROWBRIDGE, recently of New-York, whose correspondence with the rebel LAMAR lately been published, is now at Fort Warren."

27. Guest Book 8 April 1865. Note: The Eastern Townships located between Montreal and Vermont was populated by United Empire Loyalists who had been driven from the United States for supporting the Crown in the American Revolution. They were given Crown land in the Townships to act as a buffer against American encroachment. They remained viscerally opposed to Washington and plans for strengthening the central government and were instinctively supportive of the Confederacy. A small Confederate colony took root here in the years after the war that included for a time Jefferson Davis and his family.

28. Hoy, *Canadians in the Civil War*, 331; http://www.nytimes.com/1864/01/16/news/lamar-correspondence-further-interesting-developments-implications-citizens-new.html?pagewanted=all (Accessed April 2016.)

29. We do indeed find a Mr. Powell registered at St. Lawrence Hall on 5 August 1864, 29 October 1864, and 23 March 1865. See *The Lamar Correspondence* 16 January 1864, *New York Times* at http://www.nytimes.com/1864/01/16/news/lamar-correspondence-further-interesting-developments-implications-citizens-new.html?pagewanted=all (Accessed April 2016.)

30. Thomas Boaz, *Guns for Cotton*, (Shippensburg: Burd Street Press, 1996), 66. Serge Noirsain, *Blockade Runners of the Confederate Government*, 8. http://chab-belgium.

com/pdf/english/Blockade%20Runners1.pdf (Accessed Mar 2016.)

31. Baker. *History of the U.S. Secret Service*, 362-364.

CHAPTER 7
The Hidden Hand — John Wilkes Booth in Montreal

1. Sheehy, *The Booth Fragment*. Part of an entire page torn from the Montreal St. Lawrence Hall arrival book, 18 October 1864. Walter Pollack, Senior National Detective Police Detective and brother-in-law of National Detective Police Chief Lafayette Baker also checked in with Booth. Both he and Baker would be regulars at St. Lawrence Hall. Note that Pollack checked in with senior Confederate agent Luke Blackburn. They had side-by-side rooms and were just down the hall from Booth who was in room 150. Both Baker and Pollack worked for Secretary of War Edwin Stanton. (Pollack also appears to have ties to Confederate Thomas Jones who aided in Booth's escape through southern Maryland.)

2. Causey, *Historic Montgomery Theatre Partially Collapses*. <http://alabamapioneers.com/historic-montgomery-the-atre-partially-collapses/#sthash.nKwk7ywh.dpbs> (Accessed April 2016.)

3. U.S. Consul in Montreal, Congressman John Potter, wrote that Booth was in the city in the latter part of October and "probably under an assumed name at a subsequent point." Letter quoted in Mayers, *Dixie and the Dominion*, 209. After the assassination, the *Montreal Gazette* referred to Booth as being "in Montreal last winter" which would indicate a period beyond October 1864. Mayers, *Dixie and the Dominion*, 208.

4. H.S. Booth, registered on 26 January 1865, arrived at 11 p.m. from New York. The initials have been clearly tampered with but the handwriting looks much like that of the Booth signature on 18 October 1864. Booth was known to be in NYC several times in the January-February timeframe. The train trip from New York City to Montreal was 12 hours—not much different from today. More importantly, St. Lawrence Hall proprietor Henry Hogan maintained to the day he died that Booth was in the hotel in 1865 before the assassination. Kearney and Ray, *Whatever Happened to...?* 84; Graham, *Histrionic Montreal*, 145. Letter quoted in Mayers, *Dixie*

and the Dominion, 209. Finally, there is an intriguing registration for a Y/L.L. Hale and a Miss Hale arriving at St. Lawrence Hall from New York on 25 January 1865, the day before H.S. Booth checks in. Lucy Lambert Hale, daughter of Radical Republican Senator John P. Hale, was supposedly engaged to Booth. Their relationship was certainly close. Booth and the Hales stayed for a time at the same hotel in Washington while Senator Hale and his family were waiting to take up an ambassadorship in Europe. Booth's diary, recovered after he was killed at Garrett's farm in Virginia, contained Lucy Hale's picture, along with those of four other women.

5. John Rhodehamel and Louise Taper, Editors, *Right or Wrong, God Judge Me: The Writings of John Wilkes Booth*, (Champaign, IL, University of Illinois Press, 2001). Letter to Dr. G.T. Collins, dated 28 October 1864, 32.

6. Kauffman, *American Brutus: John Wilkes Booth*, 380; Michael Burgan, *The Assassination of President Lincoln*, (Minneapolis: Compass Press, 2004,) 9-13; Edward Steers, *Lincoln's Assassination*, (Carbondale: Southern Illinois University Press, 2014,) 111.

7. Sheehy, *The Booth Fragment*.

8. William Richter, *Historical Dictionary of the Civil War and Reconstruction*, (Maryland: Scarecrow Press, 2012), 200-201.

9. Tidwell, *Come Retribution*, 330-332.

10. Atzerodt's Confession see http://reasonlincoln.com/articles/george_atzerodt_confession.html (Accessed April 2016.)

11. Edward Steers, *The Assassination of President Lincoln*, 1865 testimony of Henry Finnegass regarding his stay at St. Lawrence Hall. Hoy, *Canadians in the Civil War*, 351.

12. Tidwell, *Come Retribution*, 262-263. Clinton is found in the St. Lawrence Hall guest book for 28 May, 8 July, and 24 August 1864, but with St. Louis identified as the city from which he had arrived. On 24 August he checked into St. Lawrence Hall the same day as senior Confederate Commissioner Jacob Thompson. We do not know Clinton's true identity but he was almost certainly involved with the Confederate Secret Service. We also know he traveled in interesting circles. In addition to meeting Booth in early July, he arrived in Montreal on 8 July 1864 accompanied by Mr. and Mrs. Garneau of St. Louis. Originally a Canadian, Garneau was known in

St. Louis as the "Cracker King." During the war he was one of the largest suppliers of bread and hardtack (crackers) to the U.S. Army. His trip to Montreal may have had to do with supplying crackers to the Confederacy, which was desperately short of foodstuffs for its armies in the field. Garneau was not alone in Montreal. Much of the budding U.S. "military-industrial complex" was on hand, selling their wares. In Garneau's party was a Miss Clinton, presumably the daughter of Confederate agent H.V. Clinton. Clinton is clearly an alias but his ties to Booth are undeniable and those seeking his true identity might begin looking in St. Louis, Missouri.

13. Guest Book 28 May, 8 July, and 24 August 1864.
14. Captain P.C. Martin, in addition to shipping Booth's wardrobe, provided these vital letters of introduction.
15. Mosby captures Union commander in Surprise Raid. See http://americanhistory.si.edu/blog/2013/12/meet-john-s-mosby-the-gray-ghost-of-the-confederacy.html (Accessed April 2016.)
16. Tidwell *Come Retribution*, 247-248.
17. Ibid,, 405-408, 424. George Atzerodt, in his last confession, sometimes called his lost confession, admitted knowing about another plot against Lincoln centered in New York, probably involving the mysterious 178½ Water Street. Atzerodt claimed in this confession that Booth was concerned the New York cabal would get to Lincoln before him. For the lost confession see http://rogerjnorton.com/Lincoln82.html (Accessed April 2016.)
18. Guest Book. There is an intriguing registration on 3 November 1864 for Rev. E/J Gordon from Virginia arriving from Hamilton, CW just days after Booth's departure. It matches the other Gordon signature in the guest book for 8 March 1865. The use of prefixes such as Dr. or Rev. to disguise signatures was a common practice, Beverley Tucker sometimes put Judge in front of his name and Luke Blackburn sometimes used the prefix Rev. or the first name Josiah.
19. Thomas Conrad, *The Rebel Scout*, (Washington: The National Publishing Company, 1904), 118,120.
20. Ibid.
21. John Parker was apparently charged with dereliction of duty in May 1865 but the charges were dropped the following month. The circumstances behind the dropping of the charges remain unclear. http://rogerjnorton.com/Lincoln61.html (Accessed July 2016.)
22. Conrad, *The Rebel Scout*, 118,120.
23. Ibid. There is a Victor Conrad registered at St. Lawrence Hall on 14 September 1864, shortly before Booth's sojourn in the city. He was traveling with H.E. Benson of Mobile, Alabama, indicating Conrad (whoever he was) was traveling with a fellow Southerner.
24. Singer, *The Confederate Dirty War*, 124-144. Conrad's kidnapping plot mirrored that of Booth's exactly, albeit in more professional hands. Thomas Harney had been involved in the deadly City Point explosion in August 1864 which destroyed General Grant's most important supply depot. Other Confederate torpedo efforts were aimed at sinking ships along the Mississippi with explosives that resembled coal. Once shoveled into a boiler the resulting explosion was devastating. Harney was no amateur.
25. Ibid.
26. Tidwell, *Come Retribution*, 341. Powell proved himself a man of steely courage throughout the trial. He revealed little to interrogators and maintained his stoic demeanor right to the gallows. His only plea was for Mary Surratt, who he maintained was innocent. The risks involved in attempting to kidnap the President of the United States were far greater than any he faced with Mosby's Raiders and so were the consequences. Powell was jumping from the frying pan into the fire. As for Colonel J.S. Mosby, he was in Richmond at the time of John Surratt and Sarah Slater's last visit to the city to brief Judah Benjamin. This was in late March 1865 shortly before the fall of the Confederate capital. In his confession, George Atzerodt said that Wood (Lewis Powell) was referred to as "Mosby." See Atzerodt's lost confession in *The Trial: The Assassination of President Lincoln and the Trial of the Lincoln Conspirators*, Edward Steers editor.
27. For George Atzerodt's lost confession see http://law2.umkc.edu/faculty/projects/ftrials/lincolnconspiracy/atzerodtconf.html (Accessed April 2016.)
28. Tidwell, *Come Retribution*, 415 and George Atzerodt's lost confession, see http://rogerjnorton.com/Lincoln82.html (Accessed April 2016.)
29. Frank Zornow, *Lincoln and a Party Divided*, (Norman: University of Oklahoma Press, 1954), 143.
30. Tagg, *The Unpopular Mr. Lincoln*, 412-415.

31. Ibid.

32. New York Mayor George Opdyke and Attorney David D. Field in New York City. Powerful Republicans (and some Democrats) were involved. This included Parke Godwin, G. Wilkes, Lewis Parsons, Ben Wade, Congressman Henry Winter Davis, Governor J. Andrew, Manton Marble, Theodore Tilton, Governor William Dennison, and others who attended these meetings. Salmon Chase sent observers. Senator Charles Sumner and Congressman Thaddeus Stevens were also likely involved. Sumner was in New York that summer. Even Lincoln loyalist Thurlow Weed was in attendance. http://www.mrlincolnandnewyork. org/inside.asp?ID=100&subjectID=4 (Accessed April 2016.)

33. Ibid. A possible candidate as Chase's observer would have been Simeon Draper, a New York Customs officer with close ties to both Chase and Edwin Stanton. He would later lead the expedition to Savannah (accompanied by Stanton) to retrieve thousands of bales of cotton captured at the port city. This cotton was brought north under suspicious circumstances and disposed of in New York, within Draper's jurisdiction. Secretary of the Navy Gideon Wells viewed it all as a swindle and boondoggle. Some of the owners of the cotton, such as Gazaway Lamar, later sued successfully for recompense. Since Lamar's agents were in contact with Federal officials like Draper and senior War Department detective Lafayette Baker, it raises the possibility they were part of a cabal that first sold the cotton in New York and then successfully sued the U.S. government for recompense for the supposed loss.

34. Letter Auctioned 2009: "Dear Sir, An informal meeting of citizens representing the feelings and wishes of the Democracy of various sections of the state of Pennsylvania was held in the city on the 22nd ult. The subject under consideration was the tendency of public affairs resulting from the maladministration of the Federal Government by Mr. Lincoln and his advisers, and the mode best to be adopted to prevent a continuation of executive power in unworthy hands." Signed by J.S. Black, James C. Van Dyck, C. Ferguson, William D. Reed, Richard Vaux, John C. Bullitt, Robert Krane, Samuel A. Gilmore, and William A. Wallace.

35. Cumming, *The Devil's Game*, 159. Headley, *Confederate Operations*, 257. Coffman, *Captain Hines'*, 501. See also "Report of Jacob Thompson" in *The Papers of Jefferson Davis*, Jefferson Davis, reprinted LSU Press, 25-30.

36. Zornow, *Lincoln and a Party Divided*, 113.

37. Guest Book 26 June; 22, 27 July; 13 August; 1, 3 November 1864; 18 January 1865.

38. Guest Book 17, 25 October 1864, registrations in the hotel for Mr. and Mrs. Watson and Dr. Baron C. Watson. The certificate of deposit was released to his heirs some years after the war by none other than Joseph Holt, Judge Advocate General. 178½ indicated a back door address off the lane.

39. *History of the St. Albans Raid*, Vermont Historical Society, October 1876, Hon. Edward Sowles, 27-55. A prime example would be Judge C. Coursol who dismissed the St. Albans raiders in a surprise decision regarding jurisdiction. The raiders were dressed and packed to flee the moment the decision was handed down. They stopped long enough to pick up a carpet bag of $87,000 from the Bank of Ontario, in an after-hours transaction. Coursol, Police Chief Lamothe, and Henry Starnes, president of the Bank of Ontario and later Mayor of Montreal, all came under suspicion.

40. Gray, *Conspiracy*, pp. 50, 57-59, 78, 81, 88. Larabee, *Dynamite Fiend*, 46-47. Wise, *Lifeline of the Confederacy*, 46, 158. The vessels had apparently been purchased with the help of Henry Starnes, president of the pro-Southern Bank of Ontario (Montreal Branch) and may have involved some funding from Savannah banker and blockade-runner Gazaway Lamar. Lamar and his son, Charles Lamar, ran the blockade-running *Importing and Exporting Company of Georgia*. Charles Lamar registered at St. Lawrence Hall on 21 August 1864 along with National Detective Police Chief Lafayette Baker. This suggests the two may have been involved in moving cotton from the South (particularly Savannah) to markets in the North.

41. Tidwell, *Come Retribution*, 330-331, 281, 275, 250, 187, 180, 146.

42. Ibid. 146. After the war Kane went on to become Mayor of Baltimore.

43. The calculus regarding prisoners-of-war was different in Washington than Richmond. Exchanged Union captives

were usually invalided home, while Confederate prisoners often found their way back into the lines. General Grant recognized this lethal proclivity of Confederate POW's to return to the fight. It would force him to deal with the same Confederate soldiers a second or third time. According to Grant this could only lead to "a war of extermination." In short, he would have to kill them all. Grant determined that, as a matter of military necessity, prisoner exchanges had to be ended. This decision probably shortened the war, but it led to the unnecessary deaths of tens of thousands of prisoners on both sides. Northern and Southern prisoners were left to languish in unhealthy, overcrowded prison camps all across the country. The unique horrors of Andersonville notwithstanding, death rates in both Northern and Southern prison camps were similarly appallingly high, running 12-15 percent. While the North could afford to do without these men, the South could not.

44. Confederate agents George Kane and Kinsey J. Stewart, both of whom operated in Canada, proposed clandestine operations to Jefferson Davis and Judah Benjamin in 1864. Historian William Tidwell, (Come Retribution) believes Stewart's plans were directed against Lincoln and may have been the antecedents of efforts to kidnap the President. Stewart asked General Lee his views on the "morality" of his proposed plan which certainly indicates it involved something out of the ordinary. Lee did not think much of the plan or Kinsey Stewart's ability to pull it off, but passed him on to Colonel E.G. Lee, who was soon to be senior Confederate Commissioner in Canada. Stewart also presented his plan to Jefferson Davis and Judah Benjamin. Whatever Stewart had in mind made everyone uneasy and his initial proposal was apparently shelved. But the failed Dahlgren raid on 2 March 1864, where orders calling for the assassination of Jefferson Davis and his cabinet were found on Dahlgren's body, hardened attitudes considerably in the South. The wholesale destruction of civilian property by the Union Army, including whole towns and cities, also contributed to an environment of vengeance with the South looking to strike back. It was in this atmosphere that several operations against Lincoln were organized. Once set in motion, they gained a momentum of their own making recall or reconsideration, never mind cancellation, difficult. Tidwell, Come Retribution, 274-283.

45. Guest Book: 24 August; 30 September; 1, 3, 4, 5, 7, 9, 10, 12, 14, 15, 17, 18, 25, 27, 28, and 29 October.

46. Trial Transcript: Trial and the Lincoln Conspirators 1865. Testimony of Daniel Eastwood and Bank Cashier Robert Campbell, who testified that Booth was in the bank a dozen times in October. Given that he was only in the city for ten days, the number of his visits to the bank seems excessive. Reportedly, P.C. Martin was usually with him at the bank. What could possibly have brought Booth to the bank so often?

47. Ibid.

48. Ibid.

49. Original transcript of the trial of the Lincoln conspirators, 1865 testimony of Daniel Eastwood of the Bank of Ontario 16 June 1865. Wood was in receipt of a $25,000 bank draft given him by Jacob Thompson. The cashier's check had been made out in the name of a bank employee who then endorsed it to Wood. This was the normal method for laundering money through the bank to disguise the true recipients.

50. There are two candidates for our Mr. Davis. They are H. Davis and B.A. Davis. Both have photographs in the Notman collection and both turn up at St. Lawrence Hall. B.A. Davis, however, registered at the hotel arriving from Petersburg, Virginia.

51. Steers, Blood on the Moon, 73.

52. The bank draft was entered into evidence in the trial of the Lincoln conspirators as having been signed by bank manager, "Stanus." This was clearly a misreading of the signature of Henry Starnes, manager of the Montreal branch of the Bank of Ontario and later Mayor of Montreal.

53. The Assassination of President Lincoln and the Trial of the Conspirators, Washington, 1866, testimony of E. Conger, 255.

54. New York Times. 6 May 1864. Gigantic Operative Movement. <http://nyti.ms/2naXwDC> (Accessed September 2016.) Higham, Murdering Mr. Lincoln, 116.

55. Ibid.

56. Guest Book 7 October 1864. McPhail claims to be arriving from Toronto and is accompanied by a Mr. and Mrs. George Colt from Buffalo. Colt was a successful banker.

The signature in the guest book is a good match with McPhail's surviving autographs.

57. Atzerodt's "Lost Confession" see http://rogerjnorton.com/Lincoln82.html. Surratt and Slater traveled to Richmond together just before the fall of the city and registered at St. Lawrence Hall at least twice together on 10 January and 18 April 1865. She spent much of March and April with Surratt and was apparently with him as he escaped back to Canada following the assassination. General Edwin Lee, the senior Confederate Commissioner in Canada, who lived in Montreal, apparently disapproved of Slater's relationship with Surratt. See http://bit.ly/20DhoPz (Accessed April 2016.)

58. Guest Book 15 February 1865.

59. Guest Book 11 Jun, 7 October, 1864, 15 Feb, 18 April 1865.

60. Guest Book 18 April 1865. Surratt registered as J. Harrison, his usual alias, but also as J. Surratt, using a highly calligraphic signature style. Surratt's surviving autographs show a broad range of signature styles. Right ahead of and simultaneous with Surratt's registration is that of Miss (H.C.) Slater in room 714 or 414; the obfuscation may well be intentional.

61. Chamlee, *Lincoln's Assassins*, 198. Slater's quick release suggests several possibilities: The first is that the Mrs. Slater in custody was not Sarah Slater but another woman. There were several Slater families in Baltimore in 1865. Alternatively, Burnett was new to the file and did not connect Slater to Atzerodt's and Weichmann's testimony. Monumental incompetence seems implausible, Burnett was a first-class prosecutor and a ruthless one with a good track record. The War Department's policy at the time was to arrest and hold *anyone and everyone* who might have information about the assassination. The proprietor of Ford's Theatre was imprisoned just for owning the site where the murder took place. Others were arrested and held in prison simply for knowing John Wilkes Booth or the Booth family. By the time of her arrest, Slater, or at least a bilingual courier from Montreal, had been identified by Louis Weichmann and George Atzerodt as being affiliated with both Booth and John Surratt, as well as having been at the Surratt boarding house. Slater's name would become infamous in the Lincoln and Surratt trials but by this early stage of the investigation Slater and the French-speaking courier

had not necessarily been matched. Another possibility is that Slater was a double agent like Sanford Conover and Richard Montgomery, and had to be protected by the War Department. If she was a double agent, we must wonder why Burnett did not have her testify like Conover. Alternatively, she may have been in possession of information so sensitive that she was ordered into hiding. Remember that when convicted perjurer Sanford Conover (Charles Dunham) was arrested, he began making threats of exposing Radicals and others involved in the assassination. A con man and a liar by profession, Conover either knew or could create damning information. He was an expert at lying. No one in authority was prepared to gamble on what he might say, true or otherwise. He was quickly pardoned and left town much to everyone's relief. His threats amounted to blackmail but they worked. As for Slater, she did not disappear as legend has it. She went to live with her family in New York City and divorced her husband in 1866. All this was in the public domain. If researchers 150 years later could track her down, presumably the much vaunted and feared National Detective Police could have done so in 1865/1866.

62. John Niven, *Salmon Chase: A Biography*, (Oxford, New York: Oxford University Press, 1995), 370.

63. Guest Book 25 October 1864. Sprague was also deeply involved in cotton trading.

64. Guest Book 18, 19 November 1864. The very next registration is for Mr. and Mrs. Henry Winter arriving from New York. If John Harrison Surratt could become John Harrison then Henry Winter Davis could become Henry Winter. We also find Rev H.W. Davis registered on 16 June 1864. The use of prefixes such as Dr., Rev., or Judge was a common subterfuge used by both sides in Montreal.

65. Guest Book 12 October 1864.

66. George Townsend, newspaperman, New York City wrote the first account of the Lincoln assassination and the execution of the conspirators. He signs in as George E. Townsend from New York City on 21 October. Earlier in the month, on 12 October, he signed in using his famous nom de plume "Gath." He would spend a lifetime studying and writing about the assassination beginning with his 1866 account *The Life, Crime and*

Capture of John Wilkes Booth. That Townsend may have been in Montreal at St. Lawrence Hall at the same time as Booth is an extraordinary coincidence. If that seems extraordinary, consider that Townsend ran into Booth at the Pennsylvania Hotel in Washington on 26 March 1865, only two weeks before the assassination. While he was talking with Booth, a group arrived, presumably his co-conspirators, and they adjourned to a private room. (Terry Alford, *John Wilkes Booth and George A. Townsend, A Marriage Made in Hell.* Paper delivered at the Third Biannual Tudor Hall Conference, Aberdeen, Maryland. 3 May 1992. As quoted in Arthur Loux's *Booth Day by Day* FN 296.) Townsend had just returned from Europe and was, at the time, a correspondent for the Democratic-leaning *New York World.* (John Muller, *Mark Twain in Washington,* History Press, 2013, 147.) *"By mid-1864, Townsend returned to America and took up editing and writing for a collection of New York papers..."* He wrote under pseudonyms for the Republican *New York Times* and other publications like *The New York World.* Townsend was a friend and contemporary of Mark Twain and a prolific author and journalist.

67. Guest Book 22 September 1864, Shaw arrives with J. B. or J.A. Bingham. Also J. Bingham checks in from Philadelphia on 3 October 1864. Shaw registers again on 27 October 1864

68. Tagg, *The Unpopular Mr. Lincoln,* 412.

69. Guest Book 10, 16 October 1864.

70. Guest Book 25, 26 October 1864.

71. Guest Book 24 October 1864

72. Trial of the conspirators, 1865, 38, 39

73. Guest Book 2, 10, 11 Jul; 24 Oct; 5, 15, 27 November 1864; and 28 February 1865

74. Guest Book 28 October 1864. John van Buren, sometimes referred to as "Prince John," was deeply involved in George McClellan's presidential campaign.

75. Higham, *Murdering Mr. Lincoln,* 114-115, and *John Wilkes Booth Suggests Upcoming Assassination* http://coolopolis.blogspot.com/2010/01/john-wilkes-booth-suggests-upcoming.html (Accessed April 2016.)

76. Higham, *Murdering Mr. Lincoln,* 114.

77. Guest Book 18 October 1864. *The Booth Fragment,* paper prepared for the Rare Book Department, Free Library of Philadelphia, Barry Sheehy, Cindy Wallace, March 2013. This paper discusses the fragment torn from the entire page of Montreal's St. Lawrence Hall Hotel arrival book 18 October 1864. Walter Pollack, senior National Detective Police detective and brother-in-law of National Detective Police Chief Lafayette Baker, checked in the same day as Booth. Both he and National Detective Police Chief Lafayette Baker would be regulars at St. Lawrence Hall. Note that Pollack checked in alongside senior Confederate agent Luke Blackburn. They had side-by-side rooms 158/159 and were just down the hall from Booth in room 150. Blackburn was an ardent Confederate but both Baker and Pollack worked for Secretary of War Edwin Stanton.

78. Guest Book 13 October 1864

79. Guest Book, John McCullough registered at St. Lawrence Hall on 27 June 1864 and occupied room 41. He would later go into voluntary exile in Montreal for a year or more because his friendship with Booth made him a target.

80. Graham, *Histrionic Montreal,* 142.

81. Michael Burlingame, *Abraham Lincoln a Life, Volume 2,* (Baltimore: Johns Hopkins University Press, 2008), 794. "There is much talk about the assassination of Lincoln—that if he authorizes the approval of that paper (recalling the Virginia Legislature)—the sooner he is assassinated the better." Radical Senator Benjamin Wade. Another Radical George Julian attended a meeting of Radical Republicans the day after Lincoln's assassination and recorded in his diary "Hostility towards Lincoln's policy of conciliation and contempt for his weakness were undisguised; the universal feeling among radical men is that his death is a god-send." Diary of George Julian 15 April 1865, See archive.org/stream/jstor-27785702/27785702_djvu.txt (Accessed March 2016)

82. F. Scott Fitzgerald, "The test of a first class intellect is the ability to hold two opposing ideas in the mind and still continue to function."

CHAPTER 8
Leaks, Anomalies, and Questions

1. Tidwell, *Come Retribution,* 406. After the war Colonel Robert F. Martin and Lieutenant Colonel James Gordon admitted having advance knowledge of the plot. Others

who were likely aware of these plans included agents Robert and Josephine Brown, (Robert Brown registered with James Gordon at St. Lawrence Hall, 8 March 1865), Sarah Slater, John Surratt, P.C. Martin, and most of the senior Confederate Commissioners who were in Montreal during the summer and fall of 1864. While Montreal's hotels had proven that they could protect the privacy of their guests, the Confederate Secret Service in Canada was, in contrast, a rather leaky ship regarding operational secrets.

2. *Turner-Baker Papers*, National Archives of the United States. In 1866, Stanton ordered the Turner-Baker Papers sealed. Some snippets were released for *War of the Rebellion: A Compilation of the Official Records of the Union and Confederate Armies* shortly after the war but the bulk of the files remained sequestered. It was only in the 20th century that the "Turner-Baker" files were made available to historians. These files are intriguing but lack any shocking revelations that would justify being locked away for so long. Stanton apparently planned the same fate for the Lincoln Diary which, when reluctantly surrendered, appeared to be missing pages – a controversy unresolved to this day. Horan, James David. *Confederate Agent: A Discovery in History.* (Golden Springs Publishing, 2015, xvi). See also: Wick, Rob. James Randall and the Turner-Baker papers. http://lincoln-assassination.com/bboard/index.php?topic=1664.0;wap2

3. Carman Cumming, *Devil's Game.*

4. Ibid. 70-75 cites *New York Tribune* articles on 25 Jan; 19, 24, 23 Mar; and 23 April 1864. Library of Congress: New York Tribune archives. "The Scheme to Assassinate President Lincoln.1864. The schemes exposed by me to kidnap or kill the president may shock the unsophisticated reader... The same Copperhead journals that doubt my revelations of schemes to kidnap or assassinate President Lincoln, have never questioned with a single line the statement with which the Southern papers recently teemed of plots on the part of Yankee spies and Union men in Richmond to assassinate Jeff. Davis. They can readily believe that Union men are capable of murdering the Rebel President, but cannot believe that Rebels are capable of murdering the Union President."

5. Guest Book 22 July; 8, 24 August; and 3, 14 October. There are multiple registrations in the guest book for Wallace or Wallis, with Montreal, Toronto, and even "Catchy" Mississippi as the points of departure.

6. Guest Book 24 August 1864. Here we see Wallis registering with J (obscured) Thompson, Confederate Commissioner and H.V. Clinton, a Confederate agent with ties to Booth.

7. Guest Book 24 August, the registration for Thompson reads J (obscured) Thompson; the registration for H.V. Clinton is clear. J. Wallace registered again with Thompson 14 October 1864.

8. Tidwell, *Come Retribution*, 262-263.

9. Ibid. Conover's article predates Booth involvement in the Lincoln kidnapping, which is believed to have begun at the Parker House meetings in Boston in late July 1864.

10. Cumming, *Devil's Game*, 73.

11. Ibid., 61, 70-71, 73-76, 160-180.

12. Tidwell, *Come Retribution*, 406, 407.

13. Guest Book 8 March 1865.

14. Registrations for Baker, (Munson alias), Pollack. Guest Book 4, 11, 18 Aug; 13 Oct; and 29 November 1864; and 15, 23 February 1865.

15. Guest Book 14 October 1864 He registered as Jas/Jam Wallace from "Catchy" Mississippi.

16. See *Sacramento Daily Union*. The Famous Dan Sickles Trial. October 1, 1887. <http://cdnc.ucr.edu/cgi-bin/cdnc?a=d&d=SDU18871001.2.60> (Accessed March 2016.) Note: The famous Dan Sickles trial saw the first ever plea of temporary insanity.

17. William Marvel, *Lincoln's Autocrat, The Life of Edwin Stanton*, (Chapel Hill: University of North Carolina Press, 2015), 216, 251-252, 315-316, 422-423. The author, William Marvel, has written the first biography of Stanton in fifty years. Marvel, a distinguished and accomplished historian, paints Stanton as an ambitious, unscrupulous, and duplicitous man, as well as a consummate bully. Holt and Bingham do not emerge much better. Marvel makes clear that Holt and Bingham stood ready to do Stanton's bidding.

18. Elizabeth Trindal, *Mary Surratt: An American Tragedy*, (Gretna: Pelican Publishing, 1996), 149.

19. John Chandler Griffin, *Abraham Lincoln's Execution*, (Gretna: Pelican Publishing, 2006), 323.

20. Helen Jones Campbell, *Confederate Courier*, (New York: St. Martin's Press, New York, 1964), 176. Edward Steers,

editor-contributor, and Harold Holzer, editor-contributor. *The Lincoln Assassination Conspirators: Their Confinement and Execution as Recorded in the Letterbook of John Frederick Hartranft*. (Baton Rouge, LSU Press, 2009) 102, 44-45. The sustained sensory deprivation of the canvas hoods began to affect Payne/Powell's mental stability. General Lew Wallace's sketch of the conspirator shows his face swollen and hideously distorted. Powell did retain sufficient faculties and courage to swear to a statement exonerating Mary Surratt. This was witnessed and given to Chief Prosecutor Joseph Holt. It clearly did not change the outcome which appears to have been pre-ordained.

21. Steers, *The Lincoln Assassination Conspirators*, 47. Family members were allowed to visit the prisoners with the approval of the War Department and bring in supplemental food.

22. Chamlee, *Lincoln Assassins*, 194-195.

23. Marvel, *Lincoln's Autocrat*, 377, 382. Two of those originally slated to be members of the tribunal, Generals Horace Porter and Cyrus Comstock, expressed reservation about trying the conspirators before a military tribunal rather than a civilian court as the war was over. Stanton replaced them *the next day* with officers he no doubt expected would be more pliable.

24. Ibid. 377, 382.

25. Ibid. 427.

26. Thomas R. Turner, *Beware The People Weeping,* (Baton Rouge: Louisiana State University Press, 1982). 70-71. Chamlee, *Lincoln's Assassins* 114. Frederick Hatch, *Protecting President Lincoln*, (North Carolina: McFarland & Co., 2011), 76. Joshua Sharp was afterwards reluctant to speak on the subject. Whatever happened, it would not be the first or last time a government bureaucracy failed to connect the "dots" and then sought to cover its failure.

27. Chamlee, *Lincoln's Assassins,* 114-120.

28. Cumming, *Devil's Game,* 130 Original source: Samuel Arnold, *Defence and Prison Experiences of a Lincoln Conspirator.* (The Book Farm, 1943). 12-13.

29. Ibid. 136.

30. Ibid., 139.

31. Marvel, *Lincoln's Autocrat*, 423. Stanton was clearly unnerved by Johnson's request; thus the many attempts at drafting a reply and seeking Holt's input. He perhaps never expected the existence of the diary to be revealed. He certainly appeared unprepared for the firestorm that broke when its existence became public.

32. Marvel, *Lincoln's Autocrat*, 422.

33. Cumming, *Devil's Game*, 145-147, 150-152, 155. Dunham made one last trip to Montreal in June 1865 to gather evidence for Joseph Holt. News of his testimony before the tribunal in Washington and reference to his aliases, James Watson Wallace and Sanford Conover, had, however, leaked to the press. He had no sooner arrived in Montreal than he was picked up by armed Confederates and taken to St. Lawrence Hall. General William Carroll, George Sanders, Beverley Tucker, Montrose Pallen, and others interrogated him. A strong-arm man by the name of O'Donnell threatened to shoot Dunham unless he signed an affidavit saying he did not testify at the tribunal and disavowed the accusations made against the Confederates. Recognizing his life was in danger, Dunham signed the document and then slipped out of town, only to be arrested for unpaid bills before he could get safely across the border. This triggered Stanton's panicky reaction and the Dix rescue mission.

34. Ibid., 151-152

35. James W. Thompson, "The Incredible Plot of Judge Advocate Joseph Holt." See http://chab-belgium.com/pdf/english/Judge%20Holt.pdf (Accessed April 2016.)

36. Ibid.

37. Cumming, *Devil's Game*, 252.

38. Ibid., 193. He referred to the involvement of "279 and old No 8" being implicated. This referred to Thaddeus Stevens' address 279 South B Street and Benjamin Wade's address No 8, 4½ Street. In another document he spells out the Stevens address as 279 South B Street. He also revealed that Radical Congressman James Ashley had been encouraging Dunham to produce evidence that President Johnson had been involved in Lincoln's assassination. It was clear from Ashley's correspondence he didn't much care if the evidence was factual. In approaching Dunham, he was dealing with a known perjurer, so Ashley knew what he was buying. As for Montreal in the summer and fall of 1864, the Radical Republicans and Copperhead Democrats were there and so was Dunham. Following the assassination of Lincoln,

no one wanted to talk about having been in Montreal or explain their reasons for being in Canada.

39. Ibid.

40. Ibid. 258. The Request for Pardon came from none other than Judge Advocate General prosecutor Joseph Holt.

41. Jampoler, *The Last Lincoln Conspirator*, 264.

42. Ibid., 87-91 Note: There was doubt about the willingness of the British to hold Surratt in advance of evidence and a warrant, but under the extraordinary circumstances following a Presidential assassination, Britain's cooperation was likely. At the very least, there was nothing to be lost by asking for him to be remanded. It seems inconceivable that Great Britain would have ignored this request under the circumstances, thus opening itself to be blamed for Surratt's escape.

43. Guest Book 27 October 1864. There is a registration for Pierrepont Edwards shown as arriving from New York.

44. Guest Book 18 April 1865.

45. Guest Book 7 October 1864. The name J.L. McPhail appears in the hotel register on 7 August 1864, traveling with American George Colt arrived from Buffalo, NY.

46. Chamlee, *Lincoln's Assassins*, 198.

47. Thanks to the work of James O. Hall and John Stanton, two historians who spent decades investigating Sarah Slater, we know that Slater was hiding in plain sight in New York City. She divorced her husband in 1866 in New York, and the legal paperwork is in the public domain. They were able to trace her activities in New York using existing records. If Slater could be tracked down by two historians 150 years after Lincoln's assassination, surely the much-vaunted National Detective Police could have found her had they wanted to? Sources: James O. Hall, "The Saga of Sarah Slater." Reprinted in *In Pursuit of: Continuing Research in the Field of the Lincoln Assassination* (Surratt Society, 1990). John F. Stanton, "A Mystery No Longer: The Lady in the Veil." Surratt Courier, August 2011 and October 2011. See also http://bit.ly/2oIBuFk

48. John F. Stanton, "A Mystery No Longer: The Lady in the Veil." Surratt Courier, August 2011 and October 2011

49. All the names here are discussed in the chapter "American Power" except W.B Matchett. He was a defrocked minister, swindler and lobbyist, who had once been arrested by National Detective Police Chief Lafayette Baker but later apparently worked for him and the National Detective Police. Matchett was at the center of efforts to obtain a pardon for Charles Dunham. Cumming, *Devil's Game* 209-211, 213-215. He registered at St. Lawrence Hall (with obscured initials, but his distinctive last name is clear), arriving from Philadelphia, 23 September 1864. What he was doing in Montreal, we can only guess, but it may have had to do with Democratic Party business.

50. Guest Book 10, 12 August; 1, 22, 3, 14, 18, 25 September; and 3, 14, 18, 25 October 1864. J.A. Bingham, had close ties to both the Radical Republicans and Secretary of War Edwin Stanton. J. Bingham, J.B. Bingham and John Bingham appear nearly a dozen times in the register during this period.

51. Guest Book 16 July 1864. George Ashmun was the last person to see Lincoln alive at the White House.

52. Robin Winks, *The Civil War Years: Canada and the United States*, (Montreal: McGill-Queen's University Press, 1960), 39, 40. See also Steers, *Blood on the Moon*, 104. Note: Ashmun had strong ties to Canada, where he had done legal work for the Grand Trunk Railway. Early in the war he was sent as an unofficial spokesman from the Lincoln administration to Canada. Secretary Seward terminated this assignment when news of it leaked and infuriated the British ambassador to the United States, Lord Lyons.

53. Guest Book 3 February 1865. Holt's initials in February appear to be L.J. or J.G.

54. Barnett's Museum guest book, 17 October 1864. A.J. Holt

55. Guest Book 27 July 1864. The initials appear as possibly G.G. but Eckert's particular, distinctive writing style has his "T's" look like "F" or "G." There are a number of surviving examples of Eckert's signature. His point of departure is listed as Ohio, which was Eckert's home state. In the period during which Eckert is at the hotel, 24-28 July 1864, there are a number of interesting registrations for Radical Republican George Harvey (Washington DC); obscured initial A. (S.F.) Cameron (Confederate Secret Service); John Payne (Confederate banker); Baron E. Watson; Jas. T. or F. Watson (likely ties to Confederate Secret Service,); George Wilkes (member of the August anti-Lincoln 1864 conspiracy); R.M. Peck (Republican); Rev. H.W. Davis (possibly Radical Congressman Henry Winter Davis) and L. Baker,

Philadelphia (National Detective Police Chief Lafayette Baker). Congressman and Lincoln opponent Fernando Wood was also at the hotel. Richard Parsons, a strong supporter of Salmon P. Chase, also appears to have been at St. Lawrence Hall with altered initials, which was a common enough practice for American politicians in Montreal at this time, and finally, Eckert's future business patron, Jay Gould.

56. Barnett's Museum–Niagara, 22 July 1864. The signature could be Y.F. but Eckert's writing style made his T's often appear as Y's, F's or even G's. In any case it is clearly the same man registering on 22 July in Niagara and 27 July 1864 in Montreal. There is no G.G. or Y.F. Eckert in the 1864 Cincinnati City Directory. Eckert is traveling with his son, Master Thomas (T. Eckert.) making the identification nearly certain.

57. Ibid. The chances of another Eckert from Ohio traveling with his son, Thomas Eckert, are almost incalculable.

58. Eckert and Jay Gould became close. With Gould's help Eckert became head of both *American Union Telegraph* and *Western Union* in the post-war years. Maury Klein, *The Life and Legend of Jay Gould*, (Baltimore: Johns Hopkins University Press, 1986), 200; Edward Renehan, *Dark Genius of Wall Street*, (New York: Basic Books, 2008), 235-237; Murat Halstead, J Frank Beale, Willis Johnson, *Jay Gould: How He Made His Millions*, (Edgewood, Harvard University, 1892), 122; Julius Grodinsky, *Jay Gould, His Business Career*, (Philadelphia: University of Pennsylvania Press, 1957), 221; Eckert claimed to have met Jay Gould in 1872, but their paths appear to have crossed earlier at St. Lawrence Hall in the summer of 1864. Guest Book. Jay Gould 24 June, 15 July 1864.

59. Klein, *The Life and Legend of Jay Gould*, 531. This book discusses the rumor that Gould prospered during war by speculating in stocks, currencies, cotton and gold. These fluctuated with the ebb and flow of battle, sometimes dramatically. It was rumored that Eckert, in his role as chief telegraph operator at the War Department, was the source of some of this advance intelligence to Gould. Klein, however, could not find any hard evidence of this and in the absence of such information was inclined to believe Eckert's claim to have only met Gould in the 1870's. The St. Lawrence Hall Guest Book indicates that Gould and Eckert were in close proximity in Montreal during the summer of 1864.

60. Steers, *The Lincoln Assassination Conspirators: Their Confinement and Execution*, 44-45, 102. It seems unusual for a telegraph expert, with no police or legal background, to have been assigned the interrogation of such an important prisoner, but it may reflect Stanton's particular confidence in Eckert. The sustained sensory deprivation of the canvas hoods began to affect Payne/Powell's mental stability. General Lew Wallace's sketch of the conspirator shows his face swollen and hideously distorted. (Source: *Confederate Courier*, Helen J. Campbell, 176.)
Powell did retain sufficient faculties and courage to swear to a statement exonerating Mary Surratt. This was witnessed and given to Chief Prosecutor Joseph Holt. It clearly did not change the outcome that appears to have been pre-ordained.

61. John Parker, *The Guard Who Left His Post*, http://rogerjnorton.com/Lincoln61.html, (Accessed May 2016)

62. Guest Book 15 February 1865.

63. Parliamentary Papers, House of Commons, Vol. 75, British Parliament, House of Commons, 1874, Proceedings of the mixed Commission on British and American Claims, 618-621. Witnesses state that the Confederates frequently talked of plots and raids in bars and public places. One of these witnesses was F. Gerike the proprietor of Dooley's Bar and Billiard Room in St. Lawrence Hall.

64. Guest Book 6 July 1864; a good example is Boynton, *Detroit Free Press* 6 July 1864.

CHAPTER 9
The British Players and Their Stories

1. *Memoirs of Sir Garnet Wolseley*, see http://www.british-empire.co.uk/forces/armycampaigns/indiancampaigns/mutiny/wolseleymemoir.pdf (Accessed April 2016.)

2. Ibid.

3. Ibid.

4. Halik Kochanski, *Sir Garnet Wolseley: Victorian Hero*, (Hambledon: Wiley, 1999), 248-249.

5. Ibid., 37.

6. *A Memoir of Sir Garnet Wolseley*, Charles Rathbone Low, 266

7. Sir Garnet Wolseley, *General Lee*, 45. http://www.namsouth.com/viewtopic.php?t=4360 (Accessed April 2016.)

8. Viscount Garnet Wolseley, *General Lee*. http://bit.ly/2oCZwnS (Accessed April 2016.)

9. Wolseley. see http://bit.ly/2nXNLpi (Accessed April 2016.)

10. Almond, Barrie. *Captain Lewis Guy Phillips*. American Civil War Roundtable UK. http://www.acwrt.org.uk/uk-heritage_Captain-Lewis-Guy-Phillips.asp (Accessed April 2016.)

11. John Pelham http://en.wikipedia.org/wiki/John_Pelham_(officer) (Accessed April 2016.)

12. American Civil War Roundtable hhttp://www.acwrt.org.uk/uk-heritage_Captain-Lewis-Guy-Phillips.asp (Accessed April 2016.)

13. Ibid.

14. Captain Lewis Guy Phillips http://www.acwrt.org.uk/uk-heritage_Captain-Lewis-Guy-Phillips.asp (Accessed April 2016.)

15. Ibid.

CHAPTER 10
St. Albans Raid

1. Cathryn Prince, *Burn the Town and Sack the Banks*, New York: Carroll & Graf, 2006, 143.

2. Ibid., 147.

3. Ibid., 208.

CHAPTER 11
Jefferson Davis in Montreal

1. Sheehy, *Immortal City*, 380. The children were being bullied by their guards and the local Sisters of Mercy (St. Vincent's Academy) stepped in and provided both education and protection.

2. Donald Beagle, Bryan A. Giemza, *Poet of the Lost Cause: A Life of Father Ryan*, (Knoxville: University of Tennessee Press, 2008), 201. Felicity Allen, *Jefferson Davis: Unconquerable Heart*, (Columbia: University of Missouri Press, 1999), 439: "The Catholic clergy have been so good to me..."

3. Hudson Strode, *Jefferson Davis, Private Letters*, (New York: Harcourt, Brace & World, 1966,) 281.

4. Cooper, *Jefferson Davis, American*, 200, 612-613

5. Hopper, Tristin. *National PoSt. It Happened in Canada Series*. July 25, 2014. <http://bit.ly/2naSCq4> (Accessed April 2016.)

6. Donald Davison, *Beef or Beans, Pudding or Pie*. Quebec Heritage News, Autumn, 2010.

APPENDIX A

1. Melinda Squires. *The Controversial Career of George Nicholas Sanders*, Western Kentucky University, August 2000. http://digitalcommons.wku.edu/cgi/viewcontent.cgi?article=1707&context=theses (Accessed April 2016.), 109,

2. Terry Alford, John Wilkes Booth and George A. Townsend, "A Marriage Made in Hell," a paper delivered at the Third Biannual Tudor Hall Conference, Aberdeen, Maryland, 3 May 1992, as quoted in Arthur Loux's *Booth Day by Day*, FN 296.

3. Marquis, *In Armageddon's Shadow*, 169, 175-179, 243.

4. Ibid.

5. Letter from Mr. Holcombe to Judah Benjamin, Secretary of State, CSA, dated Halifax, 26 April 1864.

   He begs that you will to each of them, Dr. Almon, Mr. Keith, Mr. Wier, and Mr. Ritchie, address officially a letter in his name, returning his thanks and those of our country for testimonials of kindness, which are appreciated with peculiar sensibility, at a juncture when the Confederacy is isolated...

   Letter from William J. Almon.

   Halifax, Nova Scotia, 26 May 1864.

   To Hon. James P. Holcombe, Special Commissioner of C.S.A.:

   My Dear Sir — Allow me to express the extreme gratification I experienced upon the receipt of your letter conveying to me the thanks of the President of the Confederate States for the sympathy and kindness he has heard I have manifested towards the Southern cause...

   See also "Bluenose Effrontery": Dr. William Johnston Almon and the City of Halifax During the Unites States' Civil War, MA Thesis Timothy R. Burge, Dalhousie University 2013, and https://maritimemuseum.novascotia.ca/event/dr-william-johnston-almon-and-halifax-during-us-civil-war (Accessed May 2016.)

6. Guest Book 12 August 1864. Churchill had signed the guest book two days earlier, on 10 August 1864.

7. Guest Book 25 July, 12 August 1864

8. Alford, Terry "*John Wilkes Booth and George A. Townsend, A Marriage Made in Hell.*" Paper delivered at the Third

Biannual Tudor Hall Conference, Aberdeen, Maryland, 3 May 1992. As quoted in Arthur Loux's *Booth Day by Day*, FN 296.

9. John Muller, *Mark Twain in Washington*, History Press, 2013, 147

10. Ibid. *"By mid-1864, Townsend returned to America and took up editing and writing for a collection of New York papers..."*)

11. J.M. McPhail, Provost Marshal of Baltimore. McPhail worked for Edwin Stanton. This McPhail, whoever he is, checked in on 7 October 1865, arriving with Mr. George Colt of Buffalo.

12. Guest Book 12 November 1864.

13. Guest Book 26 December 1864, 25 February 1865.

14. Guest Book 24 June 1864, 2-3 July, 1 August 1864, 4 August, 26 April 1865

15. Woodman, Harold. *King Cotton and His Retainers*, Lexington, University of Kentucky Press, 1968, 218-219.

16. Guest Book 30 August, 13 September, 8 October, 3 November 1864.

17. Guest Book 12 October 1864.

18. Guest Book 3 October, 19 November 1864. Noyes registered as C.W. rather than W.C., reversing his initials.

19. Guest Book 18 November 1864.

20. Another curious registration entered alongside that of Myers is D.G.C. Connes. This signature closely matches that of Senator John Connes of California. Connes was, along with Senator Henry Wilson, in the pocket of the corrupt Union Pacific run by the notorious Thomas Durant and later by Durant's stand-in, General John Dix. John Myers, *Henry Wilson and the Era of Reconstruction*, (Roman & Litttlefield: University Press of America, 2009,) 40

21. Gideon Welles, *The Civil War Diary of Gideon Welles, Lincoln's Secretary of the Navy*: 201.

22. Captain Lewis Guy Phillips hhttp://www.acwrt.org.uk/uk-heritage_Captain-Lewis-Guy-Phillips.asp (Accessed April 2016.)

23. http://www.victorianwars.com/viewtopic.php?f=21&t=6731 (Accessed March 2017.)

APPENDIX B

1. North West Conspiracy trial P2, 29 O.A.K. or O.A.X.– probable symbol for Sons of Liberty, see https://archive. org/stream/trialsfortreasonoopitma/trialsfortreason-oopitma_djvu.txt (Accessed May 2016.)

2. *Regions Financial* merges with *Union Planters Bank*.

APPENDIX D

1. Ella Leon, *Foreigners in the Confederacy*, (Chapel Hill: University of North Carolina Press, 1940), 307. Note: British Consul in New Orleans, William Mure, was said to have an interest in a blockade runner sailing out of Montreal in 1861.

2. Lamar correspondence *New York Times* 10 August 1863: *"Captain Martin has been sent to Montreal for a steamer... with £14,000"* Source: http://nyti.ms/2nKnIRo (Accessed April 2016.) See also: Carole E. Scott, *Short Biographies of 19th Century Southerners*, http://carolescott.tripod.com/figures.htm (Accessed April 2016.)The Lamar family, Gazaway Lamar and his son Charles, were active in banking and blockade running. Prior to the war, Charles had also been heavily involved in slave trading. When Gazaway sold the *Republic Bank of New York* in anticipation of returning to Savannah, he transferred the bulk of his money to a bank in Montreal to prevent it being seized by federal authorities.
Through his agent in Halifax, Alexander "Sandy" Keith, Lamar helped finance vessels for Confederate Secret Service agent and blockade runner Captain P.C. Martin who was for much of the war the senior Confederate agent in Montreal. Martin was one of John Wilkes Booth's "minders" during the actor's October 1864 visit to Montreal. Lamar ran blockade runners in and out of New York on a regular basis. The U.S. Customs staff in the city were thoroughly corrupt and had pretty much been "bought off." See http://www.nytimes.com/1864/01/04/news/blockade-running-important-developments-parties-this-city-implicated-card.html The Lamars had agents operating in New York throughout the war. One of them, Nelson Trowbridge, was captured and sentenced to death for treason. Luckily for Trowbridge, his sentence was commuted near the end of the war. Trowbridge immediately fled to the Eastern Townships of Quebec just south of Montreal where a number of Confederate refugees went into exile. He would eventually turn up at St. Lawrence Hall 8 April 1865 just before the Lincoln Assassination. While he was in the Eastern Townships,

he planned to meet with National Detective Police Chief Lafayette Baker but the latter never showed. What they were meeting about we can only guess but like so much else surrounding Baker, it is all very suspicious. (Short Biographies of 19th Century Southerners) See http://carolescott.tripod.com/figures.htm Also St. Lawrence Hall guest book, 8 April 1865. Carman Cumming, The Devil's Game, 280, note 50.

3. Webster, *Entrepot*, 231, Note: We find these two vessels occasionally sailing in tandem carrying cargoes provided by the same supplier.

4. *New York Times* Blockade Running, January 4, 1864. See Lamar Correspondence *New York Times*. Lamar's blockade runner *Wild Pigeon* was under Captain Postell who had a long association with the Lamar family. See http://www.rfrajola.com/blockade/Blockades.pdf

5. "Tales of the Blockade," http://www.rfrajola.com/blockade/Blockades.pdf (Accessed October 2016.) See also: Sheehy, *Brokers Bankers and Bay Lane*, 157.

6. Lamar Correspondence *New York Times* 23 December 1863. See http://nyti.ms/2o3jsz5.

7. St. Lawrence Hall Guest Book, 24 February 1865.

8. *New York Times* 12 September 1863.

9. http://www.nytimes.com/1863/09/12/news/canadian-blockade-runners-building.html (Accessed April 2016.) TORONTO, Friday, 11 Sep. The Evening Times published a telegram from Quebec, saying that the steamers Bowmanville and Caledonia are understood to be fitting out at Quebec to run the Southern blockade, and that Hon. Mr. CAUCHEN (sic) is interested in the speculation. Cauchon was an influential player in the politics of Canada East and served for a time as a member of the government as Minister of Public Works in the George-Étienne Cartier-Macdonald cabinet.

10. http://images.maritimehistoryofthegreatlakes.ca/ (Accessed March 2016.)

11. http://www.nytimes.com/1863/09/12/news/canadian-blockade-runners-building.html TORONTO, Friday, 11 September.

12. The *Rebels in Canada: Blockade Runners from Montreal?*, *New York Times* 17 August 1863, *New York Times* archives.

13. http://images.maritimehistoryofthegreatlakes.ca/1014/data?n=33 (Accessed April 2016.)

14. C.L. Webster, *Entrepot,* 231.

15. *The Rebels in Canada; Blockade Runners from Montreal?* The Trade Very Active--Secession up North. Correspondence of the *New York Times*. 17 August 1863 MONTREAL, Wednesday, Aug. 12, 1863. Last Winter the side-wheel steamer Arabian, of 618 tons resister, belonging to A. HERON, of Niagara, C.W., left our waters and brought up in Boston, where she put in new boilers and sailed for New York, and from thence to Nassau where she was duly installed as a blockade runner, and has made several successful trips to Wilmington and Charleston – her last being from Wilmington at Nassau, July 25. She is a light draft, ten knot vessel, very like your Sound steamers, and built in 1851 at Niagara; has a beam engine and boilers below. The Canadian steamer Boston, of 455 tons register, (American,) of same build, &c., and eleven years old, went to Sea this summer, and will, no doubt, bring up in Nassau. The Bowmansville, a side-wheel steamer, eight years old, and 508 tons, American register, is having her guards reduced, and will leave Montreal soon for the coast. The steamer Clyde, of 410 tons register, nine years old, left Montreal on the 3d instant for the coast. I have no doubt you will see the three last-named in New-York before they commence operations to and from Nassau. The close resemblance these steamers bear to our own lake and river steamers will make it difficult for our cruisers to detect them. They can steam about ten knots in smooth water, are very light draft, drawing only nine feet when deep loaded. The fore-and-aft schooner Lady Mulgrave, of Halifax, was loading at Montreal on the 1st inst., by Mr. STEVENS, with 200 tons anthracite coal, leather, boots and shoes, soap, whisky, &c., for Nassau direct. Mr. STEVENS boasts of having been in Charleston lately, and no doubt he intends to try it again. The Mulgrave takes out several passengers, among them some Confederate officers, one of whom was on STUART's Staff. So you see our Canadian neighbors are imitating their "mamma" in sending aid and comfort to the slaveocracy of America. I found but one hotel in Montreal where a Union man could stop and sojourn, without being insulted daily and hourly at the table and in the parlors. That is the Ottawa Hotel, kept by S. BROWNING, an American gentleman. The Donegana and St. Lawrence are as full of secesh as an egg is full

of meat. Sympathy or good-will toward us here in the North is a thing of the past in Canada. The war interrupts their trade, and they are constantly wishing it was closed, no matter how, so we close it up soon.

16. Guest Book 16 October 1864
17. Webster, *Entrepot*, 162 (photo of blockade-runner *Luna*)
18. See http://paperspast.natlib.govt.nz/cgi-bin/paperspast?a=d&d=THA18750202.2.9 (Accessed April 2016.)
19. https://en.wikipedia.org/wiki/USS_Kanawha_(1861) (Accessed April 2016.) and http://ebooks.library.cornell.edu/m/moawar/text/ofre0022.txt (Accessed April 2016.)
20. Webster, *Entrepot*, 231.
21. Larabee, *Dynamite Fiend*.
22. http://images.maritimehistoryofthegreatlakes.ca/37507/data?n=20 (Accessed April 2016.)
23. http://images.maritimehistoryofthegreatlakes.ca/65980/data?n=1 and http://www.maritimehistoryofthegreatlakes.ca/Documents/Scanner/07/06/default.asp?ID=c007
24. Source: Maritime Museum of the Great Lakes, Kingston Ontario, http://www.marmuseum.ca/ especially Mills List of vessels.
25. Ibid.

Bibliography

PRIMARY SOURCES

Barnett's Niagara Falls Museum Registers, Niagara Falls Museums. Niagara Falls History Museum, Niagara Falls.

Clay, Clement, Papers, collection of letters compiled by Virginia Clay. Duke University.

Turner-Baker Papers, National Archives of the United States.

Diary Notes of Reverend Stephen Cameron. Library of the Civil War, Richmond, VA.

St. Lawrence Hall Arrival Guest Books. National Archives of Canada, Ottawa, ON.

St. Lawrence Hall Departure Guest Books. McCord Museum, Montreal, QC.

Notman Photographic Collection. McCord Museum, Montreal, QC.

First Three Republican Conventions: 1856, 1860, 1864, Proceedings. (Accessed October 2016.) https://archive.org/details/proceedingsoffir00inrepu

Official proceedings of the Democratic national convention, held in 1864 at Chicago (Accessed October 2016.) https://archive.org/details/officialproce00demo

Mills List of Vessels, Maritime Museum of the Great Lakes, Kingston Ontario, (Accessed October 2016.) <http://www.marmuseum.ca/>

Accounts and Papers of the House of Commons 1865, Testimony Following President Lincoln's Assassination. <http://bit.ly/2poO1TZ> (Accessed March 2016.)

New York Tribune archives. "The Scheme to Assassinate President Lincoln." The Library of Congress, 1864. (Accessed September 2016.) <http://chroniclingamerica.loc.gov/lccn/sn83030213/1864-04-23/ed-1/seq-1/>

Maritime History of the Great Lakes. <http://images.maritimehistoryofthegreatlakes.ca/> (Accessed March, April 2016.)

Proceedings of the mixed Commission on British and American Claims. Parliamentary Papers, House of Commons, Vol. 75, British Parliament, House of Commons, 1874. Printed by Harrison and Sons, London, 1874.

Pitman, Benn. *The Assassination of President Lincoln and the Trial of the Conspirators.* New York: Moore, Wilstach & Baldwin, 1865.

United States. Naval War Records Office Official records of the Union and Confederate Navies in the War of the Rebellion. / Series I - Volume 22: West Gulf Blockading Squadron (January 1, 1865 - January 31, 1866); Naval Forces on Western Waters (May 8, 1861 - April 11, 1862). Government Printing Office, Washington, 1908. <http://ebooks.library.cornell.edu/m/moawar/text/ofre0022.txt> (Accessed April 2016.)

Washburne, E.B. *Congressional Series, The Reports of the Committees of the Second Session 38th Congress.* Government Printing Office. 1864-'65. (Accessed April 2016.) <http://bit.ly/20a4tEd>

Wolseley, Viscount Garnet. *General Lee.* (Accessed April 2016.) <http://bit.ly/20BZRrg>

SECONDARY SOURCES

Andreas, Peter. *Smuggler Nation: How Illicit Trade Made America.* New York: Oxford University Press, 2013.

Brandt, Nat. *The Man Who Tried to Burn New York.* Syracuse: Syracuse University Press, 1986.

Donald, David Herbert. *Lincoln.* London: Jonathan Cape Random House, 1995.

Mogelever, Jacob. *Death to Traitors.* Garden City: Doubleday & Company, 1960.

Scharf, John Thomas. *History of the Confederate States Navy from its Organization to the Surrender of its Last Vessel.* New York: Rogers & Sherwood, 1887.

Stewart, David O. *Impeached: The Trial of President Andrew Johnson and the Fight for Lincoln's Legacy.* New York: Simon & Schuster Paperbacks, 2009.

Swanson, James L. *Manhunt: The 12-day Chase for Lincoln's Killer.* New York, Harper Collins, 2006.

Waugh, John. *Class of 1846.* New York: Time Warner, 1994

BOOKS, THESES, ARTICLES, AND ONLINE CONTENT CITED IN TEXT

Ackerman, Kenneth D. *The Gold Ring.* New York: Dodd, Mead & Company, 1988.

Accounts and Papers of the House of Commons 1865, Testimony Following President Lincoln's Assassination. (Accessed March 2016.) <http://bit.ly/2p0O1TZ>

Adams, James Mack. *A History of Ft. Screven Georgia: Tybee Island's Military History.* Tybee Island: JMA2Publications, 1998.

Albu, Susan H. and Elizabeth Arndt. *Here's Savannah: A Journey through Historic Savannah & Environs.* Savannah: Atlantic Printing Company. Savannah, 1994.

Alford, Terry. *Fortune's Fool: The Life of John Wilkes Booth.* New York: Oxford University Press, 2015.

Alford, Terry. "John Wilkes Booth, and George A. Townsend: A Marriage Made in Hell." Paper delivered at the Third Biannual Tudor Hall Conference, Aberdeen, Maryland, May 3, 1992.

Allen, Felicity. *Jefferson Davis, Unconquerable Heart.* Columbia: The University of Missouri Press, 1999.

Almond, Barrie, "Captain Lewis Guy Phillips," *American Civil War Roundtable UK.* (Accessed April 2016.) <http://www.acwrt.org.uk/uk-heritage_Captain-Lewis-Guy-Phillips.asp>

Anderson, Nancy Scott and Dwight Anderson. *The Generals Ulysses S. Grant and Robert E. Lee.* New York: Alfred A. Knopf, 1987.

Andreas, Peter. *Smuggler Nation: How Illicit Trade Made America.* New York: Oxford University Press, 2013.

Andrews, Eliza Frances. *The War-time Journal of a Georgia Girl.* Edited by Spencer Bidwell King. Atlanta: Cherokee Publishing Company, 1976

Andrews, W.H. *Footprints of a Regiment: A Recollection of the 1st Georgia Regulars 1861-1865.* Atlanta: Longstreet Press,1992.

Andrews, William L. and Regina E. Mason, eds. *Life of William Grimes, the Runaway Slave.* New York: Oxford University Press, 2008.

Anonymous. *The St. Lawrence Hall Montreal City Guide: 1885.* Montreal: Canada Bank Note Company, 1885.

Arnold, Samuel Bland. *Defence and Prison Experiences of a Lincoln Conspirator.* Blanchester: The Book Farm, 1943.

Arnsdorff, Jimmy E. *Those Gallant Georgians Who Served in the War Between the States.* Greenville: Southern Historical Press,1994.

Bailey, Anne J. and Walter J. Fraser, Jr. *Portraits of Conflict: A Photographic History of Georgia in the Civil War.* Fayetteville: The University of Arkansas Press, 1996.

Bailey, Anne J. *War and Ruin: William T. Sherman and the Savannah Campaign.* Wilmington: Scholarly Resources, 2003.

Baker, L.C. *History of the United States Secret Service.* Philadelphia: King and Baird, 1868.

Balsiger, David. *The Lincoln Conspiracy.* Park City: Schick Sunn Classic Books, 1977.

Bancroft, Frederic. *Slave Trading in the South.* Columbia: The University of South Carolina Press, 1996.

Barnard, George N. *Photographic Views of Sherman's Campaign.* New York: Dover Publications, 1977.

Beagle, Donald and Bryan A. Giemza. *Poet of the Lost Cause: A Life of Father Ryan.* Knoxville: The University of Tennessee, 2008.

Bean, W.G. *Stonewall's Man: Sandie Pendleton.* 1959. Reprint, Chapel Hill: The University of North Carolina Press, 2000.

Bedwell, Randall, ed. *May I Quote You, General Lee? Observations & Utterances from the South's Great General.* Nashville: Cumberland House Publishing, 1997.

Bell, John. *Rebels on the Great Lakes.* Toronto: Dundurn Press, 2011.

Bell, Malcolm Jr. *Major Butler's Legacy: Five Generations of a Slaveholding Family.* Athens: The University of Georgia Press, 1987.

Bell, Malcolm. *Historic Savannah.* Savannah: Morris Newspaper Corporation, 1977.

Benjamin, L.N. *The St. Albans Raid.* Montreal: John Lovell, 1865.

Berlin, Ira. *Slaves without Masters: The Free Negro in the Antebellum South.* New York: The New Press, 2007.

Billingsley, Andrew. *Mighty like a River: The Black Church and Social Reform.* New York: Oxford University Press, 1999.

Blue & Grey Press. *The Photographic History of the Civil War. Two Volumes in One. The decisive battles. The Cavalry.* Edison: Blue & Gray Press,1987.

Boaz, Thomas. *Guns for Cotton: England Arms the Confederacy.* Shippensburg: Burd Street Press, 1990.

Boney, F.N., ed. *Slave Life in Georgia.* Savannah: The Beehive Press, 1991.

Bowman, John. *Chronicles of the Civil War: An Illustrated Almanac and Encyclopedia of America's Bloodiest War.* North Dighton: World Publications Group, 2005.

Boyd, Belle. *Belle Boyd in Camp and Prison: Volumes I & II.* London: Saunders, Otley, and Co., 2010.

Boyd, Kenneth W. *Georgia Historical Markers-Coastal Counties.* Atlanta: Cherokee Publishing Company, 1991.

Boyko, John. *Blood and Daring: How Canada Fought the American Civil War and Forged a Nation.* Toronto: Alfred A. Knopf Canada, 2013.

Bragg, William Harris. *De Renne: Three Generations of a Georgia Family.* Athens: The University of Georgia Press, 1999.

Bragg, William Harris. *Griswoldville.* Macon: Mercer University Press, 2000.

Brandt, Nat. *The Man Who Tried to Burn New York.* Syracuse: Syracuse,1986.

Bryan, T. Conn. *Confederate Georgia.* Athens: The University of Georgia Press, 1953.

Brown, Barry L. and Gordon R. Elwell. *Crossroads of Conflict: A Guide to Civil War Sites in Georgia.* Athens: The University of Georgia Press, 2010.

Brown, Russell K. *Our Connection with Savannah. A History of the 1st Battalion Georgia Sharpshooters 1862-1865.* Macon: Mercer University Press, 2004.

Browning, Orville H. *The Diary of Orville Hickman Browning.* Edited by Theodore Calvin Pease and James G. Randall. Chicago: The Blackley Printing Company, 1927.

Browning Jr., Robert. *Lincoln's Trident: The West Coast Blockading Squadron During the Civil War.* Tuscaloosa: The University of Alabama Press, 2015.

Buffalo Historical Society. *The Johnson Island Plot,* 1906. Reprinted by Cornell University, references both Captain Thomas Hines and the Northwest Conspiracy, Vol 2, *Southern Bivouac.*

Burge, Dolly Sumner Lunt. *A Woman's Wartime Journal. An Account of Sherman's Devastation of a Southern Plantation.* Atlanta: Cherokee Publishing Company, 1994

Burge, Timothy A. *"Bluenose Effrontery": Dr. William Johnston Almon and the City of Halifax During the Unites States' Civil War,* Master's Thesis, Dalhousie University, 2013.

Burke, Emily. *Pleasure and Pain: Reminiscences of Georgia in the 1840's.* Savannah: The Beehive Press, 1978.

Burlingame, Michael and J.R. Turner Ettinger. *Inside Lincoln's White House: The Complete Diary of John Hay.* Carbondale: Southern Illinois University Press, 1999.

Burlingame, Michael. *Abraham Lincoln: A Life,* Vol. 2. Maryland: Johns Hopkins University Press, 2008.

Butler, Benjamin F. *The Record of Benjamin F. Butler* Boston: publisher not identified, 1883. (Accessed March 11, 2017). http://bit.ly/2nb4PLc

Byrne, William Andrew. *The Burden and Heat of the Day: Slavery and Servitude in Savannah 1733-1865.* Ann Arbor: University Microfilms International, 1979.

Calonius, Erik. *The Wanderer: The Last American Slave Ship and the Conspiracy that Set its Sails.* New York: St. Martin's Press, 2006.

Campbell, Helen Jones. *Confederate Courier.* New York: St. Marten's Press, 1964.

Carter, Stephen L. *The Impeachment of Abraham Lincoln.* New York: Alfred A. Knopf, 2012.

Carey, Anthony Gene. *Parties, Slavery, and the Union in Antebellum Georgia.* Athens: The University of Georgia Press, 1997.

Cashin, Edward J. *Beloved Bethesda: A History of George Whitefield's Home for Boys, 1740-2000.* Macon: Mercer University Press, 2001.

Catholic Diocese of Savannah. *Savannah's Catholic Cemetery Chatham County, Georgia. Volume I: The Old Section.* 2005.

Catholic Diocese of Savannah. *Savannah's Catholic Cemetery Chatham County, Georgia Volume II: Magnolia and Palmetto Sections.* 2008.

Catton, Bruce. *The Coming Fury. Volume One: The Centennial History of the Civil War.* Garden City: Doubleday & Company, 1961.

Catton, Bruce. *Terrible Swift Sword.* Vol. 2 of *The American Civil War Trilogy.* New York: Fall River Press, 2009.

Catton, Bruce. *Grant Takes Command.* Boston: Little, Brown and Company,1969.

Catton, Bruce. *Grant Moves South 1861-1863.* 1960. Reprint, Edison: Castle Books, 2000.

Catton, Bruce. *Never Call Retreat.* Vol. 3 in *The American Civil War Trilogy.* New York: Fall River Press, 2009.

Causey, Donna R. "Historic Montgomery Theatre Partially Collapses." *The Alabama Pioneers.* (Accessed April 2016.) <http://alabamapioneers.com/historic-montgomery-theatre-partially-collapses/#sthash.nKwk7ywh.dpbs>

Chamberlain, Joshua Lawrence. *The Passing of the Armies: An Account of the Final Campaign of the Army of Potomac, Based on Personal Reminiscences of the Fifth Army Corps.* 1915. Reprint, Memphis: General Books, 2010.

Chamlee, Roy Z. *Lincoln's Assassins: A Complete Account of Their Capture, Trial, and Punishment.* Jefferson: McFarland Publishing, 1990.

Chernow, Ron. *Titan*. New York: Vintage Books, 2004.

Chittenden, L.E. *Personal Reminiscences: Including Lincoln and Others*. New York: Richmond, Croscup & Co., 1893.

Clarke, Erskine. *Dwelling Place: A Plantation Epic*. New Haven: Yale University Press, 2005.

Clay, Clement, Papers, collection of letters compiled by Virginia Clay. Duke University.

Clay-Clopton, Virginia and Ada Sterling. *A Belle of the Fifties, Memoirs of Mrs. Clay of Alabama, covering social and political life in Washington and the South, 1853-66*. New York: Doubleday, 1904.

Coffin, Charles Carleton. *Four Years of Fighting*. Boston: Ticknor and Fields, 1866.

Coffman, Edward M. *CAPTAIN HINES' ADVENTURES IN THE NORTHWEST CONSPIRACY*. The Register of the Kentucky Historical Society Vol. 63, No. 1 (January, 1965). (Accessed March 12, 2017.) https://www.jstor.org/stable/pdf/23375860.pdf?seq=1#page_scan_tab_contents

Congressional Series, The Reports of the Committees of the Second Session 38th Congress, 1864-'65. Washington D.C.: Government Printing Office. (Accessed April 2016.) <http://bit.ly/2oa3d3T>

Conner, T.D. *Homemade Thunder: War on the South Coast*. Savannah: Writeplace Press, 2004.

Conrad, Thomas. *The Rebel Scout*. Washington: The National Publishing Company, 1904.

Conroy, James. *Our One Common Country: Abraham Lincoln and the Hampton Roads Peace Conference*. Guilford: Lyons Press, 2014.

Cooper, William J., Jr. *Jefferson Davis, American*. New York: Random House, 2000.

Crocker, H.W., III *Robert E. Lee on Leadership: Executive Lessons in Character, Courage and Vision*. Rocklin: Crown Forum, 1999.

Croker, Richard. *To Make Men Free, A Novel of the Battle of Antietam*. New York: HarperCollins, 2004.

Cruson, Daniel. *The Slaves of Central Fairfield County: The Journey from Slave to Freeman in Nineteenth-Century Connecticut*. Charleston: The History Press, 2007.

Culpepper, Marilyn Mayer. *Women of the Civil War South: Personal Accounts from Diaries, Letters and Postwar Reminiscences*. Jefferson: McFarland & Company, 2003.

Cumming, Carman. *Devil's Game: The Civil War Intrigues of Charles A. Dunham*. Urbana: The University of Illinois Press, 2004.

D'Arcy, David and Ben Mammina. *Civil War Walking Tour of Savannah*. Atglen: Schiffer Publishing, 2006.

Davison, Donald. "Beef or Beans, Pudding or Pie." *Quebec Heritage News*, Autumn, 2010.

Davis, Burke. *Gray Fox: Robert E. Lee and the Civil War*. Avenel: Wings Books, 1956.

Davis, Burke. *To Appomattox Nine April Days 1865*. New York: Rinehart & Company, 1959.

Davis, Burke. *The Civil War: Strange & Fascinating Facts*. New York: Wings Books, 1960.

Davis, Burke. *Sherman's March: The First Full-length Narrative of General William T. Sherman's Devastating March through Georgia and the Carolinas*. New York: Vintage Books, 1988.

Davis, Charles C. *Clarke's Regiments: An Extended Index to the Histories of the Several Regiments and Battalions from North Carolina in the Great War 1861-65*. Gretna: Pelican Publishing Company, 2001.

Davis, George B. *The Official Military Atlas of the Civil War*. New York: Gramercy Books, 1983.

Davis, Jefferson. *The Papers of Jefferson Davis*. Edited by Linda Lasswell Crist. Baton Rouge: Louisiana State University Press, 2015.

Davis, William. *Civil War: A Complete Photographic History*. New York: Tess Press, 1981.

Davis, William C., ed. *Touched by Fire: A National Historical Society Photographic Portrait of the Civil War*. New York: Black Dog & Leventhal Publishers,1997.

Davis, William C. "Jack". *Civil War Parks: The Story Behind the Scenery*. Whittier: KC Publications, 1992.

Davis, William C. *The Orphan Brigade: The Kentucky Confederates Who Couldn't Go Home*. Mechanicsburg: Stackpole Books, 1993.

Davis, William C. *An Honorable Defeat: The Last Days of the Confederate Government*. New York: Harcourt, 2001.

Debolt, Margaret Wayt. *Savannah. A Historical Portrait*. 1977. Reprint, Gloucester Point: Hallmark Publishing Company, 2001.

DeCredico, Mary A. *Patriotism for Profit*. Chapel Hill: The University of North Carolina Press, 1990.

DeKay, James Tertius. *Monitor: The Story of the Legendary Civil War Ironclad and the Man Whose Invention Changed the Course of History*. New York: Walker and Company, 1997.

Detzer, David. *Donnybrook: The Battle of Bull Run, 1861*. New York: Harcourt, 2004.

Dery, Richard. *When War Comes Home*. Xlibris Corporation, 2008.

Deyle, Steven. *Carry Me Back. The Domestic Slave Trade in American Life*. New York: Oxford University Press, 2006.

Dick, Susan E. and Mandi D. Johnson. *Images of America. Savannah 1733-2000: Photographs from the collection of the Georgia Historical Society*. Mount Pleasant: Arcadia Publishing, 2002.

DiLorenzo, Thomas J. *The Real Lincoln*. New York: Three Rivers Press, 2002.

Diouf, Sylviane A. *Dreams of Africa in Alabama: The Slave Ship Clotilda and the Story of the Last Africans Brought to America*. New York: Oxford University Press, 2007.

Dodson, W.C. *Campaigns of Wheeler and his Cavalry 1862-1865*. Atlanta: Hudgins Publishing, 1899.

Dolson, Hildegarde. *They Struck Oil*. London: Hammond, Hammond & Company, 1959.

Donald, David Herbert. *Lincoln*. London: Random House, 1995.

Donald, David Herbert. *Lincoln Reconsidered: Essays on the Civil War*. New York: Vintage Books, 2001.

Drago, Edmund L., ed. *Broke by the War: Letters of a Slave Trader*. Columbia: The University of South Carolina Press, 1991.

Duffey, James E. *Victim of Honor: The Story of John Y. Beall and the Northwestern Conspiracy*. Westfield Center: Rion Hall Publishing, 2007.

Duncan, Alexander M. "Roll of Officers and Members of the Georgia Hussars and of the Cavalry Companies, of which the Hussars are a Continuation." *The Morning News*, Savannah, GA, 1906.

Duncan, Russell. *Freedom's Shore: Tunis Campbell and the Georgia Freemen*. Athens: The University of Georgia Press, 1986.

Durham, Roger S., ed. *The Blues in Gray. The Civil War Journal of William Daniel Dixon and the Republican Blues Day Book*. Knoxville: The University of Tennessee Press, 2000.

Durham, Roger S. *High Seas and Yankee Gunboats*. Columbia: The University of South Carolina Press, 2005.

Durham, Roger S. *Guardian of Savannah. Fort McAllister, Georgia, in the Civil War and Beyond*. Columbia: The University of South Carolina Press, 2008.

Dusinberre, William. *Them Dark Days: Slavery in the American Rice Fields*. Athens: The University of Georgia Press, 2000.

Dyer, John P. *From Shiloh to San Juan: The Life of "Fightin' Joe" Wheeler*. Baton Rouge: Louisiana State University Press,1989.

Eckhaus, Phyllis. "The Northern Slave Trade." *In These Times*. January 6, 2006. (Accessed April 2016.) <http://www. inthesetimes.com/article/2457/the_northern_slave_trade/>

Elmore, Charles J. *Black America Series. Savannah Georgia*. Mount Pleasant: Arcadia Publishing, 2002.

Evans, David. *Sherman's Horsemen*. Bloomington: Indiana University Press, 1996.

Fagan, W.L. *Southern War Songs: Campfire, Patriotic and Sentimental*. New York: M.T. Richardson & Co., 1890.

Fischer, LeRoy. "Lincoln's Gadfly." The Mississippi Valley Historical Review. (Accessed April 2016.) <http://archive. oah.org/special-issues/lincoln/bibliography/articles/pdf/ fischer.pdf>

Fishel, Edwin C. *The Secret War for the Union: The Untold Story of Military Intelligence in the Civil War*. New York: Houghton Mifflin, 1996.

Flood, Charles Bracelen. *1864 Lincoln at the Gates of History*. New York: Simon & Schuster, 2009.

Folsom, James Madison. *Heroes and Martyrs of Georgia*. Macon: Burke, Boykin & Company, 1864.

Fong, William. *Biography of William C. Macdonald*, Montreal: McGill Queen's University Press, 2010.

Foote, Shelby. *Shiloh*. New York: Vintage Books, 1980.

Foote, Shelby. *The Civil War: A Narrative. Fredericksburg to Meridian*. New York: Vintage Books, 1963.

Foote, Shelby. *The Civil War: A Narrative. Fort Sumter to Perryville*. New York: Vintage Books, 1986.

Foote, Shelby. *The Civil War: A Narrative. Red River to Appomattox*. New York: Random House, 1974.

Foote, Shelby. *Stars in their Courses: The Gettysburg Campaign*. New York: The Modern Library, 1994.

Foreman, Amanda. *A World on Fire: Britain's Crucial Role in the American Civil War*. New York: Random House, 2010.

Frajola, Richard. *Tales of the Blockade*, Exhibit. (Accessed March 2016.) <http://www.rfrajola.com/blockade/Blockades. pdf>

Franklin, John Hope and Loren Schweninger. *Runaway Slaves: Rebels on the Plantation*. New York: Oxford University Press, 2000.

Fraser, Walter J., Jr. *Savannah in the Old South*. Athens: The University of Georgia Press, 2005.

Freeman, H. Ronald. *Savannah Under Siege: The Bloodiest Hour of the Revolution*. Savannah: Freeport Publishing, 2002.

Freeman, H. Ronald. *Sherman Takes Savannah*. Savannah: Freeport Publishing, 2007.

Friedman, Saul S. *Jews and the American Slave Trade*. New Brunswick: Transaction Publishers, 2000.

Frassanito, William A. *Gettysburg, Then & Now: Touring the Battlefield with old Photos, 1863-1889*. Gettysburg: Thomas Publications, 1996.

Gallagher, Gary W. *The Confederate War*. Cambridge: Harvard University Press, 1997.

Gantt Spencer. *Why Lincoln Chose War*. South Carolina: Outskirts Press, 2011.

Gantt, Spencer. *Slavery and Lincoln's War*. People-South.com Publishers, 2013.

Gardner, Alexander. *Gardner's Photographic Sketch Book of the Civil War*. New York: Dover Publications, 1959.

Garvin, Ellis. *A Guide to our Two Savannahs*. Savannah: Garvin Publishing Company, 2010.

Gates, Henry Louis, Jr. ed. *Classic Slave Narratives*. New York: Signet Classics, 2002.

Genealogical Committee of Georgia Historical Society, compiled by, Savannah Georgia. *Laurel Grove Cemetery, Savannah, Georgia. Volume 1 12 October 1852-30 November 1861*. 1993.

Georgia Historical Society. *The Georgia Historical Quarterly*. Vol. XLI. Number 4. Athens: The University of Georgia, 1957.

Georgia Historical Society. *The Georgia Historical Quarterly*. Volume LXXXIX. Summer 2005. Number 2. Savannah: Georgia Historical Society, 2005.

Giles, William. *Disease, Starvation & Death: Personal Accounts of Camp Lawton*. Lulu Press, 2005.

Glatthaar, Joseph T. *The March to the Sea and Beyond Sherman's Troops in the Savannah and Carolinas Campaigns*. Baton Rouge: Louisiana State University Press, 1995.

Glatthaar, Joseph T. *General Lee's Army: From Victory to Collapse*. New York: The Free Press, 2008.

Gleason, Michael P. *The Insider's Guide to the Civil War, The Eastern Theater*. Manteo: The Insider's Guide, 1994.

Golden, Kathleen. Meet John S. Mosby, "Gray Ghost" of the Confederacy. *Smithsonian Museum of American History*. 2013. (Accessed April 2016.) <http://s.si.edu/2nXSE1I>

Goodrich, Thomas. *The Darkest Dawn: Lincoln, Booth, and the Great American Tragedy*. Bloomington: Indiana University Press, 2005.

Goodwin, Doris Kearns. *Team of Rivals: The Political Genius of Abraham Lincoln*. New York: Simon & Schuster, 2005.

Gottfried, Bradley M. *The Maps of First Bull Run*. New York: Savas Beatie, 2009.

Graham, Franklin T. *Histrionic Montreal*. Toronto: Ayer Publishing, 1972.

Graham, Martin F., Richard A. Sayers and George Skoch. *The Blue and the Gray: The Conflict between North & South*. Lincolnwood: Publications International, 1996.

Granger, Mary, ed. *Savannah River Plantations*. Savannah: The Oglethorpe Press, 1997.

Gray, Clayton. *Conspiracy in Canada*. Montreal: L'Atelier Press, 1957.

Greeley, Horace. *Aunt Really, Come Up! Or the Nigger Sale (1859)*. London: Ward & Lock, 1859.

Greenberg, Dolores. *Financiers and Railroads*. Newark: The University of Delaware Press, 1980.

Griffin, John Chandler. *Abraham Lincoln's Execution*, Gretna: Pelican Publishing Company, 2006.

Griffin, John Chandler. *Mr. Lincoln and His War*. Louisiana, Gretna: Pelican Publishing Company, 2009.

Grodinsky, Julius. *Jay Gould, His Business Career*. Philadelphia: The University of Pennsylvania Press, 1957.

Gross, Ariela J. *What Blood Won't Tell: A History of Race on Trial in America*. Cambridge: Harvard University Press, 2008.

Gudmestad, Robert H. *A Troublesome Commerce: The Transformation of the Interstate Slave Trade*. Baton Rouge: Louisiana State University Press, 2003.

Guelzo, Allen C. *Gettysburg: The Last Invasion*. New York: Alfred A, Knopf, 2013.

Guss, John Walker. *Images of America: Savannah's Laurel Grove Cemetery*. Mount Pleasant: Arcadia Publishing, 2002.

Guttridge, Leonard F. *Dark Union*. New Jersey: Jon Wiley and Sons, 2003.

Hain, Pamela Chase. *A Confederate Chronicle: The Life of a Civil War Survivor*. Columbia: The University of Missouri Press, 2005.

Hall, James O. *The Saga of Sarah Slater, The Surratt House Society*, February 1982.

Hall, James. *Notes of James Hall*, copied by the Camden Archives and Museum for Barry Sheehy, August 2012, in possession of the author.

Hallock, Charles. *The Hidden Way to Dixie, Confederate Veteran*, Vol. XXIV. November 1916, No. 11.

Halpenny, Francess G. *Dictionary of Canadian Biography - Volume 12*. Toronto: The University of Toronto Press, 1990.

Halstead, Murat, J. Frank Beale, and Willis Johnson. *Jay Gould: How He Made His Millions*, Philadelphia, Edgewood Publishing, 1892.

Hannon, Helen. "Colonel Charles Russell Lowell: A Death to a Soldier." *The Blue and Gray Education Society*, http://www.blueandgrayeducation.org/publications/monographs/colonel-charles-russell-lowell/

Hanckel, Thomas M. *Sermons by the Right Reverend Stephen Elliott D.D., Late Bishop of Georgia.* New York: Pott and Amery, 1867.

Harper, F. Mikell. *The Second Georgia Infantry Regiment, As Told Through the Unit History of Company D. Burke Sharpshooters.* Macon: Indigo Custom Publishing, 2005.

Harwell, Richard B. *The Confederate Reader.* New York: Longmans Green and Co., 1957.

Harwell, Richard. *Lee.* An abridgement in one volume by Richard Harwell of the four-volume R.E. Lee by Douglas Southall Freeman. Charles Scribner's Sons. 1934, 1935. Southern Living Gallery.

Hatch, Frederick *Protecting President Lincoln.* Jefferson: McFarland & Co., 2011.

Hatch, Frederick. *John Surratt: Rebel, Lincoln Conspirator, Fugitive.* Jefferson: McFarland & Co., 2016.

Haunton, Richard H. *Savannah in the 1850's.* University Microfilms International. Ann Arbor, 1968.

Hawkins, Charles, trans. *Blockade and Blockade Running.* (Accessed March 2016.) <http://chab-belgium.com/pdf/english/Blockade%20Runners1.pdf>

Headley, John. W. *Confederate Operations in Canada and New York.* New York: The Neale Publishing Company, 1906.

Hearn, Chester G. *Gray Raiders of the Sea: How Eight Confederate Warships Destroyed the Union's High Seas Commerce.* New York: International Marine Publishing, 1992.

Henderson, Tom. *The Slave Ship Wanderer.* Athens: The University of Georgia Press, 1967.

Hesseltine, William B. *Civil War Prisons.* Kent: Kent State University Press, 1962.

Higginbotham, Susan. (Accessed July 2016.) <http://bit.ly/2nEayog>

Higham, Charles. *Murdering Mr. Lincoln.* Beverly Hills: New Millennium Press, 2004.

Hill, Robert J., II *Savannah Squares.* Atglen: Schiffer Publishing. Atglen, 2004.

Hinshelwood, N.M. *Montreal and Vicinity: Being a History of the Old Town.* Stockbridge, HardPress Publishing, 2013.

Hitchcock, Henry. *Marching with Sherman.* 1927. Reprint, Lincoln: The University of Nebraska Press, 1995.

Holt, Michael. *The Rise and Fall of the American Whig Party: Jacksonian Politics and the Onset of the Civil War.* New York: Oxford University Press, 1999.

Hopper, Tristin. "Freshly Defeated in the U.S. Civil War, Confederate leader Jefferson Davis came to Canada to give the newly founded country defense tips." *National Post. It Happened in Canada Series.* July 25, 2014. (Accessed April 2016.) <http://bit.ly/2naSCq4>

Horan, James David. *Confederate Agent: A Discovery in History.* Golden Springs Publishing, 2015.

Horton, James Oliver and Lois E. *Slavery and the Public History: The Tough Stuff of American Memory.* Chapel Hill: The University of North Carolina Press, 2009.

Hoskins, Charles Lwanga. *Out of Yamacraw and Beyond: Discovering Black Savannah.* Savannah: The Gullah Press, 2002.

Hough, Elizabeth. "Josephine Noel, Camden's Confederate Spy." *UDC Magazine,* August 2007, provided by the Camden Archives and Museum 30 August 2012.

Hoy, Claire. *Canadians in the Civil War.* Toronto: McArthur & Company, 2004.

Hughes, Nathaniel Cheairs, Jr. *General William J. Hardee. Old Reliable.* Baton Rouge: Louisiana State University Press, 1992.

Hubbard, J.T.W. *For Each the Strength of All: A History of Banking in the State of New York.* New York: New York University Press, 1995.

Inikori, Joseph E. and Stanley L. Engerman. *The Atlantic Slave Trade: Effects on Economics, Societies, and Peoples in Africa, the Americas, and Europe.* Durham: Duke University Press, 2007.

Iobst, Richard W. *Civil War Macon: History of a Confederate City.* Macon: Mercer University Press, 1999.

Jacobs, Harriet. *Incidents in the Life of a Slave Girl.* Clayton: Prestwick House Literary Touchstone Classics, 2006.

Jampoler, Andrew C.A. *The Last Lincoln Conspirator.* Annapolis: Naval Institute Press, 2008.

Jenkins, Wilbert L. *Climbing Up to Glory: A Short Story of African Americans during the Civil War and Reconstruction.* Wilmington: A Scholarly Resource Inc. Imprint. 2002.

Jennison, Keith W. *The Humorous Mr. Lincoln: A Profile in Wit, Courage, and Compassion.* Woodstock: The Countryman Press, 1965.

Johns, John. "Wilmington, N.C. During the Blockade." *Harper's Monthly,* September 1866. (Accessed March 2016.) <http://bit.ly/2oad8GL>

Johnson, "Contraband Trade during the Last Year of the Civil War." *Mississippi Valley Historical Review*, June 1962.

Johnson, Ludwell. "Beverley Tucker's Canadian Mission." *Journal of Southern History* 29:1 February 1963.

Johnson, Ludwell H. "Commerce between Northern Ports and the Confederacy 1851-1865." *The Journal of American History*, 1967.

Johnson, Ludwell H. *Red River Campaign: Politics & Cotton in the Civil War*. Kent: Kent State University Press, 1993.

Johnson, Michael P. *Abraham Lincoln, Slavery, and the Civil War: Selected Writings and Speeches*. Boston: Bedford/St. Martin's, 2001.

Johnson, Robert Underwood, ed. *Battles and Leaders of the Civil War. Volume 4: Retreat with Honor*. Edison: Castle Books, 2010.

Johnson, Susan B. *Savannah's Little Crooked Houses: If These Walls Could Talk*. Charleston: The History Press, 2007.

Johnson, Walter. *Soul by Soul. Life Inside the Antebellum Slave Market*. Cambridge: Harvard University Press, 2000.

Johnson, Walter. *The Chattel Principle: Internal Slave Trades in the Americas*. New Haven: Yale University Press, 2004.

Johnson, Whittington B. *Black Savannah 1788-1864*. Fayetteville: The University of Arkansas Press, 1996.

Jones, Carmie M. *Historic Savannah: A Survey of Significant Buildings in the Historic District of Savannah, Georgia*. Savannah: Historic Savannah Society, 2005.

Jones Jr., Charles C. *The History of Georgia*. Boston: Houghton Mifflin and Company, 1883.

Jones, Charles C. *Historical Sketch of the Chatham Artillery during the Confederate Struggle for Independence*. Albany: Joel Munsell, 1867.

Jones, Charles Colcock. *Defence of Battery Wagner, July 18th 1863*. Georgia: Chronicle Publishing Company: 1892.

Jones, Jr., Charles C. *The Siege of Savannah*. Fayetteville: Americana Historical Books, 1997.

Jones, Jacqueline. *Saving Savannah: The City and the Civil War*. New York Vintage Books, 2008.

Jones, Thomas. *J. Wilkes Booth*. Chicago: Laird and Lee, Publishers, 1893.

Josephson, Matthew. *The Robber Barons*. Boston: Harcourt, 1934.

Joslyn, Mauriel Phillips. *Charlotte's Boys: Civil War Letters of the Branch Family of Savannah*. Berryville: Rockbridge Publishing Company, 1996.

Joslyn, Mauriel P. *Immortal Captives : The Story of 600 Confederate Officers and the United States Prisoners of War*. Gretna: Pelican Publishing Company, 2008.

Julian, George. *Diary of George Julian, Radical Republican*. (Accessed March 2016.) <archive.org/stream/jstor-27785702/27785702_djvu.txt>

Karson, Lawrence. *American Smuggling as a White Collar Crime*, New York: Routledge, 2014.

Kauffman, Michael W. *American Brutus: John Wilkes Booth and the Lincoln Conspiracies*. New York: Random House, 2004.

Kauffman, Michael W. *Memoirs of a Lincoln Conspirator*. Berwyn Heights: Heritage Books, 2008.

Kearney, Mark and Randy Ray, *Whatever Happened To? Catching Up with Canadian Icons*. Toronto: Dundurn Press, 2006.

Keber, Martha L. *Seas of Gold, Seas of Cotton: Christophe Poulain DuBignon of Jekyll Island*. Athens: The University of Georgia Press, 2002.

Kemble, Frances Anne. *Journal of a Residence on a Georgian Plantation in 1838-1839*. Savannah: The Beehive Press, 1992.

Keneally, Thomas. *Confederates*. William Collins Sons & Co. Great Britain, 1979.

Kennedy, Frances H., ed. *The Civil War Battlefield Guide*. Boston: Houghton Mifflin Company, 1990.

Kennett, Lee. *Marching Through Georgia. The Story of Soldiers & Civilians During Sherman's Campaign*. New York: HarperCollins, 1995.

King, Spencer Bidwell, Jr. *Ebb Tide as Seen Through the Diary of Josephine Clay Habersham 1863*. 1958. Reprint, Mercer University Press, GA, 1987.

Kitchens, Michael W. *Ghosts of Grandeur: Georgia's Lost Antebellum Homes and Plantations*. Virginia Beach: The Donning Company Publishers, 2012.

Klein, Maury. *The Life and Legend of Jay Gould*. Baltimore: Johns Hopkins University Press, 1986.

Klein, Maury. *Union Pacific*. Minneapolis: The University of Minnesota Press, 1987.

Klein, Maury. *Days of Defiance: Sumter, Secession, and the Coming of the Civil War*. New York: Alfred A. Knopf, 1997.

Kochanski, Halik. *Sir Garnet Wolseley: Victorian Hero*. Hambledon: Wiley, 1999.

Lane, Mills, ed. *Dear Mother: Don't Grieve About Me. If I get killed, I'll Only Be Dead: Letters from Georgia Soldiers in the Civil War*. Savannah: The Beehive Press, 1977.

Lane, Mills. *Savannah Revisited History & Architecture*. Savannah: The Beehive Press, 1977.

Lane, Mills, ed. *Times that Prove People's Principles: Civil War in Georgia: A Documentary History.* Savannah: The Beehive Press, 1993.

Lane, Mills. *Neither More nor Less Than Men: Slavery in Georgia.* Savannah: Beehive Press, 1993.

Lankford, Nelson D., ed. *An Irishman in Dixie: Thomas Conolly's Diary of the Fall of the Confederacy.* Columbia: The University of South Carolina Press, 1988.

Larabee, Ann. *The Dynamite Fiend.* Halifax: Nimbus Publishing, 2005.

Lawliss, Chuck. *Robert E. Lee Slept Here: Civil War Inns and Destinations. A Guide for the Discerning Traveler.* New York: Ballantine Books, 1998.

Lawrence, Alexander A. *A Present for Mr. Lincoln.* 1961. Reprint, Savannah: The Ogelthorpe Press, 1997.

Lee, F.D. *Historical Record of the City of Savannah.* Savannah: Morning News Steam Power Press, 1869.

Lee, General Fitzhugh. *General Lee. A Biography of Robert E. Lee.* 1894. Reprint. Boston: Da Capo Press, 1994.

Lee, Captain Robert E. *Recollections and Letters of General Robert E. Lee.* New York: Doubleday, Page & Company, 1904.

Leech, Margaret. *Reveille in Washington.* New York: Harper & Brothers Publishers, 1941.

Leigh, Philip. *Trading with the Enemy: The Covert Economy During the American Civil War.* Yardley: Westholme Publishing, 2014.

Lens, Richard J. *An Illustrated Traveler's Guide. The Civil War in Georgia.* Watkinsville: Infinity Press, 1995.

Leon, Ella. *Foreigners in the Confederacy.* Chapel Hill: The University of North Carolina Press, 1940.

Leonard, Elizabeth D. *Lincoln's Avengers: Justice, Revenge, and Reunion after the Civil War.* New York: W.W. Norton & Co., 2004.

Lester, Richard I. *Confederate Finance and Purchasing in Great Britain.* Charlottesville: The University of Virginia Press, 1975.

Levin, Alexandra Lee. *This Awful Drama.* New York: Vantage Press, 1987.

Lincoln, Abraham. *First Inaugural Address.* (Accessed January 2016.) http://www.abrahamlincolnonline.org/lincoln/speeches/1inaug.htm

Lincoln, Abraham. *The First Edition of Abraham Lincoln's Final Emancipation Proclamation January 1, 1863.* The Library of Congress.

Lincoln, Abraham. *Handwritten Autobiography for the Chicago Press and Tribune.* June, 1860. The Library of Congress, The Easton Press.

Lockley, Timothy James. *Lines in the Sand. Race and Class in Low country Georgia 1750-1860.* Athens: The University of Georgia Press, 2004.

Long, A.L. *Memoirs of Robert E. Lee.* New York: Crescent Books, 1994.

Lossing, Benson J. *Matthew Brady's Illustrated History of the Civil War with his War Photographs and Paintings by Military Artists.* Avenel: Gramercy Books, 1996.

Loux, Arthur, *John Wilkes Booth Day by Day.* Jefferson: McFarland & Co., 2014.

Low, Charles Rathbone. *General Lord Wolseley (of Cairo): A Memoir.* Palala Press, 2016.

Lucas, Daniel. *The Land Where We Were Dreaming* (Accessed March 2016.) <http://cw.routledge.com/textbooks/9780415537070/data/section5/lucas-in_the_land.pdf> (Accessed March 2016.)

Lucas, Daniel B. *Memoir of John Yates Beall,* Montreal: John Lovell, 1865.

Mach, Thomas S., *Gentleman George Hunt Pendleton.* Kent: Kent State University Press, 2007.

MacMillan Publishing. *The Confederacy: Selections from the Four Volume McMillan Encyclopedia of the Confederacy.* U.S.A.: MacMillan Library Reference, 1991.

Maritime History of the Great Lakes. (Accessed March 2016.) <http://images.maritimehistoryofthegreatlakes.ca/> (Accessed March 2016.) <http://images.maritimehistoryofthegreatlakes.ca/1014/data?n=33> (Accessed April 2016.) <http://images.maritimehistoryofthegreatlakes.ca/37507/data?n=20> (Accessed April 2016.) <http://images.maritimehistoryofthegreatlakes.ca/65980/data?n=1> (Accessed April 2016.) <http://www.maritimehistoryofthegreatlakes.ca/Documents/Scanner706/default.asp?ID=c007>

Markle, Donald E. *Spies and Spymasters of the Civil War.* New York: Barnes and Noble, 1994.

Marquis, Greg. *In Armageddon's Shadow.* Montreal: McGill-Queen's University Press, 1998.

Marszalek, John F. *Sherman: A Soldier's Passion for Order.* New York: The Free Press. NY, 1993.

Marszalek, John F. *Civil War Campaigns and Commanders: Sherman's March to the Sea.* Abilene: McWhitney Foundation Press, McMurray University, 2005.

Marvel, William. *Lincoln's Autocrat: The Life of Edwin Stanton.* Chapel Hill: The University of North Carolina Press, 2015.

Mayers, Adam. *Dixie & the Dominion: Canada, the Confederacy, and the War for the Union.* Toronto: Dundurn Press, 2003.

Maxwell, Ronald E., *Gods and Generals. The Illustrated Story of the Epic Civil War Film.* Introduction and screenplay. New York: Newmarket Press, 2003.

McCaig, Donald. *Jacob's Ladder.* New York: W.W. Norton & Co., 1998.

McCash, June Hall. *Jekyll Island's Early Years from the Prehistory through Reconstruction.* Athens: The University of Georgia Press, 2005.

McDonald, JoAnna, ed. *The Faces of Manassas. Rare Photographs of Soldiers Who Fought at Bull Run.* Redondo Beach: Rank and File Publications, 1998.

McDonald, John. *Great Battles of the Civil War.* New York: Collier Books, 1988.

McGee, Thomas D'Arcy. (Accessed March 2016.) <http://www.azquotes.com/author/73287-Thomas_D_Arcy_McGee>

McKenzie Martin, "Home of Thomas Hines," *Explore KYHistory,* (Accessed March 22, 2017.) http://explorekyhistory.ky.gov/items/show/374.

McKitrick, Eric L. *Andrew Johnson and Reconstruction.* New York: Oxford University Press, 1960.

McMurray, Richard M. *Footprints of a Regiment.* Atlanta: Longstreet Press, 1992.

McPherson, James M. *Battle Cry of Freedom: The Civil War Era.* New York: Ballantine Books, 1989.

McPherson, James M. *Gettysburg.* Atlanta: Turner Publishing, 1993.

McPherson, James M. *What They Fought For. 1861-1865.* New York: Anchor Books, 1995.

McPherson, James M. *Crossroads of Freedom: Antietam.* New York: Oxford University Press, 2002.

McPherson, James M. *Hallowed Ground. A Walk at Gettysburg.* New York: Crown Journeys, 2003.

McWhiney, Grady and Perry D. Jamieson. *Attack and Die: Civil war Military Tactics and the Southern Heritage.* Tuscaloosa: The University of Alabama Press, 1982.

Mellish, Gordon. *Guerrilla War in Kentucky: Burbridge and Berrys.* Victoria: Trafford Publishing, 2008.

Meredith, Frank. *The Unfinished Work.* Austin: Emerald Book Company, 2010.

Miers, Earl Schenck. *The Last Campaign: Grant Saves the Union.* Philadephia: J.B. Lippincott Company, 1972.

Miles, Jim. *To the Sea: A History and Tour Guide of the War in the West, Sherman's March to Across Georgia and Through the Carolinas, 1864-1865.* Nashville: Cumberland House, 2002.

Millard, Candice. *Destiny of the Republic.* New York: Doubleday, 2011.

Miller, Randall M. and John David Smith, eds. *Dictionary of Afro-American Slavery.* Westport: Praeger Publishers, 1997.

Minor, Capt. Robert D. *The Plan to Rescue the Johnston's Island Prisoners.* Southern Historical Society Papers. 1895. (Accessed April 2016.) <http://www.csa-dixie.com/csa/prisoners/t67.htm>

Misulia, Charles A. *Columbus Georgia 1865: The Last True Battle of the Civil War.* Tuscaloosa: The University of Alabama Press, 2010.

Mogelever, Jacob. *Death to Traitors.* Garden City: Doubleday & Company, 1960.

Montreal Daily Transcript. John Wilkes Booth Suggests Upcoming Assassination. November 11, 1854. (Accessed April 2016.) <http://coolopolis.blogspot.com/2010/01/john-wilkes-booth-suggests-upcoming.html>

Morgan, Edna Q. *John Adam Treutlen: Georgia's First Constitutional Governor, His Life, Real and Rumored.* Springfield: Historic Effingham Society, 1998.

Morgan, Phillip. *African American Life in the Georgia Lowcountry: The Atlantic World and the Gullah Ogeechee.* Athens: The University of Georgia Press, 2010.

Morris, Jeffrey Brandon. *Calmly to Poise the Scales of Justice: A History of the Courts of the District of Columbia Circuit.* Durham: Carolina Academic Press, 2001.

Muller, John. *Mark Twain in Washington D.C.* Charleston: The History Press, 2013.

Murray, Maj. J. Ogden. *The Immortal Six Hundred: A Story of Cruelty to Confederate Prisoner of War.* 1905. Reprint, Dahlonega: The Confederate Reprint Company, 2001.

Myers, John. *Henry Wilson and the Era of Reconstruction,* Roman & Littlefield, University Press of America, 2009.

Myers, Robert Manson. *The Children of Pride: A True Story of Georgia and the Civil War.* New Haven: Yale University Press, 1972.

Neff, John R. *Honoring the Civil War Dead: Commemoration and the Problem of Reconciliation.* Lawrence: The University of Kansas Press, 2005.

Nelson, Christopher. *Mapping the Civil War.* Golden: Fulcrum Publishing, 1992.

New York Times. "The Rebels in Canada; Blockade Runners from Montreal? The Trade Very Active--Secession Up North." Published: 17 August 1863. (Accessed August 2016.) http://www.nytimes.com/1863/08/17/news/rebels-canada-blockade-runners-montreal-trade-very-active-secession-up-north.html

New York Times. "Canadian Blockade Runners Building." September 12, 1863. (Accessed April 2016.) <http://www.nytimes.com/1863/09/12/news/canadian-blockade-runners-building.html>

New York Times. "Mr. G.B. Lamar and the Blockade." December 19, 1863. (Accessed April 2016.) <http://nyti.ms/2nXXMms>

New York Times. "Important Disclosures." December 23, 1863. (Accessed April 2016.) <http://nyti.ms/203jsz5>

New York Times. "Blockade Running." January 4, 1864. (April 2016.) <http://www.nytimes.com/1864/01/04/news/blockade-running-important-developments-parties-this-city-implicated-card.html>

New York Times. "Great Lakes Pilot." January 16, 1864. (Accessed March 2016.) <http://www.greatlakespilot.com/stories/JohnMurray.html>

New York Times. "The Lamar Correspondence." January 16, 1864. (Accessed March 2016.) <http://nyti.ms/203mOly>

New York Times. "Gigantic Operative Movement." May 6, 1864. (Accessed September 2016.) http://nyti.ms/2naXwDC

New York Times. "General Singleton in Richmond." January 19, 1865. (Accessed March 2016.) <http://www.nytimes.com/1865/01/19/news/gen-singleton-in-richmond.html>

New York Times. "Gen. Washburne has ordered the arrest of the chief clerk in the office of Mr. Ellery, Treasury Agent, for the purchase of cotton." March 2 and 9, 1865. (Accessed September 2017.) <http://www.nytimes.com/1865/03/02/news/sherman-s-march.html>

The New York Times. "Gen. Washburne has ordered the arrest of the chief clerk in the office of Mr. Ellery, Treasury Agent, for the purchase of cotton." (Accessed September 2016.) <http://nyti.ms/203kIlR>

Newell, Clayton R. Lee vs. McClellan: The First Campaign. Washington D.C." Regnery Publishing, 1996.

Newton, Steven H. Lost for the Cause: The Confederate Army in 1864. Boston: Da Capo Press, 2000.

Nichols, G.W. A Soldier's Story of his Regiment. Kennesaw: Continental Book Co., 1961.

Nicolay, John and John Hay, Abraham Lincoln, Carbondale: Southern Illinois University Press, 2007.

Niven, John. Gideon Welles: Lincoln's Secretary of the Navy. Baton Rouge: Louisiana State University Press, 1973.

Niven, John. Salmon Chase: A Biography. New York: Oxford University Press, 1995.

Noirsain, Serge. The Blockade Runners of the Confederate Government. Trans. Gerald Hawkins. (Accessed March 2016.) <http://bit.ly/2030k7q>

None. A Pictorial History of the Battle of Gettysburg. TEM Inc. Gettysburg, PA.

Norton, Oliver Willcox. The Attack and Defense of Little Round Top. Gettysburg, July 2, 1863. Gettysburg: Stan Clark Military Books, 1992.

Norton, Roger J. John Parker: The Guard Who Left his Post. (Accessed May 2016) <http://rogerjnorton.com/Lincoln61.html>

Norton, Roger J. George Atzerodt's Lost Confession. (Accessed March 2016.) <http://rogerjnorton.com/Lincoln82.html>

Oates, Colonel William C. and Lieutenant Frank A. Haskell. Glenn LaFantasie, ed. Gettysburg: Two Eyewitness Accounts. New York: Bantam Books, 1992.

Oates, Stephen B. The Approaching Fury: Voices of the Storm, 1820-1861. The Coming of the Civil War Told from the Viewpoints of Thirteen Principal Players in the Drama. New York: HarperCollins, 1997.

Oberholtzer, Ellis Paxson. Jay Cooke: Financier of the Civil War. Philadelphia: George W. Jacobs & Company, 1907.

Oeffinger, John C. A Soldiers General: The Civil War Letter of Major General Lafayette McLaws. Chapel Hill: The University of North Carolina Press, 2002.

Official Record of Directors and Officers of the Union Pacific Railroad, 1863-1889.

Parliamentary Papers, House of Commons, Vol. 75, British Parliament, House of Commons, 1874, Proceedings of the mixed Commission on British and American Claims.

Pember, Phoebe Yates. A Southern Woman's Story. Columbia: The University of South Carolina Press. 2002.

Phillips, Donald T. Lincoln on Leadership. Executive Strategies for Tough Times. New York: Warner Books, 1992.

Pickett, George E. The Heart of a Soldier. Intimate Wartime Letters from General George E. Pickett C.S.A. to his Wife. Seth Moyle, 1913. Gettysburg: Stan Clark Military Books, 1995.

Pitman, Benn. The Assassination of President Lincoln and the Trial of the Conspirators. New York: Moore, Wilstach & Baldwin, 1865.

Pitman, Benn. *The trials for treason at Indianapolis, disclosing the plans for establishing a north-western confederacy.* Salem: The News Publishing Company, 1865. (Accessed May 2016.) <http://bit.ly/2nY3rZH>

Poole, John Randolf. *Cracker Cavaliers: The 2nd Georgia Cavalry under Wheeler and Forrest.* Macon: Mercer University Press, 2000.

Pratt, Fletcher. *Civil War in Pictures.* Garden City: Garden City Books, 1955.

Prince, Cathryn J. *Burn the Town and Sack the Banks.* New York: Carol & Graf Publishers, 2006.

Propst, Matthew. *Savannah Cemeteries.* Atglen: Schiffer Publishing, 2009.

Randall, S.S. *History of Common School System of the State of New York,* New York: General Books, 2009.

Ransom, Roger L. "The Economics of the Civil War." (Accessed March 2016.) <https://eh.net/encyclopedia/the-economics-of-the-civil-war/>

Renehan, Edward J., Jr. *Dark Genius of Wall Street.* New York: Basic Books, 2008.

Renfro, Betty Ford. *River to River: From the Savannah River to the Ogeechee River: The History of Effingham County.* Springfield: Historic Effingham Society, 2004.

Rescher, Nicholas. *Niagara-on-the-Lake as a Confederate Refuge.* Washington D.C.: NAP Publications, 2003.

Rhea, Gordon C. *The Battle for Spotsylvania Court House and the Road to Yellow Tavern May 7-12, 1864.* Baton Rouge: Louisiana State University Press, 1997.

Rhea, Gordon C. *Cold Harbor. Grant and Lee May 26-June 3, 1864.* Baton Rouge: Louisiana State University Press, 2007.

Rhodehamel, John. *Right or Wrong, God Judge Me: The Writings of John Wilkes Booth.* Champaign: The University of Illinois Press, 2001.

Ribbens, Kim Traub, ed. *Sojourn in Savannah.* Garden City: The Printcraft Press, 2000.

Richter, William. *Historical Dictionary of the Civil War and Reconstruction.* Lanham: Scarecrow Press, 2012.

Roberts, A.S. *Northern Profit and Profiteers: The Cotton Rings of 1864-1865,* Civil War History, June 1966. (Accessed March 2017.) http://muse.jhu.edu/article/416833

Robertson, James I., Jr. *Stonewall Jackson: The Man, The Soldier, The Legend.* New York: Macmillan Publishing, 1997.

Roman, Alfred. *The Military Operations of General Beauregard. Volume II.* Boston: Da Capo Press,1994.

Rosen, Robert N. *The Jewish Confederates.* The University of South Carolina Press: Columbia, SC, 2000.

Ross, Alexander Milton. *Recollections and Experience of an Abolitionist.* Toronto: Roswell and Hutchison, 1875.

Ross, Alexander Milton. *Memoirs of a Reformer, 1832-1892.* Toronto: Hunter, Rose & Company, 1893.

Rowland, Lawrence S. *The History of Beaufort County, South Carolina.* South Carolina: The University of South Carolina Press, 1996.

Rudin, R.E. "King, Edwin Henry." (Accessed March 2016.) <http://www.biographi.ca/en/bio/king_edwin_henry_12E.html>

Rush, Daniel S. and Gale Pewitt. "The St. Albans Raiders. An Investigation into the Identities of the Confederate Soldiers who Attacked St. Albans, Vermont on October 19, 1864." *The Blue and Gray Education Society.* 2008 (Accessed March 2017.) http://www.blueandgrayeducation.org/publications/monographs/the-st-albans-raiders/

Russell, Preston and Barbara Hines. *Savannah: A History of her People Since 1733.* Savannah: Frederic C. Beil, 1992.

Russell, William Howard. *The Diary North and South (1863).* Franklin Square: Harper & Brothers, Publishers, 1863.

Ryan, Jennifer Guthrie and Hugh Stiles Golson. *Andrew Low and the Sign of the Buck: Trade, Triumph, Tragedy at the House of Low.* Savannah: Frederic C. Bell, 2011.

Sacramento Daily Union. "The Famous Dan Sickles Trial." October 1, 1887. (Accessed March 2016.) <http://cdnc.ucr.edu/cgi-bin/cdnc?a=d&d=SDU18871001.2.60>

Safire, William. *Freedom.* New York: Doubleday & Company, 1987.

Sanmann, Stefan and John Cromwell. *Savannah Then and Now.* Savannah: Savannah House Publishers, 1997.

Scaife, William R. and William Harris Bragg. *Joe Brown's Pets: The Georgia Militia 1861-1865.* Macon: Mercer University Press, 2004.

Scharf, John Thomas. *History of the Confederate States Navy from its Organization to the Surrender of its Last Vessel.* New York: Rogers & Sherwood, 1887.

Schultz, Duane. *The Dahlgren Affair. Terror and Conspiracy in the Civil War.* New York: W.W. Norton & Co., 1998.

Schofield, Nikki Stoddard. *Confederates in Canada: A Civil War Romance.* Bloomington: Author House, 2016.

Scott, Carole E. "Short Biographies of 19th Century Southerners." (Accessed April 2016.) <http://carolescott.tripod.com/figures.htm>

Sehlinger, Peter J. *Kentucky's Last Cavalier: General William Preston, 1816-1887.* Lawrence: The University of Kentucky Press, 2004.

Sexton, Jay. *Debtor Diplomacy: Finance and American Foreign Relations in the Civil War.* New York: Oxford University Press, 2005.

Shaw, Robert and Russell Duncan. *Blue-eyed Child of Fortune: The Civil War Letters of Colonel Robert Gould Shaw.* Athens: The University of Georgia Press, 1999.

Sheehy, Barry and Cindy Wallace. *Savannah Immortal City.* Austin: Emerald Book Company, 2011.

Sheehy, Barry Cindy Wallace. *Civil War Savannah: Brokers, Bankers and Bay Lane.* Austin: Emerald Book Company, 2012.

Sheehy, Barry and Cindy Wallace. *The Booth Fragment,* paper prepared for the Rare Book Department, Free Library of Philadelphia.

Sigaud, Louis A. *Belle Boyd-Confederate Spy.* Petersburg: The Dietz Press, 1945.

Singer, Jane. *The Confederate Dirty War.* Jefferson: McFarland & Company, 2005.

Sizer, Lyde Cullen and Jim, eds. *The Civil War Era: An Anthology of Sources.* Malden: Blackwell Publishing, 2005.

Skinner, Arthur N. *The Death of a Confederate.* Athens: University of Georgia Press, 2008.

Smedlund, William S. *Camp Fires of Georgia's Troops 1861-1865.* Lithonia: Smedlund, 1995.

Smith Anna Habersham Wright, ed. *A Savannah Family 1830-1901.* Milledgeville: Boyd Publishing, 1999.

Smith, David. *Sherman's March to the Sea 1864: Atlanta to Savannah.* Oxford: Osprey Publishing, 2007.

Smith, Derek. *Civil War Savannah.* Savannah: Frederick C. Beil, 1997.

Smith, Gene. *High Crimes & Misdemeanors: The Impeachment and Trial of Andrew Johnson.* New York: William Morrow and Company, 1976.

Smith, Gordon Burns. *History of Georgia Militia, 1783-1861. Volume I, Campaigns and Generals.* Milledgeville: Boyd Publishing, 2000.

Smith, Gordon Burns. *History of Georgia Militia, 1783-1861. Volume II, Counties and Commanders, Part One.* Boyd Publishing. Millidgeville, GA, 2000.

Smith, Gordon Burns. *History of Georgia Militia, 1783-1861. Volume III, Counties and Commanders, Part Two.* Milledgeville: Boyd Publishing, 2001.

Smith, Julia Floyd. *Slavery and the Rice Culture in Lowcountry Georgia 1750-1860.* Knoxville: The University of Tennessee Press, 1992.

Smith, Michael T. *The Enemy Within: Fears of Corruption in the Civil War North.* Charlottesville: The University of Virginia Press, 2011.

Sneden, Robert Knox. *Eye of the Storm.* Edited by Charles F. Bryan, Jr. and Nelson D. Lankford. New York: The Free Press, 2000.

Snow, William P. *Lee and his Generals.* Avenel: Gramercy Books, 1996.

Sowles, Hon. Edward Adams. *History of the St. Albans Raid.* Vermont Historical Society, 1876.

Spracher, Luciana M. *Images of America. Lost Savannah. Photographs from the Collection of the Georgia Historical Society.* Mount Pleasant: Arcadia Publishing, 2002.

Squires, Melinda. *The Controversial Career of George Nicholas Sanders,* Western Kentucky University, August 2000. (Accessed April 2016.) <http://bit.ly/203cNFk>

Stackpole, General Edward J. *They Met at Gettysburg.* Harrisburg: Stackpole Books, 1986.

Stallings, James E, Sr. *Georgia's Confederate Soldiers Who Died as Prisoners of War. 1861-1865.* Saline: McNaughton & Gunn, 2008.

Stanchak, John and Frank Leslie. *Leslie's Illustrated Civil War.* Jackson: University Press of Mississippi, 1992.

Stanton, John F. "A Mystery No Longer: The Lady in the Veil." *Surratt Courier,* August 2011 and October 2011.

Steers, Edward, Jr. *Blood on the Moon.* Lexington: The University Press of Kentucky, 2005.

Steers, Edward Jr. *The Lincoln Assassination Encyclopedia.* New York: Harper Perennial, 2010.

Steers, Edward and William Edwards, eds. *The Lincoln Assassination: The Evidence.* Chicago: The University of Illinois Press, 2009.

Steers, Edward and Harold Holzer. *The Lincoln Assassination Conspirators: Their Confinement and Execution as Recorded in the Letterbook of John Frederick Hartranft.* Baton Rouge, Louisiana State University Press, 2009.

Stewart, David O. *Impeached: The Trial of President Andrew Johnson and the Fight for Lincoln's Legacy.* New York: Simon & Schuster Paperbacks, 2009.

Stokes, Thomas L. *The Savannah.* Athens: The University of Georgia Press, 1979.

Stone, H. David, Jr. *Vital Rails: The Charleston & Savannah Railroad and the Civil War in Coastal South Carolina*. Columbia: The University of South Carolina Press, 2008.

Strausbaugh, John. *City of Sedition: The History of New York City during the Civil War*. New York, Hachette Book Group, 2016. (Accessed December 2016.) http://bit.ly/2nb7hRU

Strode, Hudson. *Jefferson Davis: Private Letters*. New York: Harcourt, Brace & World, 1966.

Sulick, Michael J. *Spying in America: Espionage from the Revolutionary War to the Dawn of the Cold War*. Washington, D.C.: Georgetown University Press, 2012.

Summers, Mark W. *The Plundering Generation: Corruption and the Crisis of the Union 1894-1861*. New York: Oxford University Press, 1987.

Surdam, David. "Traders or Traitors: Northern Cotton Trading During the Civil War." *Business and Economic History* 28, no. 2 (1999): 301-312. (Accessed April 2016.) <https://works.bepress.com/david_surdam/22/>

Surratt, John H. *Trial of John H. Surratt in the Criminal Court for the District of Columbia, Hon. George Fisher Presiding* Washington D.C.: Government Printing Office, 1867.

Sutherland, Daniel E. *The Confederate Carpetbaggers*. Baton Rouge: Louisiana State University Press, 1988.

Swanson, James L. *Manhunt: The 12-day Chase for Lincoln's Killer*. New York: HarperCollins, 2006.

Tadman, Michael. *Speculators and Slaves. Masters, Traders, and Slaves in the Old South*. Madison: The University of Wisconsin Press, 1996.

Tagg, Larry. *The Unpopular Mr. Lincoln*. New York: Savas Beatie, 2009.

Takagi, Midori. *"Rearing Wolves to Our Own Destruction" Slavery in Richmond, Virginia, 1782-1865*. Charlottesville: The University of Virginia Press, 2002.

Tanner, Robert G. *Stonewall in the Valley. Thomas J. Stonewall Jackson's Shenandoah Valley Campaign, Spring 1862*. New York: Doubleday & Company, 1976.

Taylor, Susie King. *Reminiscences of my Life in Camp. An African American Woman's Civil War Memoir*. 1902. Reprint, Athens: The University of Georgia Press, 2006.

The Canadian Historical Review. *The Review of Historical Publications Relating to Canada: Vol. II*. Toronto: The University of Toronto Press, 1921.

The Georgia Historical Society. *The 1860 Census of Chatham County, Georgia*. Greenville: Southern Historical Press, 1980.

The Lehrman Institute. *Abraham Lincoln and Cotton*. (Accessed April 2016.) <http://www.abrahamlincolnsclassroom.org/abraham-lincoln-in-depth/abraham-lincoln-and-cotton/>

The Lehrman Institute. *Mr. Lincoln and New York: Fernando Wood*. (Accessed April 2016.) <http://www.mrlincolnandnewyork.org/inside.asp?ID=80&subjectID=3>

The Lehrman Institute. *Mr. Lincoln and New York: August Conspiracy*. (Accessed April 2016.) <http://www.mrlincolnandnewyork.org/inside.asp?ID=100&subjectID=4>

The Lincoln Library of Essential Information. New York: The Frontier Press Company, 1963.

The National Historical Society. *The War of the Rebellion: Series I-Volume I*. Washington D.C.: Government Printing Office, 1880.

The National Historical Society. *The War of the Rebellion: Series I-Volume XLIV*. Washington D.C.: Government Printing Office, 1893.

The National Historical Society. *The War of the Rebellion: Series I-Volume IV*. Washington D.C.: Government Printing Office, 1882.

Thomas, Benjamin P. and Harold M. Hyman. *Stanton: the Life and Times of Lincoln's Secretary of War*. New York: Alfred A. Knopf, 1962.

Thomas, Don. *The Reason Lincoln Had to Die*. Bakersfield: Pumphouse Publishers, 2013.

Thomas, Emory M. *Robert E. Lee, a Biography*. New York: W. W. Norton & Co., 1995.

Thompson, James. "The Plot of Judge Advocate Joseph Holt." (Accessed April 2016.) <http://chab-belgium.com/pdf/english/Judge%20Holt.pdf>

Thompson, John Herd and Stephen J. Randall, *Canada and the United States: Ambivalent Allies* (Accessed October 2011.) <https://muse.jhu.edu/book/11562>

Thuersam, Bernhard. "Wilmington to Canada: Blockade Runners & Secret Agents." (Accessed March 2016.) <http://www.cfhi.net/WilmingtonsWartimeCanadianConnection.php>

Tidwell, William A, Hall, James O. & Gaddy, and David Winfred. *Come Retribution: The Confederate Secret Service and the Assassination of Lincoln*. Jackson: The University Press of Mississippi, 1988.

Tidwell, William. *April '65*, Kent: Kent State University Press, 1995

Tidwell, William A. *Confederate Covert Action in the American Civil War: April '65*. Kent: Kent State University Press, 1995.

Time-Life Books. *1863 Turning Point of the Civil War*. Alexandria, 1998.

Time-Life Books. *Echoes of Glory. Illustrated Atlas of the Civil War*. Alexandria, 1998.

Todd, Richard Cecil. *Confederate Finance*. Athens: The University of Georgia Press.

Toledano, Roulhac. *The National Trust Guide to Savannah Architectural & Cultural Treasures*. New York: John Wiley & Sons, 1997.

Townsend, George Alfred. *The Life, Crime and Capture of John Wilkes Booth*. New York, Dick and Fitzgerald, 1865. (Accessed March 2017.) http://quod.lib.umich.edu/cgi/t/text/text-idx?c=moa;idno=AAU8937

Trindal, Elizabeth Steger. *Mary Surratt: An American Tragedy*. Gretna: Pelican Publishing Company, 1996.

Trudeau, Noah Andre. *Southern Storm: Sherman's March to the Sea*. New York: HarperCollins, 2008.

Turner, Thomas Reed. *Beware the People Weeping: Public Opinion and the Assassination of Abraham Lincoln*. Baton Rouge: Louisiana State University Press, 1982.

Underwood, J.R. *Proceedings Democratic Convention, Chicago, 1864*.

United States. Naval War Records Office Official records of the Union and Confederate Navies in the War of the Rebellion. / Series I - Volume 22: West Gulf Blockading Squadron (January 1, 1865 - January 31, 1866); Naval Forces on Western Waters (May 8, 1861 - April 11, 1862). Government Printing Office, Washington, 1908. (Accessed April 2016.) <http://ebooks.library.cornell.edu/m/moawar/text/ofre0022.txt>

Van Der Linden, Frank. *The Dark Intrigue: A True Story of a Civil War Conspiracy*. Golden: Fulcrum Publishing, 2007.

Vandiver, Frank E. *Ploughshares into Swords*. Austin: University of Texas Press, 1952.

Vandiver, Frank E. *Civil War Battlefields and Landmarks: A Guide to the National Park Sites*. New York: Random House, 1996.

Wade, Richard C. *Slavery in the Cities: The South 1820-1860*. New York: Oxford University Press, 1968.

Walker, Scott. *Hell's Broke Loose in Georgia: Survival in a Civil War Regiment*. Athens: University of Georgia Press, 2007.

Waring, Joseph Frederick. *Cerveau's Savannah*. Savannah: The Georgia Historical Society, 1973.

Warman, Joanne Browning, ed.. *The Memorial Wall to Name the Fallen at the Warrenton, Virginia, Cemetery*. Black Horse Chapter, United Daughters of the Confederacy, 1998.

Watkins, Sam R. *Co. Aytch: A Confederate Memoir of the Civil War*. New York: Touchstone, 1962.

Waugh, John. *Reelecting Lincoln: The Battle for the 1864 Election*. New York: Da Capo Press, 1997.

Webster, C. L., III. *Entrepot: Government Imports into the Confederate Status*. Minnesota: Edinborough Press, 2010.

Weichmann, Louis J. *A True History of the Assassination of Abraham Lincoln and of the Conspiracy of 1865*. New York: Alfred A. Knopf, 1979.

Weigley, Russell F. *A Great Civil War: A Military and Political History, 1861-1865*. Bloomington: Indiana University Press, 2000.

Welles, Gideon and William Gienapp, eds. *The Civil War Diary of Gideon Welles, Lincoln's Secretary of the Navy*. Chicago: University of Illinois Press, 2014.

Wells, Tom Henderson. *The Slave Ship Wanderer*. Athens: The University of Georgia Press, 1967.

Wensyel, James W. *Appomattox: The Passing of the Armies*. Shippensburg: White Mane Books, 2000.

Wert, Jeffry D. *A Glorious Army: Robert E. Lee's Triumph*. New York: Simon and Shuster, 2011.

West, Jeffry D. *General James Longstreet: The Confederacy's Most Controversial Soldier*. New York: Simon & Schuster, 1994.

Wharton, H.M. *War Songs and Poems of the Southern Confederacy 1861-1865*. Entered according to act of Congress in the year 1904 by W.E. Scull, in the office of the librarian of Congress at Washington D. C.

Wheeler, Richard. *Sherman's March. An Eyewitness History of the Cruel Campaign That Helped End a Crueler War*. New York: Harper Perennial, 1991.

Wheeler, Richard. *Lee's Terrible Swift Sword*. New York: HarperCollins, 1992.

Whitman, Walt. *Memoranda During the War: Civil War Journals*. New York: Dover Publications, 2010.

Wikipedia. "Chesapeake Affair." (Accessed April 2016.) <http://en.wikipedia.org/wiki/Chesapeake_Affair>

Wikipedia. "Viscount Lord Palmerston." (Accessed October 2011.) <http://en.wikipedia.org/wiki/Henry_John_Temple,_3rd_Viscount_Palmerston>

Wikipedia. "John Pelham (Officer)." (Accessed April 2016.) <http://en.wikipedia.org/wiki/John_Pelham_(officer)>

Wikipedia. "The Trent Affair." (Accessed December 2011.) <http://en.wikipedia.org/wiki/Trent_Affair>

Wikipedia. "USS Kanawha." (Accessed April 2016.) <https://en.wikipedia.org/wiki/USS_Kanawha_(1861)>

Wiley, Bell Irvin. *The Life of Johnny Reb: The Common Soldier of the Confederacy.* Indianapolis: The Bobbs-Merrill Company Publishers, 1943.

Wiley, Bell Irvin. *Embattled Confederates. An Illustrated History of Southerners at War.* New York: Bonanza Books, 1964.

Wilkinson, J. *The Narrative of a Blockade-Runner.* New York: Sheldon & Company, 1877.

Wilkinson, Warren and Steven E. Woodworth. *A Scythe of Fire. A Civil War Story of the Eighth Georgia Infantry Regiment.* New York: HarperCollins, 2002.

William, T. Harry. *Lincoln and his Generals.* Norwalk: The Easton Press, 1990.

Williams, David. *Bitterly Divided: The South's Inner Civil War.* New York: The New Press, 2008.

Williams, Frank J. and William D. Pederson. *Lincoln Lessons: Reflections on America's Greatest Leader.* Carbondale: Southern Illinois University Press, 2009.

Wills, Garry. *Lincoln at Gettysburg. The Words that Remade America.* New York: Simon & Schuster, 1992.

Wilson, Harrold S. *Confederate Industry: Manufacturers and Quartermasters in the Civil War.* Jackson: The University Press of Mississippi, 2002.

Winkler, H. Donald. *Stealing Secrets: How a Few Daring Women Deceived Generals, Impacted Battles and Altered the Course of the Civil War.* Naperville: Cumberland House, 2010.

Winks, Robin W. *The Civil War Years. Canada and the United States.* Montreal: McGill-Queen's University Press. Canada, 1998.

Winther, Oscar Osburn, ed. *With Sherman to the Sea. The Civil War Letters, Diaries & Reminiscences of Theodore F. Upton.* Baton Rouge: Louisiana State University Press, 1943.

Wise, Stephan R. *Lifeline of the Confederacy: Blockade Running During the Civil War.* Columbia: The University of South Carolina Press, 1988.

Wolseley, Garnet. *Memoirs of Sir Garnet Wolseley.* (Accessed April 2016.) <http://bit.ly/2nXWasS>

Wolseley, Viscount Garnet. *General Lee.* <http://bit.ly/2oBZ-Rrg> (Accessed April 2016.)

Wood, Betty, ed. *Mary Telfair to Mary Few. Selected Letters 1802-1844.* Athens: The University of Georgia Press, 2007.

Woodman, Harold D. *Slavery and the Southern Economy, Sources and Readings.* New York: Harcourt, Brace & World, 1966.

Woodman, Harold. *King Cotton and His Retainers,* Lexington, University of Kentucky Press, 1968.

Woodward, C. Vann and Elisabeth Muhlenfeld. *The Private Mary Chestnut: The Unpublished Civil War Diaries.* New York: Oxford University Press, 1984.

Woodworth, Steven E. *A Deep Steady Thunder. The Battle of Chickamauga.* Abilene: McWhiney Foundation Press, 1998.

Zettler, Berrien McPherson. *War Stories and School Day Incidents for the Children.* Saline: McNaughton-Gunn, 1912.

Zornow, William Frank. *Lincoln & The Party Divided.* Norman: The University of Oklahoma Press, 1954.

Acknowledgements

THIS WORK WOULD not have been possible without the help of the St. Lawrence Hall Collection at the Canadian National Archives, Notman's extraordinary photographic collection, and the St. Lawrence Hall departure records at Montreal's McCord Museum, and the priceless Barnett's Museum Registers, recently acquired by the Niagara Falls Museums. This latter source has long been unavailable to scholars. These unique sources provide a powerful triangulation of names, dates, and photographs that constitute the framework for this incredible story.

I owe a great debt of gratitude to photographic partner Cindy Wallace, Scott Newman of the Savannah College of Art and Design (SCAD) who prepared the maps, and my editors: Florence Nygaard, Gene Kersey, Tim Menk, and Tim Laurence. Special thanks to Thomas Brady, LLB for his valuable insights as an attorney/historian. Thanks also to Claire Scheuren, reader extraordinaire, as well as Emma Duncan Taylor and Kimberly Safranek for their help with the bibliography. I would also like to thank Dr. David Vancil of Indiana State University and Robert Lupacchino of Savannah, Georgia. Finally, I would like to thank Jonathan Wener, Chancellor of Concordia and CEO of Canderel Development Group, for his help and support. ❧

Index

Page references in *italics* indicate an illustration.

Kane, George, 44, 46, 60, 76, 77, 138, 166, 242n76, 257n42, 258n44

Keith, Alexander ("Sandy"), 77, 124, 126, 199, 266n2

Kendall, Amos, 101, 250n54

Kennedy, Robert, 43, 50, 51, 198, 239n24, 240n43, 251n58

Kent, W.H., 205

Kerr, William, 175, 181, 182, 184,

Ketchum, E.C., 99, 202-203

King, Preston, 159, 238n5

King, William, 171

Kuhn, Louis, 96, 112, 114, 209

Lachine Canal, 29, 31

Lackey, Samuel E., 180

Laflamme, Rodolphe, 175, 181

Lamar, Charles, 49, 124, 126, 194, 198, 227, 235n10, 237n4, 239n30, 243n11, 254n8, 257n40, 266n2

Lamar, Gazaway, 49, 51, 95, 121-2, 124, 198, 211, 227, 229-30, 239n30, 243n11, 249n33, 254n8, 257n33, 257n40,266n2, 267n4

Lamon, Ward, 109, 250n43, 251n8

Lamothe, Guillaume, 185, 236n21, 257n39

Lane, G.M., 116, 210

Latham, (R.B.), 252n29

Lawley, Frank, 166-67

Lawrence, A.A., 203

Leach, D.T., 228, 230

Lee, Edwin, 21, 43, 56, 59, 66-7, 71, 87-8, 158, 175, 197, 198, 199-200, 217, 252n28, 259n57

Lee, Robert E., 51, 52, 130, 132, 167, 168, 170, 172, 174

Leech, John, 116, 209

Lehman Brothers, 96, 112, 114, 209

Lennoxville, 45, 187, 191, 236

Lincoln, Abraham: assassination, 102, 133, 160-1; celebrations of Captain Wilkes, 39; conspiracy against, 52-3, 62, 98-9, 133, 135, 261n4; control of swing states, 44; cotton pass signed by, 231; disregard for personal safety, 134; domestic policy, 33; on emancipation of slaves, 32-3; kidnapping plot, 133-7, 148-9, 150, 161-2, 261n1-2; meeting with Ashmun, 159; meeting with Eckert, 160; Morrill Tariff, 37; and patronage, 109-10; political opposition to, 27, 163; position on peace compromise, 65; prospects for re-election, 62; public image of, 22-3; Radical Republicans and, 54; response to British ultimatum, 41; trade policy, 22, 23, 108-9, 111-12; travel habits, 134; Trent crisis and, 40-1; Wade Davis Bill rejection, 53

Lincoln, Mary Todd, 208, 252n22

Lovell, John, 56, 187, 188, 189-190, 197, 199, 235n8, 235n9, 240n41

Lovell Printing advertisement, 188

Lucas, Daniel, 56, 59, 199

Lyman, S.R., 206, 250n54

Lyons, Richard, 33, 174, 201, 213

Macdonald, John A., 16, 30, 42, 53, 115, 169, 209, 246n108

Macdonald, William C., 36, 47, 236n16

Major, Mr. Minor, 199, 224

Marie Victoria, 77, 227, 230, 235n10

Marshall, S.S., 142, 206

Martin, Mrs. P.C., 75-6, 76, 77, 238n24

Martin, Patrick C.: assistance to Booth, 75, 139, 199, 266n2; career, 138, 196, 235; Confederate agent, 49, 51, 60, 132, 137, 166, 171-72, 227, 266n2; death, 67, 199; family, 44; house, 235; investments, 227; John Wilkinson and, 76-7; photograph, 46; refuge in Montreal, 44; vessels owned by (Marie Victoria), 77, 138, 227, 230

Martin, Robert, 51, 134, 150, 197, 199, 260n1

Marvel, William, 216n17

Mason, James, 38, 39, 41, 68, 190

Matamoros, port of, 126

Matchett, W.B., 159, 206, 263n49

McClellan, George, 101, 137, 142, 222

McCracken, S.B., 205

McCraig, James S., 77

McCulloch, R.G., 199

McCullough, John, 144, 211, 260n79

McGee, Thomas D'Arcy, 30, 33, 33-4, 238n8

McGill University, 36, 89, 199, 236

McMillan, L.J., 78, 78, 244n48

McPhail, James, 84, 158, 258n56